David Breakenridge Read

The lives of the judges of Upper Canada and Ontario

From 1791 to the present time

David Breakenridge Read

The lives of the judges of Upper Canada and Ontario
From 1791 to the present time

ISBN/EAN: 9783337207229

Printed in Europe, USA, Canada, Australia, Japan

Cover: Foto ©Suzi / pixelio.de

More available books at **www.hansebooks.com**

British American Bank Note Co. Montreal

Hon. William Bowder
Chief Justice

THE
LIVES OF THE JUDGES

OF

UPPER CANADA

AND

ONTARIO,

FROM 1791 TO THE PRESENT TIME.

BY DAVID B. READ, Q.C.,

HISTORIAN OF THE COUNTY OF YORK LAW ASSOCIATION.

TORONTO:
ROWSELL & HUTCHISON.

1888.

ENTERED according to Act of Parliament of Canada, in the year of our Lord one thousand eight hundred and eighty-eight, by DAVID BREAKENRIDGE READ, in the Office of the Minister of Agriculture.

PRINTED AND BOUND BY ROWSELL AND HUTCHISON, TORONTO.

CONTENTS.

		PAGE
PREFACE.		1
INTRODUCTION,		5
1. CHIEF JUSTICE OSGOODE,		17
2. JUDGE POWELL,		28
3. CHIEF JUSTICE ELMSLEY,		43
4. " " ALCOCK,		53
5. " " SCOTT		63
6. JUDGE COCHRANE,		73
7. " THORPE,		77
8. CHIEF JUSTICE CAMPBELL,		86
9. JUDGE BOULTON,		96
10. " SHERWOOD,		101
11. " WILLIS,		107
12. CHIEF JUSTICE ROBINSON,		122
13. " " MACAULAY,		148
14. " " McLEAN,		158
15. JUDGE JONES,		176
16. VICE-CHANCELLOR JAMESON,		188
17. JUDGE HAGERMAN,		201
18. CHIEF JUSTICE DRAPER,		222
19. JUDGE SULLIVAN,		237
20. CHANCELLOR BLAKE,		263

21. VICE-CHANCELLOR ESTEN, ... 284
22. JUDGE BURNS, ... 294
23. CHIEF JUSTICE SPRAGGE, ... 299
24. CHANCELLOR VANKOUGHNET, ... 314
25. JUDGE CONNOR, ... 328
26. " WILSON, ... 337
27. " MORRISON, ... 347
28. CHIEF JUSTICE HARRISON, . .. 365
29. " " MOSS, ... 387
30. " " CAMERON, ... 404
31. JUDGE O'CONNOR, ... 425
32. THE LAW SOCIETY, ... 435
33. THE ADVOCATES SOCIETY, ... 450
34. CONCLUSION—REMINISCENCES, ... 462
APPENDIX, ... 471

PREFACE.

WRITING the Lives of the Judges has been to me a work of love as well as of duty. I had long felt that a complete history of those who were distinguished in the Judicial History of the Province would fill a vacuum that had existed for too long a time, and if not soon filled up the material might be unattainable with which to supply the want. I would have been glad if some other pen had taken up the work; but as time wore on, and the prospect of fulfilment darkened, I determined to take the matter in hand. I had no sooner done so, and gone a league or two on my way, when I really became interested in the work. Being allowed access to the vault of Osgoode Hall, I dived and delved till I found hidden treasure that I determined to bring to the surface. I was surprised to find how little I had known of the early Judicial History of the Province: that being the case, I felt that there must be others in the same condition. I published the lives of the first half dozen of the early Judges in "The Magazine of Western History," published at Cleveland, in the State of Ohio, induced thereto by an agent of that periodical requesting me to contribute something to its pages—the magazine articles reached this Province and attracted the attention of many of my professional and non-professional friends—got access to the shelves of the Parliamentary Library, the Library of Osgoode Hall, the Free Library, the Library of the Law

Association of York, and other educational institutions, which encouraged me to proceed with the work. I have had also the unexpected honour of being appointed Historian of the County of York Law Association, an honour which I value, as the Directors of that body are gentlemen of my own profession, who take great interest in the legal and educational progress of this Province. The writing the Life of a Judge would be an uninviting task unless coupled with political and historical incidents. I have in every case where a Judge has been distinguished for political acumen, or military or martial pursuit, on or off the Bench, not failed to mark the circumstance. I have known no party in the progress of the work, believing that every Judge has acted throughout life conscientiously according to his light. During the course of my writing, I have come across incidents in the lives of several of the Judges which have given me a clearer insight into the early history of the Province and the War of 1812 than I possessed before. The battles of Lundy's Lane, Queenston Heights, Fort Erie, and Chrysler's Farm are memorable events in the history of the Province. They have not escaped my notice; nor has the capture of York by the Americans been forgotten. The Law Society, of which I was a Bencher for twenty-seven years, has been given a place in the pages of this work as worthy companion of the Lives of the Judges. I have ventured to give a few of my own reminiscences, no doubt the least interesting part of the volume: but added as a final winding up of what I hope may prove to be a useful work, containing matter that will, at least, keep in remembrance those of the Judicial Bench whose lights have gone out. I have not obtruded upon the reader the lives of the living Judges, for the reason that, being myself still at the Bar I perchance might be called upon to plead before them, and deem it prudent to forbear. Their conscientious discharge of duties while on the Bench will, I have no doubt, be an incentive to some other writer at some future time to do justice to the positions they have so well filled

I have, before concluding, to express my obligation to friends who have encouraged me in my work. I am especially indebted to Mr. Geo. M. Jarvis, of the Finance Department, Ottawa, for procuring me information from the archives of the Dominion, without which I could not have attained the accuracy of statement of official appointments; also, for his obtaining for me information from Australia which I have found useful and interesting in writing the Life of Mr. Justice Willis. I have to thank, the Librarian of the Ontario Assembly for ready access to the books on the shelves of the Parliamentary Library. With this short preface to the "Lives of the Judges," I commit the work to an indulgent public, asking forgiveness for omissions or defects, and hoping that some profit may be derived from a perusal of its pages, descriptive of the life and times of the Judges of Ontario.

D. B. READ.

TORONTO.

INTRODUCTION.

THE FIRST BENCH AND THE ACT OF 1791.

IN introducing to the reader the History of the Bench of Ontario, I have felt that the subject would not be complete without first explaining the Constitutional Act of 1791, as it was under that Act that Upper Canada got separate existence, and following upon that, York, now Toronto, became the capital of the Province.

Previous to the passing of the Constitutional Act, the condition of affairs—civil, political, and judicial—was so widely different at different epochs that it will be profitable, if not necessary, to pass in review the state of affairs legal in the Province of Quebec during this *ante* 1791 period.

The old Province of Quebec was, by an Act of the Imperial Parliament passed in 1791—generally referred to by the Judges as "The Act of the Thirty-first of the King," with special emphasis on the word king—divided into Provinces of Upper and Lower Canada.

The period extending from 1759, the date of the conquest, may well be termed the revolutionary period of the law of Canada.

It can easily be conceived that in a part of this intervening period—namely, the period between 1759 and 1763, in which latter year the treaty of peace was come to by Great Britain and France, by which the Province of

Quebec was ceded to Great Britain by France—the state of the law and its administration in the Province were in a very unsatisfactory state. The population was a mixed population, comprising French of France, French Canadians born in the Province, Indians, Metis or half breeds, English officers, English soldiers, and English traders, a large majority, however, being native born French Canadians. The lot of these people was not happy ; the civil government was military rule.

The country in 1760, soon after the articles of surrender were signed in Montreal, was divided by General Amherst, the then Governor-General, into three districts, and English officers were appointed to the duty of District Governor over each district, with a Lieutenant-Governor over the whole. These district officers had a council of other English officers to assist, and adjudged cases brought before them, subject to the approval of the Lieutenant-Governor.

Up to the treaty of peace in 1763 the law which governed was rather the law of might than of right. The French Canadians had become a conquered race, and were in the power of the conquerers. There was nothing to show that the law was improperly or harshly administered during this period. Nevertheless, with a French population not understanding English, and an English tribunal not understanding French, it could not be otherwise than that differences and altercations of a serious character should occur. On the one hand, the French dearly loved their own laws, and did not at all relish the change in government. The English were of opinion that British subjects, as the French had become by conquest, should be governed by and be willing to submit to the English law pure and simple.

The case stood thus : By the twenty-first article of the Articles of Capitulation entered into at Montreal, September 8, 1760, between General Amherst, Commander-in-chief of His Britannic Majesty's troops in North America, and the Marquis of Vaudreuil for the

French, it was provided that the English General should furnish ships for carrying to France the Supreme Court of Justice, Police, and Admiralty.

The Marquis of Vaudreuil, by article forty-two of the Articles of Capitulation, proposed "that the French and Canadians shall continue to be governed by the custom of Paris, and the laws and usages established for their country." General Amherst answered this forty-second article thus: "They become subjects of His Majesty." The answer of the General, it will thus be seen, was short but significant. Not only the correspondence that took place between the two commanders, but the articles of the capitulation, all go to show that on the one side the Marquis was endeavouring to have preserved to the French and Canadians their ancient laws and customs, while on the other side (the English) the commander would consent to nothing else than that the inhabitants "should become subjects of the King," amenable to the laws and constitution of England.

The French, remaining in the Province after the capitulation till the final treaty of peace was signed in 1763, were not at all satisfied.

There can be no doubt that military law is not in the general pleasing to civilians; and it may be that some of those charged with the administration of the kind of law imposed upon the Canadians were not the best qualified for the duties they had to discharge; but there is no authority for saying, as is said by at least one French writer of history, that "this martial system was adopted in violation of the capitulation, which guaranteed to the Canadians the rights of British subjects." The history of the time rather goes to show that the French Canadians, though conquered, were not subdued. They still clung to their own laws, and did not willingly submit to become British subjects, to be governed by British law. It is not surprising that this should have been the case. The French Canadian, walking in the old paths all his life, and his forefathers before him, for more than a century, could not easily be weaned from his old customs. Still, "*L'homme propose et Dieu dispose*,"—the fortunes of war were against them. Without objecting to remonstrance on the part of the French, the British officials demanded peaceful recognition of the change and respect for the newly constituted authority.

Military rule was finally brought to an end; the treaty of 1763 was signed; the English colonists had reason to believe that all would be well with them; that the French and French Canadians would be content; that there would be no protestation on the part of the French, but that all would act together for the general good.

There is nothing in the treaty which gave the French Canadians or French of France the old laws and customs of Canada, the laws and customs which prevailed before the conquest. There was a clause—clause 4—by which His Britannic Majesty agreed to grant the liberty of the Catholic religion to the inhabitants of Canada—" he will consequently give the most precise and effectual orders that his new Roman Catholic subjects may profess the worship of their religion according to the rites of the Roman Church as far as the laws of Great Britain will permit." There is not a line in the treaty about laws and customs, though special regard was paid to the matter of religion. Reading the capitulation articles and the treaty together, it is apparent that the French, both by negotiation and treaty, had the greatest solicitude for their Church and their religion; that the English appreciated this, giving them very exclusive religious privileges and rights, but always reserving the right of British law.

In October, 1763, a proclamation, under the great seal, was published erecting four new civil governments in America, namely, Quebec, East Florida, West Florida, and Grenada. This proclamation stated "that, as soon as the circumstances of the colonies would permit, general assemblies of the people would be convened in the same manner as in the American provinces, in the meantime the laws of England to be in force." The issuing of this proclamation by the King plainly shows what his view of the capitulation and the treaty was, namely, that the laws of England were to prevail in Quebec until altered by competent authority.

Not two years had elapsed after the signing of the treaty when the Governor-General, acting under instructions, formed a new executive council composed of the two Lieutenant-Governors of the two districts of Montreal and Three Rivers, into which the Province had been divided, the Chief Justice, the Inspector-General of Customs, and eight other persons chosen from among the inhabitants of the colony, who, with himself, should possess all executive, legislative, and judicial functions. This act was a remodelling of the whole previous system.

A Court called the King's Bench and another Court called the Common Pleas were established, following English precedent. Both these Courts were bound to render decisions based on the law and practice of England, subject to appeal to the Executive Council.

In an ordinance of September, 1764, it was assumed that the Chief Justice, sitting in the new Supreme Court then existing, had full power to determine all cases, both criminal and civil, conformably to English law and the ordinances of the Province. Authors (historiographers), both French and English, or rather Upper Canadian, have condemned the act of the King in issuing this proclamation of 1763 as a "rash and unwise measure, that it was a great injustice to a conquered people to compel them suddenly to submit to this law of the conqueror."

The French soon showed their disposition not to be content with government under British law. Neither the forms of procedure nor the administration of the law met with their approbation. Nothing seemed to suit them but the "old regime." They argued, they discussed, they remonstrated, they charged a breach of faith on the part of the English Government—that they were promised their own laws, including the old way of administration of those laws, instead of which they had English Courts with

English Judges and English procedure, and, to crown all, the English language. This must not be endured. Petitions must be sent to the Imperial Government setting forth their alleged grievances. The British in the colony determined to uphold British law. The conflict goes on apace. Neither party in the Province will give way. They are pulling different ways. They are at cross purposes—it is French or English, and God defend the right. There is much ado about something, and something must be done to put an end to turmoil and confusion. Both parties in the state appealed to England to settle their differences. It was great good fortune for the French party that just at this time the British colonists in New England were demanding from Old England relief for their alleged grievances. The doctrine of no taxation without representation was being pushed with great vigor. A revolution of the North American colonies outside of Quebec was looming up in the near distance. In the case of actual war it would be wise on the part of the British to keep in favor her French Canadian subjects in Quebec. Now is the time of advantage for the French. "*Nous avons l'avantage.*" A Bill is introduced into the House of Lords to provide for the government of Quebec. It passes the Lords, is sent to the Commons, meets with great opposition there; a committee is appointed, witnesses, Sir Guy Carleton and Mr. Hay, the Chief Justice, are examined before the committee; the Commons finally passes the Bill in amended shape; the Lords concur; the King assents to the Act. The British in Quebec, who believed themselves the conquering and dominant race, are to change place with the conquered and submit to French law, the authorized law for their guidance in the conquered Province, the key of the whole of Canada. This Act was passed by the Imperial Parliament in 1774, entitled "An Act for making more effectual provision for the government of North America." The eighth clause of this Act enacted as follows:

"His Majesty's Canadian subjects within the Province of Quebec, the religious orders and communities only excepted, may hold and enjoy their property and possession, together with all customs and usages relative thereto, and all other their civil rights, in as large, ample, and beneficial a manner as if the proclamation, commissions, ordinances, and other acts and instruments had not been made, and as may consist with their allegiance to His Majesty and subject to the Crown and Parliament of Great Britain, and in all matters of controversy relative to property and civil rights resort shall be had to the laws of Canada as the rule for the decision of the same ; and all causes that shall hereafter be instituted in any of the Courts of Justice to be appointed for and within the said Province by His Majesty, his heirs and successors, shall, with respect to such property and rights, be determined agreeably to the said laws and customs of Canada until they shall be varied or altered by any ordinances that shall, from time to time, be passed in the said Province by the Governor, Lieutenant-Governor, or Commander-in-chief for the time being, by and with the advice and consent of the Legislative Council of the same, to be appointed in manner hereinafter mentioned."

By enacting that "in all matters of controversy and civil rights resort shall be had to the laws of Canada as the rule for the decision of the same" the old Canada or French law was restored, and all His Majesty's subjects, French and English, in the colony were, in civil matters, placed under laws totally foreign to British immigrants and those of the old British settlers who had been accustomed to British law.

The speech of His Majesty the King to both Houses of Parliament, discloses the reason for passing that Act. In that speech His Majesty says :

"The very peculiar circumstances of embarrassment in which the Province of Quebec is involved had rendered the proper adjustment and regulation of the government thereof a matter of no small difficulty. The Bill which you prepared for that purpose and to which I have given my assent, is founded on the clearest principles of justice and humanity, and will, I doubt not, have the best effect in quelling the minds and promoting the happiness of my Canadian subjects. I have seen with concern a dangerous spirit of resistance to my government and the execution of the laws in the Province of Massachusetts Bay in New England."

The Act of 1774 enlarged the boundaries of the Province of Quebec south to the banks of the Ohio and westward to the banks of the Mississippi, thus taking into the Province of Quebec a territory and people of one of the British North America colonies to the south of the great lakes, and which afterwards, by the treaty of Versailles in 1783, became part of one of the free and independent United States of America. The Act had no sooner passed and been communicated to the provincials than the English party now in their turn set about protesting against the injustice done them in imposing the French law on His Majesty's loyal subjects, British subjects of the Province: the laws of the conquered race. Petitions were sent to the Imperial Parliament asking for a repeal of the Act. The discontented colonists of the New England States, bent on revolution, were not slow in urging the people of Canada to join them in their intended resistance to imperial authority. The Congress of the New England States, which met at Philadelphia on the 5th of September, 1774, addressed the colonists in Canada as "Friends and fellow citizens," and then endeavoured to impress them with the advantage of their confederation. During the American Revolutionary War, beginning with the affair at Lexington and ending with the treaty of peace in 1783, the law was administered in Quebec under the Act of 1774—the French law—and was most distasteful to the British residents. At the time of the passing of the Quebec Act of 1774, by which the boundaries were extended, as already stated, so as to include the inhabitants of the Ohio Valley, there were as many as twenty thousand people in that region who had emigrated thitherward from other States. These people had enjoyed the benefit of British laws as administered in colonial courts. They were not then disposed to accept in their place the "*Coutume de Paris*" or any other system of French law in place of the law to which they had been accustomed. Thus a very large auxiliary force was added to the small number of Anglo-Canadian subjects settled in the districts of Montreal and Quebec, to aid in protesting against the French law.

In 1784, following the treaty of peace between the United States and Britain, a large number of subjects of the King in the now enfranchised colonies south of the St. Lawrence and the great lakes who preferred Monarchial to Republican government, and came to Canada, settled on the banks of the St. Lawrence. These emigrants to Canada, called the United Empire Loyalists, on their arrival in Canada soon found that their situation was not much improved if they were to be relegated to the old, and, in their view, antiquated laws of France. They left the United States especially to place themselves under British law, and this they determined to have. In this particular they only held to the same opinion as had influenced the people of the Ohio Valley when they, between 1774 and 1783, made their protest against being governed by French law.

In 1788 Lord Dorchester, acting for the King, styling His Majesty King of Great Britain, France, and Ireland, issued a proclamation reciting the ordinances of the Province, dividing the Province into two districts, and proclaimed that thereafter the Province should be divided into five Provinces, namely: Lunenburg, bounded on the eastern limit by a tract of land called by the name of "The Lancaster Tract," the western limit of which should be the mouth of the Gananoque River, or as then called, the Thames River; Mecklenburg, to adjoin Lunenburg on the west, and to extend to the mouth of the river Trent; Nassau, to adjoin Mecklenburg, and extend westward to the extreme projection of Long Point into Lake Erie ; Hesse, comprehending all the residue of the Province to the west ; Gaspé, all that part of the Province on the south side of the St. Lawrence to the eastward of a north and south line intersecting the north-easterly side of Cape Cat.

By Provincial Act of Upper Canada, passed in 1792, the four districts within that Province, namely, Lunenburg, Mecklenburg, Nassau, and Hesse, were re-named in the order of these names, Eastern District, Midland District, Home District, and Western District. The period between 1774 and 1791 has generally been termed "The Legislative Council" period. This arises from the fact that by the Quebec Act a Legislative Council, who were appointees of the Crown, governed in the Province. In 1777 an ordinance was passed by this legislative body dividing the Province into two districts, and established two Courts, a Court of King's Bench and a Court of Common Pleas, for each district. The Act which placed the power of government in a body irresponsible to the people was the means of causing much contention and ill-will. The Judges for the Courts were in many instances not such as to lend either dignity or learning to the administration of the law ; they did not understand the French language ; the forms of law were wholly unfamiliar to the French ; disquietude, discontentent, and dissatisfaction prevailed in the colony. The English saw the French law, which the Judges did not understand, administered by English Judges. The French witnessed their law not interpreted correctly, and mal-administered by the Bench. Petitions were sent to England to alter this state of things. The situation of affairs was very perplexing to English statesmen. Committees were formed to examine the whole subject. Instructions were sent to the Government of Quebec to obtain a reliable report as to the cause of the discontent. English traders in Quebec and French citizens were called upon to give their evidence ; reports were sent to the English Government. After receipt of these reports, and a review of the whole question, the Imperial Government, acting on the advice of Mr. Pitt, determined to divide the Province into two Provinces, as it were to herd the French in one part of the old Province of Quebec and the English in the other part, so that each could have the laws most agreeable to the majority of the people of the respective Provinces. On this the King advised, and the Parliament passed the Act of the thirty-first of the King, 31 Geo. III. ch. 31. which replaced the legislative clauses of the Act of 1774, and divided the Province into two Provinces, one of Upper Canada (now Ontario), and the other the Province of Lower Canada, by subsequent legislation called the Province of Quebec, remitting it to the name of the two Provinces combined before the division. The Legislature of Upper Canada at their first session, held at Niagara on the 17th September, 1792, enacted that the laws of England, instead of the laws of Canada, were to govern in matters of property and civil rights in Upper Canada.

Thus we have introduced into the newly constituted Province of Upper Canada laws most congenial to the taste of the United Empire Loyalists, and to the English, Irish, and Scotch, by whom the Province was principally settled.

The United Empire Loyalists had much to do in bringing about this state of things, and the English law in the Province in which they had come to settle on being expatriated from the United States. These settlers in the Province were imbued with very strong ideas on the subject of monarchical government and British laws. To their minds the establishment of a Republican Government in America would not prove a success. Time has shown that they were mistaken in this, but letting this be granted, by adhering to British laws they have retained laws which have formed the model of American jurisprudence as opposed to the "*Coutume de Paris*" and the laws of old France.

The French in the Province of Quebec retain the laws guaranteed to them by the Act of 1774, and there can be no doubt the Act of 1774 was passed after diligent enquiry as to the propriety of the Act at the time. The Attorney and Solicitor-General of Quebec had both advised that the French should be remitted to their own law. So great an authority as Lord Thurlow had declared that every Canadian had a claim in justice to as much of his ancient laws regarding private rights as was not inconsistent with the principles of his new government. The French had loudly protested against the King's proclamation and the establishment of Courts in the Province. To administer English law, without an Act of the Imperial Parliament, was an act of despotism and wholly unwarranted. The Act of 1791, dividing the Province, enabled the French to mould the laws to their liking. The English of Ontario and of Quebec of to-day are not more content than the English of the ante-American Revolution period with this condition of affairs. The mother country has shaped the policy of Canada as a whole, and it is only Imperial legislation or a revolution that can undo what has already been accomplished.

The French in the Province of Quebec are as four to one of the English population, and strongly insist that with such a majority their French law, accorded to them by the Act of 1774, should continue to prevail, while the English minority insist that in a British Province they are entitled to have British laws, like as are in force in other Provinces of the Dominion.

I do not propose to enter into this controversy—it is a large political question, and foreign to my purpose in writing of the law.

Having thus reviewed the events of old times leading up to the Act of 1792, placing the British law on a solid foundation, it will be proper to proceed with the main subject, giving some account of those called upon to advocate and administer the law thus established, beginning with the First Chief Justice, Osgoode.

I.

THE HONORABLE WILLIAM OSGOODE, CHIEF JUSTICE OF UPPER CANADA.

 LANDSCAPE without a back ground would be wanting in one of the essentials of a complete picture. A portrait and sketch of the first Chief Justice of Upper Canada would be imperfect without accompanying surroundings. It is not of so much consequence to be informed of the antecedents of the Judge as of his judicial life after his arrival in a new and sparsely settled country. He was born in England in 1754, the twenty-seventh year of the reign of his Majesty King George II. He was called to the bar of Lincoln's Inn on the 11th of November, 1779. He had been engaged at the bar but twelve years when, at the early age of thirty-seven, he was chosen to represent his Majesty, King George III., as his chief judicial officer in that part of the old Province of Quebec, lately given a separate existence and called Upper Canada. Before being sent out to this Province as its chief judicial officer, he had, in 1779, published a work entitled, "Remarks on the Laws of Descent, and the reasons assigned by Mr. Justice Blackstone for rejecting in his table of Descents a point of doctrine laid down by Plowden, Lord Bacon, and Hale." It has been said that this work, which was much thought of at the time by men of note, probably procured for him

3—L. J.

his high position and appointment to the bench. There can be no doubt Mr. Osgoode, an equity draftsman, of Lincoln's Inn, when he wrote the work referred to, was in much favour with the King and his colonial minister. At the time of his appointment all colonial judicial appointments proceeded directly from the Crown. In inaugurating the new Province with a new order of things, new laws and new institutions, the King took especial care to name as his Chief Justice one esteemed well versed in English law, which had superseded the French law—the sequel will show the choice to have been a good one.

In the selection of Colonel John Graves Simcoe for the first Lieutenant-Governor, the King was carrying out the principles of the age and time in which he lived. It was then the custom of the British Government to appoint military men to hold the chief appointments in the civil departments of the government. Colonel John Graves Simcoe had performed important service to the Crown in the revolted States of America. What more proper then than that a man of his military experience should be at the head of the Province as its first Governor. John Graves Simcoe as Lieutenant-Governor, and William Osgoode, set out on their respective official journeys in this Province, the one as head of the civil government, and the other the judicial head of the Province, at or about the same time.

The first Parliament of the Province met at Niagara on the 15th of October, 1792. The address of his Excellency, Lieutenant-Governor Simcoe, to the members of this Parliament on his opening the first session, well exemplified the principle under which the King's deputy, acting no doubt under royal instructions, desired the government to be carried on. The Lieutenant-Governor in his address, said :

> I have summoned you together under the authority of an Act of Parliament of Great Britain, passed last year (Act of 1791), which has established the British Constitution and all the forms which secure and maintain it in this distant country. This Province is singularly blessed,

not with a mutilated constitution, but with a constitution which has stood the test of experience and is the very image and transcript of that of Great Britain.

His Excellency, in calling the Province a distant country, realized his own relative position and the position of the representatives of the people whom he addressed. But who were the people? At that early period of her history the population of the Province, all told, did not exceed ten thousand souls, and they scattered in settlements here and there along the St. Lawrence and the river on which rested Niagara, the then capital of the Province. At that time what is now Toronto was a wild wilderness, frequented by Indians of the tent and birds of the air.

Mr. Joseph Bouchette, who made the first survey of York (Toronto) harbor, in 1793, thus describes the surroundings:

> I still distinctly recollect the untamed aspect which the country exhibited when first I entered the beautiful basin, which thus became the scene of my early hydrographical operations. Dense and trackless forests lined the margin of the lake and reflected their images in its glassy surface. The wandering savage had constructed his ephemeral habitation beneath their luxuriant foliage, the group then consisting of two families of Mississagas, and the bay and neighbouring marshes were the hitherto uninvaded haunts of immense coveys of wild fowl.

If the Chief Justice's duties had been limited to Toronto they would not have been very arduous. The sequel will show that they were not so limited but that his circuit extended eastward from Newark (Niagara) to Cornwall, in the eastern part of the Province—that part of the Province which, as has already been said, had settlements of people, loyal subjects of the King.

The first mention we have of the Chief Justice of the Province, in his judicial capacity, is that on the 23rd of August, 1792, he presided in the Court of Oyer and Terminer and general gaol delivery, held in the town of Kingston, in and for the district of Mecklenburg. He had as associates on that occasion Richard Cartwright and

Hector McLeod, esquires, Justices of the Common Pleas of the district. There were at this Court twenty-four grand jurors sworn in ; the records show that of the number were Henneyral Harkamer, William Fairfield, and Donald McDonnell. The fact that there were twenty-four grand jurors sworn in shows that this part of the Province was not without inhabitants. There were grand jurors, petit jurors, tip staffs, and all the incidenta and impedimenta of the English Courts of the day. I have had the advantage of perusing a vellum covered book, which bears the impress of age, and is reported to have been brought to the Province by the Chief Justice, no doubt as a guide and faithful friend in his judicial work. This book is endorsed in large old English text, "Rough Agenda Book." It is the record of the proceedings of the English Assize Courts in various counties, commencing with Hertfordshire Summer Assizes, 28 George III., A. D. 1788, before Alexander Lord Loughborough, and ending with the Kent Assizes at Maidstone, A. D. 1791. The book possesses an interest conveying to the mind the precedents used in the establishment of the Upper Canada Courts.

But to return to my narrative : There was criminal business transacted at the first Court held by the Chief Justice. The most important of the cases tried seems to have been that of a prisoner indicted " for the felonious, wilful, and malicious murder of a certain Indian of the name of Snake." The prisoner was acquitted ; nevertheless, the trial on indictment found shows with what regard the Indian was treated in that day. The life of an Indian was held as sacred against the assassin as that of the civilized white man. There is no record of the Chief Justice holding another Court until August, 1793, when he again presided at the Court of Oyer and Terminer, held at Kingston. The most important event of this Court was that a prisoner was tried for " feloniously and burglariously breaking and entering the dwelling house of Frederick Henford, shopkeeper, and for feloniously stealing and carrying away eight muskrat skins, of the value of forty shillings currency, and six raccoon skins, of the value of five shillings currency.

The Chief Justice also presided at the Court of Oyer and Terminer for the Eastern District, held at the Court house in the town of New Johnstown, on the 14th of August, 1793, at which "twenty-two grand jurors were sworn. Amongst the grand jurors were Peter Drummond, Edward Jessup, John Dulmage, David Breckenridge, Paul Hick, Asel Landon, James Brackenridge, and John Jones." These names are all familiar to the inhabitants of the eastern part of the Province, in their day and generation pioneers of the country. David Breckenridge and James Brackenridge, who were on this grand jury, were of kin to John Breckenridge, the author of the Kentucky Resolutions of 1798. Like many other families of the Revolutionary period, the Breckenridge, or, as it is in Canada spelled, the Breakenridge, family were divided on the subject of King and country. The above named came to Canada, while the other members of the family took up their residence in Virginia and Kentucky. The family was a large one, and the descendants are subjects of more than one country. Judge Chambers of Detroit is by his mother's side a descendant of James Breakenridge. David Breckenridge was the maternal grandfather of the writer.

In December, 1793, we find the Chief Justice presiding at the Court of Oyer and Terminer, held at Newark (Niagara). The Hon. Robert Hamilton and Peter Russell, Justices of the Peace of the Court of Common Pleas for the Home District, being associates. A grand jury of seventeen were sworn in at this Court Among the jurors were John McNabb, Peter Ball, William Jarvis, Angus McDonell, Francis Crooks, Ralph Clench, William Dickson, and Thomas Butler, all prominent men of Newark, or Niagara, of that period. So far as I have been able to ascertain, the last criminal Court the Chief Justice presided at, in the Province of Upper Canada, was the Court held at the town of Cornwall, in July, 1794. The notes of the cases in the Chief Justice's book mentions the case of a prisoner tried for murder ; he was acquitted of the murder but found guilty of manslaughter. The sentence of the Court was "that the prisoner be burned in the hand," and it is added, "which was accordingly done in Court."

The burning in the hand part of this sentence and its execution, is my excuse for going back a little, and calling attention to the circumstances that in these criminal cases tried before Chief Justice Osgoode, he had as associates with him on the bench gentlemen "Justices of the Peace, of the Court of Common Pleas"—*vide* Court held at Niagara, December, 1793. As recorded, the associates were "the Honorable Robert Hamilton and Peter Russell, Justices of the Peace of the Court of Common Pleas for the Home District."

From this it is evident that there were local Justices of the Peace of the Common Pleas Court of that day, and that the Justices were prominent men of the locality.

The Act of 1791 continued, in Upper Canada, the old laws of Quebec until altered by new laws, to be passed by the Canadian Legislature. Mr. Buel, in his article on "The Bench and Bar of Detroit," in a current periodical, says :

> In 1798 regular Civil Courts were organized, and Detroit became a portion of the district of Hesse. The first term held at that place was in December of the same year, with James May as Chief Judge. In 1789 a local Court of Common Pleas was organized, having both civil and criminal jurisdiction. Appeal lay to the Governor, and the Council and the Judges were selected from among the wealthier citizens, who whipped, branded, banished, and imprisoned, as their caprice or the state of their digestive organs dictated.

It thus seems that the branding was in fashion in Detroit in 1789, when Detroit was still in possession of the British and part of the District of Hesse. Why, then, might it not be resorted to as a mode of punishment in 1794 in Cornwall of the old Lunenburg and more modern Eastern District.

While in Upper Canada the Chief Justice had other than judicial duties to perform. He was a Legislative

Councillor of the Province, appointed to the Council in July, 1792, and in September, 1792, was appointed Speaker of that body.

His active judicial duties in Upper Canada commenced in August, 1792, and terminated December, 1793, or for a period of a little over a year and three months. It is not to be supposed that during that short time he could attain any great celebrity. There was, however, one act of his which will ever be cherished by Canadians, the highest and best in his judicial history; that act was his suggestion in his charge to a grand jury that slavery ought not to exist in the colony of Canada. In consequence of this charge the Upper Canadian Legislature, at their second session, held at Niagara, on the 9th of July, 1793, passed an Act entitled, "An Act to prevent the further introduction of slaves, and to limit the terms of contracts for service within this Province." It is a pride that Upper Canadians have, and justly have, that, at a time when neither their mother country nor the new republic to the south of them had abolished the devilish traffic in human flesh, their embryo Province stepped forward and led the van in loosing the bondsman's fetters. This was freedom not in name only, but in very deed.

A friend has favoured me with a perusal of the September, 1886, number of a London periodical, "The Pump Court, the Temple Newspaper and Review of Law, Literature and Society, Art and the Drama." It is singular that at this late date it should have appeared, but in that number is published a letter from his club members congratulating Chief Justice Osgoode on his appointment, which, from its date, must have had reference to his appointment, to the Chief Justiceship of Lower Canada, which took place on the 24th of February, 1794. The letter of congratulation was as follows:

THE IMMORTAL JUPITER.
TEMPLE COFFEE Ho 15 May, 1794.

The Immortal Jupiter congratulates the Lord Chief Justice Osgoode on his appointment: Snowden Barue (President), Nat Bond, J. Floud, B-

Bathe, Wm. Pott, W. Syer, V. P., Edward Cotton, T. Partington, Richard Legard, Jno. Fondret, H. Tripp, H. C. Litchfield.

To the Honorable William Osgoode, Chief Justice of Quebec.

This letter sufficiently proves the estimation in which the Chief Justice was held by a club of a very lofty name, and no doubt lofty principles.

Having traced the judicial history of his Lordship in Upper Canada, and mentioned his promotion to the Chief Justiceship of Lower Canada, it is right to say that to secure the further mark of his sovereign's favour he must have given satisfaction to the Imperial Government while representing the Crown as their Chief Justice in Upper Canada. In entering upon his duties in Lower Canada, he would find the criminal law of England in force there. The same Government had, in yielding to the Lower Canadians the French law in civil matters, retained their own criminal law, and to the administration of this law the Chief Justice was no stranger. It happened that during the Hon. William Osgoode's administration of criminal law in Quebec, there was tried an important, if not the most important, case of the time. This was the trial of David McLane for high treason, before special commission of Oyer and Terminer, under the great seal of the Province. The Judges on the commission were the Chief Justice (Osgoode), the Hon. James Monk, Chief Justice of the King's Bench of the District of Montreal, the Hon. Thomas Dunn, Jenkin Williams, Peerie Debourne, Justices of the King's Bench of the District of Quebec.

David McLane was an American, who was accused of conspiring with other Americans in Vermont and New York, and certain malcontents of the Province of Lower Canada, to overthrow the Government. It was charged that he was holding communication with Genet, the French Minister to the United States, to the same purpose. The evidence on the part of the Crown was conclusive of guilt. The prisoner offered no evidence, but relied on the cross-examination of the Crown's witnesses, his own statement and defense made in open Court, and the effort of his counsel for his acquittal. All were of no avail, however, for he was convicted, condemned to death, and executed; and as if hanging was not enough of punishment in these barbarous days, after death his head was severed from his body, it is supposed as a terror to evil doers with traitorous designs. The report of the case describes the crime thus :

> Prisoner sentenced to death. On Friday, July 21, prisoner was hanged, his head cut off after body hanging twenty-five minutes. Executioner held up the head to the public view, and proclaimed : "Behold the head of a traitor."

On the trial of this case, the Chief Justice, it is almost unnecessary to say, acted in a fair and impartial manner. The jury were told to give the prisoner the benefit of any doubt, and that the matter of fact as to the prisoner's guilt was entirely with them to determine on the evidence ; that any observations of the Court on the facts should be regarded as observation only, and not have weight with the jury. The Chief Justice's explanation of the law of high treason was most full and comprehensive. He said in his charge to the jury :

> The point of law which ought to govern this case may be comprehended in one sentence, which is this : Every attempt to subject this Province, or any part thereof, to the King's enemies is high treason, and every step taken to further such is an overt act of treason.

The Attorney-General, in his address to the jury, after defining high treason, and that "the intention to commit the crime constitutes the offence," proceeded to say : "The jury must form their opinions on the proof of the *overt* acts charged."

The prisoner, in his address to the jury before his conviction, said : "I feel gratitude that I have been indulged in every thing reasonable. I thank the Court for its indulgence to me."

I have referred to this trial at length, as Mr. Garneau, in his history, has impeached the fairness of the trial. In his criticism there is no aspersion on the Chief Justice or his judicial conduct, but there is a reflection on the Court proceedings. Mr. Garneau says : "The choice of jurors, the testimony brought forward, the judgment passed, were all of an extraordinary character." Issue must be taken with the historian on every one of these statements, and indeed his criticism is not only extraordinary but unjust. The grand jury was a mixed one—French and English— the Court was constituted of the highest Judges in the land, the petit jury were respectable citizens of Quebec— not French, it is true, nor was McLane, the accused, French. The sentence of the Court was the only judgment that could be given for the offence of which the prisoner was found guilty—and yet with all this the severe comments of Mr. Garneau find place in his history. The reporter's account of the trial of the case, and all that took place at it, is to be found on the shelves of the free library of Toronto. It is open to any citizen, French or English, to read the report for himself. After so doing, he must of necessity conclude that the historian must have been actuated more by prejudice than a fair consideration of facts, when he undertakes to throw discredit on a trial conducted with the utmost fairness, before eminent Judges and an impartial jury.

The Chief Justice remained in Quebec in performance of his judicial duties till 1801, when he resigned his office and returned to England, where he died in the Albany Chambers, on the 17th of February, 1824, aged seventy.

I do not feel that I ought to conclude this imperfect sketch without alluding to the outward form and features of the Chief Justice. The benchers of the Law Society, the governing body of the law in the Province, and indeed the country are indebted to the Rev. Dr. Scadding, the writer of "Toronto of Old," a book which contains a fund of information, personal, topographical, and historical, appropriately dedicated to that ripe scholar and distinguished statesman, the Right Honorable, the Earl of Dufferin, K. C. B., for procuring a copy of a portrait in oil of Chief Justice Osgoode. The original of this portrait is in possession of J. K. Simcoe of Wolford, county of Devon, England, a grandson of Lieutenant-Governor Simcoe. The society have been enabled to adorn the walls of their noble hall with the likeness of the Chief Justice. The likeness was taken by Berthon, whose life-like portraits of other Chief Justices are conspicuous on the walls of the library and other suitable places in the hall. Dr. Scadding rightly thought that the hall which bears the name of the Chief Justice should have the first Chief Justice in portraiture. A study of the picture presents to the eye an English gentleman of the George III. period, a gentleman with intellectual countenance, a faultless figure, and handsome face. The portrait must have been taken when he was a young man, perhaps on his setting out from England to undertake the duties of Chief Justice of the distant colony of Canada.

I do not feel I ought to leave the subject of the first Chief Justice of the largest Province of the Dominion without saying something of the Chief Justice as a man. I must, in this particular, be allowed to quote Dr. Scadding, who, quoting, says of him: "No person admitted to his intimacy ever failed to conceive for him that esteem which his conduct and conversation always tended to augment." A friend in Quebec, who knew him in that Province, and to whom I applied for information in this regard, writes to me to say: "The Chief Justice was grave and somewhat difficult of access; during his residence at Quebec, he made himself esteemed and respected as much by his high intelligence, as by his integrity and frankness of character."

II.

THE HONORABLE WILLIAM DUMMER POWELL, CHIEF JUSTICE OF UPPER CANADA.

THE Honorable William Dummer Powell was of a very old Welsh family—the family estate in Wales was "Caer Howel." The Chief Justice's grandfather, John Powell, came from England to America as secretary to Lieutenant-Governor Dummer; his grandmother was sister of Lieutenant-Governor Dummer; his father was John Powell of Boston, Massachusetts. The Chief Justice was born in Boston in 1755. At the age of nine years he was sent to England to be educated. From England he was sent to Holland to acquire a knowledge of the French and Dutch languages, and in 1772 he returned to Boston. He was called to the Bar in 1779, by the Middle Temple. Previously to 1791 he had resided for a short time in Lower Canada, and had rendered valuable aid to the United Empire Loyalists in obtaining the Act of 1791.

On the 11th of May, 1789, he left Montreal with his family for Detroit, which was still in possession of the British, and continued in their possession till the Jay treaty of 1796. The journey of himself and family to Detroit has been most graphically described by his sister in a journal she kept of the voyage, which was made principally in boats. Some idea of the difficulty of ascending the St. Lawrence and the rapids at that day, in small boats, is made plain from the fact that it took the Chief Justice and his family ten days to reach Kingston. The journal describes Kingston at that time as "a small town, standing on a beautiful bay, at the foot of Lake Ontario." It took four days to traverse the lake from Kingston to Niagara ; there the party met the celebrated Indian chief Joseph Brant. Afterwards they visited Fort Schlosser, thence to Fort Erie by batteau. While at Fort Erie they had an opportunity of visiting an Indian council held on the opposite side of the river. There were upward of two hundred chiefs at this council, delegates of the Six Nations. I extract Miss Powell's description of this council, which shows how the councils were managed in those days. The writer says :

> Each tribe formed a circle under the shade of a tree, their faces toward each other ; they never changed places, but sat or lay on the grass, as they liked. The speaker of each tribe stood with his back against a tree. The old women walked one by one, with great solemnity, and seated themselves behind the men ; they were wholly covered with their blankets and sought not, by the effect of ornaments, to attract or fright the other sex, for I cannot tell whether the men mean to make themselves charming or horrible by the pains they take with their persons.

Referring to the squaws and their taciturnity in council, Miss Powell says :

> Their ladies (squaws) preserve a modest silence in the debates (I fear they are not like women of other countries), but nothing is determined without their advice and approbation.

Speaking of the Indian chiefs, she says :

> They are remarkably tall and finely made, and walk with a degree of grace and dignity you can have no idea of. I declare our beaux looked quite insignificant by them. One man called to my mind some of Homer's finest heroes.

One of the chiefs she met at this council was Red Jacket, whose appearance and dress she fully describes not omitting his "scarlet coat, richly embroidered, that must have been made half a century, with a waist-coat of the same." The party were at Fort Erie on the 4th of June, the King's birthday, and there did honour to the day. On the 9th of June the party reached Detroit. She says :

In drawing the line between the British and American possessions, this fort was left within their lines. A new town is now to be built on the other side of the river, where the Courts are held, and where my brother, must, of course, reside.

Detroit was at this time, 1789, included in the district of Hesse, and was the first seat of justice in that region of country. The Honorable William Dummer Powell was the first Judge who presided over this Court. He was appointed a Commissioner of the Peace of the Province of Quebec in January, 1789. On examining the archives at Ottawa, we find that in January, 1791, he was appointed Commissioner of Oyer and Terminer and gaol delivery for Quebec, and in 1792, to the same office in and for Upper Canada. On the 3rd of September, 1792, Judge Powell presided at his Majesty's Court of Oyer and Terminer in and for the district of Hesse in the Province of Upper Canada, and in October, 1793, we find him presiding Judge of the Court of Oyer and Terminer for the Western District held at the Court House of the "township of Assumption." The records say of the township of Assumption; as a matter of fact, however, there is not, nor was there, a township of Assumption in the Western District. What is evidently meant is, the parish of L'Assumption in which the town of Sandwich, on the Detroit river, is situate. At this second Court held by Judge Powell in Upper Canada, he had as associates on the bench, James Baby and Alexander Grant—a grand jury of seventeen, of whom John McGregor was one. Twelve of the grand jurors had French names. The French were still largely in the majority in that part of the Province. At this Court a prisoner was tried and convicted of manslaughter—the sentence of the Court as expressed in the record, is " To be burned in the hand, and accordingly put in execution before the Court."

Judge Powell presided in the Courts of Oyer and Terminer and Gaol Delivery yearly, and at times twice a year in the several districts into which the Province had been divided, the Eastern, Midland, Home, and Western, from 1793 down to his retirement from the bench in 1825. The records show that during this period, in a country of magnificent distances, primitive mode of navigation, stage coach, and corduroy roads, he performed all his judicial duties with regularity and constant watchfulness of the good of the people. The practice of burning convicted prisoners in the hand and sentencing them to stand in the pillory was not uncommon in these times of our judicial history. Although Judge Powell first presided at a criminal Court at L'Assumption in 1793, he had before this held the Court of Common Pleas at L'Assumption, in the western district, for I find in the archives of Osgoode Hall a book in which is contained this entry:

"PROVINCE OF QUEBEC.

"Court of Common Pleas holden at L'Assumption in the Western District, on the 11th day of August, 1791, pursuant to adjournment.

"Present, The Honorable William Dummer Powell, first Judge of the said Court."

At this Court an action on a penal statute, in the name of the King, on the information of William Gartham against William Scott, was tried. Exception was taken to the jurisdiction of the Court, and the Court said:

Although the jurisdiction given to this Court is summary and without appeal, by the ordinance of 1791 the magistrates in towns are empowered, at the request of the inhabitants, to make regulations for the police, which, being published, shall have full force of law for six months, the lower penalties to be received by plaint before one Judge of Court of Common Pleas, as in causes under £10 sterling without appeal.

At an adjournment of this Court the examination of witnesses was in French, the counsel asked the witnesses questions in French and the witnesses answered them in French.

Judge Powell held this Court again in March, 1792. He held the Civil Court of Nisi Prius in the Home, Midland, and Eastern Districts in 1795, and thence forward. In his administration of both civil and criminal law he gave great satisfaction; his manly, independent qualities endeared him to the people, and gained for him a high reputation as a Judge.

Chief Justice Powell was a prominent figure, and bore an important, if not a conspicuous, part on the British side in the War of 1812. He was during that eventful period in York, and was the principal confidential agent of the Governor at that town. We learn from a letter, written by Sir Isaac Brock to Sir George Prevost, that not only the Chief Justice, but also Mr. Grant Powell, his third son, father of Mr. Grant Powell, Under Secretary of State at Ottawa, and of Mrs. John Ridout, wife of John Ridout, Registrar of County of York, had the confidence of both the civil and military commanders of that day.

By a letter addressed to Colonel Baynes, under date of July 23, 1812, Sir Isaac Brock thus expressed himself. The letter is dated at York, and says:

I wish very much something might be done for Mr. Grant Powell. He was regularly brought up in England as a surgeon. I intended to have proposed him to Sir George to appoint him permanent surgeon to the Marine department, but I now seriously think the situation would not answer. His abilities, I should think, might be more fully employed now that so many troops have been called out.

Subsequently, Dr. Grant Powell was appointed surgeon, having charge of all hospital arrangements on the Niagara frontier. After the investment of York by the Americans, in April, 1813, the Chief Justice held very important communications with the British military commander, relative to the condition of affairs and the measures proper to be taken for the public safety. I find from a memorandum of Mr. T. G. Ridout, of the 5th of May, 1813, that on the 30th of April, 1813, this communication was held, and that his father and Dr., afterward Bishop, Strachan were engaged in the same enterprise. The memorandum of Mr. Ridout was as follows:

I (T. G. Ridout) left York on Sunday, the 2nd instant, at noon, at which time the American fleet, consisting of the *Madison*, *Oneida*, and ten schooners, with the *Gloucester*, were lying at anchor about two miles from the garrison, wind-bound by a south-east wind. All their troops were embarked the evening before, excepting a small party, who burnt the large block-house, Government house, and officers' quarters. At nine in the morning a naval officer came down to town and collected ten men out of the taverns, where they had been all night.

The commissariat magazines were shipped the preceding days, and great quantities of the provisions given to our country people, who brought their wagons down to assist the Americans to transport the public stores found at Mrs. Elmsley's house and at Boulton's barn. The lower blockhouse and Government buildings were burnt on Saturday. Major **Givin's** and Dr. Powell's houses were entirely plundered by the enemy, and some persons from the Humber. Jackson and his two sons and Ludden, the butcher, had been riding through the country ordering the militia to come in and be put on their parole, which caused great numbers to obey voluntarily and through fear.

Duncan Cameron, Esq., delivered all the money in the Receiver-General's hands (to the amount, as I understand, of £2,500) over to Captain Elliot, of the American navy, the enemy having threatened to burn the town if it was not given up.

On Friday, the 30th, the Chief Justice, Judge Powell, my father, Dr. Strachan, and D. Cameron called upon General Dearborn, requesting he would allow the magistrates to retain their authority over our own people. Accordingly, he issued a general order, saying it was not his intention to deprive the magistracy of its civil functions, that they should be supported, and if any of the United States troops committed any depredation, a strict scrutiny into it should follow. The gaol was given up to the sheriff, but no prisoners. The public provincial papers were found out, but ordered to be protected, so that nothing was destroyed excepting the books, papers, records, and furniture of the Upper and Lower Houses of Assembly. It was said they had destroyed our batteries and taken away the cannon. The barracks were not burnt. The American officers said their force, on the 27th, was three thousand land force and one thousand seamen and marines, and that their loss was five hundred killed and wounded.

Kingston, May 5, 1813. [Signed] T. G. Ridout.

As regards this attack on York in April, 1813, it has come down to us as a matter of history that in the conduct of the negotiations with the American commander for the capitulation of the place, Dr. Strachan and the gentlemen associated with him acted with great intrepidity and courage, directed to the preservation of the towns-people from carnage and their property from destruction. Dr. Strachan was much incensed at the conduct of the Americans, and did not hesitate, after the event, to say that the deputation had not received proper consideration, and had been treated with harshness; he also complained that while the negotiation was pending the ship being built in the harbor and naval store had been set on fire. But then it is to be remembered that at that time the towns-people were in very bad humor, and did not only complain of the Americans and their invasion, but bitterly complained that the town had been neglected by the British general, and not furnished with regular troops to meet the expected attack.

As a matter of fact, when the American flotilla was first discovered making for the harbor, on the 25th of April, there were no regular troops in the place ; and when the Americans landed the only opposition they met was Major Givins at the head of forty Indians and a few civilians of the town. Afterward, however, this force was supplemented by about four hundred of the Eighth Newfoundland and Glengarry regiments and five hundred undisciplined militia men—a very inferior force to the Americans. The British were obliged to retreat after the blowing up of the magazine, by which the Americans lost their general— General Pyke. The towns-people severely criticised their own general, General Sheafe, for his conduct of the defence of the town, and of his hasty retreat, leaving the inhabitants at the mercy of the American military force. Dr. Strachan, in writing to a friend in Scotland after the departure of the Americans, gave a very vivid account of this whole affair, detailing at length the incidents of the capture. In this communication he complains bitterly of the treatment the inhabitants had received, but more especially the indignity to which he had been subjected himself by General Dearborn—that he had treated him with great harshness, and spoke disrespectfully of him. But then, on the other hand, General Dearborn was met with many peremptory demands. Dr. Strachan was not a man to mince matters in anything he undertook. The account given by himself shows that his requests were couched in the language of command. The capitulators were much disposed to regulate the whole matter of capitulation. The American commander and Commodore Chauncey were not disposed to submit to this.

In reading the history of this invasion, April, 1813, I gather that the dogs of war being let loose, there was considerable barking on both sides. Happily those times have passed away, and men of the same blood, separated only by a great river, can approach each other in terms of peace and friendship as children of one mother.

In writing the judicial life of Chief Justice Powell and of the period of the war, full justice cannot be done to the subject without referring to Mr. Grant Powell, previously referred to, not only because of the relation he bore to the Chief Justice, but to the Governor General, especially as such reference will elucidate the history of the period.

The Americans in their attack on York in April, had, as has been shown, plundered the public stores and burnt and destroyed much public property, and destroyed the public library, then much prized in the town. In July of 1813, the Americans made another attack on York; the condition of matters in York after the second attack is well described in a communication made by Mr. Grant Powell and Dr. Strachan to His Excellency the Governor General, on the 2nd of August, 1813, and was as follows:

YORK, 2nd August, 1813.

SIR,—We beg leave to state, for the information of his Excellency the Governor-General, that about eleven o'clock on Saturday morning the enemy's fleet of twelve sail were seen standing for the harbor. Almost all the gentlemen of the town having retired, we proceeded to the garrison about two o'clock and watched till half past three, when the *Pyter*, the *Madison*, and *Oneida* came to anchor in the offing and the schooners continued to pass up the harbor with their sweeps, as the wind had become light, three coming to abreast of the town, the remainder near the garrison. About four p.m., several boats full of troops landed at the garrison, and we, bearing a white flag, desired the first officer we met to conduct us to Commodore Chauncey.

We mentioned to the Commodore that the inhabitants of York, consisting chiefly of women and children, were alarmed at the approach of the fleet, and that we had come to know his intention respecting the town; that if it were to be pillaged or destroyed we might take such measures as were still in our power for their removal and protection. We added that the town was totally defenceless, the militia being still on parole, and that the gentlemen had left it, having heard that the principal inhabitants of Niagara had been carried away captive—a severity unusual in war. Commodore Chauncey replied that it was far from his intention to molest the inhabitants of York in person or in property; he was sorry that any of the gentlemen had thought it necessary to retire, and that he did not know of any person taken from Niagara of the description mentioned. Colonel Scott, the commandant of the troops, said that a few persons had certainly been taken away. The Commodore told us that his coming to York at present was a sort of retaliation for the visits our fleet had made on the other side of the lake, and to possess himself of the public stores and destroy the fortifications, but that he would burn no houses; he mentioned something of Sodus, and the necessity of retaliation should such measure be taken in future. He likewise expressed much regret at the destruction of our public library on the 27th of April, informing us that he had made a strict search through his fleet for the books; many of them had been found, which he would send back by the first flag of truce. He then asked what public stores were here—a question which we could not answer. In parting, both the Commodore and Colonel Scott pledged their honour that our persons and property should be respected, and that even the town should not be entered by the troops, much less by any gentleman there. As we were quieting the minds of the inhabitants, the troops took possession of the town, opened the jail, liberated the prisoners, taking three soldiers confined for felony with them; they visited the hospitals and paraded the few men that could not be removed. They then entered the stores of Major Allan and Mr. St. George and secured the contents, consisting chiefly of flour. Observing this, we went to Colonel Scott, and informed him that he was taking property. He replied that a great deal of officers' luggage had been found in Mr. Allan's store, and that all the private property was to be respected. Provisions of all kinds were lawful prize, because they were the subsistence of armies. That if we prevailed in the contest, the British Government would make up the loss, and if they were successful their Government would most willingly reimburse the sufferers. He concluded by declaring that he would seize all provisions he could find.

The three schooners, which had anchored abreast of the town, towed out between eleven and twelve o'clock on Saturday night, and we suppose that the fleet would have sailed immediately, but having been informed by some traitor that valuable stores had been sent up the Don, the schooners came up the harbor yesterday morning. The troops were again landed, and three armed boats went up the Don in search of the stores. We have since learned that through the meritorious exertions of a few young men, two of the name of Playter, everything was conveyed away before the enemy reached the place—two or three boats, containing trifling articles, which had been hid in the marsh, were discovered and taken, but in the main object the enemy was disappointed. As soon as the armed boats returned, the troops went on board, and by sunset both soldiers and sailors had evacuated the town. The barracks, the woodyard, and the storehouses on Gibraltar point were then set on fire, and this morning at daylight the enemy's fleet sailed.

The troops which were landed act as marines, and appear to be all they had on board—not more certainly than two hundred and forty men. The fleet consists of fourteen armed vessels. One is left at Sackett's Harbour.

It is but just to Commodore Chauncey and Colonel Scott to state that their men, while on shore, behaved well, and no private house was entered or destroyed.

We have the honour to be, etc., etc.. etc.

[Signed] JOHN STRACHAN.
GRANT POWELL.

COLONEL BARNES,
  Adjutant-General.

If there is a prevalent tradition that the Americans acted with undue severity on this occasion of the capture of York, this communication should dispel any such idea if it exists in the public mind. The Americans, in fact, performed their military duty in a becoming manner and with a just regard to the rights of men. Continental wars have shown that the further east you go the less regard is paid to private rights.

That the Chief Justice was especially honoured by his Excellency, the Governor General, with his confidence, appears from several communications. As head of the law, he was in the confidence of the magistracy of the day —acting in concert with them for the welfare of the town and surrounding country.

Being at Kingston on the 4th of June, 1813, in the intervening period between the first and second attack by the Americans on York, he addressed the following letter to the Governor's Secretary—which contained a report of the magistrates resident in York, but at a meeting at which the Chief Justice was present, and took a conspicuous part in its proceedings. The letter is as follows :

KINGSTON, June 4, 1813.

SIR :—Conformably to the pleasure of his Excellency, the Governor-in-Chief, I have the honour to enclose to you a copy of the proceedings of the magistrates, etc., at York during the possession of that place by the enemy.

I beg leave to submit for his Excellency's information, that under the existing circumstances it was thought inexpedient especially to advert to the plunder or receipt of public property, which in such case would have been concealed from search or defended by force, which the police had no means to control.

But in aid of that object the sheriff was directed by the meeting to consider himself as the King's bailiff, as usual, and whenever public property was found by himself, or pointed out to him by others to take it into his hands, leaving the claimant to establish his pretentions to the possession by the ordinary Courts of law until a change of circumstances enabled the ministers of the law to act with decided power to overawe opposition. This measure was deemed merely prudence.

I have the honour to be, etc., etc.,

[Signed]   WM. DUMMER POWELL.

Edward Benton, Esq.

At a meeting of the magistrates resident in the town of York, attended by the Judges, the Sheriff, and the Rev. Dr. Strachan, the actual situation of the town and district was taken into consideration :

The enemy's fleet and army lying in the harbor, all our military defences at the port destroyed, the inhabitants disarmed and on parole, it is obvious that measures of as much energy as our circumstances admit should be immediately adopted to preserve order and prevent anarchy, to support and encourage the loyal, to supress the disloyal, and to confirm the wavering.

It is, therefore, unanimously declared that, by the eruption of the enemy and temporary possession of this port, no change has taken place in the relation of the subject to his Majesty's government and laws, except to such as were parties to the capitulation as prisoners of war and are under parole of honour not to bear arms until exchanged.

That it is equally now, as before the invasion, high treason to aid, assist, counsel, or comfort the enemy. That all felons and evil doers are equally amenable to the laws as before. That the powers of the magistrates and ministers of the law are unimpaired, and continued to be so even during the actual possession of the enemy, as the commander of the forces declared by a general military order to the troops.

That private property, having remained unchanged not only in construction of the law but by the express terms of the capitulation, the enemy himself disclaims the right assumed by some individuals to transfer it from the owner.

That it is the duty of all good subjects to declare to the magistrate all instances of such unjust possession as may come to their knowledge and of the magistrate to enforce the restitution.

That persons desirous to signify their abhorrence of anarchy, which must prevail if principles adverse to the above declaration gain ground, are called upon to associate in support of the laws and to afford their aid to the civil magistrates and their ministers.

That the high sheriff do publish and enforce this declaration.

I find the Chief Justice again on the 28th of June, 1813, and on the 1st of August, 1813, in confidential communication with Sir George Prevost relative to the American invasion of York. As the communication of the 28th of June was of a private and confidential character, I will do no more than simply refer to it without giving its full contents. The substance of the communication of the 28th of June was in regard to the state of the town, labouring under the inconveniences from the attack of the Americans, its commissariat and the accommodation that could be afforded for troops. He writes among other matters:

> The accommodation for troops is very little diminished, the two block houses being the only soldiers quarters destroyed. There is timber on the ground prepared for building ways and wharf for the ship sufficient to throw up a coarse but warm cover for a great many men at little expense. The town could not hold one thousand men without great inconvenience.

The communication of the 1st of August was as follows:

William Dummer Powell to Sir George Prevost:

NEAR YORK, August 1, 1813.

SIR:—Yesterday morning the American squadron, consisting of two ships, a brig, and twelve sail of other vessels entered the harbor of York and landed troops computed at two thousand men. As they seized upon the flour in Messrs. Allan and St. George's store and served it out to the inhabitants, it is to be presumed that they do not mean to remain long enough to consume it themselves. The male inhabitants very generally dispersed, although most on parole, alarmed at the transfer of paroled militia and non-combatants from Newark to the interior of the United States. Major Allan was considered so obnoxious that he quitted the town early. It is said this morning that a warrant is issued to apprehend him. The commissary proceeded to General de Rottenburgh. The cattle which had been provided for beef were driven off towards the head of the lake. The ammunition was removed to the safest place which could be devised. The baggage of the Nineteenth Dragoons was also secured as well as the circumstances admitted. Colonel O'Neil with three officers entered the town as the shipping was coming to, and proposed requiring to gallop through. A message has been sent to the carrier of your Excellency's despatches not to take them through York, and another to Major Herriot to use his discretion in advancing with the *Voltigeurs*. The squadron has landed a few men on the beach, supposed with intent to attack the depot at Beasley's, but Major Maul had had the precaution to embarrass the outlet so that their craft could not pass, upon which they re-embarked and proceeded to York. The same brigade would join Major Maul last night, but, being obliged to embark their guns in boats, it is possible they might not venture to proceed, as there was no person left to forward intelligence to your Excellency, unless Dr. Strachan should do it. The liberty of giving you this intelligence is taken by a person lately honoured with your commands to report confidentially on certain topics.

William Dummer Powell to Sir George Prevost :

AUGUST 1, 9 o'clock P.M.

SIR :—Since I took the liberty to write to your Excellency the particulars which had come to my hearing of the events of yesterday, at York, further intelligence has reached us that after embarking their troops yesterday, the enemy received information of all the ammunition and baggage of the Nineteenth Dragoons, which had fallen into their hands. It is also reported that several boats have been taken in the River Credit, which we think probable, as Lieutenant-Colonel Battersby wrote from the head of the lake, to Mr. Allan, that he has been constrained to leave his boats with baggage in the creek, and desired militia might be sent to secure them. This letter to Mr. Allan has not found him, as upon learning that a reward was offered to apprehend him, he retreated to the woods.

The despatch from your Excellency to the officer commanding at York, has been sent on to Burlington, there being no officer left in York. The troop of Nineteenth Dragoons on the march, halted this day at Port Credit, fifteen miles from York, and notice has been given them of the situation of that port. The enemy had furnished no guard beyond the Don bridge at six o'clock this evening, but the town was reported to be full of troops, and the inhabitants alarmed at a threatened conflagration of particular houses.

No sooner had the war of 1812 ended than Canada, that fruitful soil of rebellion, was again in a state of insurrection in the Red River country. Earl Selkirk had left his native heath to plant his clansmen along the borders of the Red River of the north. In 1816 the pibroch and the claymore were busy in their separate vocations in the neighbourhood of Fort Garry. Murder, robbery, and arson had got a foothold on the hitherto peaceful prairie Earl Selkirk had felt that he was commissioned to cause the downfall of the Northwest company of traders. The members and employees of the company resisted the Scottish earl. Riots occurred of a magnitude which in the year of grace 1886 would be called a rebellion. The rioters were arrested and taken to Montreal for trial. The accused languished two years in prison, all because his Lordship was not ready to proceed with his indictments. At last the Government intervened, the place of trial was changed to York, and the accusers and accused met face to face. The excitement waxed strong. It was a fortunate circumstance that so able and firm a Judge as Chief Justice Powell presided at the trial. The reported proceedings show that great energy and ability was displayed by so able counsel for the prisoners as Samuel Sherwood and Levius P. Sherwood in defence of their clients. The jurisdiction of the Court was attacked, and every possible device resorted to on the prisoners' behalf. The Chief Justice was obliged to rule suddenly on points of the greatest importance, and was always equal to the occasion. A review of the report of the case shows that he exhibited professional ability, and showed a firmness, coupled with impartiality, that will ever redound to his credit and to the honour and dignity of the Bench. The prisoners were all acquitted, and thus ended the troubles of the prairie country, and not till the expiring of fifty years was the peace disturbed in the country of the Indians and the Metis.

Up to the war of 1812 Chief Justice Powell had been a puisne Judge—he was not promoted to the Chief Justiceship till 1815. It will thus be seen that the major part of his judicial duties in the Province was in the capacity of puisne Judge. Whether as Judge or Chief Justice he was always conscientious in the performance of his duties. Referring to "Taylor's Reports," I find that the last time Chief Justice Powell presided in Court was in Trinity Term, 6 Geo. IV., A.D. 1825. In the proceedings of Michaelmas Term, 1825, the Reporter makes this note :

MICHAELMAS TERM, 1825.

The Honourable Mr. Justice Campbell this term took his seat upon the bench as Chief Justice in place of the Honourable Chief Justice Powell, who retired.

6—L. J.

The Chief Justice survived his retirement from the Bench nine years. Three years of this time were spent in England, where he visited, accompanied by his wife and daughter. The rest of his life was spent in quiet retirement in Toronto, where he died in his seventy-ninth year. His widow survived him, and died in 1849, in her ninety-first year. The Powells will always be remembered in Toronto as one of the good old families of the old town of York, grown to be the flourishing city of Toronto. There is no portrait in Osgoode Hall of Powell, C. J.

His granddaughter, Miss Jarvis, has favoured me with a view of the Chief Justice's portrait in oil, in her possession. The likeness affords an excellent clue to the firmness and disposition of so excellent a Judge.

This likeness is by Gilbert; represents the Chief Justice in his more advanced years, partially bald head, grey hair, and a full, florid English face.

III.

THE HONORABLE JOHN ELMSLEY, CHIEF JUSTICE OF UPPER CANADA.

THE Honourable John Elmsley, destined to be a future Chief Justice of Upper Canada, was the son and heir of Alexander Elmsley, of the parish of Marylebone, Middlesex, England. He was born in 1762, was nephew of the celebrated London publishers, Elmsley & Brother, of the like celebrated comical critic and editor, Peter Elmsley, of Oxford.

Mr. John Elmsley, as I suppose I must call him before elevated to the dignity of a Chief Justice, was called to the bar of England, at the Middle Temple, on the 7th of May, 1790. He had been at the bar only six years and six months, or about that time, when he received His Majesty's letters patent appointing him his Chief Justice of Upper Canada, to succeed the Honourable William Osgoode, who had been promoted from the Chief Justiceship of Upper Cannada to the chief judiciary of Lower Canada. The King's patent appointing Mr. Elmsley was dated the 21st day of November, 1796. The London publisher, of whom I have spoken, was a friend of the Duke of Portland, and it is said that Mr. Elmsley owed his appointment to the Bench to the patronage of the Duke. The Chief Justice first took his seat as Chief Justice at the Court House, Newark, on the 16th of January, 1797. It may be interesting, as well as instructive, to give the ceremony of the inauguration of the Chief Justice into his new office. The tendency of the present day is to do away with form and ceremony, but then it must be remembered that we live in a democratic age. It was not so at the period of the Chief Justice's appointment; indeed, if there was one thing more than another aimed at in that day, it was the preservation of kingly dignity, and following on that the dignity of the Judges who administered the laws of the state. In the "King's Bench Term Book of Hilary Term, 37 George III.," Monday, 16th of January, 1797, I find this entry:

> This day John Elmsley, Esq., came into Court, produced His Majesty's letters patent, dated the 21st day of November, 1796, constituting him Chief Justice of this Province, took the oaths of office, and subscribed the declaration against transubstantiation.

The Reporter adds an N.B. as follows:

> The ceremony on this occasion was as follows: The Chief Justice, preceded by his marshal, and attended by the officers, civil and military, of the Province, entered the Court and ascended the step of the bench at the left end. He then produced his patent, and delivered it (in the absence of Mr. Justice Powell) to the Clerk of the Crown, informing him of the nature of it, and desiring him to read it. Silence having been proclaimed by the crier, the patent was read, all persons standing and uncovered. The Clerk of the Crown having read the patent, returned it to the Chief Justice, who then took the usual oaths and subscribed the declaration against transubstantiation, the Chief Justice reading the oaths from a roll and the Clerk holding the book to him, after which the Chief Justice advanced to the middle of the Bench, and, bowing to the Bar, the officers of the Court, and the persons who had accompanied him to the Court, covered himself, and took his seat. The Attorney-General then rose and moved that the Clerk of the Crown might make the entry on the records of the Court that his Honour had taken the several oaths and subscribed the declaration of law required, to which the Chief Justice assented. The Chief Justice then informed the Clerk of the Crown that he had appointed Mr. Alexander McNabb to be Marshal to the Chief Justice and to that Court, and directed him to administer his oath of office, which was done accordingly, and the new Marshal took his seat in front of the Court, between the Attorney-General and Solicitor-General.

The reader, after perusal of this notice of ceremonial, f not exhausted in the reading, must of force admit that Canada truly had a royal judicial beginning. The only ceremonial of the present day at all equal to this is the nobility of gait and mein exhibited by "Black Rod" on occasion of the meeting of Parliament at Ottawa.

Let us not, however, make light of the precedent. Was it not always the case in the olden times that forms of law were a principle feature in the administration of justice? The more modern doctrine is that forms must give way to substance. Hence in the administration of justice, as in other matters, we have more the reality of things than of obsolete forms and worn-out precedents. Equality and justice have taken the place of the strict and technical reading of the bond. Shylock may take his pound of flesh, but if he do that, justice, which tempers the law, will overtake him. The dodger may lose his ducats, the "*Equitas sequitur legem*" doctrine is pretty well exploded.

But to return to the Chief Justice. We find that he presided in full term in T. T. 37 George III., 17th July, 1797, and that Mr. Gray (afterwards Solicitor General) moved several rules that term. He also presided in M.T. 37 George III., 8th March, 1797, in H. T. 38 George III., 1st January, 1798. E. T. 38 George III., 2nd April, 1798, and T. T. 38 George III., 2nd July, 1798.

So far as I can make out from the records, he first presided at the criminal Court of Oyer and Terminer in the Province at the Court holden for the Midland District at Kingston, on the 11th September, 1797, at which Court Richard Cartwright was one of the associate Justices. He continued in the performance of his official duty as Chief Justice to hold Criminal Courts of Oyer and Terminer in the various judicial districts of the Province, at Newark, York, Kingston, Cornwall, and Johnstown, once a year down to the Court for the Home District, held at York on the 14th of February, 1801. During this period he had as grand jurors well known men, men prominent in their day, and without naming all I might mention some whose descendants still live in the province: At the Court of New Johnstown, on the 19th of September, 1797, Ephraim Jones and Edward Jessup; at Newark, the Court for the

Home District, on the 22nd January, 1798, Andrew Heron, Mr. Crooks, George Law, Peter Ball, and Joseph Clement.

The grand jurors of these days were prominent inhabitants of the country and were summoned by the sheriff, who generally took care to summon men of intelligence having real estate in the country.

In Chief Justice Elmsley's time the practice of branding and pillorying had not yet gone out. I find that at the Court held by him at New Johnstown, on the 11th of September, 1798, a prisoner convicted of perjury was sentenced to be pilloried three times and imprisoned six months ; and at the Court held by him at York, on the 14th of November, 1798, one prisoner convicted was sentenced to be "publicly whipped," and another to be "burned in the hand." Transportation was also a sometime sentence in those days. The record of this Court holden at York on the 26th of November, 1798, states in the case of three prisoners brought up for sentence, " The Attorney General moved that they may be permitted to transport themselves "—not to be transported, but to transport *themselves.* This reminds one of Gratiano's advice to the Jew : " Beg, that thou mayest have leave to hang thyself."

The Chief Justice, while residing in York, took much interest in the material progress of the place. He acquired a large property above the McAulay property on Yonge street. His inclination as well as his interest induced him to be one of the principal promoters of the opening of Yonge street. Dr. Scadding, in his "Toronto of Old," acquaints us with the fact that in 1800 the Chief Justice presided at a public meeting to consider the best means of opening the road to Yonge street, and that he was a subscriber to the fund raised for that purpose. Government House, at the corner of King and Simcoe streets, in Toronto, was formerly the property of Chief Justice Elmsley. It is a matter of history that when the Americans attacked York in 1813 the magazine at the fort exploded. The Government House at that day was near the magazine. On the restoration of peace the Chief Justice's private house, at the corner of King and Simcoe streets, was purchased and converted into Government House. It has ever since, for the most part of the time, been occupied for the same purpose—the Governors and Lieutenant-Governors there dispensing the hospitality suitable to their station. The Governor's residence has more than once been added to and improved. There seems to be a disposition on the part of those who have the control of the vice-regal mansion to preserve in its surroundings some of its antiquity.

Captain the Hon. John Elmsley, of Toronto, was son of the Chief Justice ; in his younger days he was a lieutenant in the royal navy, and never lost his love for the water. At a time when skilful seamen were required for the lake steamers plying between Toronto and Kingston, and the St. Lawrence, the captainship of the steamer *Sovereign* was committed to the salt water sailor, Captain Elmsley ; indeed his title of captain was acquired from his having charge of lake craft ; he was a skilful and popular captain. I remember on one occasion being a passenger of his on a voyage of his vessel going from Toronto to Kingston. Before daylight of the morning we should have arrived at Kingston, the vessel (the *Sovereign*), in a dense fog, owing to no fault of the mate in charge, ran upon Nine Mile point, nine miles above Kingston. I had, on that occasion, an opportunity of observing the care and skill of Captain Elmsley in the command of the steamer, extricating her from her dangerous position after a delay of several hours. Before this, in 1839 or 1840, I had an opportunity of knowing him in another capacity. At that time I was pursuing my studies with his brother-in-law, the Hon. George Sherwood, of Brockville, when one day there appeared a stranger in the place. The good people of Brockville wondered who he might be. He was a man of manly bearing and it is said much resembled his father, the Chief Justice. It was not given to the people of Brockville to know as much of him, on that occasion, as was afforded to the writer. He had come there to augment his then dawning wealth by the accession to it of soldiers' claims. There were in the vicinity of Brockville a number of militiamen who had, as a reward for their services in the War of 1812, been granted scrip entitling them to claim land from the Government. Captain Elmsley foresaw that the ownership of these claims might be turned to good account, and so he was bent on acquiring them. Soldiers, even though militiamen, and sailors are never very provident, and claims could be had at a large discount of their real value. "Now's the day and now's the hour," see approach the Elmsley power. He came, he saw, he conquered. He procured assignment of many claims. I accompanied him on his expedition to witness the transfer. These claims were the foundation of his wealth as a large landed proprietor. I have been told by those who knew the Chief Justice that Captain John Elmsley, in a large degree, resembled his father, the Chief. If this be so, from my acquaintance of Captain Elmsley, acquired on the occasions I refer to, I can say that the Chief Justice must have been a man of goodly presence, great acquirements, and nobility of character. Captain John Elmsley did not follow in the footsteps of his father in the matter of faith and religion. The Chief Justice was a staunch Protestant and member of the Church of England. He was one of the principal founders of the building of St. James's Church, sometimes called the Cathedral. Indeed, in old times, during the bishopric of the Right Reverend John Toronto, more commonly known as Bishop Strachan, of Toronto, it was always so called. In the year 1843, Captain John Elmsley became a pervert or convert to the Roman Catholic Church, though up to that period he had, like his father and mother, been a staunch Protestant. The ostensible cause of his change of faith was the reading of the Roman Catholic Bishop of Strasburg's observations on the sixth chapter of St. John's gospel. Mr. Elmsley satisfied his own mind and published a pamphlet, which he circulated through the Province, giving the reason for his change of faith. The Bishop, then Archdeacon Strachan, felt it his duty to remonstrate with his old parishioner, and adopted the like means of refuting the doctrine of transubstantiation, which had become a matter of faith with Captain Elmsley. The Archdeacon published at the *Courier* office (owned by G. P. Bull in Toronto), in 1834, a pamphlet addressed to the congregation of St. James's Church, in which, in a very able manner, he answered and endeavoured to remove the doubts or confirmed opinion of Captain Elmsley in regard to the question which had agitated him I, by accident, picked up this pamphlet one day in a book stall of the city. I prize it as a relic of the past and remembrancer of the controversy.

In order to show the spirit in which this controversy was conducted, and the spirit that animated the good Archdeacon, I will quote but one passage in his deliverance. The Archdeacon wrote in 1833, thus:

The members of the Roman and English Catholic Churches, both clergy and laity, have always lived on the most friendly terms in Upper Canada, and I trust will continue to do so. A regard for the tranquility of their flocks and the variety and extent of their duties appeared to dictate this line of conduct to the clergy; and their situation has hitherto afforded them little leisure or convenience for polemical discussion. But new converts, anxious to spread the strange light that has burst upon them, are not easily restrained within the limits of a prudent discretion, and therefore Mr. Elmsley thought it necessary, as it would appear, even before his final conversion, to labour for the conversion of others, by publishing an English translation of the Bishop of Strasburg's commentary on the sixth chapter of St. John.

I quote the passage merely to show that, with a difference of opinion and independent thought, there may be coupled that tolerance and charity which " vaunteth not itself, is not puffed up." I would not have referred to this matter at all were it not that the secession of Captain Elmsley from the English Church at the time caused much pain to the Archdeacon and no little scandal to the Church; and, going back to the Chief Justice, his inauguration and declaration against transubstantiation, the matter is one, in some degree, akin to the subject in hand.

Captain Elmsley, notwithstanding his secession from his mother Church, continued in well-doing, in acts of charity and benevolence. Many a poor citizen, some now living, had reason to acknowledge assistance from his bounty, and the Roman Catholic Church profited largely by his benefactions.

I must pass on, as it were, changing the venue from the Province of Upper Canada to that of Lower Canada. The Chief Justice had performed his duties so much to the satisfaction of his royal master, that, on the resignation of Chief Justice Osgoode, he was appointed to succeed him in the Chief Justiceship of Lower Canada, on the 13th of October, 1802. I have before me a copy of the letter of the Colonial Minister, Lord Hobart, to Lieutenant-General Hunter, informing him of the appointment, or proposed appointment, of Mr. Elmsley to the Chief Justiceship of Lower Canada. The letter is dated Downing street, 31st of May, 1802, and reads as follows :

SIR : The office of Chief Justice of Lower Canada having become vacant by the resignation of Mr. Osgoode, in fixing on a person properly qualified to succeed him, the character and merits of Mr. Elmsley, who has discharged with so much credit to himself the duties of a similar appointment within your government, could not fail to point him out to his Majesty as in every respect worthy of his choice.

In his new office of Chief Justice of Lower Canada, Chief Justice Elmsley was conspicuous for his fidelity and zeal in the public service. In 1804 he was appointed to the speakership of the Legislative Council of that Province. The system then prevailing in the Province of Lower Canada, under which the Chief Justice was appointed member of the Legislative Council by the Crown, and was sometimes, if not always a member of the Executive Council, also appointed thereto by the Crown, was a vicious one ; but then it is to be said that this was long before the visit of Lord Durham to Canada, when the true principles of responsible government, as existing in England, did not prevail in Canada. A Chief Justice who, to his judicial duties, has superadded political duties, such as those of Legislative or Executive Councilor, is apt to have motives imputed to him which mar his usefulness as an independent Judge. This was especially the case in Lower Canada, where a vast majority of the people were French, and the officials of Government English. Even so impartial and excellent a Judge as the first Chief Justice Osgoode was not able to escape the friction occasioned by such a state of affairs. Sir Robert Shore Milnes was Lieutenant Governor of the Province during the Chief Justiceship of Osgoode, as well as of Elmsley. Sir Robert Shore Milnes was a military man, very much given to governing by military rule. In 1801 serious differences took place between him and Chief Justice Osgoode. The Chief Justice had prepared charges against another Judge—Judge DeBonne—which the Chief Justice thought called for his dismissal. The Governor took it upon himself to shield Judge DeBonne. There can be no doubt that the complaint of Chief Justice Osgoode, as to the performance of Judge DeBonne's judicial duties, was well founded. In a despatch from Sir R. S. Milnes to the Duke of Portland, on the 20th of March, 1801, he sought to bring the Chief Justice into disfavour with the home Government, and attempted to excuse DeBonne. In this despatch he wrote:

> Since the representation I made to Mr. DeBonne, respecting his non-attendance in the Courts, he has been constant in his duty, and at the opening of this Parliament he called upon me to offer his services, and to say that he had no wish but to be considered by me in a favourable light, and to give his support as he uniformly had done to the representative of his Majesty in the Province.

This despatch itself shows that the Governor knew that Judge DeBonne had been remiss in the performance of his duties, that he had made a representation to him on the subject and had received and accepted his apology. The Chief Justice Osgoode in this matter, as in all other matters, was solicitous for the honour and dignity of the Crown and its officers, especially its judicial officers. The Chief Justice came out of this affair with honour, and on his resignation, was granted a pension of eight hundred pounds sterling per year. I do not find that the path of Chief Justice Elmsley was crossed by the Governor though the same Governor reigned during his occupancy of office. There is nothing to show that Chief Justice Elmsley was held otherwise than in esteem in Lower Canada.

He had only filled the office there for a period of three years [or thereabout, when death cut short his earthly career in the month of July, 1805, at Montreal. He was a gentleman of great professional talents and application, as well as the most amiable demeanor. Mr. Morgan informs us that the Quebec *Mercury* said of him, in an obituary notice of his death : " That he was eminently distinguished not less for his private virtues than his public talents."

IV.

THE HONORABLE HENRY ALCOCK, CHIEF JUSTICE OF UPPER CANADA.

HAVE somewhere read that Charles Francis Adams, who really had reason to be proud of his ancestry, grew tired of being introduced as a grandson of John Adams and the son of John Quincy Adams. At one political meeting he said: "The fact of my ancestry has been referred to several times during the evening. I am proud of my father and grandfather, but I wish it distinctly understood that I appear before you as myself, and not as the son and grandson of any man." Chief Justice Alcock has to be spoken of in almost the same strain, for I have not been able to gather much of his history before his appearance in the official records of Canada. His father was an Englishman, residing at Edgliston, in the county of Warwick, and the future Chief Justice was called to the Bar of Lincoln's Inn in Hilary Term, 1791.

Chief Justice Alcock was one of those men so fortunate as to diversify his duties. His first appointment was on the General Commission of the Peace for the Province in 1796. On the 30th of November, 1798, he was appointed Judge of the King's Bench for Upper Canada, and on the 19th of January, 1799, Judge of the District Court of the Province. In the autumn following his appointment he entered upon his judicial duties. He presided at the Court of Oyer and Terminer, held at

Newark (Niagara) on the 15th and 16th of October, 1799. He continued holding the principal criminal Court of the Province down to the autumn of 1804. He had, in the intervening period, on the 7th of October, 1802, been promoted to the Chief Justiceship of the Province, and thenceforward he continued in the duties of his high office till July, 1805, when he was promoted to the Chief Justiceship of Lower Canada. The opinion entertained of Judge Alcock at the Colonial Office appears from a letter from Lord Hobart to Lieutenant-General Hunter, Governor of the Province at the time, dated the 31st of May, 1802. In that letter Lord Hobart thus expresses himself:

> The professional abilities of Mr. Alcock, and the high opinion you appear to entertain of him, have induced His Majesty to promote that gentleman to the situation of Chief Justice of Upper Canada, and to call him to a seat in the Executive and Legislative Council, which will become vacant by Mr. Elmsley's removal to those of the Lower Province.

During the time of his occupancy of the Bench in Upper Canada, which was but a few years, he gave every satisfaction in the performance of his duties, which consisted principally in holding the Criminal Court in the various districts of the Province. In January, 1800, he presided at the Court of Oyer and Terminer for the Home District, held at York, where he had waiting on him twenty-four grand jurors, among whom were Thomas Ridout, William Jarvis, and —— Wilcock. I have only to mention those names to show of what sterling stuff were the jurors of those days. The Ridouts and Jarvises were leading families in the early days of York. The Jarvises were New England Loyalists. The Jarvis who was Secretary of the Province, as well as Stephen Jarvis, who was in early times Registrar of this Province, were officers in incorporated colonial regiments before the independence of the United States.

In August, 1803, the Chief Justice held the Criminal Court for the London District. In Chief Justice Alcock's time the Court for the London District was held at Charlotteville. The record is "at the Town of Charlotteville,

22 August, 1803." In September, 1803, he presided at the Court holden for the Western District. At this Court two prisoners were convicted of murder, and the sentence of the Court was "both to be hung till dead, afterward to be hung in chains." I do not know why the Court was so very particular as specially to order that after the vital spark had fled the doomed men were to be hung in chains, but such was the sentence. In 1803, or January, 1804, the Chief Justice (Alcock) presided at the Court for the Home District, held at York, when a man and his wife were found guilty of a nuisance—the sentence on the wife was "six months common jail, and to stand twice in the pillory opposite the market house two hours each time during the imprisonment." The market-place was about in the same locality as the present St. Lawrence Market. In a proclamation issued by Governor Hunter, on the 26th of October, 1803, there was established in York a regular market, to be held once a week, and the boundaries of the market-place were defined. The town seems also to have enjoyed the luxury of a public pump and other great advantages. It was at or near this public pump in the market-place that the public whipping, as well as the pillorying, was enacted. Dr. Scadding, in "Toronto of Old," in his topographical sketch of the town and the public pump, says :

> And here we once witnessed the horrid exhibition of public whipping, in the case of two culprits whose offence is forgotten. A discharged regimental drummer, a native African, administered the lash. The sheriff stood by, keeping count of the stripes. The senior of the two unfortunates bore his punishment with stoicism, encouraging the negro to strike with more force. The other, a young man, endeavoured for a little while to imitate his companion in this respect, but soon was obliged to evince by fearful cries the torture endured.

What stories might not that pump at the market-place be able to tell if it had tongue to speak. At a very early period in the days of King Charles and Archbishop Laud there is said to have been a pump in Salem, Massachusetts, which for purity of water, if not for purity of language, was unsurpassed. It has been celebrated in the " Rill of the Pump." The writer of the Rill has indulged in much pleasantry on his theme. It is not to be doubted that at a later age in Toronto the town pump and its surroundings were not far behind the pump of Salem in contributing to the delectation of incipient York.

The reader must not suppose that whipping was a punishment peculiar to Canada, or that it had not age and some Puritanism to commend it to public favour. Has not that most delightful painter of New England customs, Nathaniel Hawthorne, in his tale, " Endicott and the Red Cross," written it down for our learning, that in old Salem there was in close vicinity to the meeting-house "that important engine of Puritanic authority, the whipping post, with the soil well trodden around it by the feet of evil doers who there had been disciplined : at one corner of the meeting-house was the pillory, and at the other the stocks, and that a criminal who had boisterously quaffed a health to the King, was confined by the legs in the stocks ?"

These evil doers, referred to by him, were sentenced to undergo their various modes of punishment for the space of one hour at noonday. The New England malefactors of these days had often to submit to bear a more scandalous and life-long punishment.

Hawthorne tells us that among the crowd he was describing "were several whose ears had been cropped, like those of puppy dogs ; others whose cheeks had been branded with the initials of misdemeanors ; one with the nostrils slit and seared, and another with a halter about his neck, which he was forbidden ever to take off, or to conceal beneath his garments."

The last sentence passed by the Chief Justice in Upper Canada, so far as I can ascertain from the records, was on the 5th of October, 1804, at Cornwall Court, holden for the Eastern District. Banishing was not out of vogue at that time. A prisoner named La France was convicted of stealing and sentenced to be "banished from the Province for the term of his natural life, and that he take his departure from the Province in two days from this time." Inasmuch as most prisoners who were banished from the Province were at that period almost of necessity compelled to take refuge in the United States, it seems hardly fair to have imposed upon the new Republic citizens of this class, dumping them, as it were, over the border.

Chief Justice Alcock, like other Chief Justices of the latter period of the last century and the beginning of this, was a member of the Legislative Countil of Upper Canada to which he was summoned in 1803, and, indeed, at the same time was made Speaker of that aristocratic body. After his removal to Lower Canada he was made a Legislative Councillor there also, and in 1807 was appointed Speaker of the Council. He was also a member of the Executive Council. I do not find anything in the history of the times to justify me in saying that he was a success in his political capacity, although much esteemed in his judicial. I hazard the opinion that a good deal of jealousy was at the bottom of his unpopularity as a councillor. In his day the wheels of government did not run smoothly in the Lower Province. The Legislature of the Province was filled with place-men, and the executive was often arbitrary and offensive. Mr. H. W. Ryland, in 1807, had for fourteen years been clerk of the Executive Council. The Governor of the Province, so far as England was concerned, was generally confided to a military officer. There were frequent changes of officers and as frequent changes of executive government. Mr. Ryland was there all the time—in fact and in truth he was *sub rosa*, more ruler than was the Governor. He had the ear of all the Governors during the whole time of his incumbency of office. He was afflicted largely with Franco-phobia—indeed, if he had his way he would have had nothing but military government in Lower Canada. He, however, was but one of a class, and there can be no doubt voiced the views of the majority of the English in the Province, and that view was the extirpation of the French.

In 1807 a change of officers was likely to take place, and Mr. Ryland was likely to be suspended in his office. He conceived the idea, rightly or wrongly I cannot say, that Chief Justice Alcock was desirous of getting his intended father-in-law appointed to the place. Mr. Ryland, not always very choice in his language, in writing to the Lord Bishop of Quebec, designated the Chief Justice as *a contemptible animal*, in another place he called him *a curious beast* These, however, were but figures of speech, and the Secretary was much commended by his friends for his frankness and John Bullism.

Even at the expense of prolixity, I must give the communication of Mr. Ryland to the Lord Bishop, necessary as it seems to me, in order to understand the *raison d' etre* of the undoubted historical fact, that a worthy and popular Judge, in his judicial status, was yet disliked in his political status. Mr. Ryland's letter to the Lord Bishop of Quebec is dated, Quebec, 17th October, 1807. It professes to give an account of Sir. James Craig's arrival in Canada, and is as follows :

MY DEAR LORD— I had the happiness to receive your Lordship's letter, by the Honourable and Reverend Mr. Stewart, who appears to me to merit every eulogium your Lordship can bestow on him. I admire his zeal, I venerate his principles, and from my soul I wish him all possible success in the highly laudable mission he has undertaken. The president is on every account most heartily disposed to promote the object in view, and your Lordship may be assured that no endeavour of mine will be wanting to the same end ; but you well know, long before this time, the great change that is about to take place here, and which probably will remove me from the only situation that can enable me to contribute to the accomplisment of your Lordship's wishes in any matters of a public nature.

The ministry has at length taken a most decisive step with respect to this country, and at the same time the wisest that could be adopted for its preservation and happiness, and I hope and trust that henceforth the civil government of this Province will never be separated from the military command. I can only say that during the last twelve months I have had a more difficult and arduous duty to perform than has at any time been imposed upon me during the fourteen years preceding, and I should be very glad if your lordship could obtain an opportunity of ascertaining this matter by an inspection of the correspondenc from home since the month of January last. I flatter myself the Secretary of State will have received a series of dispatches which, if read with attention, will not only give him a general and useful knowledge of the state of things here, but also a particular insight of certain leading characters, whose utmost endeavours have been to defame and injure the president (Mr. Dunn) with a view to their own private interests. I particularly allude to that contemptible animal the C. J. (Chief Justice Alcock), to his worthy friend and coadjutor * * (of whose treacherous, plausible, and selfish character I have never had but one opinion), and to that smooth-faced swindler whom the Lieutenant-Governor has taken so affectionately by the hand as the man who of all others comes the nearest, in point of knowledge, to the great Tom of Boston. To these worthies I must beg leave to add a pudding-headed commanding officer, who, if the president had given in to all his chamelian projects, would have introduced utter confusion into the whole system, civil and military. The reinforcements so prudently sent from Halifax are arrived. We look only with anxiety for the Governor-General and Commander-in-Chief, whose established fame assures us that a better choice could not have been made.

This communication was not transmitted to the Lord Bishop till after the 24th of October, when Sir James Craig was sworn in as Governor, and on the 22nd of October Mr. Ryland added to his previous communication the following:

The day after I wrote what goes before, I was awakened very early in the morning by a messenger from Mr. Dunn, informing me that he had received an express from Sir James Craig, and that the General was just at hand. I dressed myself immediately and got on board the frigate with Mr. D.'s answer to the General's despatch before the ship cast anchor, and before any other of the public functionaries knew she was at hand. I found the General, as he had stated, extremely ill, in bed; but he received me with great politeness, and, after enquiring concerning my appointment as Secretary, he begged I would do him the favour to remain in the same situation with him. I never in my life was so pleased with any person at first sight; and, although I saw him under every disadvantage, he struck me as a most amiable, intelligent, decided character. He landed about one o'clock, after which I saw him only for a minute, for he was so unwell he earnestly desired to be left alone. Yet that curious beast, the C. J. (C. J. Alcock), after intruding himself with unparalleled assurance upon the General before he landed, forced himself upon him again at the chateau, when everybody but the President had withdrawn, and most impudently sat the latter out. There is little doubt that he ventured on this proceeding for the purpose of recommending as secretaries his intended father-in-law and a young man named Brazenson, or some such name, whom he had brought out with him from England, but his scheme entirely failed and his folly will fall on his own pate.

I am tempted here to say : "*Hinc illæ lachrymæ.*" It plainly appears that office, or retention of office, was the cause of the whole difficulty. In still another addition to the communication of the 17th and 22nd of October, Mr. Ryland (after referring to the circumstance of the swearing in of the Governor the day before, and the sickness, which was so serious that his life was almost despaired of) breaks out into this rhapsody :

> Oh ! if I could but flatter myself he would regain his health, I should become a new man, different, entirely different, from what I have been during the last eight years ; I should look forward with infinite delight to the moment of my reunion with my wife and children. I should almost forget that I am surrounded by scoundrels, and for the love of this one just and honourable man I would bury in oblivion the mean jealousies of a contemptible self-sufficiency and the false professions of smiling deceit. But should it please Almighty God to remove from us this incomparable man, and should there be a chance that the civil government of this Province is again to be disunited from the military command, I do hope your lordship will favour me with your utmost interest toward enabling me to make the exchange which Mrs. R. will tell you I have in contemplation.

I think the reader, after reading Mr. Ryland's communications, will say that he understood *English as she is spoke*. It will further occur to him that the writer of the communication was no small power in the Province, both in church and state. Much more might be gathered from the historical part to show that Mr. Ryland, however excellent a man he may have been, was hardly the one to form a dispassionate judgment of the Chief Justice, who was much esteemed not only for his learning but excellent qualities.

Sir James Craig and Mr. Ryland were very much of one mind as to the mode proper to be pursued in dealing with the French in Lower Canada, and that was to treat them as a conquered people in every respect. It will be observed that Mr. Ryland, in his last communication to the Bishop of Quebec, referred to the Governor as "that incomparable man." The French have stigmatized his administration as the "reign of terror." Yet, with all this, on the return of the Governor to England, in 1811, without leave, in consequence of ill health, broken down in constitution and spirits, he was informed by Lord Liverpool "that the Prince Regent warmly approved of his conduct as Governor of Canada."

There can be no doubt that he carried on the government with much firmness, rather too much so to be pleasing to the French. In a conversation he had with Mr. Plessis, he said:

> It is a certain fact that up to the present time the country has been governed in a spirit foreign to that of the British constitution. We may let things pass here which would not be permitted in any other part of the British dominions. The Home Government will be justified in calling me to account yet for several concessions which were made contrary to its instructions. So long as the Province was not a dependency of much consequence, small regard was paid to such irregularities; but since it has become an important colony, in respect of its population, its material products, and its trade, now augmented to an extent undreamed of in former times, so great an extension in all respects having been given to the colony, it is time that its government were organized on the same plan as the other portions of the Britannic empire. Its greatest glory is that royal prerogative rules everywhere in it.

I would not have the reader suppose that the Governor's allusion to royal prerogative was directed to anything else than the matter in hand—that was the matter of appointment of the clergy in Quebec, the Roman Catholic clergy by the Bishop instead of the Crown. Sir James Craig, like Mr. Ryland, was strongly of the opinion that the act of appointment by the Bishop instead of by the Crown was a direct infringement of the royal prerogative—there is not probably a single Englishman in the Province of Quebec who does not think the same!

During the period of the occupancy of the Bench by Chief Justice Alcock in Lower Canada, events of great importance were transpiring in that Province. In 1805 the British Government had made known to the Roman Catholic Bishop an intention to reclaim, at the Papal court, the privilege accorded to the Kings of France, by the concordats, of nominating to the parochial charges in the colony. The Bishop resisted this proposal peremptorily, as it would have subordinated the Canadian

Church to an Anglican establishment. A change of government taking place in England, the British Government did not pursue the matter, and so, to this day, the Church reigns in the Province of Quebec. The Chief Justice, notwithstanding the many difficulties he had in his political capacity, bore up against them, and succumbed to the hand of death on the 22nd of February, 1808.

That he was much esteemed as a Judge will appear from the obituary notice of him, published at his death by the Quebec *Mercury*. The *Mercury* said :

In the exercise of his public duties he evinced the advantages which attend the forming of a legal scholar at the English Bar, and in all the various offices which he filled he acquitted himself an able Judge, distinguished by the most eminent rectitude and unwearied assiduity. His memory was retentive, his judgment clear and penetrating, and so profound was his knowledge of English law that the energies of his mind cast a luminous ray over the dark and abstruse code of Provincial jurisdiction. His language was classical and perspicious, nor can those who have heard his judgments remember them without a mixture at once of pleasure and regret. In the habitudes of his life his manners were those which are commonly said to be peculiar to a "plain Englishman," affable, conciliating, unaffected. In a word, his public and private virtues will long live in the hearts of both the old and new subjects of this Province, and his death will be felt with a general and unfeigned sorrow.

V.

THE HONORABLE THOMAS SCOTT, CHIEF JUSTICE OF UPPER CANADA.

THE Hon. Thomas Scott was of Scotch parentage. His father, Thomas Scott, was a minister of the Church of Scotland. The Hon. Thomas was born in the year 1746. It was the intention of his father that he should also be a minister of the gospel; he was, in fact, on probation as a minister; but became tutor in the family of Sir Walter Riddell, whose name is famous in the law Courts in Edinburgh. It was through the advice and influence of Sir Walter Riddell that he was induced to leave Scotland for London, where he studied for the law at Lincoln's Inn, and was called to the Bar in Hilary Term, 1793.

In the year 1788, when yet in his pupilage, he received employment under the Crown in the Province of Quebec. At this time the Crown, represented in the Province by Lord Dorchester, had determined to convey to Jeffrey Lord Amherst a parcel or parcels of the confiscated Jesuit estates in the Province. Accordingly Lord Dorchester, on the 2nd day of January of that year, with a view of being informed as to the nature and quality of the estates, issued a commission to Reuben Chandler, Thomas Scott (the future Chief Justice), John Coffin, Gabriel Elzeard Taschereau, Jean Antoine Panet, George Lawes, James McGill, and Messrs. De St. Ours and Rouville, commanding them, or any three of them, to make investigation into what lands and estates were held, possessed, and claimed by the order of Jesuits within the Province, and the manner and ways by which they were, and what portions or parts thereof had been by them aliened and exchanged, and what portions or parts thereof were then vested in the Crown, and which might be legally given and granted. The commissioners were further instructed that the Crown, being desirous to be apprised of the nature and quality of the said lands, and the title by which they were possessed, their value, the nature of the terms by which they were holden, and what claims were made by their heirs of the donors of such parts of the lands as were given to the religious Order of Jesuits by private persons, these several matters were not only to be inquired into, but reported on by the commissioners.

The bare fact of Chief Justice Scott, then a private citizen, plain Mr. Scott, being named on this important commission, showed that he possessed the confidence of the Government of the Province. The first appointment Mr. Scott received in Upper Canada was that of Attorney-General, in 1801. He was promoted to the Chief Justiceship of the Province in 1804. The records show that he first presided at the Court of Oyer and Terminer for the Home District, held at York, commencing the 1st of April, 1807.

Following upon this, in the summer and autumn of that year, he presided at the Court of Oyer and Terminer and General Gaol Delivery in the Newcastle, Midland, Johnstown, Eastern, Western, London, and Niagara Districts. On the 21st October, 1807, he again presided at the Criminal Court for the Home District, at which Court a prisoner, convicted of stealing five shillings, was sentenced to banishment for seven years. At this day such a sentence for such a trifling offence would be considered disproportionate to the crime. It may have been, however, at the period of this sentence, that in the mind of the Court it would be of benefit to the Province to deprive the prisoner of British air for several years, after which he might return purified and reformed.

In 1808 the Chief Justice presided at the Criminal Courts held at York, Sandwich, and Niagara. During the following years, down to the 30th March, 1812, he held the Spring and Autumn Courts at York for the Home District.

I must cry a halt here. The Temple of Janus is now about to open wide its doors and Bellona reigns supreme. The Autumn Court, it is true, was held, but amid the din of war. Before the Autumn Assize was held in the month of June, 1812, the young Republic of the United States had declared war against Great Britain. To most minds this would seem a rash undertaking. Not so, however, thought Mr. Madison, the American President, or the Congress of the United States. Had not England been at war with France, and with all her main and might, striving to curb the despotic sway of the great general of the age, Napoleon Bonaparte, there might not have been a war with America. At the present day it seems almost beyond belief that two nations of the same blood and the same lineage could, except for the gravest reasons, go to war.

It will be but right to place before the readers the causes which influenced the United States to take so important a step. The alleged cause was the Orders in Council, passed by the British Government, which prohibited all neutral nations (which would include the Republic) from commercial intercourse with France. It is true America suggested another reason for her hostile attitude to Great Britain, and that was the impressment of seamen on American vessels by the British cruisers. When it is admitted that up to March, 1811, Great Britain had impressed from the crews of American vessels, peaceably navigating the high seas, not less than six thousand mariners who claimed to be citizens of the United States, and who were denied, as asserted, opportunity to verify their claims; when it is considered further that in the exercise of the powers given by the Orders in Council, a thousand American vessels with their cargoes had been seized and confiscated, there would seem some measure of excuse, if not justification, for the Americans in the extreme act in declaring war. Nevertheless there ought not to have been any war. The Orders in Council were but an answer to France for her Berlin decrees, which were no more or less than a commercial ostracism of England. Under these decrees France excluded from her shores the merchandise of England, her colonies and dependencies. Every article of British produce was searched for, seized, and committed to the flames, while the most cruel punishments were inflicted on the subjects of France who dared to violate these arbitrary laws.

The palpable effect of these decrees was to exclude English commerce, while American commerce could flourish with renewed strength. If America could furnish France with supplies in American ships, and ships being free from capture, it is manifest that France could have prolonged her war with England, and for that matter with the world, for an interminable period and to an intolerable extent. How, then, could England, by her decrees, suffer France thus to rule the commercial world? It was certainly in the power of the United States to profit by the decrees and build up their commerce at the expense of England, but the question is or ought to be, was it right for a young Republic thus to fortify the cause of the greatest despot of the time, the tyrant and despoiler of the peace of Europe? As to the impressment of seamen, the matter being looked into, would have disclosed that the seamen impressed were in the majority of cases British seamen who had deserted their ships and taken refuge under the American flag. If England were to allow this, the supremacy of the seas, which she had acquired, would have been lost, her navy annihilated, and ships, colonies, and commerce a thing of the past; a dream that had vanished forever. But why enlarge on this? The American Congress declared war on the 18th of June, 1812, and they, the Orders in Council, were rescinded on the 23rd of June, 1812. So that before war was well set going the principal cause of this war was removed. In

American documents, acknowledging repeal of the order, it is stated :

> If the Orders in Council had taken place sufficiently early to have been communicated to the United States Government, before they had actually declared war, the repeal of these decrees against neutral commerce would have arrested the resort to arms ; and that one cause of the war being removed, the other essential causes—the practice of impressment—would have been the subject of renewed negotiation. But the declaration of war having given the practice of impressment as one of the principle causes, peace could only be the result of an express abandonment of that practice.

I think we may say that if the electric telegraph had been in existence on the 23rd of June, 1812, it is at least doubtful if there would have been a war between Great Britain and the United States. My reference to the war, its origin and cause, has been suggested by the fact that the grim visage of the demon was appearing on the stage, the judicial duties of the Chief Justice were interrupted—the peaceful quiet of the Province was disturbed by the cries of wounded men and the cannon's roar. In connection with the war and its outcomings, the Chief Justice was an impartial observer of current events. He was a witness of the acts of the Americans in the capture of York in 1813. With a sense of justice which it is well to remember, in a letter of the 30th of April, 1813, he writes : " The humane attention which General Dearborn had paid to the present situation of its inhabitants by pursuing a line of conduct so conducive to the protection of a number of individuals and so honourable to himself."

Chief Justice Scott's residence was in York ; the house was at the corner of Yonge and Front streets, in which Judge Sherwood lived while a resident in York. The house had attached to it, on the east side, garden, orchard, and pleasure ground, which extended all the way to Scott street, running from Wellington to Front street, and which is named after the Chief Justice.

He took great interest in the Loyal and Patriotic Society of Upper Canada, organized at York in 1812, and was its first chairman and president. The objects of the society were "to afford relief and aid to disabled militiamen and their families ; to reward merit, excite emulation, and commemorate glorious exploits by bestowing medals and other honourary marks of public approbation and distinction for extraordinary instances of personal courage and fidelity in defence of the Province." The society had only been formed a few days before the subscription of York to the fund had amounted to the respectable sum of eight hundred and seventy-five pounds (thirty-five hundred dollars), to be paid annually during the war with the United States. Medals were also struck in London, by order of the Loyal and Patriotic Society. These medals, however, never reached the intended recipients from the fact that there were so many candidates for the coveted honour that the difficulty of deciding who was to receive them was found to be too great. The medals were finally broken up and the bullion, augmented with what remained of the funds of the society, devoted to benevolent objects. A considerable donation from the funds was made to the York General Hospital, an institution well deserving of the favour shown to it, and the foundation of the present Toronto Hospital, which enjoys more than a provincial reputation. As a reminder of the old time of the war, and the loyalty which inspired the Canadians of that day, it will not be out of place to give a short description of this medal. It was two and one-half inches in diameter. On the obverse, within a wreath of laurel were the words " For Merit "—on this side was also the legend, " Presented by a grateful Country "—on the reverse was the following device : A strait between two lakes, on the north side a beaver (emblem of peaceful industry), the ancient cognizance of Canada ; in the background the British lion slumbering ; on the south side of the strait the American eagle planing in the air, as if checked from seizing the beaver by the presence of the lion ; legend on this side " Upper Canada preserved."

Notwithstanding the loyalty of the mass of the people of the Province of Upper Canada during the war of 1812, there were some whose American sympathies carried them so far as to subject them to the suspicion if not to the actual commission of high treason. Consequently the Legislature, on the 14th of March, 1814, passed an "Act for the more impartial and effectual trial and punishment of high treason and treasonable practices in the Province." On the 11th of April of the same year, Gordon Drummond, Esquire, then president of the Province, by and in the name of the King, issued a commission to Chief Justice Scott (and others), the Honourable William Dummer Powell, the Honourable William Campbell, Justice of the Court of King's Bench, John Small, Esquire, Richard Hatt, Thomes Dickson, and Samuel Hatt, Esquires, Justices of the Peace, to enquire, by the oath of good and lawful men, at the Court of Oyer and Terminer of the several districts of the Province, into the matter of high treason or treasonable practices committed in either of the Districts of London, Home, or Niagara. The commissioners were not only to enquire but to hear and determine the matters brought before them. It is not always the man who shouts most loyalty that is the most loyal. It is not to be questioned, however, that in the war of 1812 the great body of the Canadians were of refined gold. The United Empire Loyalists had in the American Revolution been subjected to the refining influence of a white-heated crucible, and came out as the purest of metal, battling for their country in her hour of severe trial.

Between the time of the treaty of peace, however, and the war of 1812, a great many Americans, tempted by the richness of the soil of Canada, were willing, for a time at least, to forsake the Stars and Stripes for the land protected by the Union Jack. These strangers were not, in taking up citizenship in Canada, actuated by love of the institutions of Canada, but a desire of gain. Dr. Caniff, in his history of the times, describing the men of this class, says of them: "They would talk loyalty with the Loyalists, shrug their shoulders with the doubtful, and with the well-known Yankee would curse the King." There were others who came to Canada to speculate, and at the same time preach Republican principle—men, in fact, who had no hesitation in endeavouring to seduce Canadians from their allegiance. In some parts of the Province they were but too successful, especially in the west. At Waterford, in the county of Norfolk, enrollment for service was impeded by these tactics of the men from over the border.

That true Christian soldier, Lieutenant, afterward the Rev. George Ryerson, has related that the women of that region, with loud cries and arms around their husbands' and lovers' necks, implored them not to go to the war. The result was, that many were prevailed upon, and refused to take up arms. Some of these men were arrested and taken in a schooner to Niagara. The Ryersons were United Empire Loyalists, always to the front on Britain's side.

As I am now writing of the disaffected element, and to show that there was good reason for the commissions issued to Chief Justice Scott and others to try traitors, I will again quote Dr. Caniff. He says:

> We must not omit to mention the name of William Ryerson (brother of Egerton Ryerson, the Superintendent of Education), who, although young at the time of the war, and not enrolled, was a participator in the strife. It was known that a party of Canadian traitors were collected at the house of one Dunham, at Port Dover. One of the Bostwicks, without any authority, determined, with a number of volunteers, to ferret them out. William Ryerson was one of the volunteers. They succeeded, after a sharp encounter, in which some were killed, in taking a number of them prisoners. There were some forty of them, and they were planning the destruction of the houses of certain leading men in the neighbourhood. Nine of them were subsequently hanged at Burlington (Hamilton).

I think I may now take leave of this subject and the loyal Methodist, the Rev. George Ryerson, who not only fought but bled for his country in the War of 1812, wounded at Fort Erie, the mark of which he carried about him all of his most useful life.

In writing the life of Chief Justice Powell, I made reference to the conspicuous part taken by Bishop Strachan, at York, in the negotiations with the American commander for the capitulation of the town in 1813. Chief Justice Scott was one of Dr. Strachan's prominent parishioners, and a pew-holder in St. James's Church. The Bishop, ever mindful of the good to be done for his people in life, and never forgetful of them after death, in the case of the Chief Justice, after his death, visited William Scott, a brother of his, in Scotland, in 1825. In a letter, bearing date the 9th of October, 1826, the Bishop, writing to a friend in Scotland, says :

> I left St. Andrews on Tuesday, the 10th. On Wednesday, at Dundee, I went with Mr. Kerr, a writer, to Meigle to see William Scott, brother of our late Chief Justice, whose mind is enfeebled. I carried with me his father's and brother's watches, some rings, and other little matters.

In another passage of the letter he says :

> Mr. Kerr, of Dundee, who is our man of business, and of good repute, has the general charge and attends to the payment of expenses. We have left plenty of money in his hands, and all the instruction I gave him as to its application was simply this, to treat William Scott as he would treat his own brother in the same situation.

I would like to be able to say that there was a portrait of Chief Justice Scott in Osgoode Hall. Such, however, is not the case. The only portraiture I can present of him is such as I gather from the recollections of those who knew or have seen him. He is represented as having been in appearance not unlike the eminent American jurist, Chancellor Kent. He was a man of cultured mind, of retiring disposition and thoughtful expression of countenance.

He died at Toronto, on the 28th of July, 1824, at the age of seventy-eight years, and his remains were committed to the tomb in that town, where they now rest, in St. James's cemetery. Loving friends have placed a tombstone at the head of his grave, with an inscription which not only marks his age, but, I believe, truly represents the man and Chief Justice as he was. The inscription reads as follows :

Sacred to the Memory
of
THOMAS SCOTT,

Late Chief Justice of this Province, who departed this life July 28, 1824, at the advanced age of seventy-eight years. This amiable man will be long remembered for the sweetness of his disposition and suavity of manners as a companion, his uprightness as a Judge, his amiable and endearing qualities as a friend, and his charity and truth as a Christian.

VI.

THE HONORABLE THOMAS COCHRANE, JUDGE OF KING'S BENCH, UPPER CANADA.

THE Honorable Thomas Cochrane was a member of the English Bar, receiving his call at Lincoln's Inn. His father was the Hon. Thomas Cochrane, Speaker of the Nova Scotia Assembly in 1784, and, 1788, a member of the Council of that Province. The Cochranes were a distinguished family. William, a brother of the Judge, was a general in the army, and another brother, Sir James Cochrane, Chief Justice of Gibraltar. One of his sisters married Commodore, afterward Sir Rupert George, and another, Dr. John Inglis, the second Bishop of Nova Scotia. Before Judge Cochrane's appointment to the Bench of Upper Canada he was Chief Justice of the Supreme Court of Prince Edward Island, to which office he was appointed on the 24th of October, 1801. The patent of his appointment as Judge of the King's Bench of Upper Canada is dated the 25th of June, 1803, and Judge of Oyer and Terminer and General Gaol Delivery on the 20th of July, 1803. He was not more than thirty years of age when appointed to the Bench of Upper Canada. Lord Hobart, in writing to Lieutenant-General Hunter, making him acquainted with Judge Cochrane's appointment, expressed himself as satisfied with his ability for the post. Lord Hobart's letter is dated the 31st of May, 1802, and in it he says: "Mr. Cochrane, at present Chief Justice of the Island of Prince Edward, will proceed to your Government as *puisne* Judge in the room of Mr. Alcock. These arrangements will, I trust, ensure a continuance of that regularity and ability with which the business of the Courts in the two Provinces have so long been conducted."

Judge Cochrane is styled Judge of the King's Bench, Upper Canada, and not Judge of Upper Canada, as a few years before his appointment the Provincial Legislature had passed an Act constituting a Court of Record, to be styled "His Majesty's Court of King's Bench for Upper Canada." This Act was passed in the thirty-fourth year of the reign of George III., on the 9th of July, 1794. The first Parliament of the Province declared that this Court should possess all such powers and authority as by the laws of England were incident to a Superior Court of civil and criminal jurisdiction, and should have and exercise all the rights, incidents, and privileges as fully to all intents and purposes as the same were at the time the Act took effect, used, exercised and enjoyed by any of His Majesty's Superior Courts of law at Westminster, in England.

Judge Cochrane was only Judge in the Province for little over a year when his career was cut short by an accident, which I will describe further on. I cannot find from the records that he presided at more than one Court in the Province previous to his sudden taking off, and that was at the Court of Assize and *nisi prius* for the Newcastle District, held the 26th of September, 1803. There is, indeed, no official record of his having presided at any Court, but Mr. Alexander McDonell, senior clerk in the Crown office, has in his possession, and which he has shown me, the docket of causes kept by his uncle Angus McDonell, in which is an entry of his that he was engaged in a cause at the Newcastle Court, of which I have spoken, and that Judge Cochrane presided at that Court. The fact that there is no official account of his judicial acts may be accounted for by the probability that his own note book perished with the Judge when he was drowned in the waters of Lake Ontario. It is not often that a whole Court, Judge, counsellor, crown officer, high sheriff, and prisoner to be tried are all drowned at one and the same time. This, however, was an event that occurred in Upper Canada in 1804. It happened that in the month of October of that year the administration of criminal justice required that investigation be made into the circumstances connected with the death and alleged murder of one Thorp, a white man, said to have been murdered at Ball Point, on Lake Scugog. The crime, if such it was, had been committed in the year previous. An Indian who passed by the name of Whistling Duck, a brother of Ogetonicut, had been murdered by a white man ; and as in those days before missionaries had softened and enlightened the heart of the Indian, revenge was a prominent article of the red man's creed, an Indian, Ogetonicut, of the Muskrat branch of the tribe of Chippewas, determined to have his revenge, and so to carry out his purpose he murdered another white man, one John Sharp. Governor Hunter had promised that the murderer of Whistling Duck should be punished. The law's delay had, however, intervened, the prospect of punishment being meted out to the guilty was not encouraging. Chief Wabasheco, of the Muskrat branch of the tribe referred to, conceived it to be his duty to interview the Governor. He and his tribe, Ogetonicut among the number, voyaged in canoes from the mouth of Annis Creek, near Port Oshawa, to Gibraltar Point, opposite York, where they encamped. The arrival of the dusky sons of the forest became known to the authorities, the machinery of the law for the arrest of Ogetonicut was set in motion. Constables were ordered to their duty, with the aid of a guard of soldiers Ogetonicut was lodged in jail at York. It afterwards appeared by actual survey that the offence was not committed in the Home District, but in the Newcastle District. The trial, therefore, must take place in the latter district. In those days the voyage down the lake was mostly made by canoe or schooner. The schooner *Speedy* was chartered to convey the Court from York to the camping place, where the investigation was to be held. It was the 7th of October, 1804, the weather was stormy, and the *Speedy* not being oversea-worthy was not able to withstand the gale. In the dead of night the vessel suddenly went down, buried in the waters of Lake Ontario, not far from Presque Isle harbour. The captain of the schooner, Judge Cochrane, Solicitor-General Gray, Angus McDonell (whom I have previously named), the Indian prisoner, two interpreters, several witnesses, Mr. Herchmer, a merchant of York, in all thirty-nine persons, were swallowed up in the deep. No trace of them or the vessel was ever after discovered. It was a short summons and mournful fate which overtook the passengers and crew on the *Speedy*.

> There are those who go down in the dead, wild sea
>   When storms have wrecked proud ships,
> With none to heed what the words may be
>   That break from their gurgling lips.
>
> No anthem peal flows sweet and loud,
>   No tablets mark their graves,
> But they soundly sleep in a coral shroud
>   To the dirge of the rolling waves.
>
> 'Tis well to find our last repose
>   'Neath the churchyard's sacred sod,
> But those who sleep in the desert or deep
>   Are watched by the self-same God.

VII.

THE HONORABLE ROBERT THORPE, JUDGE OF THE COURT OF KING'S BENCH, UPPER CANADA.

JUDGE THORPE, Mr. Stewart in his history of the Laws of Prince Edward Island states, was an Irish lawyer. He, like Judge Cochrane, had been a Judge of the Supreme Court of Prince Edward Island, before his appointment to a Judgeship in Upper Canada. His appointment as a Judge of the Supreme Court of Prince Edward Island took place on the 10th of November, 1802, and to the Judgeship of the Court of the King's Bench of Upper Canada on the 24th of January, 1805. He also received a commission to secure titles to lands on the 11th of April, 1805. The first entry I find of his having presided in Court is that he held the Criminal Court at York, on the 25th of March, 1806, and had as his associate W. Willcocks. At this Court, William Warren Baldwin, the father of Robert Baldwin, was sworn in as acting Clerk of the Crown and Common Pleas. *En passant*, I may remark that the William Warren Baldwin here named was the well known and much esteemed Dr. Baldwin, the third Treasurer of the Law Society. Judge Thorpe presided again at the York (Home District) Assizes on the 28th of October, 1805, when, as the record states, "a negro, 'Jupiter,' on the complaint of John Denison that he had threatened to poison him, was bound over to keep the peace towards him and his family." Jupiter, though high sounding, is not an everyday name. I strongly suspect this Jupiter, charged as aforesaid, was the very Jupiter, or of kin to a black Jupiter, the son of a slave woman named Peggy, owned by ex-President Peter Russell. In 1806 in several numbers of the York Gazette appeared the advertisement " To be sold, a black woman, named Peggy, aged about 40, and a black boy, her son, named ' Jupiter,' aged about 15 years, both of them the property of the subscriber. The boy is tall and strong of his age. The price of the woman is $150 ; for the boy $200—one-fourth less for ready money. Signed, Peter Russell." The introduction of slaves into the Province had been interdicted by the Act of 1793. That Act, however, confirmed the right of property in slaves then in servitude, hence we find Mr. Russell endeavouring to turn his property to account.

Judge Thorpe again presided at the Assizes for the Western District, held at Sandwich on the 1st of September, 1806, and for the last time so far as I can discern, at the Assizes for the London District, held at Charlotteville, on the 13th of September, 1806.

It was during the occupancy of the Bench by Judge Thorpe that Lieutenant-Governor Francis Gore was appointed to the chief executive office of the Province. Mr. Francis Gore had been Lieutenant-Governor of Bermuda before being appointed to the Governorship of Upper Canada. He was a man endowed with many good qualities, but much given to prerogative right and arbitrary rule. It was no fault of his that his predecessor, Governor Hunter, had, by his administration, stirred up a spirit of hostility to the reigning powers that seriously interfered with equable administration of Governor Gore. The immediate successor in the Governorship to him was Commodore Grant, whom I think we may call sailor, soldier, and statesman, as he at one time and another filled all these positions—first a sailor in the merchant service, then a midshipman, then a soldier in a highland regiment, and then in the war of 1812 put in command of a sloop of 16 guns to operate on the lakes. In 1806 he was an Executive Councilor, and by an understood rotation became temporary Governor. He was more a man of science than politician, though somewhat engaged in politics. During his temporary administration of the government he had not been able to allay the excited and clamorous (for reform) feeling of the people. In July, 1806, Lieutenant-Governor Gore assumed the reins of government in succession to President Grant. Great expectations were aroused by the arrival of the new Governor. It was thought that he would speedily set things to right. Captain Green, who had been military secretary to Governor Hunter, in August, 1806, writes to Mr. McGill of York: "Of course, I may congratulate you on the safe arrival of your Lieutenant-Governor, whose amiable manners will, I think, conciliate the various points that have been in opposition to that cordiality which must ever reign in societies well regulated." Again, in September, in reply to a communication from York, Captain Green writes: "It gives me very sincere satisfaction to find that the Lieutenant-Governor is so well liked. I think he will put the axe at once to the root of the tree of discord and anarchy which lately has raised its head amongst you; that done, you will succeed and prosper."

Now the reader may well inquire what was the discord, anarchy, and confusion alluded to all about? It was just this: At this time the minds of numbers of the people, and even the minds of certain officials of the Government were impressed with the idea that there was too much oligarchical rule in the Province; that the executive authority set at defiance the will of the people, as expressed through their representatives. It was not in those days as it is now. Then, not now, the Judges were eligible for election as members of Parliament. Judge Thorpe had not allied himself so much with the governing powers of that day as with the Willcocks and the Wyatts, men of independent thought, and firm in their resolves whenever an issue occurred between the Governor and the people. Yielding to these impulses, Judge Thorpe accepted the candidature to Parliament offered him by the people of the Home District. This fired the breast of the Governor and oligarchy of the period. Mr. Surveyor-General Wyatt and Sheriff Willcocks were of one mind with the Judge, and therefore opposed to the Governor. The Governor, carrying out the doctrine of the time, the divine right of kings and their satraps, that might makes right, determined to rid himself both of the Judge and the Surveyor-General. He consequently suspended both of them from their high offices, subject to the confirmation of the English Government. In 1807 the Judge was relieved, and in the same year the Surveyor-General, Wyatt, was suspended. Nothing daunted, the Judge appealed not only to the home Government but to the law for satisfaction, and so also did Mr. Wyatt. Mr. Wyatt sued the Governor in an action at law in England, which came down to trial before Chief Justice Gibbs in 1816. A study of that case shows how the matter stood between the Judge and the Governor.

The third count of the declaration sets out the principal complaint of Mr. Wyatt, the Surveyor-General. That count alleged: "That the defendant (Governor Gore) to cause the plaintiff to be deprived of his office, and to induce the King to confirm the suspension, wrote to the Secretary of State certain false letters representing that the plaintiff had been generally hostile to His Majesty's representative, and was engaged with disaffected persons; and that plaintiff, moreover, had erased the name of a person from the plans in the office of the Surveyor-General, who had settled and made improvements in a favourable location of land, and had declared the lot to be vacant, and had obtained a grant of it to himself. That by means of said letters the King confirmed the suspension, and revoked his appointment, and the plaintiff was prevented from enjoying another office, viz.: the office of Receiver-General of the said Province." The defendant, in his pleadings, justified the charge. At this trial the Attorney-General of the Province was a witness to prove publication of the pamphlet. The name of the Attorney-General is not given in the reported case, but I suppose it was the Hon. D'Arcy Boulton, who was appointed Attorney-General in 1814, and was the immediate predecessor of the Hon. John Beverley Robinson, appointed in 1818. The counts in the declaration which charged that the defendant, the Governor, had acted wilfully, maliciously, and without probable cause in suspending the plaintiff from his office was not, in the opinion of Chief Justice Gibbs, sustained, but he thought the matter contained in the pamphlet which contained the libel in question was libellous. The jury awarded the plaintiff £300 ($1,500) damages for the wrong done him by the Governor.

It is the boast of English law that the same measure of justice is meted out to the rich and the poor, to the high and the low, to the King and his subjects. In the case of the legal war which waged between the King's Surveyor-General of the Province and his Governor of the Province, it was a case of Greek meeting Greek, but the Canadian came out triumphantly in his action with the King's executive head of the Province.

I have said that Judge Thorpe and Mr. Willcocks were very much of one mind in regard to popular rights and executive power exercised in those days by an officer, the holder of the colonial office in Downing street. The days of responsible government had not yet come upon the infant Province. The Governor was King, and the officials of the Government his satraps. Mr. Justice Thorpe, in his charge to the grand jury of the London district, in 1806, said to them :

> The art of governing is a difficult science. Knowledge is not instinctive, and the days of inspiration have passed away. Therefore, when there was neither talent, education, information, and even manners in the administration, little could be expected, and nothing was produced. But there is a point of depression, as well as of exaltation, from which all human affairs naturally advance or recede. Therefore, proportionate to your depression, we may expect your progress in prosperity will advance with accelerated velocity.

So far as this charge had reference to rulers, information,

manners, and all that, it was not so much intended for Governor Gore as for Lieutenant-Governor Hunter and his rule. The new Governor, Gore, had not yet crossed the path of the new Judge, Thorpe, for in the same address, in reply to the grand jury, who expressed their approbation of the fact that Mr. Gore, a civilian, had been appointed Governor, the Judge said :

> I shall lay before the Governor everything you desire, and I have not the slightest doubt but that I shall find in him such power of mind, such political acquirements and official habits, and such good dispositions as are fitted to make an infant Province a permanent state, wealthy and powerful, abounding in blessing to the inhabitants, and so valuable to that great empire from which we receive everything estimable, and to which we are anxious to make the most grateful return.

It does seem unfortunate that the prevailing idea at this period of the history of the Province that there was no impropriety in the Judges—appointees of the Crown—also becoming candidates for Parliament, and being elected representatives of the people. Judge Thorpe, who had only entered the Province in 1805, had so much earned the confidence of the people that he was elected a member to the Parliament which met at York on the 2nd of February, 1807. Judge Thorpe, not only in the Parliament, had been very free in his criticisms of the acts of the executive ; his charge to the grand jury of London, to which I have referred, shows pretty well how caustic and incisive the Judge could be. The Anglo-Saxon stolidity and solidity of his race crops out in every passage of his address.

Governor Gore, though of a genial disposition, was not one to be thwarted in his purpose, or unduly criticised in his conduct, without resenting it. He did not at all like the Judge's espousing the popular side. In those days, one who espoused the popular side in opposition to the powers regnant were apt to be called, and even treated, as rebels, if not something worse.

After the close of the session of Parliament, which took place in March, 1807, the Governor proceeded to Montreal

On his way down the St. Lawrence he stopped at Kingston, and there dined with Chief Justice Scott, who was holding the Court at that town.

We are indebted to Dr. Scadding for giving us the means of judging of the estimate in which both Mr. Wilcocks and Judge Thorpe were held by the Governor, this estimate being made more on political than personal grounds. Dr. Scadding tells us that the Governor wrote his friend, Mr. McGill, a very expressive letter, in which he said :

> I received most sincere satisfaction in finding that our good and worthy friend, the Chief Justice (Scott), had got on very well ; that at Newcastle the jury was respectable, and approved of their Judge, not one word being uttered respecting that other execrable monster who would deluge the Province with blood.

The execrable monster here referred to was, no doubt, Mr. Willcocks, who, after having been deprived of the shrievalty of the Home District, had set up an opposition newspaper, *The Upper Canada Guardian*, a freeman's journal, the large circulation of which gave the Governor much uneasiness. In another part of the letter to Mr. McGill to which I have alluded, the Governor says :

> "At Kingston everything went off, as might have been expected, well; the Chief entertaining a party of about forty at dinner. A number of the rebel papers (meaning Mr. Wilcock's newspaper) were distributed to poison the minds of the people, but, I hope, without effect. The object of T.'s emissions (Mr. T. is Judge Thorpe, and his emissions would be his charges to jurors and his speeches in the House and elsewhere), appear to be to persuade the people to turn every gentleman out of the House of Assembly. However, keep your temper with the rascals, I beseech you. I shall represent everything at St. James,"—*i. e.*, headquarters in London.

The language of the Governor certainly was not very dignified, however his sense of prerogative right gave him the right to use it. The Governor did represent everything at St. James, and the result was, that in the following October the following paragraph appeared in the York *Gazette* : " His Majesty's pleasure has been received by the Lieutenant-Governor to suspend Mr. Thorpe from the office of Judge in Upper Canada, and measures are to be taken for appointing a successor. The

Secretary of State has also signified to the Lieutenant-Governor His Majesty's approbation of his having suspended Mr. Wyatt from the office of Surveyor-General of lands in the Province."

We have seen the approbation of the Sovereign, of the act of Governor Gore in suspending Mr. Wyatt, the Surveyor-General, which act afterwards in a trial at law cost the Governor £300 sterling money of Great Britain. Now let us see how the matter ended as between the Governor and the Judge. This resulted also in an action of libel brought by Judge Thorpe against the Governor, in which the Governor was again mulcted in damages at the suit of the Chief Justice.

These proceedings only show that a case as between a Governor and a Judge or other official when seen through the spectacles of a British jury, instead of the eyes of a colonial minister, may present a very different aspect.

The sequel was, that the Chief Justice regained the confidence of the British Government; and although not restored to the office of which he had been deprived, he was afterward appointed to the Chief Justiceship of Sierra Leone, where he remained twenty years, when ill health caused his return to England. Chief Justice Thorpe was a very upright and conscientious man—most independent in character and conduct, he asked no favour, and feared not the power of the colonial oligarchy or the Governor of the colony. He was very unfortunate; for the rulers of the day and he could not hold the same opinion of public affairs. The Governor leaned to the side of his Executive Council, which was incensed at the Chief Justice because he could not conscientiously subscribe to the acts of the Government. As one writer expresses it: "His only object was to effect the strict and upright discharge of his duty uninfluenced and unbiased by party or by prejudice." Governor Gore did not fare as well as the Chief Justice. Although he was caressed by the Government and the time-serving powers of the Day, he was in turn recalled from the government of the Province by the Government of England. I forbear to enter into the differences between the Governor and the Chief Justice. Impartial history compels us to say that they were both men of much independence of character — perhaps too much alike to agree. The Governor, from his position, had the advantage of the Chief Justice, but the Chief Justice on appeal to his compatriots, was vindicated in his official conduct in Upper Canada.

VIII.

THE HONORABLE SIR WILLIAM CAMPBELL, CHIEF JUSTICE OF UPPER CANADA.

THE Honorable Sir William Campbell was the son of Alexander Campbell, who was the son of Captain Alexander Campbell, of the Royal Navy. The family of Campbells, of which the Honorable Sir William Campbell, Chief Justice, was a branch, was for the first half of the last century heritable commoners and sheriff's clerks of Caithness, Scotland, also supposed to be sub-cadets of the Buey-Campbells, and believed to be descended from the family of Quoy Crook, their immediate ancestor, Donald Campbell, Jr., a son of William Buey-McIver, or of John, his brother. The progenitors of the Campbell family were descended from Kenneth Buey-McIver, who emigrated from Argyle to Caithness between 1775 and 1778, and obtained a charter of Quoy Crook in Halkirk. The Honorable Sir William Campbell, Chief Justice of Upper Canada, was one of those men who could adapt himself to circumstances, equally at home, in the battle-field, the Senate, or on the judicial Bench. Not born to greatness, had not greatness thrust upon him, but with true Scotch perseverance may be said literally to have risen from the ranks to fill one of the highest of colonial positions, that of the Chief Justice of the King's Bench in the dependency of Upper Canada, once called by Queen Victoria the brightest jewel in her queenly crown.

William Campbell, afterwards Sir William Campbell, was born in Scotland in 1758. Wolfe had not yet taken Quebec; within a year afterwards the second strongest fortress in the world had fallen before the irresistible force of British arms. Of the regiments which took part in the capture of Quebec, none was more conspicuous than the Scotch Highlanders—the Seventy-eighth Regiment. The boy William Campbell was but a baby in arms at this time. As time wore on, and the sounds of war continued to echo in the woods and ways of America, the boy Campbell was growing from infancy to youthful manhood. When a Highland regiment was ordered to America to quell the strife existing in the colonies, the future Chief Justice, fired with military ardor, enlisted as a private in a Highland regiment. He came to America with his regiment to take part in the Revolutionary War. Engaged in the conflict: was in the battle of Yorktown in 1781: here his military career ended; the fortune of war was against the British—Lord Cornwallis was obliged to surrender, when the young soldier Campbell became a prisoner with the rest of that General's command. When this event occurred William Campbell was but twenty-three years of age. When peace was proclaimed in 1783 Campbell got his discharge, and determined to make British America his future home.

It occurred to him that Nova Scotia, England's oldest colony, might afford him a field for future action, if not in a civil capacity. Impelled by this idea, he made his way to the land of the Acadians; here he devoted himself to the study of the law; was called to the Bar in that Province, and after nineteen years' practice was appointed Attorney-General of Cape Breton, and was also elected a member of the Assembly of that Province. On the 18th of November, 1811, he was promoted to a puisne Judgeship in Upper Canada. He was the first of the Upper Canada Judges appointed to the Bench of that Province from the Bar of a Maritime Province. He did not attain to the Chief Justiceship till 1825, on the retirement of Chief Justice Powell.

There is a folio volume of reports in the Osgoode Hall Library called "Campbell's Manuscript Reports," which contains the cases decided by the Judges of the King's Bench, beginning Trinity Term 4th George IV. (1823), and ending Trinity Term 8th George IV. (1827). There are no Upper Canada Reports extant of the period 1811 to 1823. The "Campbell Manuscript Reports," containing the first record of decided cases in the Province, have for the most part been printed, and now form the first of the series of the Upper Canada Court Reports, under the name of "Taylor's Reports." Thomas Taylor was a Barrister of the Inner Temple, called to the Bar of Upper Canada in 1819. He was the first authorized Court Reporter of the King's Bench, having been appointed to that office under the Provincial Statute 4 George IV., cap. 3, entitled "An Act for providing for the Publication of Reports of Decisions of His Majesty's Court of King's Bench in this Province." It is a singular fact that in England there has been no public Reporter since the reign of James I., who at the instance of Lord Bacon appointed two with a handsome stipend. The Canadian Legislature seems to have followed not only the advice but the example of Lord Bacon in providing for official reports. Lord Bacon was himself much imbued with the idea of the necessity of such an officer, for in his "*De Argumentis Scientiarum*" he wrote:

> Above all, let the judgments of the Supreme and principal Courts be diligently and faithfully recorded, especially in weighty causes, and particularly such as are doubtful, or attended with difficulty or novelty, for judgments are the anchor of the laws, as laws are the anchor of the state.

The most important cases with which Judge Campbell had to deal were those tried at York in 1818, growing out of the riots on the Red River, sometimes called the Red River Rebellion. In the life of Chief Justice Powell, I have referred to, and given some account of the trial of the rioters in these cases. As then related, the presiding Justice at the trial was Chief Justice Powell, but he had with him on the Bench Judge Campbell, then a puisne Judge, not many years after to succeed the Chief. The record of these trials shows that he, equally with Chief Justice Powell, was firm in his rulings tending to the elucidation of all the facts connected with the riotous proceedings on the Red River caused by Lord Selkirk's introduction into the country of Scotch emigrants to till the soil in place of hunting deer and buffalo.

The Earl of Selkirk (Thomas Douglas) was a descendant of that Archibald Douglas, ten generations back, who obtained the *sobriquet* of " Bell the Cat."

The Earl was the seventh son of Dunbar, fourth Earl of Selkirk. While a young man he shewed the ability and industry of his race. His name is found upon the class-books of various Professors of the Edinburgh University from the year 1780 to 1790, and while pursuing his academic career there he was known as one of a band of illustrious young men earnestly engaged in literary and learned pursuits. He was a friend of the poor, and it was in order to better the condition of poor starving tenants in Scotland that induced him to enter upon the work of colonizing. His advent to Canada was caused by a desire to colonize a distant land. He was not long, however, in the country before he engaged in a conflict bordering on war with the traders of the Northwest Company. Reading an account of the occurrences of these days wherein what is now Manitoba and the Northwest Territory, the rival Companies, the Hudson Bay and the Northwest, contending for the mastery, is like reading a novel. When we come to read the trial of Paul Brown and Francis Boucher for murder, tried at York in October, 1818, before Chief Justice Powell and Justices Campbell and Boulton, William Allan, Esq., Associate, we can see the bitter enmity that existed between these rival trading companies, culminating in rebellion. Paul Brown and Francis Boucher were half-breeds, tried for the murder of Robert Semple, Governor of the Territory. It was argued at the trial that the appointment of Governor Semple was invalid. This was the contention of the Northwest Company and their partizans.

The bloody conflict that took place between the partizans of the rival companies was something like the clashing of the clans in Scotland.

If the colonists sent out by Earl Selkirk could have had full scope and been allowed to till the soil in peace, it would have been of great advantage to the country. The trappers and the traders would have given way to the plow and the reaper.

On the trial to which we have referred, some idea of the kind of settlements there were on the Red River, may be gathered from the evidence.

The Attorney-General for the prosecution was arguing that the prisoners were interfering with the settlers in their peaceable possession of their lands at Fort Douglas (for the rival parties had forts, such as they were; the Hudson Bay Company Fort Douglas, and the Northwest Company Fort Gibraltar). Mr. Sherwood, the counsel for the prisoners, challenged the Attorney-General's statement that there was a settlement, that in fact the so-called settlement was but a camp of traders, living and trading in tents. The Chief Justice, addressing the Attorney-General, then said: "It appears rather, Mr. Attorney, to have been habitations than a settlement."

The Hudson Bay Company had provided themselves with arms for the protection of what they claimed as their territory.

One Heden, in giving his evidence, said: "I was in the battle of the 10th of June. The Bois Brulés did not come to our fort. They kept about a quarter of a mile distant from it, and passed it. We had cannon in the fort."

The Northwest Company and their retainers were ready in charging that the proceedings of Lord Selkirk in the western country were of a lawless character. As a matter of fact, there was lawlessness on both sides. Lord Selkirk thought proper to invoke the law against those accused of crime in connection with the disturbances, insurrection, or rebellion, or whatever term may be applied to the occurrences, which took place in the neighbourhood of Fort Garry.

Lord Selkirk after laying charge of murder, burglary, and arson, all at that time capital offences, against partners of the Northwest Company and their retainers on the Red River and at Fort William, delayed the prosecution for nearly two years, the accused being all the time in prison. The prisoners were never in fact brought to trial by him; he left the country without proceeding with the prosecution, and the Government had, for very shame's sake, to place the accused on their defence, when, after a prolonged trial, they were triumphantly acquitted at the Court of Oyer and Terminer at York in October, 1818.

At the following Assizes for York two civil cases of importance were tried arising out of the proceedings of Lord Selkirk. One of these was an action brought by William Smith against the Earl for false imprisonment. The circumstances, were that Smith was under-sheriff of the western district, and was the bearer of a writ of restitution founded on a verdict of a special jury at Sandwich in October, 1816, granted by the sitting magistrates ordering the restoration of Fort William to the Northwest Company; also a warrant for the arrest of several persons at Fort William. When Smith arrived at the Fort and produced his writ Lord Selkirk refused to comply, and when he and the others were arrested under the warrant, which was for a felony, they put Smith out of the Fort, and placed him under military guard, and he was not liberated till the evacuation of the Fort by Lord Selkirk in May, 1817. For this Smith brought his action against the Earl, and obtained a verdict of £500 ($2,000). Daniel McKenzie also brought an action against the Earl for throwing him into a dungeon at Fort William without legal proceedings, for which he obtained a verdict of £1,500 ($6,000).

Notwithstanding the apparent lawlessness to which I have referred we must recollect that all these proceedings took place in a new and uncivilized country—a country of half-breeds, traders, and Indians. Several interests of a conflicting nature were at war with each other. The traders' interest was clearly opposed to a *bona fide* settlement of the country by either English or Scotch farmers. Lord Selkirk was in very deed a colonizer, and a brave and good one at that. No one can read the history of Prince Edward Island without acknowledging the good done by Lord Selkirk there, by importation into that island of his hardy highlanders. There is reason to believe that if he had been let alone in the Northwest the valley of the Red River would have been a flourishing and rich State a century before it became a Province of the Dominion.

Judge Campbell was promoted to the Chief Justiceship of the King's Bench in 1825, on the retirement of Chief Justice Powell. It is said by those who profess to speak with knowledge of the time, that had it not been that John Beverley Robinson, then Attorney-General, was considered too young for the Judgeship, he would have been elevated to the Bench, indeed made Chief Justice at the time of Judge Campbell's promotion. Judge Campbell was sixty-six years of age when he was appointed Chief Justice. It was a saying of the wags of the day that he at that age was so appointed to keep the place warm for the Attorney-General, whom it was well understood would succeed him in the office when he should have arrived at a judicial age. Judge Campbell had not been long promoted to the Chief Justiceship before it became within his province to preside at important civil trials at York, which were of much interest to the whole community and the cause of much acerbity of feeling. In 1826 the old system of might governing right was still in the ascendant in the Province. The officials of those days held an undisputed sway in the Province. There was no responsible government: the people might be in accord in one way of thought and action, but if the Executive were of a different way of thinking it was the Executive that governed; not the people, representatives of the people, or a government possessing the confidence of the people.

William Lyon Mackenzie was a politician and publisher rapidly gaining the voice of the people. He had removed his *Advocate* newspaper, a Liberal organ, from Queenston to York. While Mr. Mackenzie was absent from York on business, young men of the town, principally sons of officials, fired with zeal for the cause of oligarchical rule, thought it a noble thing to invade the office of the *Advocate*, throw the type into "pi," break up the press, and throw these, with some other *impedimenta* to what they considered true government, into the beautiful bay that faces the town. This act of lawlessness would at this day be visited with something more than a civil action. Mr. Mackenzie did not, however, nor did the Queen on his behalf appeal to the Criminal Courts for redress, but brought a civil action. J. B. Macaulay, afterwards Chief Justice Macaulay, after making many attempts to get a settlement, offering money as compensation, was at last called upon to defend the rioters before Chief Justice Campbell and a special jury, which resulted in a verdict against the defendants of $2,500. This verdict did not however, trouble the rioters much, for their sympathizers in the cause of responsible government raised the amount by subscription, and thus not only saved them from loss, but glorified them in the bargain.

Looking back to the time and the circumstances of this case, one can easily see that the soldier of the Highland regiment and Chief Justice, who has come down to us described as a man of "great force of character, sterling integrity, and personal worth," so conducted the minds of the jury that Mr. Mackenzie obtained a measure of justice, though opposed by the might and power of officialism. Among the defendants, the rioters, were two sons of the Inspector-General, a son of a Judge, a son of a Justice of the Peace, and the confidential secretary of the Lieutenant Governor, Sir Peregrine Maitland, as well as others intimately connected with the reigning powers. The parties who committed these acts of violence quite overshot the mark. Great indignation was excited in the minds of the people, sympathy was created for Mr. Mackenzie, the people of the county of York took up his cause, and in the year 1828 returned him to Parliament over his opponent, himself a Liberal, but who happened, to be one of the Counsel for the gentlemen of York in their trial of strength with the man who afterwards became first mayor of Toronto, but who is better known as the leader of the Rebellion of 1837.

Mr. Mackenzie was a remarkable man. Up to the Rebellion his pen was his sword, the sharpness of which no doubt so incensed the young gentlemen of York that they took the law into their own hands. The rebellion and all that took place in connection with it is more for the general historian than for judicial history. I shall therefore leave it to the historians of the time to speak of that eventful period of our history.

The Chief Justice visited his native land in 1828. On this visit not unmindful of his father who died on 23rd September, 1782, at the age of fifty-eight, he had erected in St. Peter's church yard, Thurso, Caithness, a tomb stone to mark the place of his father's burial. He had the following engraved on the tomb stone: "This tribute of filial affection is dedicated by his son William Campbell, Chief Justice and resident of York, Upper Canada." The tomb stone is still standing as a monument to his father's memory.

When Judge Campbell in 1829, owing to ill health, retired he had the honour of knighthood conferred upon him, and thenceforward was Sir William Campbell. He was the first of our Judges who was knighted, and the fact on that account deserves mention. It cannot be said the title was undeserved by the soldier who had fought under Cornwallis, had abandoned the profession of arms for that of the law, and in time had become the Chief Justice of a Province, the early home and cradle of the United Empire Loyalists.

Sir William Campbell's residence was in Duke street, Toronto, and is still standing. The Chief Justice died in Toronto in 1834. Dr. Scadding, in his " Toronto of Old," in referring to this melancholy event, says : " The funeral of Sir William Campbell in 1834 was one of unusual impressiveness. The Legislature was in session at the time and attended in a body, with the Bar and the Judges."

IX.

THE HONORABLE D'ARCY BOULTON, JUDGE OF THE KING'S BENCH, UPPER CANADA.

THE Honorable D'Arcy Boulton was of a Lincolnshire family of long pedigree, the son of Henry Boulton, an English barrister. He was married on the 18th of December, 1782, at St. George's Church, Bloomsbury, London, to a daughter of James Forster, sergeant at law. He came to America in 1797. We find him in 1803 settled in the township of Augusta, in the district of Johnstown, and moved to York in 1807. The reason for Mr. Boulton's leaving Augusta for York in 1803 seems to have been that in that year, during the administration of Peter Hunter, Esquire, as Lieutenant-Governor, it was found that there was a scarcity of Barristers in the Province, and so the Legislature thought fit to create certain gentlemen Barristers by Act of Parliament. Mr. Boulton was one of those called to the degree of Barrister on his English training alone. The Act to which I have referred was passed in the third session of the third Parliament of Upper Canada, forty-third George III., Cap. III., and was entitled " An Act to authorize the Governor, or person administering the government of this Province, to license Practitioners in the Law." The Act recited :

> Whereas, great inconvenience has arisen and is now experienced by His Majesty's subjects in several parts of this Province to practise the profession of the law, and unless the number can be speedily increased justice will, in many cases, be with great difficulty administered.

It then proceeded to enact that from and after the passing of the Act it should and might be lawful for the Governor to authorize by license under his hand and seal such and so many of His Majesty's liege subjects, not exceeding six in the whole, as he from their probity, education, and condition in life should deem fit and proper persons, to practise the profession of the law in the Province ; that before applying for license to the Governor, the Judges of his Majesty's Court of King's Bench should certify under the hand of the Chief Justice that such Court was satisfied of the ability and fitness of the party so applying to be admitted to practise as a Barrister or Attorney of the Province. On this certificate being obtained, the Law Society was to admit such person on subscribing the rules.

A good deal of pleasantry used to be indulged in by the wags of the day at the expense of these lawyers created by Act of Parliament, calling them the heaven-made lawyers. When we see, however, that men of ability and probity were to be selected from the body of the people and that His Majesty's Court of King's Bench had to certify to their fitness, we may conclude that none but gentlemen of intelligence and learning were in this manner called to the Bar ; an improvement even upon the old English system of regulating the talent of the men by the number of the dinners eaten in Hall. Mr. Boulton was very well qualified to be called to the Bar, and had very rapid promotion. In 1805 he was appointed Solicitor-General. In 1807 he had a commission of Oyer and Terminer and General Gaol Delivery given to him. In 1810 Mr. Solicitor-General Boulton sailed for England, but when off Dungeness, the vessel was sighted by a French privateer, the *Grand-Duc-de-Berg*, and chase given. Though the captain had arms on board he refused to fight, preferring a French prison to the dangers of an engagement. Mr. Boulton, and, for that matter, too, the passengers did not agree with the captain—they were for fighting, and fighting they were determined to have. Mr.

Boulton was possessed of true courage. The passengers, headed by the Canadian Solicitor-General, resisted the privateer, engaged with the enemy, but were, after a short contest, overpowered by a party of boarders, who obtained a footing upon the vessel. Mr. Boulton, wounded and a prisoner, was conveyed to Verdun, where he remained until the temporary peace of 1814, gave him his release. On Mr. Boulton's return to Upper Canada in this year, he was made Attorney-General. I take pleasure in expressing my obligation to Colonel D'Arcy Boulton, of Coburg, a grandson of the Judge, for information of family history of the Judge, which it would have been difficult to obtain but through a relative. Colonel D'Arcy Boulton himself is not without military experiences, having for some years commanded a cavalry corps, called "the Prince of Wales Canadian Dragoons," which he was principally instrumental in raising. His son, Major Boulton, in 1870, while doing duty in the Northwest, was made prisoner by Louis Riel in the first Riel rebellion, and confined in Fort Garry, sentenced to death by Riel, and only escaped death by the heart of Riel being softened by the appeals made in his behalf by friends of the Major, and the respect which his bravery excited in the minds of his greatest enemies. The Major has so well told his sufferings in his book, "Reminiscences of the Northwest Rebellion," that I need not repeat them here. Judge Boulton was elevated to the bench in 1818, and appointed Judge of Assize and *Nisi Prius*. He was in 1818 associated with Chief Justice Campbell as one of the Judges in the trial of Paul Brown and F. F. Bourcher for the murder of Robert Semple, Esquire, in the Red River country on the 18th of June, 1816, and of Cooper and Hanneman for taking, on the 3rd of April, 1815, with force and arms, eight pieces of cannon and one howitzer, the property of the Right Honorable Thomas, Earl of Selkirk, from his dwelling house, and putting in bodily fear of their lives certain persons found therein. I have already referred to these trials shortly in the life of Chief Justice Powell, and more fully in the life of Chief Justice Campbell, making any further reference thereto unnecessary. The judgments of Mr. Justice Boulton are to be found in "Taylor's Reports." During his time the litigation of the day was principally confined to John Doe and Richard Roe, cases of arrest, bail, and matters of practice. There were not many cases of much importance—at least so considered at this time. The most important was the case arising out of the Red River riots, which he assisted in adjudicating. The Judge used to drive on the circuit in his day under great difficulties, always carrying an axe and a rope for emergency, often having to cut through trees fallen across the road, and having to swim his horses across the Trent on going Eastern Circuit. Mr. Justice Boulton during his residence in York was ever on the *qui vive* for the material advancement of the place. Having land in the vicinity of the marsh at the east end of the town he, at great expense, cut an open channel through a portion of this marsh, on the eastern side of the Don River, in front of this property. This channel has continued open ever since, and is known as "Boulton's Ditch." Fishermen and skiffmen along the Don appreciate the ditch, however, as it forms a communication between the Don and Ashbridge's Bay. The Judge was a strong supporter of St. James's Church, built in 1818, and contributed liberally to the funds raised for the erection of the church. Mr. Justice Boulton, as I learn from those who knew him and enjoyed the pleasure of his society, was a good specimen of the English gentleman of his day. Dr. Scadding, in his "Toronto of Old," writes of him: "Like many of his descendants, he was a lover of horses and a spirited rider; a man of wit, too, and humor, fond of listening to and narrating anecdotes of the *ben trovato* class." The Judge was fond of entertaining the military and other prominent people of York, and was always a welcome guest at the garrison mess. He was not without experience of the military, not only of his own country but of other countries. In the engagement with the French privateers, to which I have referred, he received a severe sabre cut on the arm, from which he suffered much. In 1829 the great surgeon, Sir Benjamin Brodie, performed an operation on this wound in the arm, which was thought necessary for the preservation of the patient's life, the wound being in dangerous proximity to the artery. It may have been that this French experience of his induced him on his release from imprisonment to give the name of Bonaparte to one of his famous horses; he certainly had two carriage horses; one he named Bonaparte and the other Jefferson. These two horses of the Judge acquired quite a notoriety in their day. The Grange at the head of John street, now the residence of Professor Goldwin Smith, was formerly the property of Mr. Justice Boulton, and extended south as far as Lot, now Queen street. Bonaparte and Jefferson, not to be outdone in military prowess by their namesakes, the General and the President, were, on a certain occasion, attacked in these grounds by a bear coming out of the wood to the north. The bear was a very large one, and the horses were put on their mettle in self-defence. Bonaparte and Jefferson knew how to use their fore feet; made violent plunges therewith on the attacking enemy, and utterly routed Mr. Bruin, chased him down what is now called Bay street (and from this chase was originally called "Bear street") into the waters of the bay. Mr. Justice Boulton at first resided in a frame house, white painted, standing on the lot where Holland House, (now the Reform Club,) stands. Several children survived the Judge. The Honorable Henry John Boulton, sometime Chief Justice of Newfoundland and successively Solicitor-General and Attorney-General of Upper Canada, was one of his sons.

I am not able to fix the exact date of Judge Boulton's death. I have it from descendants, members of the family, that he died in York before the first cholera year of 1832—in 1830 or 1831. He was buried in St. James's churchyard and afterwards removed to St. James's cemetery on the banks of the Don, his final resting place.

X.

THE HONORABLE LEVIUS PETERS SHERWOOD, JUDGE OF KING'S BENCH, UPPER CANADA.

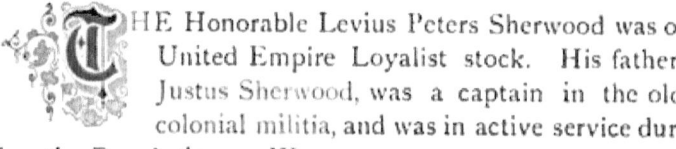HE Honorable Levius Peters Sherwood was of United Empire Loyalist stock. His father, Justus Sherwood, was a captain in the old colonial militia, and was in active service during the Revolutionary War.

Mr. Justus Sherwood, father of the Judge, came into the Province of Quebec on the 6th December, in the year 1777. He remained for some time at St. Johns in that Province, and afterwards, like a good many others of the United Empire Loyalists, settled in the township of Augusta. He was one of the first members of the Upper Canada House of Assembly, which was convened at Newark, now Niagara. He had two sons, Samuel and Levius Peters, afterwards made Judge. Both sons were educated for the Bar of the Province of Upper Canada. Levius Peters, the second son, was called to the Bar in Hilary Term 43 George III., A. D. 1803, and is number nineteen on Barristers' Roll, Osgoode Hall. Both Samuel and Levius Peters were prominent members of the Bar, and both were of counsel for the defence of the Red River rioters in 1818, at their trial in York before Chief Justice Campbell, to which I have made full reference in the life of the last named Judge. Levius Peters Sherwood was elected a member of the Upper Canada House of Assembly by the electors of the County of Leeds, and in the year

1822 was elected Speaker of that House. In 1841, during the administration of Lord Sydenham, Mr. Sherwood was elected Speaker of the Legislative Council of Canada. Levius Peters Sherwood was appointed Judge of the King's Bench on the 17th of October, 1825, and took his seat on the Bench in Michaelmas Term, 1825. The entry in "Taylor's Reports" is: "Michaelmas Term, 1825, Levius P. Sherwood took his seat as Judge in the place of the Honorable Mr. Justice Campbell." The reader going back, and referring to the life of Mr. Justice Campbell, will see that he had been a Judge since 1811. In 1825 he made way for Mr. Sherwood, himself on the 17th of October, 1825, being appointed to the Chief Justiceship of the same Court.

Before Mr. Sherwood's elevation to the Bench, and while he was Speaker of the Legislative Assembly, a most "important Act was passed, making permanent a previous Act passed for levying and collecting rates and assessments in Upper Canada, and further to provide for the more equal and general assessment of lands and other ratable property." This Act was passed in the sixth, George IV., 1825, and for a long time formed the foundation of the tax system of the Province. In Hilary Term, 1829, a case came up before the King's Bench which at the time was not only considered important in itself, but gained importance from the fact that Judge Sherwood dissented from the Chief Justice Robinson and Judge Macaulay. The case to which I refer was Evans *vs.* Shaw, in which the question was, whether a bond to the limits given under 2 George IV., cap. 6 and 7, George IV., cap. 7, by a debtor prisoner enjoying the benefit of the limits, leaving the same without knowledge of his bondsmen or bail to the limits, but afterwards returned again to the limits of his own accord and there was surrendered by his bail, given up to the sheriff and lodged in jail, was forfeited, or whether or not the surrender saved the bail from liability. The majority of the Court held the bond forfeited without redemption, but Mr. Justice Sherwood in a long and elaborate judgment maintained that so long as the Sheriff had the prisoner in close custody the bail should be protected, and not held liable for the act of the debtor in leaving the limits without their knowledge. The letter of the bond, however, was given effect to, and the bail held liable. The case is reported in "Draper's Reports," and is interesting as showing the strictness of law which was given effect to. There was, at the time, no Court of Equity in the Province. Mr. Justice Sherwood was eminently a fair man ; rather given to take an equitable view of matters when it was possible to do so, and still justify the same under the principles of law that then prevailed. If in any case he thought he had erred he would reverse his own decision. A case of this kind occurred, and was tried before him, also reported in "Draper's Reports." In writing the life of Chief Justice Campbell I made reference to William Lyon Mackenzie, and also to the candidature of Mr. James Small for the Home District, County of York representation in Parliament. In connection with this candidature Mr. Small had reason to complain of Mr. Mackenzie, and to settle the matter brought an action at law against him—Small *vs*. Mackenzie. The action was for libel of Mr. Small as an Attorney and Candidate for Parliament. The publication given in evidence was a report of a trial of Small *vs*. Hogg. At the trial of Small *vs*. Mackenzie the defendant, Mackenzie, gave in evidence in justification under the general issue that the report of the trial was correct, and obtained a verdict. Judge Sherwood tried the case, and admitted this evidence. On a new trial being moved for in Term he granted a new trial on the ground that he had improperly admitted the evidence. He held in effect that in making the comments he did in his report of the case of Small *vs*. Hogg, Mr. Mackenzie had gone beyond his privilege and had made comments reflecting on the plaintiff's honesty and his being an honorable man. That, however he might be entitled to report the proceedings of the trial, he had no right to make comments of his own opinions of the plaintiff, such as the libel in question. I refer to this case because of the prominence of the parties, and also as showing that Mr. Justice Sherwood was one of those administrators of the law who was not so self-sufficient as to believe he was always right, but was willing, on being convinced, to modify or alter his opinion. It was Mr. Justice Sherwood who was the first to decide in Upper Canada that lands which had descended to the heir could, on a judgment recovered against the executor or administrator of a deceased debtor, be sold and absolutely disposed of on execution on the judgment against the executor or administrator. He so decided in Forsyth *vs.* Richardson in "Draper's Reports." There was an important principle involved in that case which the professional reader fully understands. It was there first contended that for a simple contract debt the lands of the heir could be seized to satisfy the debt for which he had in no way become personally bound, and that, too, on a judgment, not against him, but the executor or administrator of the deceased debtor. That was held to be the effect of the Imperial Act, 5 George II., cap. 7, and was subsequently followed by the Canadian Courts as establishing the law in Upper Canada. The subsequent case of Gardner *vs.* Gardner, which has often been supposed to be the first case on this point, was not the first case, but followed the decision of Judge Sherwood in Forsyth *vs.* Richardson, but gave it strength by the judgment of a full Court.

The correctness of the decision in these cases was rudely shaken in 1863, on an appeal to the Privy Council from New South Wales, the question arising on a similar statute. The case from New South Wales was Bullen *vs.* A'Beckett, reported in 9 Jurist N. S. 973. So important was the principle involved and so serious was it thought to be, that the Legislature of Canada in 1863, at once thought it necessary to act, and passed an Act (27 Vic. Cap. 15) to *confirm* the titles acquired by purchasers at sales so made under execution against executor or administrator. Strong V. C., now Judge of the Supreme Court, in Willis *vs.* Willis,

19 Chy. (Grant) 573, after referring to Gardner *vs.* Gardner, proceeds to say :

> Some doubt which was cast on the case of Gardner *vs.* Gardner, by the decision of the Privy Council in the case of Bullen *vs.* A'Beckett on appeal from New South Wales, led to the passing of the Act 27 Vic. Cap. 15.

Judge Sherwood, from one cause and another, had to sit alone, being, in fact, the whole Court. When I come to write the life of Judge Willis, it will be seen that exception was taken to this in some quarters. I find him holding the Court alone when the case of Prentiss *vs.* Hamilton ("Draper's Reports," 398,) was before him when he was called on to decide as between two clerks in the Receiver-General's office. One clerk had said to the Receiver-General that another clerk, the plaintiff, had stolen $300 from the Receiver-General. An action of slander was brought, and one of the questions which came up was whether the communication made to the Receiver-General was privileged or not. Judge Sherwood held that it was not privileged. He said :

> Such communications possess a sort of public character, and, in that respect, essentially differ from those which are ordinarily made by servants to their master in private life.

Mr. Justice Sherwood was a painstaking Judge, and gave general satisfaction. He was very conservative in his opinions, not given to change. In 1828 he was obliged to defend the constitution of his Court, the Court of King's Bench, against an assault made upon it by his brother Judge, Willis. Judge Willis had been sent out from England, appointed to a puisne Judgeship in the King's Bench, Associate to Judge Sherwood. The Chief of the Court was Chief Justice Campbell. The Chief obtained leave of absence, and went to England. Judge Willis came to the conclusion that the Court could not be held in the absence of the Chief. This was a novel and startling doctrine to Mr. Justice Sherwood. His answer was, that it had frequently happened before that the Court had been held without the Chief, and that even Judge Willis himself had so held the Court, and that he, Judge Sherwood, would continue so to hold regardless of the opinion of Judge Willis. This he did very much to the advantage of litigants whose cases were then before the Court. A different holding would have blocked the legal business of the Province. When I was quite a lad I remember to have seen Judge Sherwood on the Bench, holding the Assizes at Brockville. I well remember with what awe I looked upon his dignified form and gray locks of flowing hair. Near to him was Adiel Sherwood, the Sheriff of the county, with a sword at his side, knee-breeches, and buckled shoes. The scene comes back to me now, an impressive one. It was the first time I ever entered a Court of Justice. I little thought then I should live to write the life of the Judge. Mr. Justice Sherwood had four sons and three daughters. Henry Sherwood, his eldest son, at one time represented Brockville and afterwards Toronto in the Upper Canada Parliament. In 1842, Henry Sherwood became the Honorable Henry Sherwood, was appointed Solicitor-General of the Province, and in 1847, he was appointed Attorney-General. The Honorable George Sherwood, second son of the Judge, represented Brockville in Parliament for nearly twenty years, and was Receiver-General and Commissioner of Crown Lands in the administration of Sir George Cartier and Sir John Macdonald. He retired from Parliament in 1863, and in 1865 was appointed Judge of the County Court of the county of Hastings.

The Honorable George Sherwood was a man of great probity, universally respected. In his Bar days he ever set his face against all sharpness in practice, having a great regard for the dignity of his profession. I was a student of his for two years, and avail myself of this opportunity in writing the life of his father, the Judge, and referring to him, to say that I always found George Sherwood not only a tutor in the law but a friend. He died a few years ago in Toronto, where he was buried. His father, the Judge, died in Toronto in 1850, and was buried in St. James's Cemetery.

XI.

THE HONORABLE JOHN WALPOLE WILLIS, JUDGE OF THE KING'S BENCH, UPPER CANADA.

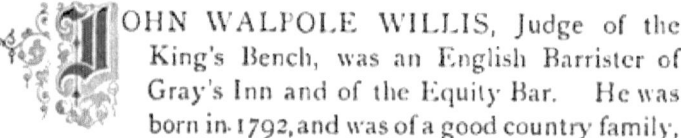

JOHN WALPOLE WILLIS, Judge of the King's Bench, was an English Barrister of Gray's Inn and of the Equity Bar. He was born in 1792, and was of a good country family, but not of a family of rank. He was the son of Dr. Willis, who as the body physician of good old King George III. achieved a considerable success in the treatment of the insane. In early life he began the study of Equity. Feeling that his future success in life depended on his own exertions, he applied himself assiduously to the study of his profession. By the time he reached his majority he was well skilled in Equity, and no sooner had he been called to the Bar than he showed the good effect of his early training and studious life in publishing a work on the "Law of Evidence." In 1820 he published his valuable work on equity pleading—"Willis's Equity Pleading"—a work which was for a long time a standard work on this branch of the science of Equity. In 1827 he published that other valuable work, his treatise "On the Duties and Responsibilities of Trustees." No doubt these writings of his, added to the circumstance that he married the daughter of an earl, procured for him early promotion from the Bar to the Bench. In 1823 he married Lady Mary Isabella Bowes Lyon Willis, one of the daughters of the Earl of Strathmore. By this marriage into a family of rank he secured an influence which he turned to account, when he thought it well to seek a Judgeship. When he married he had a good practice in London, but his flight of marriage was too high for his means; the result of the marriage was expensive and extravagant habits, finally ending in an impoverishment which caused him to be but too ready to accept a position on the Bench.

In the year 1827 it was a matter of speculation in the Colonial Office, leading to a belief in its reality in the minds of influential persons, that Upper Canada was sighing for the establishment of a Court of Equity in that Province. As yet the benighted people of that distant colony had traveled along on the old beaten paths of common law, with such of the statute law of England as they had introduced plus their Canadian statute law, which, in the minds of those in England who wanted office in the colony, was not satisfactory. Unfortunately Mr. Willis either persuaded himself, or was persuaded by others, that a Court of Chancery was necessary, and must at once be created to settle the differences of litigants in the Province. Mr. Willis having conceived this idea, and that he would be a good man to assist in the establishment of such a Court and himself be the head of it, came out to Upper Canada, leaving his wife in England, his mother and sister living with her, as they had with him before he set out for Canada. On the 18th of September, 1827, he presented to Sir Peregrine Maitland, the Lieutenant-Governor of the Province, the royal warrant appointing him to a Judgeship of the King's Bench in the expectation that in the near future a Court of Chancery would be established and Mr. Willis appointed its Chief. At this time John Beverley Robinson was Attorney-General, and it was not at all his opinion that the country was yet ripe for the creation of a new Court. The opinion of the Attorney-General was shared by many others, especially by the Executive Council. The first official reception Judge Willis had, was by the Lieutenant-Governor at Stamford Cottage, and being introduced by a royal warrant he was, of conrse, well received. After good entertainment the question of the establishment of a Court of Chancery was mentioned over the wine and walnuts. Sir Peregrine said to the new made Judge : " Sir, you have not got your Court of Equity yet!" Sir Peregrine well knew that Parliament was not yet prepared to create such a Court : hence his remark to Judge Willis.

Judge Willis found a bitter opponent to the scheme in Attorney-General Robinson. He tried every legitimate means to influence Parliament to adopt his views, but signally failed ; he always met a doughty opponent in the Attorney-General. The antagonism did not create the best of feeling between the Judge and the Attorney-General. Matters rapidly came to a head. On the 10th of April, 1828, a well-known citizen of York, Francis Collins, editor of *The Freeman* newspaper, was brought before the Court of Oyer and Terminer for a libel preferred against him by the Attorney-General. Judge Sherwood was the only Judge presiding. The next day Judge Willis presided, and this was the first time he ever presided at a Court of Assize. He in fact had no experience in criminal law or the matters of practice in common law. At this sitting Collins applied to be heard personally. The Judge gave him leave, when he launched forth into a violent tirade of abuse of the Attorney-General, charging him with breach of duty in not entering prosecutions against certain parties for supposed offences. The Attorney-General, who had been in consultation with a member of the Bar in an adjoining room, hearing of this came into Court and claimed its protection. Mr. Collins was, however, allowed by the Judge to proceed. The Judge was but too willing to listen to Collins's abuse of the Attorney-General, and said : " If the Attorney-General has acted as you say, he has very much neglected his duty." This was too much for the Attorney-General, and he at once vindicated his course in these words : " It is not my place," said he, "to play the part of a detective, or to hunt about the country for evidence of voluntary prosecutions. I have now discharged the duties of Crown officer for nearly thirteen years, and this is the first time that a failure in my duty has been imputed to me. I have already conceived it my duty to take official cognizance of offences against the state. As to other cases I have been accustomed to proceed only upon informations and complaints placed in the hands of Justices of the Peace, and upon presentments of grand juries. In cases of injuries to individuals and their property, such as assaults, riots, when a double remedy is afforded by action and indictment, I have not been accustomed to set the law in operation on my own motion."

Judge Willis interrupted the Attorney-General, saying "that the Attorney-General's statement of his practice merely proved that this practice had been uniformly wrong," and said he, "I take leave to remark that you have neglected your duty." The Judge continued in this strain with further offensive remarks. The Attorney-General could endure it no longer and in tones of hot anger and manly independence he burst forth, saying:

> My Lord, I know my duty as well as any Judge on the Bench. I have always acted in the way I have indicated, in which respect I have followed the practice of all my predecessors in this Province, and I shall continue to act in the same manner as long as I am prosecuting officer for the Crown.

A few days afterward in another criminal case at the same assizes the Judge again undertook to lecture the Attorney-General as to his practice, saying:

> The practice in this country, as stated by the Attorney-General, does not agree with my notions as to the duty of that officer, and I have laid a statement of the question before His Majesty's Government here for the purpose of having it transmitted to England, where it will be decided how far the Attorney-General is right in expressing his sentiments as he has done.

Whereupon the Attorney-General remarked that he was Attorney-General to his Majesty, and not to Judge Willis, and that he would act as he believed to be right, even though he should differ in opinion from his lordship. Judge Willis then addressing the Attorney-General, said :

> Mr. Attorney-General, I am one of His Majesty's Justices in this Province. As such it is my place to state to the Crown officers what their duties are, and it is for them to perform those duties according to direction. If the interests of the Crown had not been concerned, I would not have permitted any discussion on the question. But I am sure His Majesty's Government will protect me from insult in the exercise of my judicial functions, and in stating to any public officer what I conceive to be his duties.

The Attorney-General answered the Judge by saying that his Majesty's Government would "also protect his Majesty's officers in the execution of their duty."

This episode in the Court and judicial history of the Province had its origin in the Attorney-General's refusing to be a party to the fishing out of criminal cases, and was especially directed to a case of a duel that had been fought some thirteen years before. The duel unhappily ended in the death of one of the principals. Mr. Francis Collins seems to have thought that the Attorney-General should, of his own motion, take the matter in hand and have the seconds brought to trial. No friend of any of the parties to the duel sought to open the wounds long since closed. No information before a magistrate had been laid. Nor had a grand jury made a presentment. Duelling at that time was considered the gentlemen's court of honor, and many agreed with the cavaliers of old that when that Assize had disposed of the case there was to be no further controversy. The Attorney-General would not be a party to an appeal from the court of honor without the positive and active prosecution of the friends of the duelist. Mr. Collins further urged that the persons who demolished Mackenzie's printing press, and threw the type in the bay, a full account of which I have given in the life of Chief Justice Campbell, should have been prosecuted criminally at the voluntary motion of the Attorney-General, though Mackenzie himself took no steps towards a criminal prosecution. Here again the Judge supported Mr. Collins in his contention, and the Attorney-General disputed it. The Attorney-General had said to the Judge when taken to task:

> In cases of injuries to individuals and their property, such as assaults and riots, where a double remedy is afforded by action and indictment, I have not been accustomed to set the law in operation on my own motion.

I will not dwell on these incidents of very unpleasant Court proceedings. It must have been a sorry spectacle for the spectators. The Bar generally supported the Attorney-General. Some of the Bar supported the Judge. As for the people, it was something new to them to hear the Attorney-General berated by a Judge. The independence of the Bar is thought to be one of the safeguards of English liberties. I will leave it to the reader to judge if such independence could be maintained if the doctrines laid down by the Judge were to have weight. He said as I have related: " Mr. Attorney-General, I am one of his Majesty's Judge's in this Province. *As such* it is my place to state to the Crown officers what their duties are, *and it is for them to perform those duties according to direction.*" These were plain words of the Judge. They were not words of wisdom, however, and were neither acceded to, nor did they operate as a deterrent to the Attorney-General. The Canadian Attorney-General was not prepared to be dictated to by an English Judge fresh from the Equity Bar, with no experience of criminal law.

The friction caused by the disputings between the Attorney-General and the Judge was soon to bear fruit. If Judge Willis had acted with prudence he might have done good service in the colony. He was not without talent, though just at that time the talent he possessed was not available. There was no Court of Equity, or his career might not have ended as it did. Getting into disfavor with the Attorney-General brought down on him all the antagonism of the government party. Sir Peregrine Maitland, the Lieutenant-Governor, leaned to the side of the Attorney-General. Judge Willis also assumed a superiority over Chief Justice Campbell and Judge Sherwood, his brother Judge on the bench. It was not long before an opportunity presented itself, eagerly taken advantage of, to make the Judge feel that he had missed his mark in falling foul of the Attorney-General. The Judge was for reform—all well enough if he had not descended from his dignity, availing himself of the newspapers to bolster up his cause. He announced through this channel that he was preparing for publication a work on Upper Canadian jurisprudence, which the authorities questioned as aiming at a revolution of Canadian law, as it existed. This conduct of the Judge did not comport with the sense of propriety entertained by Sir Peregrine Maitland, who represented the matter to the English Government. The Judge, by his own conduct, was directing events likely to lead to his removal from office, which afterwards actually took place.

The summary dismissal of a Judge is a proceeding so unusual that it becomes absolutely necessary to make careful inquiry into the cause and circumstances connected with such dismissal, before coming to a conclusion on its justice or propriety. There are not wanting writers who have in the most unmeasured terms condemned his dismissal, imputing it to political motives, and stigmatizing the dismissal as the base and unprincipled treatment of the family compact. I shall proceed, therefore, to give the facts connected with his displacement from office, leaving each reader to draw his conclusion as to him seems best. The ostensible cause of the Judge's removal was his persisting in his refusal to perform judicial acts which belonged to the Court of King's Bench, of which he was a Judge, unless the Court was fully constituted, the Chief Justice presiding. In Michaelmas, 1827, and Hilary Terms of the year 1828, Mr. Justice Willis took his seat and officiated with the Honourable Chief Justice Campbell and the Honourable Mr. Justice Sherwood, in the course of which Terms differences of opinion on legal points of much public importance in several causes arose. In Easter Term following, Chief Justice Campbell was absent, having a few days before this Term of Easter set off for England.

In this Term of Easter, Mr. Justice Sherwood and Mr. Justice Willis presided, and in the course of this Term the varying opinions of these two honorable Judges were publicly discussed and publicly felt. Mr. Justice Willis, under these circumstances, examining into the constitution of the Court of King's Bench in the Province, and adverting to that clause of the Provincial Statute which required " that his Majesty's Chief Justice, together with two puisne Judges, shall preside in the said Court," resolved not to sit in the Court while it continued, as he contended, thus illegally constituted in the absence of the Chief Justice, though expressing himself willing and desirous of fulfilling all other duties which the law might permit him to do as a single Judge. This opinion of Mr. Justice Willis came to the knowledge of the Provincial Government previous to Trinity Term, in which that opinion was expressed. The Provincial Government, although thus aware of the difficulty and objection raised by Judge Willis as to the constitution of the Court, took no steps to supply this alleged defect in the Court—no Chief Justice being appointed in the place of Chief Justice Campbell, absent from the Province.

In this state of things, Mr. Justice Sherwood, in Trinity Term, June 1828, took his seat on the bench, and Mr. Justice Willis, impressed with the opinion which he entertained of the illegality pursued, declared in an emphatic and grave argument, his reasons why he could not conscientiously proceed to hear causes or give judgment under such circumstances. For the better elucidation of this extraordinary case, I can not do better than refer the reader to the Journals of the Legislative Assembly of the Province of Upper Canada, First Session, Tenth Parliament, page 21 Appendix, where will be found Judge Willis's reasons, as expressed by him in Court, for thinking he was bound to take the course he did, and that conformably to law he could not act otherwise. The arguments advanced by the Judge were, in the opinion of some of the best lawyers of the day, sound. This much in any event may be said, that they were honest opinions, honestly and independently expressed as becomes a Judge of the bench of any country. A different practice had hitherto prevailed, and inasmuch as the ruling of the Judge would create a complete block in the Court, the Lieutenant-Governor, Sir Peregrine Maitland, was appealed to. He advised, with his Attorney-General, who wholly differed from Judge Willis in his exposition of the statute. The Lieutenant-Governor, acting on this opinion, summarily dismissed the Judge. Judge Willis, in defending the course he took in refusing to sit in a Court, as he contended, illegally constituted, took the further ground that the act of the Governor in giving leave of absence to Chief Justice Campbell was his individual act and not the act of the Governor in Council as the law required, and so illegal. The Executive Council of the Province made a full report of the case to the Home Government, to which the Judge made reply from Bath, in England, on the 23rd of September, 1828, which will also be found in the Journals of the House of Assembly, to which I have referred. From this reply to the report may be gathered the grounds assumed by the Council for the removal of the Judge. The Judge in his reply reiterates the arguments he advanced from the bench for the course he pursued, challenged the right of the Governor of the Province or his Council to deprive him of his position of Judge without good and sufficient cause, and above all defended his right to give a judicial opinion which he judged to be right without interference of any person, and in that respect proclaimed his independence of the King, let alone his Governor of a Province. I do not propose to go into the reply at length. Suffice to say, it repudiates the charge that he was in any way actuated by a desire for popular applause or that he had acted in any way but the one dictated by his conscientious conviction that he was doing just what was right and according to law. The concluding part of his reply is as follows:

> As to the imputation so treacherously insinuated that I have been aiming at popular applause, I observe, in the language of that great and learned Chief Justice of England, Lord Mansfield, "It has been urged against me as a crime, that I have courted popularity. I never did court it, but I have always studied to deserve it. Popularity will always pay the pursuer. This must follow. I do not mean to say I despise it; on the contrary, I sincerely wish for it, if not purchased at too dear a price, at the expense of my conscience and my duty."

So much for Lord Mansfield.

Mr. Justice Willis goes on on his own behalf to say:

> Protesting, therefore, once more against the illegality of my removal, as well as against the liability of a Judge to be called in question for the effects or consequences, nay, even for the correctness of his judicial opinions, I have, nevertheless, submitted to the foregoing ample refutation of such charges as have been brought against me, both as respects the soundness of my interpretation of the law, and also the time, place, and manner of pronouncing it. I have discharged myself of an imperious duty, which, under my conviction of justice, I was bound as an honest man and a Christian to perform.

It was charged against the Judge that his comments on the Bench upon the conduct of the Crown officers, as to prosecutions, were expressed in an unusual and unbecoming manner. Mr. John Carey was examined before a Committee of the House of Assembly as to this by direct interrogatory. His answer was as follows:

> I was present when the conduct of the Crown officers relating to prosecutions was brought under the notice of Mr. Justice Willis, and saw nothing unusual or unbecoming in the conduct of the Judge, if I except the marked lenity with which he treated the Attorney-General when he, in a most uncourteous and unbecoming manner, told the Judge that he would persist in conducting criminal prosecutions contrary to the rule pursued by His Majesty's Attorney-General in England—and that he knew his duty as well as Judge Willis or any Judge on the Bench.

Anyone who knew Sir John Beverley Robinson knows that it was not in his nature to be uncourteous to anyone. That he was firm in his opinions, and had unbounded confidence in the specialties of Canadian law, and the manner in which prosecutions should be conducted tending to the due administration of justice, there can be no doubt. I have it from those who were well acquainted with the circumstances that Judge Willis's conduct, not so much in matter as in overbearing manner, provoked the retort of the Attorney-General. Everything goes to show that although Judge Willis may have been a learned man, he was regarded as not adapted to a colonial Court, or agreeable to colonial authorities. The Judge's commission as Judge was revoked on the 26th of June, 1828, when he was removed from his office, the patent of amoval being signed by Sir Peregrine Maitland as Lieutenant-Governor—J. B. Robinson, Attorney-General.

Immediately after his amoval the Judge proceeded to England, laid his case before the Home Government—the whole matter of his administration of justice in Canada. Charges made by the Government and counter-charges made by the Judge were investigated by the Government of England and by the Privy Council. The result of the enquiry was, that the Judge had erred in his construction of the Statute regarding the Court of King's Bench, and that he should have continued to hold the Court with Mr. Justice Sherwood, notwithstanding the absence of the Chief Justice. The Privy Council were, however, of opinion that his amoval from office was too summary; that he should have had charges regularly laid against him, and been given an opportunity of discussing them before removal, though true it was that his tenure of office was during pleasure only. The confirmation of the view of the Provincial authorities as to the constitution of the Court of King's Bench was very satisfactory to the colonial Government, the Court thus gaining additional strength. The British Government gave the Judge another appointment, sending him as Judge to Demerara. He was not there long before he ceased to be a Judge in that colony— for what reason I am unable to say. Judge Willis seems to have had many judicial appointments and many amovals. After his removal from Demerara he was appointed Judge of the Supreme Court of New South Wales. By patent under seal of the colony of New South Wales he was, on the 8th of February, 1841, appointed Resident Judge for the district of Port Philip, repaired to Melbourne in that district, and officiated as Resident Judge therein till the 24th of June, 1843, when he, while sitting in Court at Melbourne, received a dispatch written by the Colonial Secretary, by direction of the Governor, Sir George Gipps, announcing to him that it had been deemed expedient to submit to the Executive Council of the colony representations which had been addressed to the Governor respecting Mr. Willis (Judge), and that after mature deliberation the Council had advised that in conformity with the provisions of the Act of Parliament (22 Geo. III., Cap. 75) the Judge should be forthwith removed from the office, not only of Resident Judge of Port Philip, but as Judge of the Supreme Court of New South Wales. The packet containing the dispatch enclosed in addition a copy of a writ issued by the Governor-in-Council of the colony, tested the 17th of June, 1843, whereby, after setting forth that it had been sufficiently made to appear to the Governor-in-Council that Mr. Willis had misbehaved himself in his office, the Governor and Council did revoke his appointment, and inhibited him from the exercise of all power and authority as a Judge of the Supreme Court. Against this decision of the colonial authorities Judge Wiilis appealed to the Privy Council. The appeal was heard on the 24th and 25th of June and 8th of July, 1846. The report of their Lordships of the Privy Council, made on the 8th of July, 1846, and which was confirmed by Her Majesty, was:

> That in the opinion of their Lordships, the Governor in Council had power in law to amove Mr. Willis from his office of Judge under the authority of the statute 23 Geo. III., cap. 75, and upon the facts appearing before the Governor in Council and established before their Lordships in this case, *there was sufficient ground* for the amotion of Mr. Willis; but their Lordships are of opinion that the Governor in Council ought to have given him some opportunity of being previously heard against the amotion, and that the order of the 17th of June, 1843, ought therefore to be reversed.

I have been in communication with friends in New South Wales, one of whom has furnished me with information in regard to Judge Willis while in that Colony, which I will not withhold from the reader. It will be found to be not essentially different from the estimate I had formed of him while exercising judicial functions in Canada. It will also be found interesting as giving more details connected with his administration in New South Wales and Port Philip. My correspondent says of him :

> Before coming to New South Wales, he had held a judicial office in British Guiana, where he soon embroiled himself in a public quarrel which brought about a memorial, and ended in his recall.

Referring to his being sent out as Judge to New South Wales he writes :

> He made himself so disagreeable to his brother Judges that they were glad to get rid of him, and when the Port Philip opportunity offered, he was appointed to the billet. He was, it is admitted, a man of much legal acumen, great application, and considerable powers of composition ; but he was, says the authority from which I quote, who knew him well, impotent to control a bad temper, lacking in dignity, and capable of being easily prejudiced—in politics he was a partizan, an intermeddler in other people's affairs, and always eager to over-step the bounds of judicial propriety and dabble in matters not regularly before him.

In another part of the correspondence he states, on the authority of a gentleman who had been Clerk of the Legislative Council, and who had written a series of papers first begun in a Melbourne paper called " The World " on the 28th November, 1881, under the title of " The Chronicles of Early Melbourne," under the " Nom de plume " of Garryowen.

> That after the appointment of Charles Joseph LaNobe as Superintendent of Port Phillip his Honour had made himself so thoroughly obnoxious to Bar, press, and public that his Court was the scene of most unbecoming exhibitions. He was never in a state of peace, and the hatchet was not only never buried but daily brandished over the head of some one. It must certainly have been a trying time for him, for according to all accounts, the lawyers were worse than the clients, and the colony was in a state of insolvency. At length the crisis came. In

November, 1842, a public meeting was held to express confidence in the Judge's administration of justice, but a breach of the peace was anticipated, and his Honor had the good sense to insist on its abandonment. An address, however, was quietly arranged, and when three hundred names were obtained a deputation waited upon him at his chambers on 11th March, 1843, to present it. John Pinney Bear, a cattle salesman, was the Chairman, and presented it. His Honor was much gratified by the compliment, and in reply intimated that he had applied to the Secretary of State for the Colonies, soliciting an enquiry into his conduct. On the other hand, four memorials were transmitted to Governor Bourke in Sydney, praying for the recall of Willis. One of these bore the names of five hundred and twenty three persons, including eighteen magistrates. It was forwarded through, and recommended by W. LaNobe, the Superintendent of Port Phillip. This was in May, 1843, by which time the Judge had quarrelled with the Governor, the Executive Council, and the Judges of New South Wales, the Superintendent of Port Phillip, the magistracy, the legal profession, the press, and was distasteful to more than one half the community. He was presiding in his Court on 24th June, 1843, and was engaged in "slating" the Crown Prosecutor (Croke) when the Sydney mail was delivered. It brought news of his suspension pending the Queen's pleasure.

In vain were the subsequent indignation meetings of his friends. In vain the presentation to him of an address signed by fourteen hundred persons. He sailed for home in the *Glenbervie* on the 18th July, 1843, and commenced his appeals to the Colonial Office. Interminable motions and arguments before the Judicial Committee of the Privy Council followed, and it took nearly three whole anxious, doubtful years to decide it. At length, on 1st August, 1846, judgment was given, reversing the order of the amotion of Judge Willis from office on the 17th June, 1843, on the ground that some opportunity of being previously heard against the amotion ought to have been given to him by the Governor and Executive Council of New South Wales, but reporting to Her Majesty in their opinion that the Governor in Council had power by law to amove Mr. Willis under the authority of 22 George III., and that upon the facts appearing before the Governor in Council and established before their Lordships in this case, there were sufficient grounds for the amotion of Mr. Willis. The Queen approved, and an order was transmitted from the Secretary of State revoking the appointment of Willis as a puisne Judge of New South Wales and resident Judge of Port Phillip. Mr. Willis applied to the Secretary of State for permission to resign his office, for a retiring allowance or pension, and also reimbursement of the expenses incurred in prosecuting the suit. To these demands a courteous but decided refusal was given, and all he obtained was his back pay on account of salary computed from the date of last payment to the date of the warrant of revokement, and such he was given only because of the reversal of the amoval order. It was a dear quarrel for the colony of New South Wales, who had to pay :

Arrears of ex-Judge's salary	£4852	10	0
Costs in defending Governor Gipps	865	4	2
Ditto through postponement on behalf of defendant	22	12	8
	£5750	6	10

The Judge made several efforts to obtain official employment; but the Downing street authorities, taught by the past, would have nothing to do with him. He died in 1877.

XII.

Sir John Beverley Robinson, Baronet, Chief Justice of Upper Canada.

SIR JOHN BEVERLEY ROBINSON was the son of Christopher Robinson, Esq., who was fourth in descent from Christopher Robinson, Esq., of Cleasby, in the West Riding of Yorkshire, England—a brother of the Right Reverend John Robinson, D.D., Lord Bishop of Bristol, and afterwards of London, in the reign of Queen Anne—and who was first Plenipotentiary at the Congress of Utrecht. Christopher Robinson of Cleasby, above named, came out to America in the reign of Charles II., as private Secretary to Sir William Berkeley, Governor of Virginia, and subsequently became Governor of that Colony, his residence being near the Rappahannock, Middlesex County, rendered familiar to every reader of the Virginia Campaign of the Federal Army during the War between the Northern and Southern States of the United States. The second son of Christopher Robinson was John Robinson, President of the Council of Virginia, who was born in that Colony, and married Catharine, daughter of Robert Beverley, Esq., formerly of Beverley in Yorkshire, but then a resident of Virginia. This John Robinson had several sons, one of whom was Colonel Beverley Robinson of the British Army, who raised and commanded a regiment during the Revolutionary War. He was father of General Sir William

Robinson, and of General Sir Frederick P. Robinson, G. C. B. From another of these sons was descended Christopher Robinson, the father of Chief Justice Sir John Beverley Robinson. The father of the Chief Justice was born in Middlesex County, Virginia, and received his education at William and Mary College, of which venerable institution, his ancestor Christopher Robinson had been one of the first trustees.

During the American Revolution Sir John's father, at the age of seventeen, left college and obtained a commission as ensign in Colonel Simcoe's regiment of Queen's Ranger's, which formed a part of Sir Henry Clinton's army. He served in this corps until the peace of 1783, when, on the regiment being reduced, he emigrated with many other Loyalists to New Brunswick. While there he married Esther, daughter of the Reverend John Sayre. The Reverend John Sayre, when the war of the Revolution commenced, was Rector of Trinity Church, Fairfield, Connecticut. J. W. Lawrence, of St. John, New Brunswick, in his "Footprints, 1783-1882," states that the reverend gentleman removed to Maugerville, on the River St. John, and died August 5th 1784, in his forty-eighth year; and his daughter Esther married Christopher Robinson, and shortly after left with him for Upper Canada; that he was appointed Deputy Surveyor-General, and was father of Sir John Beverley Robinson. It would seem, however, that Mr. Robinson first settled in Lower Canada, at L'Assomption, in 1788, and having remained for a time at L'Assomption, removed shortly afterwards to Berthier, where his second son, John Beverley, the future Chief Justice, was born on 26th July, 1791. In 1792 Major General Simcoe came out from England as the first Governor of Upper Canada. He had, as we have seen, been Mr. Robinson's commanding officer during the Revolution. The Major-General induced his quondam ensign Christopher, to remove from Lower Canada and take up his residence in Kingston, which he did, and lived there six years. He was admitted a Student of Law in

Trinity Term, 1797, 37 George III., and was called to the Bar of Upper Canada in Trinity Term, 1797. He stood No. 6 on the Barristers' Roll at Osgoode Hall, and also No. 6 on the Benchers' Roll. He continued in the practice of his profession till 1798, during which period he was elected a Member to the first Parliament of Upper Canada, held at Newark, to represent the counties of Lennox and Addington. In 1798 he removed with his family to York, now Toronto, intending to settle on a place which he had bought below the Don on the Kingston Road, and on which he had built a small house. He died on the 2nd of November of the same year after a short illness, having suffered from the gout for many years.

Sir John Robinson received his education principally at the hands of Dr. Strachan, and was entered as a Student-of-the-Law in Hilary Term 48 Geo. III. A.D. 1808. He studied under the auspices of Attorney-General Macdonell, who was Provincial Aide-de-Camp to Sir Isaac Brock, and who was killed a few minutes after his gallant Chief had fallen at the battle of Queenston on the 13th October, 1812. Sir John was called to the Bar in Hilary Term, 1815, 55 Geo. III. He stands No. 40 on the Barristers' Roll, and 23 on the Benchers' Roll. He was three times elected Treasurer of the Law Society, *i.e.*, in the years 1818-1821, and 1828-1829. While yet a Student Sir John in 1812 entered the service of the Militia in defence of the Province in the War of 1812. He served as Lieutenant in the York Militia, and was present at the surrender of General Hull to Sir Isaac Brock, at Detroit, in August of that year, and drew up the terms of surrender. He was also at the battle of Queenston Heights, where Brock so nobly fell, and was one of the officers of the detachment which after that battle escorted a number of American prisoners to Quebec, among whom was Colonel, afterwards General Scott of the United States Army. He was mentioned in despatches for his gallant conduct in that battle. On his return from this service he was, before he was actually called to the Bar in due form of law, appointed acting Attorney-General for Upper Canada, the Solicitor-General Boulton being then a prisoner of war in France. On the 14th March, 1815, the Legislature of the Province passed an Act reciting :

> *Whereas* the glorious and honorable defence of this Province in the war with the United States of America hath necessarily called from their usual occupations, and professions, most of the inhabitants of the Province, and amongst them very many Barristers, Students-at-Law, Attorneys, and Articled Clerks of Attorneys, whereby the regular meetings of the Benchers of the Law Society of the said Province, being for many terms past interrupted, several young gentlemen have been prevented from making due application for admission on the books of the said society as Students-at-Law, and several Students-at-Law have in like manner been prevented being called to the Bar to their manifest and great injury: *and whereas* this evil, as far as in them lay at a meeting of the said Law Society, held as of Hilary Term in the fifty-fifth year of his present Majesty's reign, did enter upon their books the names of several persons who have been prevented in manner aforesaid from obtaining their due admission as Students, and Barristers, as aforesaid : therefore to remove all doubts as to the legality of such entry; it is enacted that all those persons whose names were then entered on the book of the Law Society as Students-at-Law, and Barristers, should be deemed, and held to be legally and regularly entered on the said book, and are thereby declared to be Students-at-Law, and Barristers, within the Province, and of such standing as to time as is now allowed to each respectively upon the book of the Society.

Sir John Robinson was one of the gentlemen who being in active service at the front during the war was prevented going up for call at the regular time, and so was entered on the books of the Law Society in Hilary Term, 55 George III., and his admission confirmed by this Act of Parliament.

We find that in his case a tribute was paid to his talent while yet a student: his appointment as acting Attorney-General taking place 19th November, 1812, before he was called to the Bar. On peace being proclaimed, Mr. Solicitor-General Boulton (who on a voyage to England had been made prisoner by a French privateer and taken to France) obtained his liberty and on his return from France to Upper Canada in 1815, was created Attorney-General, Sir John Robinson taking his place as Solicitor-

General. In 1817 Mr. Boulton was elevated to the Bench, and Mr. Robinson was again appointed, and this time permanently, to be Attorney-General of Upper Canada. He entered the House of Assembly of Upper Canada in 1821 as member for the Town of York, then the seat of Government, and was twice re-elected, continuing to be a member of that branch of the Legislature until he was summoned to the Legislative Council on the 1st of January, 1830, of which branch of the Legislature he was appointed Speaker on the 2nd of January, 1830.

In his professional practice at York, Mr. Robinson had the confidence of a great number of people, and on the circuits he had many friends. I have heard him say that in going on circuit he had often to travel on horseback with saddle bags as receptacle of his briefs and his books for ready reference. There are no published reports of decided cases from his call to the Bar till 1824, but the records in Osgoode Hall shew he had a large established practice, the largest of his day. His name appears in Taylor's Reports, 1824 to 1829, arguing cases in opposition to the Solicitor-General and other prominent Barristers of the time. He was during that time Attorney-General and head of the Bar.

I will not dwell now at large on this period of his life as it was in his character of Chief Justice that he gained his great distinction.

It will not be irrelevant to refer to Mr. Robinson's parliamentary career, as in some measure affording a key to his subsequent judicial life. If I might venture an opinion I should say that there was no more devoted a King's man in his Majesty's dominions. I might add that a reverence for established authority was one of the distinguishing traits of his life. Mr. Robinson was a Tory of the old school. Church and State had a charm for him which, to men of the present day, seems a relic of feudalism. Well!—it may be so, but in the days of feudalism there were many knights-errant who fought their country's battles bravely and well.

"*Tempora mutantur et nos mutamur in illis.*"

Since the American and French Revolutions the world has witnessed great changes, the most significant of which is the spread of democracy. In Mr. Robinson's parliamentary day the voice of the people was first beginning to be heard, but it was a small voice. In Upper Canada it was stifled by a system of autocracy which prevailed in Upper Canada as in other colonies.

In writing the lives of previous Judges I have referred to the pernicious system which prevailed of Judges being members of Parliament. I have now to refer to what I conceive to have been another dangerous element in the administration of affairs, and that was that the Chief Justice of the Province was a member of the Executive Council, frequently, if not always, the head of the Council and the adviser of the Lieutenant-Governor of the Province, this was the state of things in 1828 when Mr. Robinson was a member of the Legislature and Attorney-General. It was part of a system which did not strike him as contrary to principles of good government. The Roman Catholic Bishop and Archdeacon Strachan were both members of the Legislative Council, the higher branch of the Legislature. I can quite understand, considering the school in which Mr. Robinson was educated, that he could easily convince himself that in a country where the Governor came as a stranger to the Province, its habits and customs, it was not incompatible with good government that he should have as his adviser one intimately acquainted with the condition of affairs, and none so likely to fulfil the requirement as the Chief Justice. That was not, however, the view entertained by the majority of the members of the Legislative Assembly. On reference to the Journals of the Assembly, 4th Session, 9th Parliament, 9 George IV., A.D. 1828, 15th March, it will be seen that the Assembly passed the following address:

To THE KING'S MOST EXCELLENT MAJESTY.

MOST GRACIOUS SOVEREIGN :—

We, Your Majesty's dutiful and loyal subjects, the Commons of Upper Canada in Parliament assembled, beg leave most humbly to approach Your Majesty upon a subject of the deepest interest connected with the administration of justice :

We would again humbly and earnestly represent that the Executive Council is appointed by Your Majesty to advise His Excellency upon the affairs of the Province, and that the connection of the Chief Justice with it, wherein he has to advise His Excellency upon executive measures, many of which may bear an intimate relation to the judicial duties he may have thereupon to discharge is highly inexpedient, tending to embarass him in his judicial functions, and render the administration of justice less satisfactory if not less pure.

Your Majesty's faithful Commons represent their deep sense of the expediency of rendering the Judges in the Province as independent of the Crown as the Judges of England.

The prayer of this address was, that His Majesty would be pleased to discontinue to impose on the Chief Justice a duty so incompatible with his judicial character.

Mr. Rolph, seconded by Captain Matthews, moved the adoption of the address. The yeas were : Baby, Beardsley, Bidwell, Clark, Hamilton, Horner, Lefferty, and nine other members, names well known in Canadian Parliamentary History, in all sixteen. The nays were : the Attorney-General, John Beverley Robinson, and five others, six in all. The address was carried by a majority of nine.

As we have seen Mr. Robinson voted with the minority. This vote is singularly illustrative of the spirit of the times actuating those who wished to preserve the " *status quo.*" We find here the Attorney-General voting against a measure calculated to dissever the administration of justice from the executive and political head of the Province, and in the same division others of the members who usually voted with the Attorney-General are found voting for the measure. This like many other measures passed upon and reported in the Journals shew that at that time it often occurred that *Tories and Reformers* voted on the same side. There was not nearly so much partisanship then as now, every man voted according to his conscience, there was no man in Parliament big enough to hold in his pocket the votes of his fellow members, or curb the aspirations of a progressive people.

In the same session of the same Parliament we find the Religious Denominations Bill passed, the object of which was to enable religious congregations, Presbyterians, Lutherans, Calvinists, Methodists, Congregationalists, Independents, Anabaptists, Quakers, Menonists, Tunkers, or Moravians, to appoint trustees, and their successors in perpetual succession to hold land for the purpose of their meeting house, chapel, or burying ground. We find the Attorney-General, (Robinson,) Bidwell, Perry, and McDonald, of Glengarry, voting on the same side for this measure, while we find Rolph and nine others on the opposite side. The measure seems to have been carried by a majority of nine, and amongst these Episcopalian, Roman Catholic, and Methodist members. This rule shews that Mr. Robinson by his acts evinced his high regard for the early settlers of the country of whatever faith or political complexion. Mr. Robinson, a noted Tory, is found voting on the same side as Bidwell and Perry, the most pronounced Liberals of their day.

A great deal has been said and written in Canada about family compactism—that there was a family compact, and Mr. Robinson the head of it. This is all very true. At the same time it must be remembered that the chief men of the Province were called " Family Compact " thirty years before Mr. Robinson came upon the scene. The old family compact was something like the F. F. V's of Virginia They were a party of themselves, and monopolised the most and best offices of the state.

Much has been written about Mr. Robinson's Parliamentary treatment, sometimes called bad treatment, of Barnabas Bidwell, the father of the distinguished lawyer Marshal S. Bidwell. A close examination of the facts, however, will dissipate any such erroneous idea. The Journals of Parliament, A.D. 1821, tell the whole story. Barnabas Bidwell was in 1821 elected Member of the Assembly to represent Lennox and Addington in Parliament. Mr. Bidwell was born in the British Province. of Massachusetts Bay before the American Revolution

17—L. J.

He remained in that Province during the rebellion of the British colonies, being under age, and without taking up arms against the mother country. After arriving at the age of twenty-one years he was appointed Treasurer of the county of Berkshire, Attorney of the State of Massachusetts, and Member of Congress. He took an oath to support the Constitution of the United States. He came to Upper Canada in 1810, and constantly thereafter remained therein, and took the oath of allegiance to His Majesty the King of Great Britain. On the 29th December, 1821, the petition of Timothy Stong and one thousand other electors of the counties of Lennox and Addington, praying for the expulsion of Mr. Bidwell from the Assembly on the above recited facts, which he admitted, came up.

On that occasion the Attorney-General (Robinson) moved that the 29th December be appointed for taking into consideration the petition of Mr. Stong and others against Mr. Bidwell's election.

It was moved in amendment by Mr. Jones, of Grenville, that it be resolved: "That this House is of opinion that Barnabas Bidwell, not being naturalized by any British Act of Parliament, is an alien, and therefore incapable of being elected to serve in the Parliament of this Province," (Upper Canada). Twelve Members, including the Attorney-General, voted for the amendment and nineteen against. The amendment was therefore lost, and the original motion was carried.

No one can say that the Attorney-General and twelve others most of whom were United Empire Loyallists were influenced by any other motive than to purge Parliament of the presence of a gentleman however estimable who had taken the oath of allegiance to a Government formed on the wreck of the British Colonies, and with which Government their country had been at war, but seven years previously. A country of which Mr. Bidwell had been a Member of Congress, and so in a measure responsible for the hostility of the United States in the war of 1812. We must view these matters as they struck the men of that day, and not as it could strike men who live half a century afterwards. In the following year there were found more members who were willing that Mr. Bidwell should retain his seat in the House.

On the 4th of January, 1822, the question for the avoidance of the election of Mr. Bidwell again came up, and his election was avoided by but one vote. Dr. Baldwin, Mr. Baby, and Col. Nichol voted that Mr. Bidwell should retain the seat, while the Attorney-General voted for the avoidance of the election.

It may be that the closeness of the vote exasperated the liberals of that day. Still when they had voting with them several supporters of the Attorney-General, as well as personal friends, it may well be conceived that there was room for divergence of opinion, and that those who voted either way were acting according as their conscience dictated. Col. Nichol, who, as we have seen, voted against the Attorney-General on the Barnabas Bidwell motion on the 9th January, 1822, five days after the vote on the Bidwell motion, brought up the report of the Joint Committee of both Houses appointed to draft an address to His Excellency the Lieutenant-Governor praying him to appoint John B. Robinson, Esq., Attorney-General as Commissioner to take to England and present at the foot of the Throne the Joint Address of both branches of the Legislature to His Majesty relative to the financial concerns of the Province of Upper Canada ; the Committee reported that they had agreed to a draft which was read, and is as follows :

> *To His Excellency* SIR PEREGRINE MAITLAND, *Commissioner of the Most Honorable Military Order of the Bath, Lieutenant Governor of the Province of Upper Canada, and Major General Commanding His Majesty's Forces therein, &c.*
>
> MAY IT PLEASE YOUR EXCELLENCY :
>
> The Legislative Council and House of Assembly while concurring in a report, and in an address to our Most Gracious Sovreign on the subject of our Provincial relations with Lower Canada, have also united

in a desire that on an occasion of such vast importance to the interests of this Province some person of talent and consideration may be appointed to lay this address at the foot of the Throne.

The Legislative Council and House of Assembly while they disclaim all desire of interfering with an appointment which by their joint resolution, rests solely with Your Excellency: and repose the fullest confidence in your Excellency's wisdom to select a person fully qualified for this important mission on considering the magnitude of the subject, have agreed in opinion, from the experience of the extensive information of his Majesty's Attorney General on the affairs of this Province that the duties suggested by the report will be fulfilled by him in the manner most conducive in the attainment of the important end they have in view.

Now as the resolution expresses this *was* an important mission—there was considerable friction between the Province of Upper Canada and the Province of Lower Canada; the duties on goods coming to Upper Canada from England were levied in Montreal or Quebec in Lower Canada. These duties largely tended to swell the revenues of Lower Canada, while Upper Canada contributed she had not received her proper share of the revenue. Other questions of great moment affected the body politic of both Provinces. Committees of the Legislature of the two Provinces had been appointed, met, received evidence, and reported. It became necessary that England should be called in to adjust the difficulties that had sprung up in the Provinces.

It was no small compliment to Mr. Robinson that he at this epoch at the early age of thirty years, should in such flattering terms have been selected to represent so important interests to the Parent State. Mr. Robinson immediately, on receipt of the resolution, wrote a letter to the Speaker of the House acknowledging the honor done him by appointing him commissioner, and then went on to say:

> I trust that it will be believed that on an occasion of this kind considerations of a personal nature would not have more weight with me than it is necessary to give them, but having no private interest or object to advance by discharging the duty committed to me, I owe it to myself to represent that however willing I may be to incur the inconvenience which must attend my immediate departure for Europe, my present circumstances do not admit of my making any considerable

sacrifice, and that I cannot meet the expenses which must attend the commission and sustain the loss which must arise from an immediate abandonment of my public emoluments, and the total interuption of my professional pursuits for an indefinite time without an adequate provision.

Subsequently adequate provision was made, he undertook the commission, and fully satisfied the expectations of the Legislature in his manner of performing the duty entrusted to him. On his return to the Province he received the thanks of both branches of the Legislature couched in the strongest language of approval. During his stay in England he was called to the English Bar by the Honorable Society of Lincoln's Inn, and shortly after the Imperial Government offered him the valuable appointment of Chief Justice of the Mauritius which he declined, perferring to follow the career he had so successfully begun in Upper Canada.

Colonel Nichol, whose name I have mentioned as moving the address to which I have referred on the subject of Mr. Robinson's mission to England, was one of the ablest and most noted members of the Assembly, and a companion in arms with Mr. Robinson and the gallant General Brock on the occasion of the capture of Detroit and the surrender of General Hull in 1812. In the possession of the family of his son is a gold medal specially awarded to Colonel Nichol for his service on that occasion. On one side is inscribed " DETROIT," on the obverse side is the figure of Britannia ; and inscribed on the outer edge of the medal " Lieutenant-Col. Robert Nichol Quarter Master General to the Militia."

This medal was awarded Colonel Nichol for special services. It was a rich souvenir of the past and no one congratulated the recipient of it more heartily than Mr. Robinson.

In the year 1829 was held the Assembly which surpassed all others up to that time in advocating those principles of reform, which had got a fast hold on the people. At the first session of this Parliament Marshal S. Bidwell, son of the Barnabas Bidwell to whom I have previously referred, was a Member of the House, and elected Speaker. A large majority of the Members of this House were opposed to the policy of previous Legislatures, mainly guided by John Beverley Robinson, then and still, Attorney-General.

The proceedings of the House show that the popularity of the Attorney-General was visibly on the decline. It was not without a protest that he had gained his seat for the town of York. He was, however, sworn in as Member on the 8th January, 1829. No sooner, however, had he secured the position than he found his place an unenviable one. Attacks fast and furious were made on him and his policy, which must have been truly galling ; and yet the Attorney-General stood manfully to his guns. On the 12th January, 1829, a resolution was passed in the House :

> That although the House sees his Excellency, (Sir John Colborne, Lieutenant Governor), unhappily surrounded by the same advisers as have so deeply wounded the feelings, and injured the best interests of the country, yet in the interval of any necessary change this House entertains an anxious belief that under the auspices of his Excellency the administration of justice will rise above suspicion, the wishes and interests of the people properly respected, the constitutional rights and independence of the Legislature be held inviolable, the prerogative and patronage of his Most Gracious Majesty be exercised for the happiness of the people and the honor of the Crown, and the revenues of the colony be hereafter sacredly devoted to the many and urgent objects of public improvement, after making provision for the public service upon the basis of that economy which is suited to the exigencies of the country and the condition of its inhabitants.

This resolution was strongly opposed by Mr. Robinson (Attorney-General) and five other Members, but in a full House of forty-eight Members was carried by a majority of forty-two. The resolution speaks for itself. Every word, and every line of it indicate that the Legislature (the Assembly) was hot-afoot after reform—it was a direct stab at the Attorney-General, and the existing order of things, expressing that : "His Excellency is *unhappily surrounded by the same advisers* as have so deeply wounded the feelings and injured the best interests of the country."

The reference in the resolution to the **administration of justice** was doubtless aimed at the Attorney-General.

In the life of Judge Willis I have referred to the conviction of Francis Collins for a libel on the Attorney-General ; the case was tried before Mr. Justice Sherwood, and resulted in Collins being subjected to a fine of £50, and sentenced **to twelve months** imprisonment. During the Session of 1829 the matter of the conviction was brought up in the Assembly, Collins had petitioned the Lieutenant-Governor for remission of his sentence, and the prayer of the petition was refused. The Legislative Assembly undertook to second **the** application of Collins for executive clemency, but met with a rebuff from the Governor, and that not in very mild **terms. Events were** proceeding rapidly to a crisis. On the 26th January, 1829, the Assembly passed a **resolution** :

> That they owe it to their own dignity and honor to declare that by their application for the exercise of the royal clemency towards Francis Collins they have not merited the imputation which they apprehend to be conveyed in his Excellency's message, that their request was inconsistent with the due support of the laws, and their duty towards society.

This resolution **was carried,** twenty-four Members voting for it, and nineteen against. The **Attorney-General** voted with **the minority.** The carrying of this resolution shews that **the** Attorney-General had lost his hold **on the House, and that,** in a matter in which **he was** personally concerned, the Legislature **were** desirous of condoning the offence of Collins, the libel on the Attorney-General.

On the 16th January, 1829, the Sedition Law Repeal Bill was read a third time **and** passed in a full House, forty-one Members voting for the Repeal, and *one* (the Attorney-General) against the Bill. By these proceedings it became quite evident to the Attorney-General that he should no longer oppose the will of the people as expressed in Parliament.

At the close of the session, in July, 1829, **an** offer of **the** Chief Justiceship, (become vacant by the retirement of Chief Justice Campbell,) having been made to him, he accepted the office, not displeased to be rid of the turmoil of political life.

On his elevation to the Bench the Chief Justice found himself called upon to administer and interpret laws, a very considerable part of the Canadian statutory portion of which he had either framed or assisted in framing. A reference to the Statute Book for the term he was in Parliament will shew that during that period many laws of a truly practical and beneficial character were passed, especially laws relating to legal procedure and the administration of justice. It can well be understood, then, how much at home Sir John found himself on the Bench. It would be idle to attempt to give even a synopsis of the judicial decisions come to by him during the thirty-three years he was Chief Justice of the Queen's Bench. It is sufficient to say that during this whole period, the longest ever attained by any Chief Justice or Judge in the Province, he was looked up to, as indeed he was the head of Bench, and that his decisions, contained in thirty volumes of the Reports, uniformly had the respect of the Bar. He had much to do in giving interpretation to the laws regulating the division of lands in the Province, and was familiar with all the intricacies of the boundary laws. In commercial law he was ever for a liberal interpretation of the laws affecting banking and commerce, regarding these matters as of the utmost importance to the advancement of the Province. He had no difficulty in bringing his mind to a clear conception of the different circumstances of the mother land and the colony in relation to land matters. Evidence of this is found in his decision in *Dean* v. *McCarthy*, 2 Q. B. 448, where he made a bold attack on the English law in regard to the owners of land kindling fire on their own land whereby a neighbour's fence was burned, holding that in Canada, where such fires were useful or necessary to clear the lands, such owner was not an insurer that no injury should happen to his neighbour, but was responsible only for negligence. This decision was followed, and in effect its correctness affirmed by the subsequent case of *Gillen* v. *North Grey R. W. Co.*, 33 Q. B. 128, affirmed in Appeal, 35 Q. B. 475.

In the administration of Criminal Law the Chief Justice was strict to a degree. Before promotion to the Bench his long practice in Crown Law, as Attorney-General, had directed his mind in channels that ever after pursued their even course. Having practised before him for seventeen years of my professional life, and in my early professional career engaged in a great many criminal cases, I can bear testimony that while the Chief Justice was strict he was ever ready to hear what counsel had to say in defence of a prisoner, giving due weight to all counsel's arguments in his charge to the jury. I am aware that there are those who think that his bias was unduly to the Crown. I can not say this, but can say that I do not believe he ever forgot his duty to the Crown in this or any other matter. I was once concerned in a criminal case, the eminent counsel Henry Eccles, Q. C., and myself being for the prisoner, and on the trial before Judge Draper, at Toronto, were unsuccessful in procuring an acquittal. The charge was embezzlement, and from the position of the prisoner, a clerk in a bank, was a serious one. After conviction we moved Draper, J., to arrest the judgment, but failed again, the Judge sentencing the prisoner to seven years imprisonment. We were then entitled to carry the case into the Queen's Bench, presided over by the Chief Justice, which we did ; and there again failed to convince the Chief Justice that the ruling of Judge Draper was erroneous. We then carried the case to the Court of Appeal, then composed of the Judges of the Courts of Queen's Bench, Common Pleas, and Chancery, when the case received much consideration, the points were much debated at the Bar. The Court of Appeal (the Chief Justice assenting), was at first disposed to confirm the opinion of the Judge who made the ruling at the Court of Oyer and Terminer confirmed by the decision of the Court of Queen's Bench, but after much difference of opinion on the Bench, and much discussion there, just before giving judgment the Chief Justice reversed his previous ruling, admitted that the ruling at the trial had been wrong, that the ruling of the Court of Queen's Bench confirming that ruling and in which he concurred was wrong. The majority of the Court adopting this view the conviction of the prisoner was quashed, the judgment arrested, and he was saved from the severe infliction of imprisonment for the term of seven years to which he had been sentenced. I think in this case the Chief Justice shewed the highest attribute of a Judge in reversing a decision which he had come to when a fuller investigation and argument satisfied him that the decision was wrong. I mention this case as shewing that the Chief Justice was capable and willing, in all cases, to answer the demands of justice.

In the Rebellion of 1837 the Chief Justice doffed the ermine for the sword. The morning after the College bell called the citizens of Toronto to arms to meet the invaders marching down Yonge street to disturb the city's quiet, he was at St. Lawrence Hall, where the Governor had taken up position to meet those who were willing to defend the town from attack. I was a College boy at the time and well remember with the enthusiasm of youth applying for arms to shoot down the rebels, and being rejected on the ground of being too young for the service, the Governor saying that the arms could better carry me than I carry arms. The Chief Justice was there as a volunteer, making common cause with his fellow townsmen in defence of hearth and home. As to the rebellion itself I say nothing. Mr. Dent has so well written of the events of the time in his History of the Rebellion, that it is quite unnecessary to enlarge on the subject.

In 1838 it fell to the lot of the Chief Justice to have to try a number of persons charged with treason in the rebellion of 1837. Two prisoners William Lount and Peter Matthews were arraigned before him charged with this offence; the prisoners candidly and honestly admitted the charge, and pleaded guilty. They were in fact some of the principals in an armed force destined to attack Toronto, seize all the public property, overthrow the Government, and inaugurate a Provincial Government for the direction of the affairs of the Province. There never has been a doubt in the minds of any one that had the insurgents been successful in their attack on Toronto, not only the public property of the place but the public men would have been made subject to the invading force. However that may be the indictment against the prisoners was full and comprehensive, they admitted the charge and all the Chief Justice had to do was to pass the sentence of the law, which was capital punishment.

The Chief Justice, in passing sentence on the prisoners, expatiated at large on the crime of High Treason ; and in a touching manner referred to the misery and ruin entailed upon the families of the prisoners, and not only on their families, but the families of others engaged in the rebellion.

The *Christian Guardian* newspaper of April 4th, 1838, in a three column article, published in full the remarks of the Chief Justice on that melancholy occasion. After dealing in generalities the Chief Justice addressed each of the prisoners separately in the following words :

With respect to you William Lount, you are known to have held that station in this Province, that you must have taken, and probably on more than one occasion a deliberate oath to bear true allegiance to that Sovereign against whom you are convicted of having levied open war. I hope you have now some sense of the aggravated guilt of violating so solemn and express an obligation. In a country in which you had been admitted to the honorable privilege of making laws to bind your fellow subjects, it was due from you to set an example of faithful obedience to public authority ; instead of combining with desperate unprincipled men to overthrow the Government of your Sovereign, and to set the laws at defiance, you should have been found to resist such an attempt by every sacrifice of life or property. You are too intelligent not to have known your duty. The signal fidelity of thousands of people of this Province of humbler station than your own shews that there was no room for doubt as to the part which it became you to act as a man, as a subject, and as a Christian. That you have so fully deviated from that course must now be the occasion of bitter remorse to yourself, as I have no doubt it is the occasion of sorrow to most, if not all of those who were exposed to danger from the wicked rebellion in which I fear I must say you took a very prominent part.

In addressing Peter Matthews the Chief Justice said :

With regard to you, Peter Matthews, it is not unkown to me that in one period of your life, you proved yourself willing to render useful service in defence of your country. You certainly are not ignorant of that duty of allegiance which binds a subject to his Sovereign, and it is to be deplored that you should have so freely betrayed it. I fear that the part which is known to have been borne by you in the late miserable rebellion was too conspicious to allow it to be supposed that you were a reluctant or unwilling agent. But I take it for granted that the evidence of these facts which, if you had not confessed your guilt, would have been laid before a jury on your trial, will be submitted to consideration in the proper quarter.

Addressing both prisoners the Chief Justice thus delivered himself:

I need hardly tell you, prisoners, that the painful duty which your conviction of the crime of treason imposes on this Court is marked out to them by the law. We have no discretion to exercise. The awful sentence of death must follow your conviction. But although a power to pardon resides only in the Sovereign whose authority you endeavoured to subvert, if I could conscientiously encourage in you a hope that pardon could be extended, I would gladly do so, for it would render infinitely less painful the duty which the Court has to discharge. I know no ground on which I can venture to hold out to you such a hope, and I do therefore most earnestly exhort you to prepare yourselves for the execution of the sentence which is about to be pronounced. In the short time that may remain to you I pray that you may be brought to a deep sense of the guilt of the course of which you are convicted, and that you may be enabled to address yourselves in humble and earnest sincerity to the infinite mercy of the Saviour whose Divine commands you have transgressed.

No one, the most hypercritical can take exception to this charge. It was no doubt a painful thing to the Chief Justice to be obliged to sentence men who in other days had well served their country ; in Peter Matthew's case, no doubt, in the militia in the War of 1812. I have it from the best authority that in the evening after the sentence was passed the Chief Justice said to an old friend that he had never performed a more painful duty in his life.

It has been supposed by some laymen, and it may be by others, that the Chief Justice should have in some way interposed to save the lives of the prisoners. It seems to be forgotten by such persons that the province of mercy is exclusively with the Crown. The Court after condemnation has but to pass the sentence of the law.

Sir George Arthur was Governor of the Province, and it rested with him to have extended the clemency of the Crown if he had reason to believe that the public interest demanded or even warranted its exercise. The Governor was much importuned to spare the lives of the prisoners. As many as thirty thousand people petitioned him to extend the mercy of the Crown to the prisoners. All attempts to procure a commutation of the sentence proved to be of no avail. The prisoners were subjected to the extreme penalty of the law. The Governor might, and probably did, call on the Chief Justice for a report of the case as it stood before him; and it would then have been the duty of the Chief Justice to say whether or not he saw any ground for recommending a pardon or reprieve.

Mr. Lindsey, in his life of Mackenzie, has written (referring to Lount and Matthews):

> There was indeed no question about their guilt, but the Chief Justice afterwards performed the ungracious office of assuring the Executive that he saw no ground upon which he felt that he could properly recommend a pardon or respite.

To say "that there was indeed no question about their guilt, but the Chief Justice afterwards performed the ungracious task," &c., is something akin to a *non sequitur*.

However that may be, the Chief Justice in reporting as he did, or is said to have done, to the Governor was but performing a plain duty. Without travelling out of the record, what other report could he have made? The prisoners had admitted guilt, and the Chief Justice had a duty to perform to the Crown and the country. Unless he admitted that rebellion was justifiable, which he was not likely to do, he could not have done otherwise than he did. Even if rebellion could be justified it had not been set up as a defence. The Chief Justice at this time was a Legislative Councillor. He had been for many years a member of that body and its Speaker. As a member of the Legislative Council he was sworn " to defend the Crown against all traitorous conspiracies and attempts whatever which should be made against the Queen's person, Crown, or dignity." This oath the Chief Justice under all circumstances religiously observed.

The *Christian Guardian* newspaper, the influential organ of the large body of Methodists in the Province, in an editorial under date of April 18, 1838, affected to give some reasons why Sir George Arthur could not see his way clear to exercise the clemency of the Crown. The editorial reads as follows :

> We understand that several petitions, praying for the exercise of the Royal prerogative in their behalf, were sent in to the Governor, who expressed his deep regret that the circumstances were such as to render his interference improper, and that a sense of public duty constrained him to allow the law to take its course in relation to them. This decision was probably founded mainly upon the consideration that Lount was the leader of the band of rebels who marched to Montgomery's on the fatal night in which the gallant Colonel Moody was murdered, and that no facts have transpired to elicit the actual perpetrators of that horrid deed ; and that Matthews was the leader of the party who burned the property of Mrs. Washburn, attempted to burn the Don bridge, killed a man, and fired upon a woman who expostulated with them. With these particulars before them, and many others which have not yet been made public in consequence of the prisoners having avoided a trial by pleading guilty. It appears that the Executive deemed it imperative that such an example should be made as would be likely to deter persons in time to come from entering upon a project so fraught with evils of the highest magnitude, and so utterly subversive of everything that is essential to the good order of society.

The members of the Executive Council at this time were :
    The Honorable Robert B. Sullivan.
           " William Allan,
           " Augustus Baldwin,
           " John Elmsley,
           " William H. Draper.
I do not call this a Family Compact council.

In writing the life of Chief Justice Robinson the work would be unfinished if some allusion were not made to the Family Compact, of which he was the recognized chief;

and there are not wanting writers who have laid to the door of the Family Compact all the sins that flesh was heir to in those days, including the non-reprieve of Lount and Matthews. After all, what was the Family Compact? It was an organization composed of those who had originally settled the Province, and no doubt thought they had at least a pre-emptive right to it, many of them having occupied positions of trust in the old colony. They were men not of the same family or always of kin to each other, but like the soldiers of old, when they had conquered a place they meant to hold it. The government of the country got into their hands, and they were determined to hold it against all comers. The citadel had many defenders, Beverley House one of the principal bastions, no doubt, being held by the Chief Justice, who never surrendered till the last gun was fired.

In 1839 Mr. Charles Poulett Thompson, an English merchant, was appointed Governor General. In pursuance of instructions of the English Ministry he proposed for the acceptance of the people of Canada a measure which united the Provinces of Upper and Lower Canada, provided for the equal representation of both Provinces in a conjoint Legislature, and conceded the full acknowledgment of the long wished for right of Responsible Government.

Mr. Poulett Thompson, the Governor General, afterwards Lord Sydenham, in his message to the Legislative Council said: "I have been instructed by her Majesty to administer the government in accordance with the well understood wishes of the people, and to pay to their feelings, as expresssed through their representatives, the deference that is justly due to them." This message was a sad blow and great discouragement to the Tory party. The practice heretofore had been not to pay to the feelings of the people, as expressed through their representatives, the deference that was justly due them. On the contrary, the Executive and the Governor had over and over again totally disregarded the will of the people, as expressed through their representatives in Parliament. The "vox populi" of those days was as so much thin air, evanescent and unsubstantial.

Mr. Robinson was startled, but not discouraged by the action of the governor, Poulett Thompson. In the following year, 1840, we find him in England, when he wrote a pamphlet entitled "Canada and Canada Bill, being an examination of the proposed measure for the future Government of Canada, with an introductory chapter containing some general views respecting the British Provinces of North America." In this pamphlet he took the ground that a union of the Provinces was in every way unwise, inconvenient, and would turn out to be impracticable.

A perusal of this pamphlet will shew that some of his prognostications have proved but too true; the racial prejudice in the Province of Quebec has been so great that the existence of an Englishman in that Province has become well nigh intolerable. The Chief Justice had a prescience of this, and was therefore for the adoption of some other scheme. The Imperial Federation Act, which superseded the Act of Union of 1841, had not been enacted in his lifetime.

In 1850 he was appointed a Companion of the Bath, and in 1854 received the high distinction of being made a Baronet of the United Kingdom. In 1856, on the occasion of his last visit to England, the honorary Degree of D. C. L. was conferred on him by the University of Oxford.

Sir John Beverley Robinson, in the performance of his public duty as Judge and in his private life, was one of the most courteous of men. The junior Barrister as well as the senior recognized that the Chief Justice always heard all he had to say in advocating the cause of his clients. The Chief was always dignified in manner, adding dignity to the Court over which he presided.

In 1862 the Chief Justice retired from the chief justiceship of the Queen's Bench and was appointed presiding

Judge of the Court of Appeal, (18th March, 1862,) which office he held up to the time of his death.

On Sir John's retirement from the Chief Justiceship of the Queen's Bench the Bar of the Province entertained him at a banquet of the most distinguished character at Osgoode Hall. The banquet was in June 1862, and was of the most *recherché* description. The Bar had given many invitations to guests, and the company numbered two hundred ; the military, the Church, clergy of more than one denomination, the Provost of Trinity College, the Bishops, and the Chief Justice's brother Judges, graced the occasion. It was a memorable event, the first great banquet given in the new library of Osgoode Hall. Those of us who were there have some recollection of the speech made by the Chief Justice in response to the toast in his honor. It was full of tenderness and made a lasting impression on all those present. In it the Judge gave a short synopsis of the history of his early life and subsequent judicial career. I will only give the peroration of his speech. The speech itself was lengthy, and every word was of great interest. Concluding, he said :

> They (the Bar) would recollect, and he would remind some of the younger members of the profession, that it was the solemn oath administered to all Judges for more than five hundred years, framed in the reign of Edward III., and worded in the plain, expressive language of that time : "That he will well and lawfully serve our lord the King, and his people in the office of justice ; that he will do equal law and execution of right to all the King's subjects, rich and poor, without having regard to any person.

Sir John Beverley Robinson through his whole judicial career paid the utmost regard to this oath. The *Globe* newspaper of Toronto, after the great banquet given in his honor, thus wrote :

> We are not of the school of politics to which Sir John B. Robinson belonged, and were he in public life now, it is certain that we should differ widely from his views. But that ought not, and shall not prevent us paying a tribute of praise to a well spent and honored life. Sir John B. Robinson in his speech of last evening gave cordial thanks to the late Rev. Dr. Stewart, of Kingston, and to the Rev. Dr. Strachan, who sat

beside him, a hale man of 84 years, for their kind protection and training bestowed on him in his early years when left an orphan; and doubtless to them he owed something of his early rise. But it is evident that the youth who distinguished himself on the field of Queenston at the age of 25, and was thereafter made Attorney General, ere he had been actually called to the Bar in a formal manner, needed but little help in life. He was the architect of his own fortune. Possessed of a ready and clear, if not a profound intellect, a steady will, great activity, will and perseverance, Mr. Robinson would doubtless have succeeded in any country, but in a backwoods region like Canada, it is not wonderful that he rapidly took the first honors of profession and was called to the Bench at the early age of 40. He was at that time, and remained for some time after, the head of a powerful political party, and shewed invincible determination and courage in advocating its views. Doubtless he was often in the wrong—who has not been proved by time to be in the wrong?—but no one will deny to him the credit of being perfectly sincere and honest in his convictions, and having laboured for them with conscientious zeal and assiduity. In reference to one part of his public career no limit need be placed on our praises. He was a strong friend of British connection, and defended this outpost of England with a courage which knew no difficulty. As the acknowledged head of society in this Province, Sir J. B. Robinson has exercised as great an influence as in his political sphere, and has used it in an eminently beneficial manner. In his own personal habits, temperate, frugal, chaste, and dignified, liberal in his hospitality, a friend of morality, and an enemy of excess, there can be no question that his example has had a powerful influence on social habits, not only in this city but throughout the whole Province. As subject, parent, and member of society, he stands before his countrymen *sans peur et sans reproche*, worthy of the honors bestowed upon him by his Sovereign, and of the esteem and respect of his fellow citizens.

I will not let any words of mine weaken this noble tribute to departed worth, not written as an obituary, but in the full blaze of light, during the lifetime of the Chief Justice, and at a time when the great organ of public opinion declared itself as not of the school of politics to which the Chief Justice belonged.

Sir John in his latter days was a martyr to the gout, and died at Beverley House on the last day of January, 1863, in the 72nd year of his age, "*Pallida mors æquo pulsat pede.*"

The Bar, the Bench, and general public testified the respect in which they held him by attending his funeral obsequies in St. James's Church of which he had been a member for many years, in large numbers. It is doubtful if ever before in Toronto so large a cortege followed to the grave the bier of any citizen. His memory will be held in affectionate remembrance by all who knew him.

The portrait in oil by Berthon, hanging on the western wall of the library of Osgoode Hall, is a very perfect likeness of him as he was at the time it was taken.

I have been able to give but a brief memoir of a life full of interest and incident. It may serve as a foundation at least on which some future writer may raise a superstructure more worthy of so distinguished a Judge.

XIII.

THE HONORABLE SIR JAMES BUCHANAN MACAULAY, KNIGHT, CHIEF JUSTICE OF THE COURT OF COMMON PLEAS.

SIR JAMES B. MACAULAY was the son of James Macaulay, Esquire, M. D., of the 33rd Regiment of Foot. Dr. Macaulay came to Canada soon after the formation of the Upper Canada Government in 1792.

At that early period Niagara was the chief town and the seat of Government of the Province. It was there Governor Simcoe had his headquarters, before spying out York as a future capital. The Queen's Rangers, Governor Simcoe's old regiment, was stationed at Niagara, and the father of the Chief Justice, being attached to that regiment, came out with the regiment from England. Dr. Macaulay was afterwards appointed Inspector General of Hospitals. James B. Macaulay, the second son of Dr. Macaulay, and afterwards Chief Justice, was born at Niagara on the 3rd of December, 1793. He received his early education from Dr., afterwards Bishop Strachan, in Cornwall, and was a life-long friend of the Bishop.

Mr. Macaulay had no sooner completed his education with Dr. Strachan than he longed to enter the army. He had not long to wait, and soon obtained a commission as ensign in the 98th Regiment of Foot. Not only at this early period of his life, but ever afterwards, every movement of Sir James was that of a soldier. He had all the instincts of the true soldier—brave, manly, ingenuous, and of such sterling honesty that his name has been, continues to be, and will continue to be, as long as his name is remembered, a household word in Canada.

When the War of 1812 broke out Mr. Macaulay, though then but nineteen years of age, with alacrity entered into the military service of the Canadians, called upon unexpectedly to take up arms for the defence of their beloved Province. A regiment, the Glengarry Fencibles, having been raised for the special defence of the Province, the ensign (Macaulay) obtained a Lieutenancy in that valiant corps; and so much of a soldier was he, that he was afterwards appointed Adjutant of the regiment. He was with the regiment on that cold winter morning in February, 1813, when, Col. McDonald in command, they made a spirited and dashing attack on Ogdensburg, crossing the ice in deep snow, charging the batteries on the American shore with much heroism, if not complete success. Captain Jenkins had the command of the right wing in this engagement, and made a gallant charge on a seven gun battery, covered by a body of infantry two hundred strong.

David Thompson, of the Royal Scots, in 1832, wrote a most excellent history of the events of the then late war. Writing of this charge of Captain Jenkins, he says:

> At the very commencement of this charge the brave Jenkins received a wound with a grape shot in his left arm, which literally shivered it to pieces, still his courage nothing abated he continued to lead on his gallant followers to the assault when he received a severe wound in his right arm, yet with the most enthusiastic gallantry did he continue to advance at the head of his little band of Spartans, cheering them forward, until by the loss of blood and the increasing pain of his wounds he fell in the rush, completely exhausted. The command of the right wing then devolved on Lieutenant Macaulay, of the same corps, who continued the charge on the enemy's works.

We thus find the future Chief Justice in the front of the battle at a very critical point in the history of the Province.

Lieutenant Macaulay was at the battle of Lundy's Lane, fought on the afternoon and night of the 25th of July, 1814.

The battle of Lundy's Lane was the most hotly contested of all the engagements which took place in the War of 1812. The invaders of Canada forming the centre division of the American army under the command of General Brown; and the Canadians under the command of General Drummond, fought for superiority with a courage which was truly heroic. This battle was not a long range engagement, but a hand to hand, bayonet to bayonet, muzzle to muzzle conflict. The American army had for a considerable time before the battle formed their line in rear of Fort George (Niagara), with the purpose of capturing that fort: in this, however, they were not successful, and were retreating up the road leading from Niagara to Niagara Falls and Fort Erie. They were unexpectedly intercepted by a portion of the British and Canadian forces under General Riall at the point of intersection of Lundy's Lane with the main road to the Falls. Just below the point of intersection of the lane with the main road there is a rise of ground. The column of British, under the command of Lieutenant Colonel Morrison, following up the Americans in their retreat, formed in line on the north-east or Niagara river side of the height, their left resting on the Queenston road. The troops from the Twelve and Twenty-Mile Creeks, together with a detachment of the King's regiment as they arrived, were formed on each side of Lundy's Lane.

The battle between the contending armies raged most fiercely in their contest for the commanding position of the brow of the hill at the east end of Lundy's Lane.

David Thompson previously quoted, states:

The enemy (the Americans,) on this quarter (the brow of the hill), for a length of time directed his whole efforts; and notwithstanding the carnage was truly appalling, no visible impression had yet (afternoon) been made, still on this part of the field did the whirlwind of the conflict continue to rage with awful and destructive fury. Columns of the enemy (the Americans) not unlike the undulating surge of the adjacent cataract, rushed to the charge in close and impetuous succession.

When the shades of night had covered the contending forces the battle was continued till midnight with increased fury. The writer, Thompson, says:

> Charges were made in such rapid succession, and with such determined vigor that often were the British Artillerymen assailed in the very act of sponging and charging their guns; and often were the muzzles of the guns of the contending armies hauled up and levelled within a few yards of each other.

General Drummond's report of this action stated the number of killed, wounded, and missing on the side of the British to have been 836. General Brown in his report of the killed, wounded, and missing on the side of the Americans stated the number to have been 858.

The American General, Brown, was himself wounded in this engagement, and so was also General Scott, who commanded a brigade during the action.

Another writer, in describing this battle a few years after it was fought, states:

> Of all the battles fought in America the action at Lundy's Lane was unquestionably the best sustained, and by far the most sanguinary. The rapid charges, and real contest with the bayonet were of themselves sufficient to render this engagement conspicuous. Traits of real bravery and heroic devotion were that night displayed by those engaged which would not suffer in a comparison with those exhibited at the storming of St. Sebastian, or the conflict at Quatre Bras.

The Americans had much the larger force at Lundy's Lane.

The result of the engagement is best described by General Brown, the American Commander. In his report to his Government, after describing the battle, he said: "I therefore believed it proper that General Ripley and the troops should return to camp." The camp here referred to was beyond Chippawa, a distance of nearly four miles from Lundy's Lane (the field of action.)

On the day after the battle the Americans continued their retreat, the British force remaining in possession of the field.

The reader will conclude from this, that the victory was with the British. The Americans, nevertheless, were able to make good their retreat to Fort Erie the day of the battle.

The quotations I have made, drawn from history, shew that the Americans, the British, and the Canadians, all fought with desperation in this battle. It is the part of a good soldier to be generous to those whom he may have opposed and overcome in the heat of battle. David Thompson, the Royal Scot, has not forgotten this trait of a soldier in his relation of the battle. Dr. Canniff, whose father was at the battle of Lundy's Lane, in a paper read by him to the York Pioneers on Queenston Heights in 1877, the sixty-third anniversary of the battle, in his turn, also bears witness to the courage of the Americans in this battle. He said : " It can not be denied that the Americans fought with the most distinguished bravery, in fact, they fought with desperation." And these admissions only go to shew how great is the credit due to the British regulars and the Canadian militia who encountered them, and held their ground that eventful night.

On the Plains of Abraham has been raised a monument to Wolfe and Montcalm, the rival commanders of the English and French armies. It may be that at some future day a monument may be placed on the battle ground of Lundy's Lane, to commemorate a battle described as second to none during the American War.

Old veterans like to fight their battles over again. Not long since I had a conversation with old Mr. John Bright, 93 years of age, then living below the Don, Toronto, a veteran of the War of 1812, who was wounded at the battle of Lundy's Lane, for which he received a pension. His eye brightened when his mind was stirred by recalling the scenes of the eventful night of the 25th of July ; and he could tell how, with the blessed moonlight shining on the combatants, the moon's pale light was lightened by the blaze from the cannon's mouth, a sheet of flame : how man met man in the fearful carnage of bloody war !

The War of 1812, the cause of so much bloodshed, was not a popular war ; it was a war of ambition.

Had there been no Napoleon Bonaparte there would probably have been no war between England and the United States. The Northern and Middle States of America were opposed to the war—if not a majority, at least a large minority, of the people of those States. Resolutions were passed at a convention of delegates from several counties of the State of New York, held at the Capitol in the city of Albany, on the 17th and 18th September, 1812, of which one was :

Resolved, that, without insisting on the injustice of the present war, taking solely into consideration the time and circumstances of its declaration, the condition of the country, and the state of the public mind, we are constrained to consider, and feel it our duty to pronounce it a most rash, unwise, and inexpedient measure.

The Canadians were on the defensive in this wretched War of 1812. The Americans had no heart in the business. Egged on by Napoleon Bonaparte, they continued a struggle which resulted in uniting Canada more firmly to the English Throne. In 1791 the United Empire Loyalists had obtained for themselves a constitution which was modelled on British lines, free from French influences. They were not likely in 1812 to give up their free constitution to satisfy the machinations or intrigues of Napoleon Bonaparte, even though Mr. Madison was prevailed upon to give countenance to the great despot of the age.

Very soon after the battle of Lundy's Lane we find Lieutenant Macaulay with the troops who made the attack on Fort Erie, occupied by the Americans, on the 15th of August. This battle, which was fought with great fury, was disastrous to the British. Sir Gordon Drummond with the force under his command, or so much of it as remained after the bloody onslaught at Lundy's Lane, thought to capture the army of General Brown in the strong-hold of Fort Erie, and thus at one blow end the war. The attack was a spirited one, General Drummond himself, during the conflict performing most extraordinary acts of valor, all, however, of no avail. The British, after succeeding in gaining admittance within the fortifications, were compelled to retire, owing to an accidental explosion of gunpowder which literally blew into the air the greater part of the attacking force. The fort was thus left in possession of the Americans.

It was now the turn of the Americans to attack the British, which they did on the 17th September, with their forces reinforced by General Brown who had recovered from his wounds, and again took the field. The attack was not, however, so successful as had been the defence of the fort. After about half an hour's desperate fighting the Americans retired under cover of their works and into the fort. Shortly after this the Americans evacuated Fort Erie, and thus ended the campaign of 1814.

It is something to be remembered, that in all these engagements, Ogdensburg, Lundy's Lane, and Fort Erie, Lieutenant Macaulay the future Chief Justice did his part well, doing his duty as a soldier, as he afterwards did in his professional career as a lawyer and Judge, in the Province.

On the restoration of peace the Glengarry Fencibles were disbanded, and the Lieutenant exchanged his sword for Blackstone. In 1818 he became a student of law and was called to the Bar in Hilary Term 1822.

At this period of the legal history of the Province the lawyers were but few in number. So great was the dearth of professional men, owing principally to the war, that it had become necessary to pass an Act of Parliament under which doctors were transformed to lawyers, and students made barristers without the usual formalities of examinations. Mr. Macaulay was not one of them, and went through the usual course; but on his call to the Bar the competition was not so great as in a later period of professional life. He had not long to wait for clients. Taylor's Reports abound with cases in which he was counsel for one party or the other, frequently in opposition to the law officers of the Crown, and he rapidly rose in his profession, constantly gaining the respect and confidence of all with whom he came in contact in a professional way.

Mr. Macaulay had been but seven years at the Bar when, in 1829, he was elevated to the Bench as one of the Justices of the Court of King's Bench. He was Associate of Chief Justice Robinson in that Court till the constitution of the Court of Common Pleas in 1849 when he was made Chief Justice of that Court. The unbounded confidence which the people had in his integrity singled him out as the one who ought to be Chief Justice of this newly created Court, and his appointment was hailed with satisfaction by the whole profession, as well as by the body of the people. In the Court of King's Bench he had been most assiduous in the strict performance of his duties. Many litigants, who were so unfortunate as to lose their cases by the decision of the majority of the Court, were pleased to suffer the loss if they had the judgment of Judge Macaulay in their favor. On his elevation to the Court of Common Pleas he brought to the discharge of the duties of Chief Justice of that Court the same untiring industry which had distinguished him as a Justice of the Queen's Bench. He had a habit of not only consulting the principal cases on any given question, but seemed to have gone over every case to be found in any way bearing on the subject : so conscientious was he in the full discharge of his duty. An examination of the cases in which he gave judgments and reported in the Common Pleas Reports, will shew a library of cases cited by him *pro* and *con*, in support or defence of his judgment

Mr. Macaulay continued to hold the place of Chief Justice of the Common Pleas till 1856, when he retired from the Bench, the cause of his retirement being defective hearing which he thought necessitated his withdrawal from judicial duty. On his retirement from the Bench he was elected Treasurer of the Law Society, and subsequently a commission having being formed for the revision of the long accumulated Statutes of the Provinces of Upper and Lower Canada as well as of the

Statutes of Canada since the Union of 1841 he was appointed Chairman of that Commission. No better appointment could have been made: his long occupancy of the Bench, as well as his well known habit of industrious application to detail afforded a guarantee that under his guidance nothing would be left undone to make consolidation and revision of the statutes a successful work.

As I was one of the Commissioners, and also Secretary of that Commission, it would be unbecoming in me to express an opinion on the performance of that trust. I can, however, say that Chief Justice Macaulay, during the whole period of the Commission, upwards of two years, left nothing undone to make the work command success. He continued to do duty when, as I know, his health was such that it was with the greatest difficulty he could concentrate his mind on the work. I have watched him over and over again, going over the frequent revises submitted to him by others of the Commissioners to whom portions of the work had been submitted, with a carefulness and conscientious regard for the correct interpretation and consolidation of the body of the law, which well justified his selection as a safe guide in so important an undertaking. The altering of the language of the law in the revision and consolidation gave him great concern, fearing that the Commissioners in adopting Coode's system, substituting the present for the future tense in the Criminal Acts, might by mischance fall into error, or misconstrue the law in some case. This difficulty was, however, got over by the Parliament of the Province giving legislative sanction to the work of the Commissioners.

Chief Justice Macaulay refused to accept any compensation from Government for the work done by him on the Commission. He was in receipt of a retiring pension as ex-Chief Justice of the Common Pleas, and ex-Judge of the Queen's Bench. His sense of right dictated to his mind that as he was in receipt of a pension he ought not to receive pay from the Government for revising the Statutes. So high a sense of duty as this does not in a majority of cases affect the mind of man.

A few months after the completion of the revision of the Statutes he received the honor of knighthood, and was, on the 27th of July, 1857, appointed a Judge of the Court of Error and Appeal, a position held by him till a few months before his death. He died at Toronto on the 26th November, A.D. 1859, and was buried in St. James's Cemetery.

A whole community mourned his loss. He will be ever remembered as one of the most upright of men and a most conscientious Judge.

The Law Society have a well executed portrait of the Chief Justice on the walls of the Library of Osgoode Hall.

XIV.

THE HONORABLE ARCHIBALD MCLEAN,
CHIEF JUSTICE.

THE Honorable Archibald McLean is entitled to be placed in the first rank in the company of those who have occupied the Bench in Upper Canada.

His career from early boyhood to a green old age was surrounded with many difficulties which only a man possessed of great determination and indomitable courage could overcome. Although born in Canada he was of Highland stock: his whole life shewed that he had in him all the characteristics of the northmen of Scotland—bravery, endurance, steadfastness of purpose, and sterling integrity were among his many virtues.

He was the son of Colonel Neil McLean of St. Andrew's, in the County of Stormont, Upper Canada, who was born at Mingarry, in the Island of Mull, Scotland. Colonel Neil McLean was born in the same year (1759) that Quebec was compelled to surrender to British arms. He was a soldier almost from his infancy. He at an early age obtained an ensigncy, and afterwards a lieutenantcy in the Royal Highland Emigrants or 84th Regiment.

We find Colonel N. McLean in 1796 a captain in the Royal Canadian Volunteers in which corps he served in Montreal, Quebec, and York, doing duty as a volunteer officer until the regiment was disbanded, when he was appointed sheriff of the Eastern District. When the war of 1812 broke out Colonel McLean, ever ready to do service for the Crown and his native Canada, again went on active service as Colonel of the Stormont Militia and commandant of the district. He held this position at the time that Major General James Wilkinson, of the centre division of the American army formed for the conquest of Canada, issued his famous proclamation urging the Canadians to quietly submit to the invading force. The proclamation of Major General Wilkinson was as follows:

Proclamation of JAMES WILKINSON, Major General, and Commander in Chief of the expedition against the Canadas, to the inhabitants thereof:

The Army of the United States which I have the honour to command, invaded the Province to conquer, and not to destroy, to subdue the forces of his Britannic Majesty, not to war against unoffending subjects. Those therefore amongst you who remain quiet at home, should victory incline to the American standard, shall be protected in their persons and property; but those who are found in arms must necessarily be treated as avowed enemies. To menace is unmanly, to seduce, dishonorable. Yet it is just and humane to place these alternatives before you.

This proclamation was issued by the Major General at or in the vicinity of Fort Wellington when he and his division of his army of the Republic for the subjection of Canada were about starting on their proposed tour of conquest down the St. Lawrence, to terminate in the capture of Montreal. The undertaking, however, was not as successful as the Americans desired. On the 11th November, 1813, a superior force of the Americans who had landed on Canadian soil in the neighborhood of Fort Matilda between Prescott and Cornwall were marching down the north shore of the St. Lawrence *en route* for Montreal when, arriving at a place called Chrysler's farm, they were met by the Stormont Militia, commanded by Colonel McLean, and other troops prepared to dispute the undisturbed march of the Americans.

Here, at Chrysler's farm, was an engagement between the opposing troops on an open campaign, the battles of the contending parties having heretofore been principally bush fighting. General Wilkinson, writing of the engagement, said : " All was conducted in open space and fair combat." The Canadians were fighting in defence of their country, their homes, and their firesides: the invading force, as the proclamation of General Wilkinson shews, though not for plunder was for conquest. The fortunes of the day went against the Americans in what has since been called the battle of Chrysler's Farm. The Americans were impeded in their advance on Montreal, and compelled to retreat across the river to their own country. Major-General Wilkinson got a severe handling from his Government for this engagement, and was subjected to a court-martial. It is but right that I should give his estimate of the Canadians, who were constantly placing obstructions in his way from the time he left the head of the St. Lawrence till his arrival at the point of battle. In his despatch to the American Secretary of War (intended to account for his defeat), dated at Headquarters, French Mills, (adjoining the Province of Lower Canada), 16th November, 1863, he wrote:

> The enemy deserve credit for their zeal and intelligence, which the active universal hostility of the male inhabitants of the country enabled them to employ to the best advantage.

What I have written thus far is important as leading up to the career of Chief Justice McLean, which will be found to follow in some respects, especially in the military part of it, that of his worthy and patriotic father. Besides his military career, Colonel Neil McLean will be remembered in his civil capacity of member of the Legislative Council of Upper Canada. Colonel McLean was married to the youngest daughter of John McDonell, of Leek, by whom he had three sons and five daughters. His sons were John, the eldest, Archibald, the second, born at St. Andrews on the 5th April, 1791, and Alexander. John was Sheriff of the Eastern District. Alexander, the youngest, was for some time M. P. for Stormont, and also Commandant of the Eastern District

Archibald, the future Chief Justice, received his early education at Dr. Strachan's school in Cornwall. Dr. Strachan, afterwards Archdeacon of York, and afterwards Bishop, had the honor of educating and, in a measure, moulding the lives of several of the older Judges of Upper Canada. Chief Justice Robinson, Chief Justice Macaulay, and Chief Justice McLean were all pupils of this celebrated and accomplished scholar.

At sixteen years of age young McLean had acquired sufficient knowledge to warrant him in striking out for himself in pursuit of the purpose he had formed, of becoming a member of the Bar. To carry out this purpose he proceeded to York, and in Trinity Term, 1808, was entered a Student of the Law in the books of the Law Society. On being admitted he immediately entered the office of Mr. Firth, the then Attorney-General, where he continued to pursue his studies until the breaking out of the War of 1812. By this time Mr. Firth had gone out of office, the Honorable John McDonell appointed Attorney-General, 28th November, 1811, succeeding him.

It will thus be seen that the Student McLean and the Attorney-General McDonell had been brought in very near relation; a relation only terminated by the melancholy death of the Attorney-General not long afterwards. When the 3rd York Militia was ordered to the front in 1812, Mr. McLean was given a commission in that regiment. When on the 13th October, 1812, General Van Ranselaer's army, under Brigadier General Wadsworth, affected a landing at the lower end of the village of Queenston (opposite to Lewiston), and made an attack on the small handful of British troops stationed there (the flank companies and such of the militia forces and Indians as could be collected in the vicinity), young McLean was on the ground. Attorney-General McDonell by this time had been appointed Provincial Aide-de-Camp, and was in attendance on Major General Sir Isaac Brock. On the morning of the 13th October, before day-light, the Americans attempted to force a passage of the river at Queenston;

the attempt to force a passage here was for some time successfully resisted, and several boats were either disabled or sunk by the fire from a one gun battery of the British on Queenston Heights, and from a masked battery about a mile below the Heights. Following the example, however, of that Highland force which climbed to the plains of Abraham by what was supposed an impracticable path, and so contributed largely to the taking of Quebec, a considerable force of the Americans effected a landing some distance above by a path which had long been considered impassable, and was therefore unguarded, and succeeded in gaining the summit of the mountain. This force which made good their ascent to the top of the heights carried the battery there and turned the right of the British position, compelling them to retire with considerable loss. History has recorded that the flank companies of the York militia to which Lieutenant McLean was attached much distinguished themselves in their encounter with the opposing forces on the memorable 13th of October. Auchinleck, in his history of the first attempt to drive the Americans from the heights on this eventful day on which the noble General Brock and his brave Aide-de-Camp (Attorney-General) Colonel McDonell both lost their lives in defence of the Province, thus describes the engagement :

> On retiring to the north end of the village on the Niagara road, our (the British) little band was met by General Brock, attended by his A. D. C., Major Glegg and Colonel McDonell. He was loudly cheered as he cried "Follow me, boys," and led us at a pretty smart trot toward the mountain, checking his horse to a walk, he said, "Take breath, boys, we shall want it in a few minutes." Another cheer was the hearty response both from regulars and militia. At that time the top of the mountain and a great portion of the side was thickly covered with trees, and was now occupied by American riflemen. On arriving at the foot of the mountain where the road diverges to St. Davids, General Brock dismounted, and waving his sword, climbed over a high stone wall, followed by his troops ; placing himself at the head of the light company of the 49th he led the way up the mountain at double quick time, in the very teeth of a sharp fire from the enemy's riflemen, and ere long, he was singled out by one of them, who, coming forward took deliberate aim,

and fired ; several of the men noticed the action and fired—but too late—
and our gallant General fell on his left side, within a few feet of where I
stood. Running up to him, I enquired " Are you much hurt, sir?" He
placed his hand on his breast, but made no reply, and sunk down. The
49th now raised a shout " Revenge the General," and regulars and militia,
led by Colonel McDonell, pressed forward, anxious to revenge the fall of
their beloved leader and literally drove a superior force up the mountain
side to a considerable distance beyond the summit. The flank companies
of the York Militia, under Captains Cameron and Heward, and Lieuten-
ants Robinson, McLean, and Stanton, besides many others whose names I
forget, eminently distinguished themselves on this occasion. At this
juncture the enemy was re-enforced by fresh troops, and after a severe
struggle, in which Colonel McDonell, Captains Dennis and Williams, and
most of the officers were either killed or wounded, we were overpowered
by numbers, and forced to retreat, as the enemy had outflanked us, and
had nearly succeeded in gaining our rear. Several of our men were thus
cut off, and made prisoners, myself among the number.

This description of the first engagement was furnished to Auchinleck by Mr. G. S. Jarvis who was on the ground. It was also confirmed by Captain Crooks, Colonel Clark, Colonel Kerby, and Captain John McMicikin, all of whom were present on the occasion.

Colonel McDonell, about the same time that General Brock was shot, received a wound from which he afterwards died. Lieutenant McLean was wounded in the same conflict. After Colonel McDonell received his wound which proved mortal he called out to Lieutenant McLean : " Archie, help me." Lieutenant McLean's wound also came nearly proving to be mortal. Owing to delay in extracting the ball, his life was for a time despaired of, and for several months he could not return to duty.

When the Americans made their attack on York Lieutenant McLean was at his post. He carried the colours of the 3rd York Militia to a place of safety, burying them in the woods behind McGill's house, the site where the Metropolitan Church now stands. York being in the hands of the Americans the Lieutenant made good his escape, and reported himself at Kingston. We next find him at the battle of Lundy's Lane, so fully described by me in the life of Chief Justice Macaulay, that I need not here refer to it more at large. Lieutenant McLean was made prisoner at this battle, was detained part of the time in close confinement, and did not obtain his release till the end of the war. After the Declaration of Peace he was offered, but refused, a commission in the regular army.

Having thus traced out his military career, we will return to his civil occupation. As seen, he had lost his old master. Still, determined to pursue his legal studies, he entered the office of Dr. Baldwin, father of the Hon. Robert Baldwin, and finished his legal studies with him, and was called to the Bar in 1815, Easter Term, 55 George III. On being called to the Bar he returned to Cornwall, where he had received his early education, and commenced to practise his profession in that town, and continued to practise there down to 1837.

During this period he had a very considerable legal business. The counties around Cornwall are populated mostly by Highland Scotch; and, if there be any truth in the clannishness of the Highlanders, we may be sure that McLean the barrister was in as much favor with them as was McLean the soldier, fighting side by side with them in defence of the Province.

In 1807 Mr. McLean was retained by the Hudson Bay Company to take evidence relating to the difficulties between that company and the North-West Company, which difficulties led to the killing of General Semple and his men in the Selkirk riots at Red River. It was a difficult business to get to the Red River from York or Cornwall at that date. The long journey had to be made by canoe, and the party suffered a great deal of hardship, the scarcity of provisions, it is said, compelling them to live three weeks entirely on cat-fish.

In 1820 Mr. McLean was elected Member of Parliament to represent the county of Stormont in the Legislative Assembly of the Province. He retained the confidence of the electors, and continued to represent Stormont in Parliament down to his elevation to the Bench. While a

Member on the floor of the House he was a strong adherent of the Tory party, generally acting with Attorney-General Robinson, the Leader of the House. He was twice elected Speaker of the House. His dignified appearance and manner in the Speaker's chair added dignity to the House itself.

The veterans of 1812 had reason to be devoted to him then as they had been in the field of battle. In 1825 he went to England to press their claims for pensions, and he succeeded in having their claims allowed.

In 1837 he removed from Cornwall to Toronto, arriving at that place about a month before the breaking out of the Rebellion. Colonel Fitzgibbon and he being well acquainted with the dissatisfaction at the state of affairs existing in the country fully appreciated the situation. Colonel Fitzgibbon especially was called a croker on this subject, the inhabitants of Toronto generally thinking they had nothing to fear, though rebellion was at their very doors.

Mr. McLean expressed his fears that there would be a breaking out of the slumbering fires of revolution. Some good citizens charged him with too much concern in this matter, when he replied : " I am afraid we will be caught napping." He was right—there was not a soldier in town when William Lyon Mackenzie assembled his forces at Montgomery's Hill on the confines of Toronto.

On the night of the uprising, in December, when the city bells rang out the alarm, he was the first to respond to the call of arms. Immediately the alarm was sounded he and his son John took his horses, and going to the Old Fort, they got artillery harness, and limbering up a twelve pounder drove to the City Hall where the loyalists were assembled. As they drove up, the word was passed : " Here comes the rebels," and a hundred guns were levelled, when fortunately they were recognized by Chief Justice Robinson who told the men who they were. In the attack on Montgomery's Hill Mr. McLean, with the rank of Colonel, commanded the left wing.

He was afterwards sent with despatches to the British Minister at Washington, and when *en route* would have been taken prisoner as a hostage by the sympathizers on the border (Mackenzie then being on Navy Island) had it not been for the good offices of Marshal Spring Bidwell, who, though a staunch liberal and political opponent of his, was his personal friend.

Mr. McLean was first appointed to the Bench, on the 23rd March, 1837, when he received his patent as Judge (puisne) of the King's Bench. It cannot be said that the service he had rendered his Sovereign and country did not entitle him to this mark of favor.

In the year 1850, (19th January,) Judge McLean exchanged his place in the Queen's Bench for a Puisne Judgeship of the recently formed Common Pleas Court. From a junior Judge of the Queen's Bench he thus became a senior Judge in the Common Pleas under a new Chief, Chief Justice Macaulay.

Again, on the 5th February, 1856, he exchanged back again, taking his place as senior however, of the Court of Queen's Bench under his old Chief, Sir John Robinson, and on the 18th March, 1862, was appointed Chief Justice of that Court (the Queen's Bench).

I will not deal with his Common Pleas Judgeship, any more than to say that he gave his valuable assistance to Chief Justice Macaulay in his headship of that newly constituted Court, to give confidence and weight to the decisions for the six years he was Judge of that Court. I need only refer to the adjudged cases which will be found in the first volume of the Common Pleas Reports.

Established again in the Queen's Bench in 1856 he was not now disposed to accept the conclusions of his Chief as always right, though treated with the greatest respect. The most important case in the Queen's Bench in which there was a difference of opinion among the Judges was the case of John Anderson, a negro slave of Missouri in the United States charged with the murder of Seneca T. Diggs, of Missouri, and who had escaped to Canada, his return to the United States being claimed under the extradition treaty. The facts of the case were simple enough : no doubt Anderson was a slave in bondage according to the laws of Missouri and the United States ; it was equally clear that in attempting to escape from slavery and to regain his freedom he had killed Diggs : that in such attempt Diggs without warrant, but justifiably, according to the State laws and United States law was endeavouring to prevent Anderson making his escape ; and that Anderson, being pursued by Diggs, in order to secure his liberty, and prevent his return to his master from whom he had escaped, stabbed Diggs with a dirk knife, from which wound Diggs died. Anderson on his final escape and coming to Canada was on the information of James A. Jenning, of Detroit, in the State of Michigan, taken before a Magistrate at Brantford, in Canada, on the 30th April, 1860, charged :

> That he John Anderson did on the 28th day of September, 1853, wilfully deliberately, and maliciously murder one Seneca T. P. Diggs, in the County of Howard, in the State of Missouri, one of the United States of America.

On the argument of the case in the Queen's Bench, on a habeas corpus which had been issued for the extradition of Anderson after commitment on the charge by the Brantford Magistrates, many questions presented themselves : 1. Was the warrant of commitment sufficient, and if not sufficient should it not be amended if the information and depositions established the charge? 2. Could the Court interfere at all in the matter, or was it not exclusively the business of the Government to decide whether the prisoner should be extradited or not without the aid of the Court ? Lastly, and the greatest question of all was, whether or not the offence of murder, if committed, must have been murder according to the laws of Upper Canada, where the prisoner was found after his escape from slavery, or according to the laws of Missouri, where the offence was committed.

At the time the question came up, which was just before the American Rebellion, in 1860, there was great excitement in the United States caused by slaves escaping in a mysterious way, commonly known as "the underground railway," and in other ways to Canada, defying the laws of the State from which they came, and the Federal laws of the United States. The excitement was no less in Canada, where attempts were made to again deprive such persons of their hard-earned freedom, and restore them to bondage. I will not refer in detail to the various questions presented to the Court, the important one involving the general right of surrender being the last. This question rested on the construction to be placed on the Ashburton Treaty, made 9th August, 1842, and ratified October, 1842, and the 89th chapter of Consolidated Statutes of Canada, taken from 12 Vic. cap. 19.

The treaty provides that the Governments of the two countries shall, upon mutual requisition, deliver up to justice persons charged with any of the crimes specified in the treaty committed within the jurisdiction of either of the contracting parties, who should seek an asylum, or be found within the territories of the other:

> Provided that this shall only be done upon such evidence of criminality as, according to the laws of the place where the fugitive or the person so charged shall be found, would justify his apprehension and commitment for trial, if the crime or offence had been there committed.

Statutes of Canada, cap. 89, for carrying out this treaty, provides, sec. 1, that upon complaint made under oath or affirmation, charging any person found within the limits of the Province with having committed within the jurisdiction of the United States of America, or of any of such States, any of the crimes enumerated in the treaty:

> Any of the Judges of His Majesty's Superior Courts in this Province, or any of His Majesty's Justices of the Peace in the same, may issue his warrant for the apprehension of the person so charged, that he may be brought before such Judge, or such Justice of the Peace, to the end that the evidence of criminality may be heard and considered; and if, on such hearing the evidence be deemed sufficient by him to sustain the charge

according to the laws of this Province, if the offence had been committed therein, he shall certify the same, with a copy of all the testimony taken before him, to the Governor, that a warrant may issue upon the requisition of the proper authorities of the United States, or of any such States, for the surrender of such person according to the stipulation of the said treaty, and the said Judge, or Justice of the Peace, shall issue his warrant for the commitment of the person so charged to the proper gaol, there to remain until such surrender be made, or until such person shall be discharged according to law.

Looking at the proviso of the treaty and that part of section 1 of the statute to which I have referred, it will be seen that the wording affords much room for doubt whether the treaty makes and the Legislature meant that the various offences, mentioned in the treaty, must be offences of the same class in the country where committed, and in the country where the escaped offender is found and his extradition demanded ; or, does it mean only that if the evidence of the offence were such as to prove an offence in the country (United States) where committed, and the same evidence did not prove the offence to be one of the same class in the country where the accused is found, the treaty or Act of Parliament demands that he should be extradited ?

The case was very ably argued by Harrison, Q. C., afterwards Chief Justice, and Henry Eccles, Q.C., for the Crown, and by Freeman, Q.C., for Anderson, who was accused of murdering Diggs.

The conclusion arrived at by the majority of the Queen's Bench, Chief Justice Robinson and Mr. Justice Burns, was, that if the offence was an offence of murder in Missouri, although the same facts did not establish the crime of murder in Canada the prisoner must be extradited ; that the killing of Diggs would have been murder in Missouri, although Anderson was endeavouring to relieve himself from the shackles of slavery ; that slavery was lawful in Missouri, and an attempt to capture a slave trying for his freedom there was lawful, and therefore that Diggs was killed while in exercise of his lawful powers in his effort to capture Anderson and return him to slavery.

Mr. Justice McLean dissented from the judgment on several grounds, and especially on the main ground, holding that Anderson was in unlawful bondage, and that his case was in no way different from a white man endeavouring to escape unlawful custody who was entitled to use all necessary means even to the taking of life in assertion of his liberty; that there was not and could not be such a thing as slavery in Canada, that Anderson's case must be governed by the law of Canada, that he would have been in unlawful custody if in bondage in Canada, and would have been entitled in Canada, and according to her laws to obtain his release even by taking life if necessary, and therefore was not guilty of murder according to the laws of Canada, and so was not within the treaty or Act of Parliament.

The reader will find a full report of this case, with all the arguments *pro* and *con* in the published Queen's Bench Reports, and will there see, not only the able and fair manner in which the questions presented were considered both by counsel and bench, but the elaborate judgments of all the Judges.

I will only give the concluding part of Judge McLean's judgment in which he explains the position he took in holding that Anderson was entitled to his freedom, and should be discharged, and his reasons for his judgment. In concluding his judgment Mr. Justice McLean said:

> The law of England, or rather the British Empire, not only does not recognize slavery within the dominions of the Crown, but imposes upon any British subject who shall have become the owners of slaves in a foreign State the severest penalties, and declares that all persons engaged in carrying on the slave trade when captured at sea shall be liable to be treated as pirates. In all the British possessions the institution of slavery, which, at one time prevailed to a certain extent, was abolished at the enormous expense of twenty million pounds sterling in remunerating the holders of slaves. An immense amount has since been expended in efforts to suppress the African slave trade, and by every possible means the British Government has put down and discountenanced the traffic in human beings. Even when slavery was tolerated in some of the British possessions no person could be brought into England without becoming free the moment he touched the soil; and though other nations have not

chosen to follow the noble example of the **British nation, and some are** yet embarking in nefarious and unchristian attempts to import human beings from the east coast of Africa to be held in perpetual bondage, **for** the purpose of this world's gain, at the risk of being regarded as pirates, happily the traffic has **become** too uncertain and too hazardous to be **carried on** to so great an extent as **formerly prevailed.** In the adjoining Republic the evils and **the curse of** slavery are every day becoming more manifest, and even now threaten to lead to a dissolution of the Federal compact of the United States, under which the several States have enjoyed an unexampled **degree** of prosperity. **The evil is not less** revolting in a social point of view, for the laws of some of the States of the Union may tolerate the dealing in human beings as if they were sheep or **oxen.** The **best** feelings of our nature must shudder at the severance of those endearing relations which usually form the solace and happiness of mankind. A father and mother, husband and wife, are liable **at** the caprice of a master, or perhaps from his necessities, to be separated from each other and from their children ; and they are bound **to** submit ; or if **they attempt** to escape from bondage, and to consult their own happiness **in preference to the gain** of their masters, are liable to be hunted **by any white or black man** who chooses to engage in the **pursuit, and when cap**tured are liable **to** severe punishment and increased severity **from their** task-masters.

The prisoner Anderson, as appears by the statement of Baker, had felt the horrors of such treatment. He was brought up to manhood by one Moses Burton, and married a slave on a neighbouring property, by whom he had one child. His master, for his own **purposes,** disregarding the relationship which had been formed, sold and transferred him to a person at a distance, to whose will he was forced to submit. The laws of Missouri enacted by their white oppressors, while they perpetuate slavery, confer no rights on slaves unless it be the bare protection of their lives. Can it, then, be a matter of surprise that **the** prisoner should endeavour to escape from so degrading a position ; or, rather, would it not be a cause of surprise if the attempt was not made ? Diggs, though **he** could have no **other** interest in it than that which binds slave holders for their common interest to prevent the escape of their slaves, interfered to prevent the prisoner getting beyond the bounds of his bondage, and with his slaves pursued and hunted with a spirit and determination which might well drive him to desperation ; and when at length the prisoner appeared within reach **of capture he with a stick in his** hand crossed over a fence and advanced to intercept and **seize him.** The prisoner was anxious to escape, and in order to do so made every effort to avoid his pursuers. Diggs, as their leader, on the contrary, **was** most anxious to overtake and come in contact with the prisoner for **the** unholy purpose of riveting his chains more securely. Could it be expected from any man indulging in the **desire** to be free, which nature has implanted in his breast, that he should quietly submit to be returned to bondage and to stripes if, by any effort of his strength, **or** any means within his reach, he could emancipate himself ? Such an expectation, it appears to me, would be most unreasonable, and I must say that in my judgment the prisoner *was justified* in using any necessary degree of force to prevent what must have proved a most fearful evil. He was committing no crime in endeavoring to escape and to better his own condition; and the fact of his being a slave cannot, in my humble judgment, make that a crime, which would not be so if he were a white man. If in this country any number of persons were to pursue a colored man with an avowed determination to return him into slavery, it cannot, I think, be doubted that the man pursued would be justified in using, in the same circumstances as the prisoner, the same means of relieving himself from so dreadful a result. Can, then, or must the law of slavery in Missouri be recognized by us to such an extent as to make it murder in Missouri, while it is justifiable in this country to do precisely the same act? I confess that I feel it too repugnant to every sense of religion and every feeling of justice to recognize a rule, designated as a law, passed by the strong for enslaving and tyrannising over the weak—a law which would not be tolerated for a moment, if those who are reduced to the condition of slaves and deprived of all human rights were possessed of white instead of dark complexion.

This judgment of Mr. Justice McLean, although he was in the minority on the Queen's Bench, received the highest commendation in England, the English press pronouncing it a judgment worthy a Mansfield. As slavery has been abolished in the United States the reasons of his decision, or for that matter of the judgment of the Court which was adverse to his conclusion, are no longer of importance on the particular question involved, though the judgment might be of supreme importance in another class of cases, offences within the treaty, but not involving the question of slavery.

Mr. Justice McLean, with his other good qualities, possessed the quality of endurance in a remarkable degree. On the trial of Dr. Dill at, Hamilton, for a capital felony, his conscientious sense of duty in the administration of criminal law caused him to give undivided attention to the case from nine o'clock in the morning till four o'clock the next morning without a break for even a taste of food.

I have frequently been on the circuit, when he presided at the Assizes, when he, day after day, commenced the Court at nine in the morning and sat till twelve at night without a recess. He had to try a remarkable case in the

County of Haldimand. The people of this county had for a long time been subjected to annoyance caused by desperadoes going through the country committing all kinds of offences, murder, arson, rapine, and other equally heinous crimes. The leader of the desperadoes was supposed to be a man named Townshend. At length a man, supposed to be Townshend, was arrested after the murder of a man named Beldon, and was tried for the murder before Judge McLean. He was not only tried once but several times: as was said at the time one hundred witnesses swore one way, that the prisoner was Townshend, and a hundred others were equally clear that he was not Townshend. All the marks and moles that Townshend ever had were given in evidence to prove the man's identity, and the proofs of identity were most conflicting.

Judge McLean sat week after week for several weeks at Cayuga Assizes, trying with great patience and endurance, day and night, to fathom the mystery. The jury did not agree, and the man was discharged. Shortly afterwards the same man, or a man supposed to be the same man, shot a constable at Port Colborne, and was again tried for his life at Welland, and was acquitted. A large number of the people of both counties were convinced that the man who committed the crimes was Townshend, but whether the man tried was Townshend or not was never solved. He claimed that he was a mariner named McHenry, and after his acquittal turned his trial to account by going round the country with a sister of Townshend exhibiting himself for money much after the manner of Sir Roger Tichborne of English notoriety. The Judge at the time was much commended for his physical endurance.

In Church matters Mr. Justice McLean was a staunch Presbyterian of the Old Kirk. When the disruption took place in the Presbyterian Church, the Free Churchmen seceding from the Old Kirk, the Judge remained firm in his adherence to the Church of his fathers. He even when called on for opinion expressed his regret at and disapprobation of the secession; his strong views on this subject frequently brought him into conflict with those who could not see eye to eye with him; he nevertheless had the respect and high regard of all right thinking Scotch people.

He was more than once honored by being elected President of the St. Andrew's Society. At their annual banquets on St. Andrew's day he graced the festive board with his presence, as President, doing all the honors of so loyal and patriotic a body.

In his own house the Judge was the ever gracious and kindly host. On New Year's day, that day so much celebrated by Scotchmen, and which used to be as much celebrated by Canadians, he made welcome to his hospitable board the many citizens of Toronto who knew how to appreciate a Highland heart.

Nor must we here forget the Chief's amiable wife who so nobly shared in the Chief's hospitality on recurring New Year's days. Mrs. McLean was of Highland stock. She was the daughter of John McPherson, of Three Rivers, and grand-daughter of that McPherson who was in the company of the chivalrous Donald Cameron of Lochiel, who, history tells us to the very last in his devotion aided Charles Edward Louis Philip Casimer Stuart, the Pretender, in his desperate but foolhardy attempt to gain the throne of his ancestors in 1745. For this aid and comfort this Donald Cameron sacrificed his life. The grandfather of Mrs. McLean was pardoned after his daring attempt had failed.

After Mrs. McLean's grandfather was pardoned he was offered a commission in the army which he declined. He emigrated to Canada, assisted in the defence of the Sault au Matelot, Quebec, when Montgomery was killed. One of his sons was killed during the siege. He was offered payment for his services and for his house which was burned by a shell, but he refused and replied: "I take nothing from the House of Hanover."

Chief Justice McLean will long be remembered in Canada as an upright Judge and Highland gentleman, a worthy representative of the chiefs of his nation.

The Law Society have preserved his likeness in a portrait of him which is at the head of the east stairway leading to the Library of Osgoode Hall. The large, life-size portrait is in a most excellent position, the sunlight streaming through the glass in the dome frequently surrounding the portrait with a radiance which adds a charm to his genial face.

The Chief Justice died on the 24th October, 1865, in the 75th year of his age. At the request of the Law Society, and the legal profession generally, his funeral was a public one. In commenting on his death the *Upper Canada Law Journal* wrote as follows:

The manner of the late President of the Court of Appeal (The Chief Justice McLean had been made President of the Court of Appeal on the 22nd July, 1863, a short time before his death) upon the Bench was dignified and courteous, unsuspicious and utterly devoid of anything mean or petty in his own character, his conduct to others was always what he expected from them. The profession generally, the young student as well as the old practitioners will long remember his courtesy and forbearance in Chambers and on the Bench ; others will think of him as an agreeable and entertainig companion and a true friend, while others will call to mind the stately form of the old Judge as he approached and entered St. Andrew's Church where he was a constant and devout attendant, rain or sunshine, until his last illness which terminated in death. Archibald McLean was a man of remarkable and commanding presence, tall, straight, and well formed in person, with a pleasant handsome face and a kind and courteous manner, he looked and was every inch a man and a gentleman. He belonged to a race most of whom have now passed away, the giants of early history of Canada. He was one of the most brave, honest, enduring, steadfast men sent by Providence to lay the foundation of a country's greatness. The funeral proceeded to the Necropolis where amidst the sorrow of all who knew him were deposited the mortal remains of the Honourable Archibald McLean, the brave soldier, the upright Judge, and the Christian gentleman.

XV.

THE HONORABLE JONAS JONES, JUDGE OF THE QUEEN'S BENCH, UPPER CANADA.

THE family of Jones is a very large one in the Province of Upper Canada. The particular branch of this large family to which the Honorable Jonas Jones belonged is not buried in obscurity. The special knowledge, however, is most, confined to the lineal and collateral relatives of the Judge. In the early days of the Province when its principal inhabitants were United Empire Loyalists, the Joneses in the County of Leeds and Grenville were as well known as the difficulties which confronted the early settlers, or the war-whoop of the Indians which disturbed their midnight slumbers. The Joneses were people who did not fear the war-whoop, or any other whoop of the Indians, for they came from the Mohawk Valley, the original home of the chiefest tribe of the Six Nation Indians, in the State of New York, when a British Province. The first immigrants of this branch of the Jones family which came to America, like many others of that day, had Biblical and Puritan names. I do not know that they had any other characteristic of the Puritan than that indomitable spirit of independence which was the mainspring of Puritan action.

Josiah Jones, the first of the family who came to America from England to Boston, crossed the Atlantic for his New England home about the year 1640. This

Josiah married, and had a son Josiah, who had a son Josiah, who also had a son Josiah, whom we may call Josiah the 3rd. Josiah the 3rd, in the latter part of the last century, settled at Weston, near Boston. He had several sons, of whom Elisha was the youngest. Elisha married and had several sons, of whom Ephraim was the 10th.

It is related that one of the Jones family, during the Rebellion period of the United States, 1774, was hanged three times by the Rebels, (Continentals), and as many times cut down before life was extinct, in the vain hope that information relative to the King's forces might be obtained from him. This man so thoroughly gained the enmity of the Continentals by his adherence to the King's cause, that he was hunted by the Revolutionary Authorities like a a wild beast. After the close of the war he made his way to New Brunswick, and died at a ripe old age.

Ephraim Jones, father of Jonas Jones, at the time of the Revolution, was a resident of the Mohawk Valley. Not inclining to the Continental cause, but thoroughly imbued with love for England, notwithstanding the eccentricities of a British Ministry, he made his way to Montreal, so as to be within the British, or more properly speaking, so as to be without the Continental lines. Two of the brothers of Ephraim Jones succeeded in reaching Nova Scotia.

People of the present day can scarcely conceive the great sacrifice made by those who adhered to the King's banner in the Revolutionary days. It is but little to say they sacrificed all the comforts of life, they also in many cases sacrificed their friendships, their family ties, some members of a family going one way and some another, and more than this they sacrificed their possessions in the New England Colony, and all they had on earth, for the sake of the Royal cause. It does seem strange, too, that those who came to Canada did so knowing that they were coming to a Province a large majority of the inhabitants of which were French ; French too, of the most pronounced type ; French who had been at war with the New England Colonies, then Colonies of Great Britain.

For several years before the French Revolution the New Englanders in aid of the British in the parent state were at open war with Quebec, and yet it was to Quebec that the United Empire Loyalists of New England and and other States flocked in large numbers on the breaking out of the Rebellion. And why was this ? It was because the Continentals were not in agreement among themselves, some were for Paul, and some for Apollos, some for present submission relying on future reform, others for immediate revolution and shaking off the British yoke.

It was of great importance to the British in the Revolutionary War to have the neutrality if not the active assistance of the French of the Province of Quebec. This they succeeded in securing. And so it happened that the Non-Revolutionary Continentals came to Canada to get rid of their revolutionary brethren of the New England and other Colonies now the United States. They came not because they loved Cæsar less, but because they loved Rome more. England had to gain the affections and assistance of the French in the Province of Quebec, who had been granted privileges not guaranteed to them by treaty. The United Empire Loyalists, rather than rebel, came to such a Province with such privileges, trusting to that perseverance for which they were so eminently distinguished, to extort from England in Canada that British system under British laws that they so much cherished. How much more is it to their honor then that they should have endured all they did in such a cause.

The United Empire Loyalists were not long in Quebec before they demanded of England to be free of French laws and French customs, so liberally accorded to the French by the Canadian Constitutional Act of 1774, and by their demand gained a severance of the Province into two Provinces of Upper and Lower Canada, and the Constitutional Act of 1791.

The adherence of the United Empire Loyalists to the King's cause entitled them to all they acquired thereby in the British Provinces. Theirs was not a beggar's petition, but a right acquired as a reward of patriotism.

It was not till 1790 that Ephraim Jones, better known as Commissary Jones, in consequence of his having charge of the supplies granted to the settlers in Canada by the British Government, took up his residence in the Province, still the Province of Quebec. I was born in the same township in which he settled on coming to the Province, not far from where he took up his land (300 acres) for services rendered the Crown, a little to the east of Maitland, in the Township of Augusta.

When Ephraim Jones arrived in the Province of Quebec he was still a bachelor, but shortly after married one of Canada's daughters, Miss Coursoll, of Montreal. By this union he had four sons and four daughters; the sons were Charles, in due time the Honorable Charles Jones; William Jones, who became Collector of Customs in Brockville, a few miles from the old homestead; Alpheus, who settled in Prescott; and Jonas Jones, who was numbered among the earliest members of the Bar of the Province of Upper Canada. Jonas Jones was born in the year 1791.

Jonas Jones was a pupil of Dr. Strachan when he kept his school at Cornwall. From him he received a liberal education from which he profited, as did his comrades John Beverley Robinson and Archibald McLean, both afterwards Chief Justices. In Easter Term, 1808, 48 George III., he was entered a Student of the Law, commenced and pursued his studies in Brockville till the breaking out of the war. When the war of 1812 broke out he was but twenty-one years of age, not thought too young, however, to be offered a commission in the militia of the Province. He received his first commission as Lieutenant of Cavalry, on the 22nd of June, 1812, (signed by General Brock) and was attached to the First Regiment of Leeds Militia, commanded by Colonel Breakenridge. He received his second commission on June 18th, 1822, as Colonel of the Third Regiment of Leeds. He was at the attack on Ogdensburg, under Lieutenant-Colonel McDonell, on the 22nd February, 1813. On the landing of the attacking force in the environs of the Village of Ogdensburg, he and Duncan Frazer were despatched by Colonel McDonell, under a flag of truce, to the American head-quarters at the Stone Garrison, with a demand for an unconditional surrender. Forsyth, of the American defenders of the village, made answer to this demand: "Tell Colonel McDonell there will be more fighting." The bearer of the reply had no sooner entered the ranks than the battle commenced. After a sharp encounter, Forsyth was driven from his position to Thuber's tavern, near Black Lake. Fifty-two marines were taken and conveyed to Canada. Besides, the Americans lost five killed and eighteen wounded. Most of the prisoners were paroled and sent to Montreal. The British held possession of the village during the day, securing a large amount of public stores and munitions of war. Before re-crossing the river, the barracks were burned, and an attempt made to destroy the bridge.

On the conclusion of the war, and the people having settled down to peaceful pursuits, Mr. Jones availed himself of the education he had received in Brockville, proceeded to York, and in Hilary Term, 55 George III., 1815, was called to the Bar. He at once opened an office for the practice of his profession in Brockville, where he had a successful practice. In politics he was a decided Tory. What time he could spare from his profession, he employed in supporting and strengthening the Tory party in the Counties of Leeds and Grenville. He had not many years to wait for recognition of his services, the electors of Leeds and Grenville returning him to the Provincial Parliament, the first time as member of the eighth Provincial Parliament in 1821, and again for the ninth Provincial Parliament in 1825 and 1826.

On referring to the Journals of the House, I find Mr.

Jones, during these two Parliaments, in his place in the House promoting beneficial legislation. He was, in 1821, one of the Commissioners appointed by the House to confer with the Commissioners of Lower Canada on the subject of duties collected at the Port of Quebec. This was a matter of much concern to the people of the Province of Upper Canada. I have referred to the difficulties at large in the life of Sir John Beverley Robinson. The selection of Mr. Jones as one of the Commissioners by the House shews that he was esteemed a man of business capacity, well qualified to perform his duty to the Province on this important subject.

In 1821 there was an agitation existing which extended to the House on the subject of the Sedition Laws. In the minds of some a more speedy mode of trying and punishing seditious people than the ordinary Courts was required. That was not, however, the opinion of Mr. Baldwin, then a member of the House, as I find that on the 1st December, 1821, he moved :

That it be resolved that the Commons of the Province, well knowing the ample sufficiency of the ordinary Courts of law for the security of the Province against all seditious attempts whatever, view with reluctance any obstacle presented to their reasonable wishes for a recurrence to that ordinary course, from whence no deviation can be justified but by temporary law in times of danger and violence.

Mr. Jones voted for Mr. Baldwin's resolution.

In the Session of 1823 Mr. Jones supported a bill brought in by Mr. Burwell "to authorize the appointment of District Attorneys." As a matter of fact District Attorneys were not appointed till a much later date.

In 1832 the lines of parties were beginning to be more closely drawn. Thus we find a stormy meeting being held in Brockville in March, 1832, in which Mr. Jones took a prominent part, espousing the Tory cause. A requisition had been circulated signed by Charles Jones (Honorable Charles Jones), Jonas Jones, John L. Read, (my father), and eighteen others, calling a meeting to be held in Brockville, for the formation of an Emigrant

Society in compliance with the recommendation of Sir John Colborne. After the meeting was over it was proposed to draft an address to be presented to His Majesty the King, stating :

> That the Province was in a most flourishing condition, enjoying the blessings of a free constitution and a government most liberally and impartially administered.

That was not at all the opinion of the malcontents of that day, who, led by Mr. Buell, organized an opposition meeting at which a petition was prepared of a diametrically opposite character. A historian writing of these events says :

> Year after year the contest increased in bitterness until Mackenzie and a few followers were driven into rebellion, and it ended in a mad attempt to capture Little York.

The election of Leeds again sent Mr. Jones to Parliament in 1836. The sessions of 1836 and 1837 were the most important of all the sessions of the Old Parliament of Upper Canada before the Union. Great discontent prevailed in the country, arising from the fact that the people were getting uneasy at being ruled by an irresponsible executive. At last a remedy was sought in the Union of the two Provinces of Upper and Lower Canada. The proposition to unite the Provinces was violently opposed by Sir John Robinson, and by a majority of the then Houses. On the 3rd March, 1837, Mr. Jones voted for a resolution of the House, that an address be presented to His Majesty stating :

> That this Province we believe to be quite as large as can be effectually ruled by one Executive Government. The population which Upper Canada contains is almost without exception of British descent. They speak the same language and have the same laws, and it is their pride that these laws are derived from the Mother Country, and are unmixed with rules and customs of foreign origin, wholly and happily free from the causes of difficulties which are found so embarrassing in the adjoining Province, we cannot but most earnestly hope that we shall be suffered to continue so, and that His Majesty's paternal regard for his numerous and loyal subjects in this colony will not suffer a doubtful experiment to

be hazarded which may be attended with consequences most detrimental to the peace, and injurious to the best interests of themselves and their posterity.

This resolution was carried by a small majority. Twenty days afterwards on the 23rd March, 1837, Mr. Jones was appointed a Puisne Judge of the Court of Queen's Bench.

When appointed to the Supreme Court Bench, Mr. Justice Jones had had a great deal of experience of judicial duty as Judge of the District Court, and so brought to the Bench a mind well trained, with a discernment which well fitted him for his position. He was eminently a practical man, and well acquainted with the ways of the Country. His military and cavalry experience had given him a jaunty air, and a spring that would have done credit to the modern athlete.

It was very much his custom in hearing cases to interrupt counsel in their argument by putting to them a suppositious case. He would say, "Now Mr. ———, suppose it was the case of a horse." The old counsel of his day were always familiar with this fondness of his of intruding a horse into the case whatever it might be, and were not slow to follow his example in putting the case of a horse in argument, which was sure to catch the Judge's ear.

He had not been long on the Bench before called upon to give judgment in a horse case which at the time was the subject of much comment. The case was Gorham v. Boulton, 6 U. C. O. S. Races were got up in Toronto by the Toronto Race Club, of which William Boulton was treasurer. The race was for a purse of one hundred guineas, to be paid to the winner if the stewards decided in favor of the party claiming the money; the one hundred guineas being deposited in the hands of the treasurer of the course. The race was run, and the plaintiff claimed the stakes, the plaintiff's horse won the first heat, and came in first on the second, and it was alleged there had been foul riding. The case is only important as deciding that where the decision as to who won the race was left to the stewards, who had not decided that plaintiff had won, though he proved that in fact there was no foul riding, he was not entitled to sue the treasurer for money had and received till he had got the decision in his favor.

Judge Jones, in giving judgment, said :

<blockquote>
The defendant having received the money as an officer of the club as proved by their orders, he cannot be liable for money deposited in his hands as stakes to be paid to the winner of the race, until the race is decided in favour of the plaintiff by the person authorized to decide. When money is deposited in the hands of a trustee for a specific purpose, the depositor cannot recover it back till the trust is at an end, as a part, unless as a balance in discharge of the trust. There is no express undertaking on the part of the defendant to pay the money to the plaintiff, and none can be implied by law until, according to the terms of the deposit, the stewards have decided in favour of the plaintiff. The stewards have *not* decided in his favour, but on the contrary have decided against him, and if the decision is not final, not being by a majority of the whole club, the matter is still undecided. In either case it appears to me that this action cannot be maintained for the purse. I think the parties submitted to the decision of the acting steward, that the plaintiff is bound by such decision, and can bring no action against the defendant.
</blockquote>

I selected this case out of many others in which Judge Jones gave judgment, because of its directness, perspicuity of language, and plain, understandable expression of opinion.

There was another case in the Queen's Bench, about 1842, but not reported till four years afterwards, 2 U. C. Rep. 224, the case of Doe Irvine *v.* Webster, which was the topic of much legal discussion at the Bar. The more important as it settled a principle by a majority of the Court, the Court itself being divided on the main question. In this case one Knapp, the nominee of the Crown of certain land, had, before the patent issued, on 3rd November, 1880, executed a deed poll by which he "granted, bargained, and sold," the premises to one Wood, who conveyed by deed of bargain and sale to another, and by regular assignments the land was conveyed to the lessee of the plaintiff, who claimed under this chain of title. On 1st November, 1803, nearly three years after Knapp made the deed to Wood, letters patent were completed in Knapp's name for the land, and remained in the Provincial Registry Office, having been duly enrolled. Knapp having been made aware of this fact on 10th September, 1824, disregarding his first deed, executed a deed of Release and Quit Claim to one Philips, who conveyed to the defendant. It will thus be seen that the principal contention was, whether a party in possession of land claiming under a deed made by the patentee of the Crown after the Crown had parted with their title to the patentee, had a better title than a party claiming by deed from the same patentee before the patent had issued, when the patentee was but a nominee of the Crown, and had not acquired the legal estate from the Crown, or ever been in possession. The question resolved itself into a question of estoppel. Whether or not the party in possession claiming through the same patentee, Knapp, who had made the deed of bargain and sale to Wood, through whom the plaintiff claimed, was estopped from disputing the title of the plaintiff claiming under the first deed, though as a matter of fact Knapp had not the Crown title when he conveyed to Wood.

The question was a most important one and as expressed by Chief Justice Robinson in the case of McLean v. Laidlaw, subsequently decided, (but reported first in the same volume of Reports) the decision was "the result of a long and anxious consideration." Chief Justice Robinson in Doe Irvine v. Webster held that there was an estoppel, and that the defendant was not at liberty to go into evidence: that Knapp had no title when he conveyed to Wood, but was estopped from disputing his title, and so the title of the plaintiff claiming through him. Judge Macaulay, the senior Puisne Judge, held that no estoppel was created. Mr. Justice Jones while leaning to the opinion that there was an estoppel, held that it was not necessary to decide the question of estoppel, and the plaintiff was entitled to recover on other grounds. He said:

> Although in this case the defendant takes from Phillips, who also holds under Knapp, it appears to be unimportant to determine whether the defendant is bound by the estoppel, because if the interest acquired by Knapp under the patent enured to Wood by reason of his prior deed it gave Wood the estate in fee, which he could convey to McLean and McMillan without entry, there being at that time no person in actual possession of the lot. For the same reasons the deed of Bargain and Sale from McLean and McMillan to Bowman and Smith, the lessors of the plaintiff, was effectual to convey the estate to them, and therefore they had a right to recover in this action.

Although the case is reported as Doe Irvine *v.* Webster, it would have been better to have been reported as Doe Bowman and Smith *v.* Webster as it appeared in evidence that Wood, in 1816, conveyed to McLean and McMillan, who in 1817, conveyed to Bowman and Smith, (Judge Macaulay's Judgment, p. 248). One of the demises laid in the action was that of Bowman and Smith who were the real plaintiffs, no deed to Irvine having been proved, so that Judge Jones must be understood as deciding that the interest acquired by Knapp under the patent enured to Wood by reason of his prior deed, and so Wood got the estate which he could convey to McLean and McMillan, which they could convey to Bowman and Smith, and so the plaintiffs were entitled to recover possession of the land.

I doubt not, but that the reference to this case will be more interesting to the professional than to the lay reader. I give it, however, as it established the principle of estoppel on a basis which I believe has never been shaken as applied to similar deeds under similar circumstances in Canada. The case was elaborately argued, and much considered, judgment being given by four Judges, Judge Jones being one of those deciding a principle ever since maintained.

The Honorable John Hilyard Cameron was Reporter of the Court in 1846, and has appended this note to Doe Irvine *v.* Webster :

> Judgment was given in this case in Hilary Term, 1842, before the commencement of the publication of these reports, but the great importance of the question adjudicated upon and the reference to it by the

Court in the preceding case (McLean *v.* Laidlaw) has induced the reporter to introduce it here.

One has only to read the judgments of all the Judges to shew the interest taken in the question involved, and besides, they shew that Mr. Justice Jones, as well as every other Judge on the Bench, felt it his duty to give all the arguments and reasons which induced the conclusion to which the several Judges arrived, though not agreeing in their decision.

The Honorable Jonas Jones will long be remembered by those who knew him. The active life he had led before being promoted to the Bench, he retained after his promotion. His ambition was to keep up with the other Judges his confreres on the Bench. He would often, in early morn, wend his way to the Judges' Library at the Hall, to be armed at every point for a conference with his brother Judges.

It is to be feared he taxed his strength too severely in the performance of duty. A plethoric man, such as he, could scarcely do without his old time exercise. He was suddenly struck down by apoplexy in Toronto, in 1848, when away from his own house, He never recovered from the stroke: died, and was buried in St. James's Cemetery. He left a large family of children, several of whom are still living. I have read a historical memoir of him, written by a Brockville gentleman in 1879, which I think but expresses the truth as I knew him. The memoir says:

> His great knowledge of the way and manner of the people caused his judgment in the District Court and in the Queen's Bench to give great satisfaction. His manliness of character and honesty of purpose caused him to beloved by the people of the United Counties of Leeds and Grenville, and his removal from Brockville was much regretted by all classes. His advice and assistance to the early settlers of Leeds and Grenville is not yet forgotten.

XVI.

The Honorable Robert Sympson Jameson, Vice-Chancellor of Upper Canada.

IN writing the life of Vice-Chancellor Jameson, we travel out of the dull routine of Common Law into the broader pastures of Equity. Vice-Chancellor Jameson was the first Judge that ever presided in an Equity Court in Upper Canada. Judge Willis hoped to have been the first Judge of a Chancery Court in the Province; a reference to his life, however, will shew how much he was disappointed in such hope, and the embroglio he got into with his brothers of the Common Law Bench, resulting in his amoval from his Judgeship of the King's Bench.

Historically speaking our earliest acquaintance with Mr. Jameson, V. C., was about the same period (1820), that he made the acquaintance with Anna Murphy, his future wife. He is at this time represented as "a young barrister of good family, handsome appearance, and fascinating manners, that his powers of conversation were exceptionally brilliant, his morals irreproachable, and his learning much beyond that of the average even of professional men of his age."

Mr. Jameson was a barrister of the Middle Temple. He was the son of Thomas Jameson. Mr. Jameson was admitted into the Society of the Middle Temple in 1818, and in 1824 was a Reporter in Lord Eldon's Court, who was doubtless his friend and patron. In that year (1824), there was published in London a volume of Reports with this designation: "Cases in Bankruptcy by Thos. C. Glyn, Esq., of Lincoln's Inn, Barrister at Law and Commissioner of Bankruptcy, and Robert S. Jameson, Esq., of the Middle Temple, Barrister at Law, containing Reports of Cases decided by Lord Chancellor Eldon and by Vice Chancellor Sir John Leach. From Michaelmas Term, 1821, to the sitting before Michaelmas Term, 1824, and a Digest of all the contemporary cases relating to the Bankruptcy Laws in the Courts."

Although Mr. Jameson has been represented in his early days at the Bar to have had "learning beyond that of the average professional man of his age," it has not been represented whether this average was general average or special average. However this may be, Mr. Jameson was not a success in his profession as a barrister, his bright anticipations on setting out in his career of practice at the Bar were not destined to be fulfilled. It was a fortunate circumstance for him that he had so influential a patron as Lord Eldon, the Chancellor, and that there were outlying Colonies of the Empire where he might possibly obtain greater success than in England. In his early life he had friends, literary men, who in the field of literature gained great renown. Himself born in the Lake Country of England, he was naturally intimate with the poet Wordsworth, who loved to roam over that region, and commit to verse the beauties of the scenery.

He was also the familiar friend of Coleridge and of Southey. What wonder then, living as it were in the realms of poetry, that he should have accepted with kindness the regard of a romantic young lady even before he was out of his teens in the law.

In 1820 he met Anna Murphy, the daughter of Bromwell Murphy, an Irish artist, a miniature painter, described as a "brilliant, unstable, impecunious Irishman," a very Captain Costigan of a man, full of fun and fury.

The life of V. C. Jameson would not be of absorbing interest without bringing into it the story of Anna Jameson, *neé* Anna Murphy, so well known as the Authoress of "Winter Studies and Summer Rambles in Canada," a book written in a lively animated style, and which was well received, and had many readers in Britain and the United States.

Although Mr. Jameson became engaged to Anna Murphy in 1820, the engagement was not of long duration. A few weeks had only elapsed before a lover's quarrel occurred, and the engagement was broken off. Mr. Jameson soon after commenced and continued his reporting; while the lady took the place of governess in the family of a lady who visited France and Italy. The governess, during the tour, keeping a diary of her travels, which she subsequently published under the title of "The Diary of an Enuyeé." On her return to England Anna Murphy accepted the situation of governess in another family, that of Mr. Littleton, Member of Parliament for one of the Ridings of Staffordshire, who was subsequently raised to the Peerage by the title of Lord Hatherton. Colonel Edward George Henry Littleton, who was in Canada as Secretary to Lord Dufferin, was a grandson of Lord Hatherton.

The position of governess becoming irksome, in 1826, or about that time, she renewed her engagement with Mr. Jameson, and they were married. The marriage was not a happy one. The parties to it thought they were, but really were not, suited to each other. In her mature years Mrs. Jameson referring to her girlish life, wrote of herself: "I was an affectionate but not, as I now think, a lovable or attractive child." Again writing of herself as she was at the early age of eight years, she wrote: "I always fancied evil and shame and humiliation to my adversary, to myself the role of superiority and gratified pride."

Mr. Dent, in his history, has well said of the life of Mrs. Jameson: "Such a person was not likely to make a man happy as a wife when grown to womanhood."

The father of Mrs. Jameson was, during the period of his daughter's girlhood, in straitened circumstances, this added to his unsympathetic nature was not likely to contribute to the happiness of the future authoress.

During the residence of her father in London in 1806, when his daughter was but twelve years of age, she, no doubt, foreseeing that her future life depended on her own exertions, applied herself to education, and acquired a high degree of proficiency in Latin, Italian, and other languages.

Mr. Jameson had not been long married, before something more than a lover's quarrel occurred between this unhappy couple—the union was not a happy one from the beginning—four years had not passed over their heads in married life when the husband and wife thought it well to separate, for a season at least. Mr. Jameson was glad to expatriate himself for a time, and through influence obtained the appointment, in 1829, to a puisne Judgeship in the Island of Dominica, one of the British possessions in the West Indies.

Mrs. Jameson remained in England, and betook herself to travel and her favourite literature. She made a tour of the continent, accompanied by her father and his patron Sir Gerard Noel. On the continent she made the acquaintance of Goethe. She spent some time at Weimar, where she first met Goethe and other members of the brilliant circle of the Grand Duke. In 1831 she wrote the "Memoirs of the Lives of Celebrated Sovereigns." Her husband, in Dominica, either from neglect or indifference, contributed but little to her support. She was glad to write for a living. In 1832 she published her "Characteristics of Women," a series of disquisitions on the female characters in Shakespeare's plays. It is a well written work, possessing great interest to any reader who desires to cultivate an acquaintance with the female characters of the great dramatist. Mrs. Jameson never joined her husband in the West Indies.

In 1833, Mr. Jameson resigned his Judgeship in Dominica, and returned to England. He remained there a few weeks in the society of his wife at the house of Mrs.

Bates, a married sister of Mrs. Jameson. In the same year, 1833, he came to Upper Canada, and took up his residence in York, having on the 21st June, 1833, been appointed Attorney-General of the Province, owing his appointment to the British Government. His was the last appoinment made to that office for Canada by the British Government. In Trinity Term, 1833, he was entered a member of the Law Society, and on the same day was called to the Canadian Bar. While holding the position of Attorney-General he followed the English practice of having a chief clerk; his chief clerk was William Keele, remembered as the author of a work on Justices of the Peace. Mr. Keele was himself an attorney, and was of great service to the Attorney-General (Jameson) in his practice. As a matter of fact the practical knowledge in law which Mr. Jameson had, was acquired while on the Bench in Dominica. He had never practised common law, civil or criminal, while in England. His practice in Upper Canada as Attorney-General was not seriously large, nor did it last for a long time.

Mr. Hagerman, afterwards Mr. Justice Hagerman, was Solicitor-General during Mr. Jameson's incumbency of the office of Attorney-General. At this period of the history of the Province, the Crown practice was divided between the Attorney and the Solicitor-General.

In 1835, Mr. Jameson was elected a member of the Legislative Assembly to represent the County of Leeds. I have a distinct recollection of the election, living as I did in Grenville, the adjoining county for which my father was returning officer at the general election of 1836, then for the first time held at the village of Merrickville, in the rear of the county. The Attorney-General might have found some cause for writs arising out of that election, as at about the fourth day of the polling, a body of men came down from Leeds, and as the returning officer and his clerk (the village schoolmaster) were crossing the common, after their mid-day meal, (the clerk, with poll book in hand), the invaders from Leeds seized the poll book, tore it into a thousand fragments, and thus broke up the election.

Mr. Jameson sat in Parliament for Leeds until the general election of 1837, to which I have referred, and on the 23rd of March, 1837, he was appointed Vice-Chancellor.

The want of a Court of Equity in this Province had begun to be seriously felt, consequently the Legislature on the 4th March, 1837, enacted :

> That there be constructed and established a Court of Chancery, to be called and known by the name and style of "The Court of Chancery of the Province of Upper Canada," of which Court the Governor, Lieutenant Governor, or person administering the Government of the Province, shall be Chancellor. And that for the better administration of justice in the said Court, the judicial powers thereof, both legal and equitable, shall be exercised by a Judge, to be appointed by His Majesty under the Great Seal of the Province, and to be called and known as "The Vice-Chancellor of Upper Canada," and who shall hold his office during good behaviour ; which said Court shall be holden at the seat of Government in the said Province, or in such other place as shall be appointed by proclamation of the Governor, Lieutenant-Governor, or person administering the Government of this Province.

Mr. Jameson was the first Vice-Chancellor of this Court. In 1836, before his appointment to the Bench, he was Treasurer of the Law Society. He was also elected Treasurer of the Law Society for the years 1837, 1838, 1839, 1840, and 1845.

During the time Mr. Jameson was Attorney-General he wrote to his wife more than once soliciting her to join him in Canada. She, however, clung to her gods of literature, making another tour of the continent, spending a considerable time in Germany, keeping up an occasional correspondence with her husband, not, however, of a character shewing much wifely affection. The relation which subsisted between the husband and wife may best be judged of by a letter Mrs. Jameson wrote Mr. Jameson in answer to a letter he wrote to her in May, 1835, in which he had jokingly told her he intended ere long to take another wife. This was written, no doubt, to rouse her jealousy, and attract her to Canada ; the effect is shewn by her answer. She wrote, after some months, and which must have been shortly before Mr. Jameson was appointed Vice-Chancellor :

> You say it is your intention to marry again. My dear Robert, jesting apart, I wish it only depended on me to give you that power. You might perhaps be happy with another woman. A union such as ours is, and *has been ever*, is a real mockery of the laws of God and man. You have the power to dispose of our fate as far as it depends on each other. I placed that power in your hands, and had you used that power in a decidedly manly spirit, *whether to unite or part us*, I had respected you the more, and could have arranged my life accordingly. But what an existence is this to which you have reduced us both. If you can make up your mind to live without me, if your vague letters signify a purpose of this kind, for God's sake speak the truth to me ; but if, on the other hand, if it is your purpose to remain in Canada, to settle there under any political charge, and you really wish to have me with you and, make another trial for happiness, tell me so distinctly and decidely, tell me what time to leave England, tell me what things I ought to take with me, what kind of life I shall live, that I may come prepared to render my existence and yours as pleasant as possible.

Her husband then wrote her to join him, having previously informed her that he had secured about three acres of eligible ground on Brock street, on which to build a cottage to her taste, and which he wished her to occupy with him, if possible to illuminate it with her presence. The result was, that in September, 1836, she sailed for New York, *en route* for York, to join her husband. Her husband did not meet her at New York, nor on her arrival at York, then truly muddy York, as Mrs. Jameson described it in her "Studies and Rambles in Canada."

It is no pleasant task to write of these divergences between a public man who attained the position of Vice-Chancellor and his clever wife. I may, however, say, quoting the language used in the introductory chapter to the life of Wordsworth (the Vice-Chancellor's friend) in "Morley's English Men of Letters," "I have endeavoured to write as though the subject of this biography were himself its auditor, listening, indeed, from some region where all of truth is discerned, and nothing but truth desired."

Mr. Dent, in his life of Mrs. Jameson, has already published very much of what I have written in regard to the gifted authoress. It is fitting that I make my acknowledgment to him for much of the knowledge I have acquired of Mrs. Jameson, so well known in years gone by in the society of York.

The Vice-Chancellor, presiding in his Court, was a model of gentlemanly dignity, and was ever willing to give all attention to those who had business in his Court. He had pleading before him as counsel several barristers who were distinguished at the Bar, and who afterwards attained eminence on the Bench. I will mention but some of the names as I gather them from the reports: William Hume Blake, afterwards Chancellor; J. P. Esten, afterwards Vice-Chancellor; Robert Baldwin Sullivan, afterwards Judge Sullivan. There were others, but these are the most prominent names of those practising in his Court. During the time he sat alone as Vice-Chancellor, before the reorganization of the Court under Chancellor Blake, the Rebellion of 1837 was in full blast in the Province for at least a considerable part of that period, so that Chancery proceedings had a comparative lull; there are not, during this time, more than thirty reported cases heard before Mr. Jameson, Vice-Chancellor, and some of these were appeals in bankruptcy. None of the decisions were such as at this day are regarded as affording precedents for future decision. The Vice-Chancellor himself was a great stickler for precedents, not given to striking out in new paths, or venturing to establish a principle unfortified by past authority. A friend of mine, who knew the Vice-Chancellor well, says, that Mr. Jameson told him that he thought the principal duty of a Judge was to follow precedent.

On March 15, 1837, Mrs. Jameson writing to her sister Charlotte wrote:

> You will be glad to hear that Jameson is appointed Chancellor (*sic*) at last. He is now at the top of the tree, and has no more to expect or aspire to. I think he will make an excellent Chancellor; he is gentlemanlike, *and*

will stick to precedent, and his excessive reserve is here the greatest of possible virtues. No one loves him, it is true; but every one approves him, and his promotion has not caused a murmur."

This letter in its language certainly bears testimony to the fact that in some way his wife knew that he meant to make precedents his guiding star. It was, perhaps, well that he should have done so, for it has never been ascribed to the Vice-Chancellor that very great industry or very great originality were his principal characteristics. Robert John Turner, who practised in his Court, was wont always to ply him with precedents, having a full appreciation of the Vice-Chancellor's regard in this direction. If by any possibility a reference, even a dictum of Lord Eldon, could be found bearing on the subject in question, knowing the Vice-Chancellor's partiality for Lord Eldon, at whose feet he sat before leaving England, the dictum was eagerly seized upon as a precedent which ought to sway the judicial mind of the Vice-Chancellor.

In very fact the counsel got too strong for the Vice-Chancellor, and the Court had not been in existence more than four years before it became necessary to reconstruct the Court, placing at the head of it the then leading counsel, Mr. Blake: the Vice-Chancellor being relegated to second place.

The Vice-Chancellor was fond of music, literature, and the fine arts. He entertained liberally while his wife was with him, which, however, was for less than a year. Arriving in York in November of 1836, Mrs. Jameson managed to live through the winter with Mr. Jameson, in a cold, formal way. She wrote:

> I could almost wish myself a dormouse, or a she-bear, to sleep away the rest of this cold, cold winter, and to wake only with the first green leaves, the first warmth of summer wind.

She found time, however, during the winter to visit Niagara Falls. A gentleman is still living in Toronto who accompanied her on that journey. Like many others who have visited Niagara Falls, her first impressions of that great cataract were disappointing, as she expresses her wish that the Falls were like Yarrow, yet unvisited, unbeheld—" no, it must be my own fault," she cries:

> The reality has displaced from my mind an illusion much more magnificent than itself. I have no words for my utter disappointment. Oh! I could beat myself! and there is no help! The first moment, the first impression is lost; though I should live a thousand years, as long as Niagara itself shall roll, I can never see it again, for the first time. Something is gone that cannot be restored. What has come over my soul and senses? I am metamorphosed; I am translated; I am an ass's head, a clod, a wooden spoon, a fat weed growing on Lethe's brink, a stock, a stone, a petrefaction. For have I not seen Niagara, the wonder of wonders, and feel, no words can tell *what*, disappointment.

When Spring came Mrs. Jameson, desiring to be released from her surroundings, the official circle of York, and a not too happy home ventured on an expedition through the Western District, and made her way to Sault Ste. Marie, which at that time was a very arduous undertaking for a man, much more so for a lady, surrounded by comparative strangers. Her great desire, however, to see Indian life overcame all obstacles: she made the journey, shot the rapids of the Sault in an Indian canoe, and thus accomplished a feat which astonished the stay-at-homes of York, and excited some surprise with her home friends accustomed to continential pleasure trips, but not to so difficult or hazardous an undertaking as Mrs. Jameson took on herself to perform.

This trip is a memorable one in many ways, not only in the incidents of travel and the notoriety Mrs. Jameson gained thereby, but because while moving about among so many scenes, her niece, in the history of her life, tells us, "arrangements were going on for her final separation from her husband, and the establishment of her future independence;" indeed, the many letters of Mrs. Jameson which have been published prove conclusively that independence was what she sighed for, independence of her husband was what she prayed for. She was wont in early life to declaim on independence.

> "Thy spirit, independence, let me share,
> Lord of the lion heart and eagle eye;
> Thy steps I'll follow with my bosom bare,
> Nor heed the storm that howls along the sky."

All we know of the cause of the Vice-Chancellor and his wife's disagreements is, that there was that kind of incompatibility between the two that made both of them desirous of release.

On May 26th, 1857, she wrote to Mr. Noel from York:

I shall be in England about October or November next. The Winter has been beyond measure dreary and lonely; *but one of the objects of my coming will be, I think, accomplished*, and my future life more easy, and my conscience clear. It was worth the sacrifice to purchase all I *can* have of peace and independence for the rest of my days, and what we do from a principle of duty turns out well surely. So I put my trust in God and my own firm will, and will not fear what man can do unto me.

From this it is clear that from the time she set out from England for Canada till her return, she had but one object in view, separation from her husband. Mrs. Jameson, before leaving America, paid a visit to Miss Sedgwick, who took a lively interest in her, and treated her with marked respect, indeed, with affection. Mrs. Jameson was much courted by American Society, and made a very favorable impression on the *literati* of the Republic.

At length, early in the year 1838, the time came for her final departure from America. Before she left the country legal papers had been drawn up, assuring to Mrs. Jameson an allowance of three hundred pounds a year; and she took her leave in the possession, if not happy possession, of a letter from her husband the Vice-Chancellor, dated September 21st, 1837, which was as follows:

My dear Anna—In leaving Canada to [reside among your friends in England or elsewhere, you carry with you my most perfect respect and esteem. My affection you will never cease to retain. Were it otherwise I should feel less pain at consenting to an arrangement arising from no wish of mine, but which I am compelled to believe is best calculated for your happiness, and which therefore I cannot but approve.

The obtaining this letter was a victory for Mrs. Jameson. Mrs. Jameson and her husband never afterwards met, they were separated for ever. Coleridge, one of Mrs. Jameson's early friends, in his poem of the "Quarrel of

Friends," has written lines which may not be inaptly applied to the case of the Vice-Chancellor and Mrs. Jameson.

> Alas ! they had been friends in youth
> * * * *
> They parted—ne'er to meet again,
> But never either found another
> To free the hollow heart from paining,
> They stood aloof, the scar remaining
> Like cliffs which had been rent asunder ;
> A dreary sea now flows between,
> But neither heat, nor frost, nor thunder,
> Shall wholly do away, I ween,
> The marks of that which once hath been.

The Vice-Chancellor died in Toronto, in 1854. He left considerable property in real estate, the house and premises on Brock street, and several acres of valuable land in what is now Parkdale, bordering on Jameson Avenue, named after the Vice-Chancellor. Mrs. Jameson survived her husband several years. In her latter years she took great interest in what is termed the "Woman's Rights" question. She had a thorough conception of the idea, since become a fixed fact, that many employments then confined only to men, could and should be shared by woman. Her niece, Gertrude Macpherson, in the history of her life, says, on the authority of a Mrs. Parkes, that :

> She attended a Local Science meeting at Bradford, in October, 1859, and sat during the whole of one day in the Section B, where papers on the employment of women were being read, and occasionally joined in the discussion which ensued. When Mrs. Jameson spoke, a deep silence fell upon the crowded assembly. It was quite singular to see the intense interest she excited. Her age and the comparative refinement of her mental powers, had prevented her sphere of action from being "popular" in the modern sense ; and this, of course, created a stirring desire to see and hear her of whom they knew little personally. Her singularly low and gentle voice fell like a hush upon the crowded room, and every eye bent eagerly upon her, and every ear drank in her thoughtful and weighty words.

Alas ! she had not many months to live after this meeting. What time was left to her she employed in good works, writing a series of books intended to exhibit the manner in which Art had told the history of our Lord had engaged her thoughts and attention. She did not live to complete the work. In March, 1860, she was seized with an attack of bronchitis, which settled on her lungs, and produced fatal results She passed quietly away, and thus ended an active and troublous life. Her Niece, in the preface to the memoir of her life, thus wrote of her :

> The story of one who kept a stout heart through all the troubles that befel her, who kept her unhappiness to herself, and sought unceasingly to give happiness to all who belonged to her; who never used a pen to strike or to wound, nor took advantage of its power to avenge herself on any one who wronged her; and who was all her life long the chief support and consolation of her family, must possess some interest for all good people.

In concluding the life of the Vice-Chancellor, intertwined as it has been, with what may be considered by some, irrelevant matter relating to Mrs. Jameson, only referred to because history had already recorded the principal events of her life, I must remind the reader that when Vice-Chancellor Jameson was appointed to the Bench, the old English system of Equity, with its interrogatories and cross-interrogatories and all other dilatory paraphenalia of the time prevailed. Mr. Jameson was compelled to follow this antiquated "Jarndyce v. Jarndyce" system. It was too absurd to last long, and had finally to give way to an entirely different state of things. The system was too heavy for one man to carry. A great improvement took place when the Court was re-constructed, with Chancellor Blake at its head.

I have mentioned that the Vice-Chancellor died in 1854. His last resting place was in Toronto where he had lived so many years. Mrs. Jameson was buried in Kensall Green, London.

XVII.

The Honorable Christopher Alexander Hagerman, Judge of the Queen's Bench.

THE Honorable Christopher Alexander Hagerman, born at Adolphustown on March 28th, 1792, was the son of Nicholas Hagerman, of Adolphustown, in the County of Lennox, who was a United Empire Loyalist. Mr. Nicholas Hagerman came to Canada after the American Revolution. He was among the refugees who followed that portly Dutchman, Major Vanalstine, who will long be remembered by the inhabitants living on the Bay of Quinte, as one of the first settlers in Adolphustown. Revered and respected by all the country round, Major Vanalstine was one of nature's noblemen, giving succour and assistance to all who were in need when Adolphustown was a wilderness, and the Bay of Quinte the home of wild fowl and Indians. Hagerman's Point is a well known locality in Adolphustown, and got its name from Nicholas Hagerman, who settled there, near the old United Empire burying grounds. Mr. Hagerman built his house near the water's edge, but time and tide wait for no man, and not only has the burial place of Mr. Hagerman, the founder of the settlement, been well nigh blotted out, but the house where he lived, and the land on which it stood, been effaced by devouring time and the waters of the bay.

Judge Hagerman's father, though driven to cultivating the soil for a living on coming to Canada, impelled thereto by his devotion to the King's cause, was a man of education, and it is said studied law before leaving New York. I find Nicholas Hagerman was called to the Bar in Trinity Term, 37 George III., 1797, and was appointed a Bencher of the Law Society Michaelmas Term, 40 George III., 1799. After his call he commenced the practice of his profession in Adolphustown, and continued to be a successful practitioner there till his death. Nicholas Hagerman had only two sons, Daniel and Christopher Alexander, the latter in due time Judge of the Queen's Bench.

Dr. Canniff, who wrote the history of the Quinte Bay settlers, says he knew both Christopher and Daniel as small boys. That Daniel was a sedate, quiet boy, but as he has written it, " Chris was a saucy boy." However this may have been, Christopher, saucy and self-asserting as he was, had a large head and plenty of brains. As soon as he had grown out of his pinafore life he was sent to school in Kingston, where he finished his education, acquiring a sufficient knowledge of the classics to enable him to pass the Curriculum of the Law Society. He studied law for a part of the time of the course with his father at Adolphustown, and for the balance of his time with Mr. Allen McLean, of Kingston.

Christopher Alexander Hagerman was admitted a Student at Law Michaelmas Term, 49 George III.. 1808 : was called to the Bar, Hilary Term, 55 George III., 1815, and was appointed a Bencher in Easter Term, 1 George IV., 1820.

After Christopher (the son) was called to the Bar, it happened that sometimes the father and son came across each other as advocates of opposing parties in the Courts. On one occasion at Kingston this opposing of interests occurred, in a well contested case, the father being on one side, and the son on the other. Much to the annoyance of the father, Christopher won the suit for his client. On the result being proclaimed, the father said to the son,

"Have I raised a son to put out my eyes?"—"No!" replied the son, "to open them, father."

At the commencement of the War of 1812 Christopher went as Lieutenant with a company from Adolphustown to Kingston, and was shortly afterwards chosen Aide-de-Camp to the Governor General. This promotion, taking place just about the time of his becoming of age, was the means of bringing him into prominence, for we find that as soon as the War was over he was appointed Collector of Customs at Kingston. The Gazette of September 5th, 1815, announces that Christopher Hagerman had been appointed to His Majesty's Council in the Province of Upper Canada. As he was then but twenty-three years of age, it may readily be conceded that there is great significance in "now and then." What a glorious thing for young men is War!—the plain but ambitious young man of yesterday becomes the hero of to-day.

Mr. Hagerman was appointed to the Bench in 1828: this was, however a temporary appointment, only till the King's pleasure should be known. I have, in the life of Mr. Justice Willis, given an account of the difficulties Judge Willis brought upon himself in insisting that the Court of King's Bench could not be held constitutionally without the presence of the Chief Justice, who had gone to England on sick leave, and how ultimately those difficulties culminated in the amoval of Judge Willis. At that time Mr. Hagerman was an available man for the Bench, and was appointed to fill Mr Justice Willis's place. The British Government did not restore Mr. Willis to his place, but sent him to another Colony; at the same time they thought proper not to confirm the appointment of Mr. Hagerman. In this way they paid but a left-handed compliment to the Governor in his action in regard to Mr. Willis. The action of the Governor was, no doubt, thought to be precipitate: especially was it so considered by those who had espoused Judge Willis's cause, and they were those who were opposed to the Government of the day.

Although Mr. Hagerman, in the disruption that took place, lost the Judgeship, he secured another Government appointment. We find him on the 13th July, 1829, appointed Solicitor General. This office he held until, on the representation of William Lyon Mackenzie, the Colonial Secretary thought proper to cancel the appointment.

William Lyon Mackenzie had been repeatedly expelled from the House of Assembly, to which he had been sent as representative by the County of York. As a consequence of these proceedings Mr. Mackenzie visited England, bearing many petitions to the King and the British Parliament praying for redress of grievances. Lord Goderich, the then Secretary of State, gave much attention to Mr. Mackenzie's representations. One result of these representations was, the removal from office of the Attorney-General, H. J. Boulton, and the Solicitor-General, Mr. Hagerman. Mr. Stanley who succeeded Lord Goderich restored Mr. Hagerman, and appointed Mr. Boulton to the Chief Justiceship of Newfoundland. The reason assigned for the removal of the Crown officers was, that they had "permitted the repeated expulsion of a member of the Assembly, although the constitutional objections to that course had been conveyed to His Excellency by His Majesty's Government."

Mr. Hagerman was elected a member of the Legislature to represent the town of Kingston for the first time in 1819. His appointment as Solicitor-General, as well as his practice, requiring his constant attention at the capital, induced, indeed required that he should change his place of residence from Kingston to York; he consequently shortly after removed with his family from Kingston to York, and built for himself a very fine brick house on the corner of Simcoe and Wellington Streets, not far from Government House. He also built for himself a convenient office just north of the house where he carried on his practice for some years. The house and office are still standing, the former being used for the office of the Attorney-General and the latter for the Ontario Government Emigration Agency.

In the year 1835 Mr. Hagerman formed a partnership with Mr. Draper. The firm of Hagerman & Draper were well known in their day, not only for the large business they did, but as having as heads of the firm two of the most brilliant lawyers of the time. Mr. Hagerman holding the office of Solicitor General, had to give much of his time to Crown business, advising with the Government on all the multifarious matters that came up in the administration of the law department of Government.

Passing over his earliest Parliamentary career, I pass on to the exciting Session of 1836, in which he sat in the Opposition benches, the Reformers, a party to which he was opposed, having then a majority in the Assembly.

As we see things now-a-days, it seems strange that the Solicitor-General of the Province should be in the party of the minority of the Assembly; yet such was the case of Mr. Solicitor-General Hagerman. He was Solicitor-General and a member of the House in the Session of 1836, which was unequivocally a Reform house, while Mr. Hagerman was so much of a Tory that he would not allow himself to be called a Conservative, but a Tory out and out. I have not anywhere read so clear an exposition as his of the then agitated question as to whether the Governor was bound in all cases to consult his Council in governmental public questions; whether his Council had at all times a right to control him in the public business; or whether the Governor was only bound to listen to them when he asked for or required their advice. It was a very important question, and on which hinged the principles of Responsible Government afterwards adopted and carried out ever since the Union of the Provinces of Upper and Lower Canada in 1841.

In this Session of 1836, a Select Committee of the House made a long and voluminous report on the subject, claiming that the Governor's advisers, his Council, and the Governor himself, were responsible to the people, and that the Governor performing acts of Government without the advice and counsel of the Council, was contrary to the Colonial Constitution ; this gave an opportunity to the Solicitor-General to give to the House his views of constitutional rights and practice.

Looking to the past, and to the acts of Government of that day, Mr. Hagerman's speech in Parliament will throw much light on a very much misunderstood subject. I will, therefore, place before the reader, not the whole but part of the substance of the relative and important parts of his speech in the Assembly on this question. He said :

It appeared to him that the point on which the committee should have turned their attention was the origin of the Executive Council in the Colonies, the duties originally assigned to them, and the responsibility, if any, which attached to them as Councillors. An advantage which would have resulted from this plan of investigation had it been adopted would have been that the Committee would have informed themselves of the utter impossibility of the Lieutenant-Governor's divesting himself of the responsibility, and that by the laws and constitution he is emphatically and distinctly responsible to the King as Head of the Empire, politically ; and to the people of this Province individually in his private capacity, for every act of his government, and that the Executive Council are not and can not be made responsible to the people for any acts of theirs. Without further remark he, the Solicitor-General, would proceed to show on what grounds and upon what authority he rested these opinions.

There were not many works extant containing a history of the constitutions and forms of government in the Colonies but there were a few, and some of them giving a very explicit account of the Councils appointed by the Crown, their duties and responsibilities especially in the Colonies of America, and in order to attract the attention of the House to the line of argument he intended to pursue he begged honorable members would bear in mind that it would eventually appear that the Executive Council of Upper Canada which it was contended, was created by, as well as identified with, the Constitution of the Province (as conferred by 31 George III.) was merely the constitution of a body that had existed in Canada from the first moment of an organized Government, after the conquest down to the passing of the Act which divided the Province of Quebec into Upper and Lower Canada, and which was precisely similar to those existing in the old Colonies on this Continent and the West Indies. The first authority he should cite in support of this argument was that of a gentleman who held the office of Chief Justice of Georgia during the time that State was a Colony of Great Britain, and subsequently held high legal appointments in the West Indies. This gentleman in his remarks on the Council says: "They are to give advice to the

Governor or Commander-in-Chief for the time being when thereunto required, and they stand in the same relation to the Governor in a Colony that the Privy Council does to the King in Great Britain. In some cases the Governor can act without their advice and concurrence, and there are other cases in which the Governor is required by his instructions not to act without the advice and concurrence of his Council. Which (instructions) every Governor and Commander-in-Chief should carefully attend to. The Council sit as Judges in the Court of Errors or Court of Appeal. The Council are named in every Commission of the Peace as Justices of the Peace throughout the whole Colony;" Stoke's Constitutions of the British Colonies, pp. 239, 240. Thus we see the origin of Councils in the Colonies, and the duties assigned to them, and how completely the duties heretofore performed by the Council in this Province correspond with those imposed on the Councils in the old Colonies now separated from Great Britain as well as those which remain appendages of the Empire. In the old Colonies they advised the Governor when required by the King's instructions, they do so here; in the old Colonies they constituted a Court of Appeal, by our Constitution that duty is imposed on them here; and in this Province as in the other Colonies their names appear as Justices in every Commission of the Peace throughout the Province. The same author observes that when a new Governor came to a Province the names of the persons who were to constitute his Council were named in his instructions and that no other appointment or commission was necessary; but this practice has now fallen into disuse, at least in this Province. The last set of instructions containing the names of the Council, were those brought out by Sir Peregrine Maitland; but it should be borne in mind, that those very instructions are those now laid on the table by command of Sir Francis Head, that they contain the names of the Councillors then existing in Upper Canada and prescribed their duties. These instructions and these duties have undergone no change since that period.

Governor Simcoe the first Governor that came to this Province brought with him the first instructions that were designed to direct the King's representative, the Council, and other officers of the Government in their duties and as they were in the adjoining building on record in the books of the Council it was somewhat strange that the Committee did not examine them. They would be found to be the same as those delivered to Sir Peregrine Maitland.

In some of the old Colonies the Council was possessed of legislative power conjointly with the Governor, and sometimes formed an intermediate legislative branch between the Governor and an Assembly elected by the people. Of course in all matters relating to the enactment of laws the Governor could not act independently of the Council, except in so far as respected the assenting to or refusing of bills. Upon the death, removal, or resignation of the Governor, the senior Councillor, by the King's instructions, assumed the Government, as in this country, unless the senior Councillor happened to be Superintendent of Indian Affairs or Surveyor-General of the Customs, (which officers were always extraordinary members of the Council,) in which case the government devolved on the ordinary member of the Council next in seniority.

Such was the nature and constitution of the Executive Councils in the old Colonies of America, and although in the majority of those Governments, Legislative Assemblies existed, one branch elected by the people as in this country, yet there is no trace of any pretence that those Councils were responsible for their official acts to any other person or party than the King. Responsibility to the elective branch of the Legislature was never thought of; and the Chief Justice of Georgia, whose work he had quoted, and who had resided and held office in several of the other Colonies, distinctly states, that the Executive Council were guided by the King's instructions, and were therefore responsible to His Majesty only. They were appointed as in this Province by the King, and removed at his pleasure; they advised his representative, when required, in secrecy; their acts could be known to the King only, and to him only were they accountable for them. Let us now consider the origin and constitutional powers of the Executive Councils in these Provinces, they will be found to be precisely similar to those already described.

It would be recollected that Canada was obtained by conquest from the Crown of France, in 1759, and that by the treaty of Paris in 1763, it, together with other territories in America, was finally ceded to Great Britain. The form of Government in Canada between the years 1759 and 1763, was a course of purely military despotism, regulated by the terms of the capitulation. In the year 1763 the King issued his proclamation, in which he declared, that the territory in America ceded by the treaty of Paris, should be erected into four separate Governments, viz: Quebec, comprising the whole of Canada; East Florida; West Florida; and Grenada. For the purpose of shewing clearly the views of His Majesty with respect to the form of Government intended by him to be established in those territories, it would be proper to refer to the proclamation itself, which contains the following passage:

"And whereas it will greatly contribute to the speedy settling our said new governments, that our loving subjects should be informed of our paternal care for the security of the liberty and prosperities of those who are and shall become inhabitants thereof, we have thought fit to publish and declare by this our proclamation that we have, in the letters patent under our Great Seal of Great Britain by which the said governments are constituted, given express power and direction to our Governors of our said Colonies respectively, that so soon as the state and circumstances of the said Colonies will admit thereof, they shall with the advice and consent of the members of our Council, summon and call general assemblies within the said governments respectively, in such manner and form as is used and directed in those Colonies and Provinces in America which are under our immediate government; and we have also given power to the said Governors with the consent of our said Councils and the representatives of the people so to be summoned as aforesaid to make, constitute, and ordain laws, statutes, and ordinances for the public peace, welfare, and good government of the said Colonies, and of the people and inhabitants thereof, as near as may be agreeable to the laws of England, and under such regulations and restrictions as are used in other Colonies, and in the meantime, and until such assemblies can be called as aforesaid, all persons inhabiting in or resorting to our said Colonies, may confide in our royal protection for the enjoyment of the benefit of our laws of our realm of England ; for which purpose we have given power under our Great Seal to the Governors of our said Colonies respectively, to erect and constitute, with the advice of our said Council respectively, Courts of Judicature and public justice within our said Colonies, for the hearing and determining of causes, as well criminal as civil according to law and equity, and as near as may be agreeable to the laws of England, with liberty to all persons who may feel themselves aggrieved by the sentence of such Courts, in all civil causes, to appeal, under the usual limitations and restrictions to us in our Privy Council."

Here then was the root from which sprung our present constitution. In the above extract it will be observed that in the Patent constituting the Government of Quebec, allusion is made to "a Council ;" and that the Governor, with the advice of such Council, might summon and call a general assembly, "in such manner and form as is used and directed in those Colonies and Provinces in America which are under our immediate government." Now it would scarcely be contended that the Council thus created by the King, could be responsible to any other power than himself. There was not at that time, nor for years afterwards, any representative body in the Colony; and it might be further remarked, that had an assembly been convened in pursuance of the power contained in the proclamation, it (the assembly) was to be constituted as in the "other Colonies and Provinces of America ;" and it does not appear that it was not to be clothed with greater powers than they possessed. No assembly, however, was ever called under the authority of the proclamation, and Canada continued to be governed by a military officer, assisted by a Council until the year 1774. For eleven years an Executive Council did exist clearly and positively irresponsible to any power but the Crown, and possessed, too, of powers greatly transcending those of the present Council, for it appears by the 4th section of the Act 14 George III., ch. 83, that with the Governor it had power to enact laws by which the inhabitants of the Colony were bound. This Act the 14 George III., was the first passed by the British Parliament giving a settled form of government to Canada, and in it allusion was made to the existence of a Council, possessing the powers just mentioned. The Act authorized His Majesty to appoint a certain number of persons as Legislative Councillors, who when appointed should hold their office for life ; and ordained that the laws and ordinances passed by them, and assented to by the Governor on behalf of the King, should supersede all ordinances previously made by the Governor and the Executive Council. The Executive was not, however, done away with ; on the contrary it continued to exist to advise the Governor ; and by an ordinance passed in the year 1785, by the Council and Governor, it was constituted a Court of Appeal as in the old Colonies, which ordinance is recognized and confirmed by our constitutional Act 31 George III., ch. 31, sec. 34. Before proceeding to examine the provisions of the important Act last mentioned it might as well be asked whether the Executive Council of Quebec between the years 1774 and 1791, could be said to be responsible to any other power than the King for their official conduct? It would be manifestly absurd to say that it was responsible to the people, at a time when the people had no voice in the government. The Governor and the Legislative Council were both appointed by the King; the Executive Council was a body created by the King which he could continue or suppress at his mere will and pleasure, there being no law or ordinance that required their existence. Being appointed their duties were defined by the King, and lessened or extended according to his sole decree, unless where particular duties were imposed by ordinance; and when so those duties were of a character distinct from those of advisers of the King's representative. Where then should we seek for their responsibility to the people? It could no where be found. (Hear, hear). If then up to the time of passing the Constitutional Act the Executive Council were only responsible to the King, the next and most important question to be decided was, whether by that Act their character was changed, whether in fact, as is now alleged, "The Executive Council of this Province is by the Constitution responsible to the people and not to the Crown, and like the Cabinet in England should go out of office upon a vote of the Assembly, and that the Governor is bound by their advice, and is not responsible for his acts any more than the King is for his acts." Those who blindly contended for a principle so dangerous to the peace, welfare, and good government of this Province, would search in vain for support from the great charter conferred upon its inhabitants for the protection of their liberties. That Act recognizes a Council to be appointed by the King, but it creates no such body. It was manifest that when the 31 George III. was passed, the British Parliament had before it the King's proclamation of 1763, the Royal Instructions to the Governor, the Act of 14 George III. ch. 83, and the Ordinances of the Province of Quebec, passed in virtue of the last mentioned Act; each of which was specifically referred to in the Constitutional Act; and Parliament assuming that the King in the exercise of his royal prerogative would continue a Council which had previously existed, required of it when created certain specified duties, but no where making it a Cabinet which by its advice was to govern the Province, and assume the power and responsibility of the Crown, rendering the King's representative a mere cipher, subject to its domination and control. A principle so preposterous as this could no where be found in the Constitution. (Hear, hear). Nothing could be more clear than that it never was intended that the Council should have greater powers than were intrusted it prior to the passing of the Constitutional Act; which powers were defined in the King's Instructions, and the laws and ordinances then in force in the Colony, passed in pursuance of the powers given by the 14 George III. By an Ordinance of the Province of Quebec the Governor and Executive Council were constituted a Court of Appeals, and were continued such by the 34th section of the Constitutional Act, and by another section the Governor was required to act with the advice of his Council in erecting parsonages and endowing them; these are the only duties specifically required of the Council; all others depend on the will of the Sovereign. If, as is contended, it was meant that nothing could be constitutionally done without the advice of the Council, was it to be believed that so important a principle would have been left in doubt by the eminent statesman who framed the Constitution? It was inconsistent with common sense to suppose they would have been so blind to their duty. (Hear, hear).

But in truth there could be no doubt in the minds of dispassionate and intelligent men, the Constitution itself gave a plain and distinct negative to the assertion, that the Governor is at all times and upon every public occasion to consult the Council. It would be admitted that no duty which a Governor has to exercise can be of greater importance than deciding on the laws presented to him by the other branches of the Legislature for the royal assent; and it may be fairly argued that if upon any one point more than another he stands in need of the advice of a council it must be in coming to a decision on questions which may involve the safety of the liberties and property of the people of the country; notwithstanding this, however, he is not to be guided by his Council, but by the Royal Instructions. This was a provision in the Constitution itself, and in the following clear and intelligible words:

"Section XXX. And be it further enacted by the authority aforesaid, That whenever any bill, which has been passed by the Legislative Council and by the House of Assembly in either of the said Provinces respectively, shall be presented for His Majesty's assent, to the Governor or Lieutenant-Governor of such Province, or to the person administering His Majesty's Government therein, such Governor or Lieutenant-Governor or person administering the Government, shall, and is hereby authorized and required to declare, according to his discretion, but subject nevertheless to the provisions contained in this Act, and to such instructions as may from time to time be given in that behalf by His Majesty, his heirs or successors, that he assent to such bill in His Majesty's name, or that he withholds His Majesty's assent for such bill, or that he reserves such bill for the signification of His Majesty's pleasure thereon."

This section of the Constitutional Act was important for several reasons but principally because, in the first place, it at once overthrows the doctrine that the Governor is on all occasions to consult his Council or act by its advice; and secondly, as shewing that the King's instructions from time to time given were recognized by Parliament, and embodied in the Constitution as binding on the Governor. (Hear, hear). The clause just quoted required the person administering the Government to assent to or reject bills "according to his discretion," not by and with the advice of his Council, but in conformity with the instructions he may "from time to time" receive from His Majesty. How absurd would it then be for a Governor, were he to apply to his Council in a doubtful case for advice and acting upon it assent to a bill contrary to the orders contained in his instructions which by the express terms of the Constitution were to be his guide, how would he excuse himself by alleging that he acted upon the advice of his Council, instead of his instructions? Where then must the responsibility rest? Upon himself, of course; and it would be out of his power to rid himself of it and cast it upon another. (Hear, hear).

The Constitution having thus emphatically recognized the Royal Instructions, as binding upon the Governor and forming a part as it were of the Constitution itself, it would be proper again to refer to those instructions for the purpose of placing before the House in a clear and connected manner the duties required by the Sovereign of the members of his Council when he appointed them to their office; The following were the words used:

"To the end that our said Executive Council may be assisting to you in all affairs relating to our service, you are to communicate to them such and so many of these our instructions, wherein their advice is mentioned to be requisite, and likewise all such others from time to time as you shall find convenient for our service to be imparted to them."

Language could scarcely be more intelligible or free from ambiguity than was here employed, and let it be borne in mind, that these instructions were brought to this country by Governor Simcoe, who was also the bearer of the Constitution conferred upon this Province and which he was charged to put in operation. They were moreover delivered to him after the Constitutional Act had passed the British Parliament, and by the statesman who had conducted that great measure to maturity. (Hear, hear).

On Friday, the 16th December, 1836, Mr. Hagerman made his celebrated speech in the Assembly on the Clergy Reserves question, arguing forcibly that the Reserves set apart for the support of a Protestant Clergy in the Province should not be diverted from their original purpose to promote general education, or for any other purpose. As I write I have the speech before me; it was one of Mr. Hagerman's most able efforts. Happily the Clergy Reserves question, which caused so much bad feeling at the time, has been long since settled. I need not encumber the life of the Judge by any further reference to this great politico-religious controversy.

Mr. Hagerman was a man of very independent mind, and would not surrender his independence even if thereby he lost position or secured favor. This trait of his character is strongly exemplified in the action he thought proper to take during the Session of the Upper Canada Parliament in 1839. He was then Attorney General. His Excellency the Governor General had sent a message to the House recommending a Legislative Union between the Provinces of Upper and Lower Canada. Mr. Hagerman was opposed to the Union of the Provinces. While the House was in Session on 19th December, 1839, Mr. Hagerman gave his reasons for opposing the union. Some of which I will give as illustrating his independence of character, but which may be read with profit as of historical importance. He said:

> As it was my duty, I at a very early period after the arrival of the Governor-General, sought an interview with His Excellency, and respectfully but plainly stated the opinions I entertained on this great question, and declared that I should feel it my duty, as a matter of principle and honor, to vote against it, should it be brought under discussion. *I felt then, as I feel now, that upon receiving this communication his Excellency would have been fully justified in immediately dispensing with my services*; and that he did not do so I impute to the entire absence of that unjust and arbitrary disposition that would persecute a public servant for maintaining a long expressed opinion upon a question of vital interest to his country and which, until within a few months, had been concurred in by a government of which he was a member. Under these circumstances, I find myself for the first time during a Parliamentary career which commenced just twenty years ago, in direct opposition to a measure proposed by the authority of the Crown * * It may reasonably be supposed I would not now depart from my usual course, but for reasons of a very powerful nature; and this I may truly and emphatically declare to be the case. In the vote I am about to give, I firmly believe is involved the question of allegiance and as far as depends on my humble advice, the integrity of the Empire. Sir, I believe that the union of the Provinces of Upper and Lower Canada will place in imminent peril the connection of this country with the Parent State; and believing this, I cannot, I dare not, without violating the oath of allegiance I have so frequently and so willingly taken, vote in favour of this measure.
>
> The main grounds on which the union of the Provinces is recommended and advocated, are; First, that a Constitutional Government may be restored to Lower Cauada; and second, that the Province may be relieved from its financial difficulties by charging its public debt on the joint revenues of Upper and Lower Canada.
>
> I will endeavour to examine these two propositions separately; and with respect to the first, I desire to ask what claims Lower Canada has on this Province to consent to peril its very existence as a dependency of the British Crown for the purpose of restoring to it a government it has lost by open rebellion to its Sovereign, and which for years past it has used for the most factious and ungrateful purpose, and with singular

disregard for the peace, welfare, and prosperity of this Province? Sir, if we look back to the history of Lower Canada, it may be fearlessly asserted that no people on the face of the globe ever exhibited such proof of ingratitude to the best, and noblest, and most disinterested of benefactors. Nor did a people so recklessly and wickedly cast aside and repudiate the blessings that were offered for their acceptance, and never did a case occur in which fewer claims to the sympathy of loyal subjects have been established. When England became possessed of the Canadas by conquest, it might be said that its inhabitants were by that event emancipated from a state of thraldom approaching to slavery; and the freedom conferred upon them was that of British subjects, released from the vassalage in which they had been previously held by the feudal laws of the French Empire. The Criminal Law of England was speedily introduced, life and property were made secure, and the blessing of the British Constitution were gradually and generously conferred. Step by step did the Imperial Government proceed in its earnest desire to raise the Canadian people to the same social and political condition enjoyed by British subjects, and which would place within their reach the happiness and prosperity which the institutions of England are alone calculated to secure and perpetuate. The proclamation of 1763, the Act 14 George III., which established a Legislative Council, composed of persons resident in the Province, and who enacted some of the best laws on the Provincial statute book, and lastly granting the Constitution of 1791, the most perfect and liberal ever before or since conferred on any Colony, are striking and conclusive proofs of this assertion; and to that may be added the undeniable fact, that the government of the Province from the conquest to the present time, has been conducted with mildness and justice, and without affording the slightest ground for the factious and violent opposition that successive Governors have experienced from an ungrateful and unjustly dissatisfied people. Indeed it may be said that in proportion as benefits were heaped upon them did the hatred of the Lower Canadians toward everything British, the source of all their blessings, go on increasing, until at last they rose in open rebellion against their government and benefactors, and evinced that hatred to all of British origin that even Lord Durham has declared to be incredible * *

It is my belief that the best means for reconciling the Lower Canadians to British authority, British institutions, and British society, is by introducing a well organized system of education and by employing the resources of the country in improving the roads, forming canals, and making other obvious improvements, the benefits of which can be seen and felt. By this means you may at last convince these people, if any thing will convince them, that it is far better and more to their advantage to attach themselves to a party which is plainly seeking to preserve their peace, and increase their wealth and comfort, than to one that would embroil them in rebellion and misery. Let this experiment be tried for a few years, and then it will be fit to consider whether the Constitution of 1791 may not again be introduced.

The peroration of Mr. Hagerman's speech was eloquent, and secured the applause of the whole House. He said:

So strongly do I feel the fatal consequences of the measure, that were I permitted to approach my gracious Sovereign, I could, on my bended knees, implore Her Majesty to withhold her assent to it. I could humbly say to Her Majesty : I am the son of one of those loyal and devoted men who hazarded their lives, and shed their blood, and forfeited their estates in support of their allegiance to your Majesty's revered and illustrious ancestor. Driven from their once happy homes, they, in numberless thousands, took refuge in this Province, which was assigned them by their justly beloved King, where they and their descendants might live as British subjects, in the enjoyment of British laws, and British institutions. At the time of their first settlement the whole country was a wilderness, and the means of subsistence was for years scanty and precarious. They complained not of their privations, but laboured on in their endeavoring to establish their children in peace and independence, and to imbue their minds with love to their Sovereign, and a dutiful obedience to the laws and constitution of their Country. As they left this world—few, very few of them are living now—they had the happiness of seeing their most sanguine hopes of prosperity to their children fully realized. The forests had disappeared, fertile fields had spread over the land, and the whole Country was dotted with the habitations of half a million souls, possessing every comfort that could be desired by reasonable men, and a greater share of the blessings of this world than is to be found within the same space of the habitable globe. Too much prosperity led them to engage in undertakings for the improvement of their country, which has involved them in temporary embarrasments— and in a moment of despondency, they besought your Majesty to unite them with Lower Canada, and place under the control of the Legislature the Sea Ports of the Provinces. They were not insensible to the peril to the institutions of their Country, and the dangers that would be incurred by separation from Your Majesty's Crown and Empire, by becoming thus identified with half a million of people who had evidenced by open rebellion, their desire to be released from their allegiance, and gladly would they have sought and accepted any other means of relief. I would humbly remind Her Majesty that the British Nation did not think it too much to give twenty million sterling to release the slothful African from compulsory labour imposed upon him by long existing laws, and to wipe out the foul stain of domestic slavery, that rested upon the British Empire ; and I would venture to implore that £100,000 might be given, or the credit of the Nation might be pledged for that sum to her industrious, and enterprising and devoted subjects in this Province ; I would represent, that this favor granted, joy and happiness, contentment and prosperity would be extended to half a million of as devoted subjects as are to be found within the limits of Her Majesty's extensive and mighty Empire. The present dangerous weapon would then be no more thought of; the integrity of the Empire would be established, and secure in the permanency of their institutions and their connection with the parent State, Her Majesty's grateful people in Upper Canada would redouble their exertions to repay the generous gift, and the glory of having placed them in security and prosperity, would be no slight reward to Her Majesty, for her noble and parental interference in their behalf.

By the time the Rebellion of 1837 had broken out, Mr. Hagerman had succeeded to the Attorney-Generalship, to which place he was appointed on the 23rd March, 1837. Mr. Hagerman, in performing the duty of Crown officer at the Assizes, was generally considered to be more pungent than polite. He was a man of good presence, about six feet in height, with a large head and massive forehead, with intellectual organs all well developed. He was a formidable man for any one to meet, whether in the forensic arenas or on the floor of Parliament. What he wanted in grace of manner, he made up in intellectual strength. He was a wonderfully persuasive speaker, and could hold a jury of twelve, or a jury of a hundred, in or out of Parliament, spell-bound with his flow of eloquence and persuasive oratory. He was not unlike the Honorable William Ewart Gladstone in public discussion. He could, if need be, roar as a lion, or entrance an audience with silvery tones of the most mellow modulation. I have frequently heard him, when addressing the House, and even now bear in memory the hard hits of invective he used to indulge in when he thought it necessary to do so ; and then again the smooth, soothing sentences with which he would cover over the invective, leading on his auditory to adopt his view of the subject of debate.

In prosecuting those who were engaged in the rebellion of 1837, Mr. Hagerman brought down upon himself many a stricture and hostile criticism from those of the people and profession whose sympathies lay in the direction of the revolters to constituted authority. It was thought by them that milder doses of legal medicine might well have been administered than he was in the habit of prescribing.

Appeals made to him as Crown officer did not, as a general rule, receive a favorable response; he went on in the even way of prosecuting the offence whatever it might be, leaving the consequences to others.

People of the present day can hardly realize the state of things that existed then. Society seemed heaved up from the foundation; the terms Loyalist and Rebel were bandied about in wild confusion. Men as loyal as their neighbors with more pretension, were as loyal as they in heart, and loved their country as well; it was the administration of the affairs of the Country they complained of. All that then occurred must be left to history. Good men on both sides were not agreed, they seemed but to agree to disagree.

Mr. Hagerman, the Attorney-General, was no doubt a pronounced Tory, and would give no countenance to those he esteemed rebels. As Attorney General he had a difficult duty to perform, and it is not surprising that in the performance of it he incurred the odium of many who sympathized with those he was called on to prosecute.

Mr. Hagerman received his Patent as a Puisne Judge of the Court of Queen's Bench on the 15th of February, 1840. The cases of any importance in which Mr. Justice Hagerman gave judgment will be found in the second volume of the Upper Canada Reports. He was the Puisne Judge giving judgment in the case of Doe Irvine *vs.* Webster, reported in that volume and which I have referred to at large in the life of Mr. Justice Jones.

In this case Mr. Justice Hagerman differed from Chief Justice Robinson. In his judgment he argued the case at large giving very sound reasons for his conclusion, which was the same as that arrived at by Judge Macaulay the then senior Puisne Judge of the Court.

Any one reading these judgments will be of the opinion that the points involved are just such points as it would be desirable to have settled by the Privy Council, and indeed Sir John Robinson, in McLean *vs.* Laidlaw where the same point came up, expressed a wish that sometime the question should be reviewed by the Court of Appeal. The Chief Justice said:

> The doctrine of estoppel is likely to have a much more extensive application in this country than in England; and it has therefore been always much desired by the Court that the parties in some case would by a special verdict or otherwise place the question upon record in such a shape that the opinion of the Privy Council might be taken upon appeal.

In Doe Irvine *vs.* Webster, Mr. Justice Hagerman commenced his judgment by saying:

> It would be presumptuous in me to say that I have arrived at these conclusions free from all doubt as to their correctness, the difference of opinion which prevails among my learned brothers, and the able manner in which they have sustained their views, shews how much may reasonably be said on both sides, and sufficiently evinces the difficulty of coming to a determination altogether satisfactory on the important questions raised for the decision of the Court; but believing that certain admitted principles are opposed to the plaintiff's right to recover in this action, I have no alternative but to pronounce a judgment to that effect.

Chief Justice Robinson came to the exactly opposite conclusion. To shew how near they were to an agreement, we must refer further to Mr. Justice Hagerman's judgment, which demonstrates that if the party to whom the first conveyance was made had gone into possession, Judge Hagerman would have held that there was an estoppel. He says:

> I do not wish it to be understood that I give any opinion that would affect this case *if the party to whom the first conveyance was made had gone into possession,* and the attempt were made to eject him by the patentee of the Crown after obtaining his patent, or by any subsequent assignee or purchaser under him. In the first case the law of estoppel would probably be held to apply, and in the second the statute forbidding the purchase of pretended titles to land would very likely invalidate the conveyance. These, however, are cases that must be adjudicated as they arise. In the present instance, I am of opinion, upon the foregoing grounds, that judgment should be for the defendant, independently of any consideration that may arise from the operation of the Statute of Limitations.

Not only on the ground that there was no estoppel, but for other reasons, Mr. Justice Hagerman was of opinion that judgment should go for the defendant. His opinion was, that no title ought to be said to be acquired in Crown lands by a party dealing with them before the patent issued. He said :

> But there is a further consideration which in my opinion would be conclusive against the plaintiff in this case and which has been adverted to by his Lordship the Chief Justice, namely, that it must be regarded as most unreasonable, [and as I think against all law that any agreement, covenant, or conveyance entered into between two persons for the disposal of the Queen's domain, in the occupation of neither of them, and which it must have been known to both it was unlawful for them to interfere with, could attach to the land, or at any time constitute a legal title or give a right of occupation either to the grantee or any one claiming under him.

I will not quote from this judgment further—sufficient is shewn to prove that Mr. Justice Hagerman could have very decided opinions, and express them in very decided language.

There was another case in which Judge Hagerman gave judgment in which a point was determined, possessing some interest as regards claims against deceased persons' estates. The question was, whether in the case of a debt barred by the Statute of Limitations, an acknowledgment of the existence of the debt given by the executor without an express promise to pay the debt, was sufficient to take the case out of the Statute of Limitations ; and it was held that it was not, but an account stated by the executor of a debt due by his testator which had never before such accounting been ascertained or determined, was sufficient to charge the executor as a substantive debt without an express promise to pay. This case is reported in Upper Canada Queen's Bench Reports, 291. The judgments were by Chief Justice Robinson and Mr. Justice Hagerman, who took pains to examine into the authorities carefully before coming to a conclusion.

There are now only two parties living who were concerned in the case, namely, Clarke Gamble, Q.C., who was a witness; and Sir J. Lukin Robinson, who was Counsel for the plaintiff. A written acknowledgment of the debt was put in as given by Mr. Morrison, as agent for the executrix of Mr. Washburn, Attorney-at-Law. This was Mr. Justice Morrison, since deceased. Mr. Blake, afterwards Chancellor Blake and now deceased, was Counsel for the defence. The Judges who heard the case, and gave judgment, are no more.

I well recollect Judge Hagerman, and have practised before him. I remember him as a powerfully built, thick-set man, who filled his place on the Bench with dignity, and gave attention to arguments of the Bar. I find a case reported in 1846 where I moved a rule before him to set aside an arrest. The case is Barry *v.* Eccles, 2 U. C. Q. B. Rep. 383. After the arrest the parties had left all matters to arbitration. An award was made for a much smaller sum than the defendant had been arrested for. Judge Hagerman, on this ground, set aside the arrest. The case is impressed on my memory from the fact that it was the first in which I had ever moved to set aside an arrest; and also gives an opportunity of saying that the vile law of arrest as it then existed, by which a party could be arrested for debt on the ex parte affidavit of a plaintiff, and without the intervention of a Judge, has happily long since been repealed.

I do not find that Judge Hagerman was, for the few years he was on the Bench, called on for his judgment in very many important cases. He frequently held the Practice Court, which did not give much scope for the exercise of talent, and for a part of the time that he had the appointment of Judge he was absent in England. I believe he gave satisfaction as a Judge. I never in his life time heard that he was considered other than a painstaking upright Judge.

Mr. Hagerman was three times married. His first wife, Elizabeth Macaulay, was a sister of Sir James B. Macaulay, by whom he had three daughters and one son. Mrs. John Beverley Robinson, wife of the Hon. John Beverley Robinson, late Lieutenant-Governor of Ontario, was his daughter by his first wife. It may occur to many that the sweet voice with which she used to delight the people of Toronto when singing for charities, was a family gift, inasmuch as her father was likewise so gifted.

Judge Hagerman, after the death of his first wife, married Emily Merry, who died, leaving one daughter, and in 1846, after his appointment to the Bench, he went to England, where he married Caroline Tysen, an English lady, who, on her introduction to Toronto, was pronounced a lady of that English type, which is generally considered *par excellence* the perfection of womanhood.

The Judge did not long survive his third marriage. He died at Toronto on the 14th May, 1847. I may be permitted to quote from the monument erected to his memory in St. James's Cemetry by his daughter Mrs. Beverley Robinson without giving the whole inscription. After the heading of " Sacred to the memory, &c.", the inscription states that he " died in Toronto on the 14th May, 1847. Endowed with a quick and clear perception and a strong understanding and by nature eloquent, he discharged his duties with credit to himself and advantage to the Province."

The inscription contains other terms of endearment which I need not transcribe. I think Mrs. Robinson has, in that part of the inscription I do quote, given what was the general estimate of the Judge, by those who knew him, and is deserving of regard for so perpetuating the memory of her distinguished father. A daughter's sacred tribute to his worth, the conclusion of the inscription is as touching as it is responsive. " His affectionate daughter erected this to his memory."

XVIII.

The Honorable William Henry Draper, C.B., Chief Justice of Upper Canada.

WILLIAM HENRY DRAPER was an Englishman, the son of English parents, and was born in the Surrey Suburbs of London, on the 11th March, 1801. His father was a clergyman of the Church of England, the Reverend Henry Draper, who was successively Rector of St. Anthony's Church, in the heart of London, and of South Brent, in Devonshire. It was while the Reverend Henry Draper was Rector of St. Anthony's that William Henry Draper was born. He had not yet got out of his teens, had, indeed, but just entered them, when he, like many another boy of the great metropolis of the world, conceived a passion for a seafaring life. To gratify this passion he is said to have taken French leave, and run away from home. The sea, the open sea, had a charm for him which he could not resist. He had not long to wait before an opportunity offered itself of securing a Cadetship on an East-Indiaman. How many voyages he made I have not been able to ascertain. He, it is certain, stuck to the ship till he was eighteen years of age, when he made a pause, and soon after emigrated to America. He arrived in Canada early in the summer of 1820, then in his twentieth year. Stranded on the shores of this to him unknown land, with a scant purse, but a good deal of experience, he looked about him for some occupation to gain a livelihood. He made his way to Port Hope, in the County of Durham; not a considerable place at that time, but a place where the people had a proper appreciation of education.

Young Draper was of manly bearing and good attainments. In his early youth he had been given a good education; was no stranger to the dead languages, and proficient in the living tongues. He soon secured employment as a school teacher, at Port Hope, and faithfully pursued this employment for two or three years, when he tired of it, aiming at higher things. Mr. Thomas Ward was at this time a practising barrister in Port Hope who was well esteemed, and had a good practice in his profession. Mr. Ward took a lively interest in the young sailor and school teacher, and offered Mr. Draper a place in his office if the young man could gain admission to the Law Society.

Mr. Draper's school teaching was a good introduction for him in his new venture of becoming a Law Student. He proceeded to York, and in Easter Term 4 George IV., 1821, he was duly admitted a Student of the Law by the Benchers of the Law Society. Returning to Port Hope he continued his studies with Mr. Ward till 1825, when he entered the office of the Honorable George Boulton for the completion of his studies. His aptitude for business while here, and general knowledge soon secured for him an appointment which not only gave him steady employment but some emolument. While yet a student of Mr. Boulton he was appointed Deputy Registrar of the United Counties of Northumberland and Durham. He did more than this, for, during the same time he became a married man, taking to himself a wife in the person of a Miss White, daughter of Captain George White of the Royal Navy. In 1828 he made another trip to York, passed his examination, and in Trinity Term 9 George IV., 1828, was called to the Bar.

Mr. Draper had prepared himself for the hard work of the Bar, not only by his experience at sea, but by hard work on land. While he was Deputy Registrar he resided at Port Hope: the Registry Office was at Cobourg, seven miles away. It was his custom to make daily visits to his office, walking both ways: being of vigorous constitution and robust habits he had no difficulty in doing this. He was one of those who then and ever after during life believed in healthy exercise, "*Mens Sana in Corpore Sano.*"

Those who knew him in after life, as I did, will bear testimony to this in the recollection of the skill and endurance he exhibited in the manly game of cricket.

Mr. Draper had only been a short time at the Bar when the then Attorney-General, the Honorable John Beverley Robinson, afterwards Chief Justice, had occasion to be at the Coburg Assizes. A brief had been prepared for him in a case which he was conducting; the brief was so well got up, shewing so much knowledge and skill, that the Attorney-General at once determined to have its compiler in his office in York. The Attorney-General at once made an offer to Mr. Draper of a good position in his office which the young barrister accepted. He removed to York and entered on his duties with the Attorney-General, opening up to himself an avenue which led to his future success in life. The Attorney-General had at this time an immense business, and thus was afforded to Mr. Draper a chance of making his mark. Applying himself diligently both to civil and criminal law he soon gained a reputation second to none of his time. In November, 1829, he was appointed Reporter of the King's Bench. Draper's Reports on the shelves of the Library of Osgoode Hall, are evidence of his work as Reporter. In Hilary Term 5 William IV., 1830, the Benchers of the Law Society appointed him one of their body.

It will thus be seen that the promotion of Mr. Draper was as speedy as it was deserved. Few men starting as he did, literally casting himself on the sea of life, voyaging on the great deep, have come to port with more flying colours than he.

In politics he was a Tory.

The Tories on the the arrival of Sir Francis Bond Head in the Province, in 1836, determined if possible to capture the new Governor who had come out under Reform auspices. It is a matter of history that when Sir Francis Head assumed the reins of government there were only three Executive Councillors, and that he, deeming it expedient to increase the number, invited Mr. Robert Baldwin to a seat in the Council, which Mr. Baldwin at first declined, as he did not find that he was in accord with the Governor as to the theory of Responsible Government. The Governor having secured the services of two other prominent Reformers, the Honorable J. H. Dunn, Receiver-General, a Liberal Englishman, and Doctor Rolph. Mr. Baldwin consented to act with their addition, and the three were accordingly sworn in.

These Councillors had not been in office many days before they ascertained that, after all, the Governor instead of consulting his Council on the public affairs of the Province, had made up his mind to follow in the wake of his predecessors, and, by the uncontrolled exercise of the Royal Prerogative, to govern the country in his own way, irrespective of his Council. On this stand being taken the Council resigned in a body. This brought about a crisis in the affairs of the country, and parties became completely divided. The Prerogative men stood by the Governor, while the Reformers claimed that they had been deceived by his Excellency. The only way out of the difficulty was to appeal to the people. This brought about the exciting elections of 1836.

Mr. Draper was a candidate for the suffrage of the electors of Toronto in this election, and received a majority of votes, and was returned to represent the capital in the Assembly: this was the beginning of Mr. Draper's political life.

Mr. Draper, being now in Parliament, was ripe for a government appointment, nor had he long to wait. In 1837, Lord Glenelg, the then Colonial Secretary wrote a despatch to the Governor, Sir Francis Bond Head, in answer to a despatch of Sir Francis to him, in which, after recommending three judicial appointments, he recommended Mr. Hagerman and Mr. Draper as Attorney and Solicitor-General. On this recommendation Mr. Draper was, on the 23rd March, 1837, appointed Solicitor-General, an office which he was eminently qualified to fill.

Sir Francis Head, however, by this time was beginning to disregard the instructions of the Colonial Office, and was forced to resign the Governorship. The Colonial Secretary, Lord Glenelg, on the 24th November, 1837, accepting his resignation very plainly gave him to understand that while he confirmed Mr. Hagerman and Mr. Draper in their appointments of Attorney and Solicitor-General, he totally disapproved of the removal from office of another official, Mr. George Ridout, whom he had removed for political reasons. In the Autumn of 1837 Mr. Draper was appointed a member of the Executive Council.

After the resignation of Sir Francis Head as Governor, and his exit, the incoming Governor Sir George Arthur, on assuming office appointed Mr. Draper his aide-de-camp which appointment he continued to hold during the Rebellion, and, in 1838, was appointed Colonel of a York battalion. In 1840 he was appointed Attorney-General, as successor to Mr. Hagerman who was appointed to the Bench.

The time was now approaching when it was evident to most men that a change must take place in the management of Canadian affairs. During the Session of the Imperial Parliament 1839, a Bill for re-uniting the Provinces of Upper and Lower Canada had been introduced into the British Parliament by Lord John Russell.

It was thought, and properly thought, desirable before passing such a bill to obtain the formal concurrence of the Canadians, as expressed through their respective Legislatures. To obtain the consent of those Legislatures it was deemed essential to send out a properly authorized officer to Canada, who should be able to explain the views of the British Government in regard to a Union of the Provinces.

The person selected for this office was Mr. Charles Poulett Thompson, a member of the British Parliament, of acknowledged tact and ability. Perhaps no better man could have been selected for the work to be done. He sailed for Quebec on the 17th October, 1839, and summoned the Lower Canada Council to meet on the 18th November, 1839. The Upper Canada Parliament, in Session the same year, had the Draft Bill of Union sent out by the British Parliament submitted to them also. The Bill was not in itself acceptable to either the Lower or Upper Canada Representatives; but still, with the powerful influence of Mr. Poulett Thompson, afterwards Lord Sydenham, the Bill, with some amendments, was sent back to England crystallized into an Act of Parliament (the Act of Union), which was finally passed by the British Parliament, and by a Proclamation of the 5th February, 1841, issued under the hand of Dominick Daly, Provincial Secretary, declared to come into effect on the 10th February, 1841.

On the 13th February, 1841, three days after the Proclamation of Union took effect, His Excellency Lord Sydenham called to his Executive Council eight gentlemen who already occupied the highest offices of State, namely, Messrs. Sullivan, Dunn, Daly, Harrison, Ogden, Draper, Baldwin, and Day; and on 17th March, 1841, added H. H. Killaly. It is thus seen that Mr. Draper, who, before the Union, had occupied one of the highest offices of State as Attorney-General, becomes a member of a Coalition Ministry after the Union; many of the members, Mr. Baldwin among the number, having been pronounced Reformers, while Mr. Draper had all his life been a pronounced Tory.

Mr. Draper, at the request of Lord Sydenham, retained his office of Attorney-General for Upper Canada in this Ministry for a brief period, sharing the Leadership of the Ministerial party in Upper Canada with the Honorable S. B. Harrison.

The elements of discord were not long, however, kept under in a Ministry so composed. There is no doubt the members of the Ministry were actuated by the desire to promote the interests of their common country. There was no man in it, however, of more independent mind, or more resolved to have the Goverment carried on in strict accordance with British precedent, than the Honorable Robert Baldwin. It was simply a question with him whether the Governor was to rule, or the people through their responsible advisers.

At the beginning of the Session of 1842 Mr. Baldwin resigned his position as member of the Ministry.

Mr. Draper from the first had opposed the union of the Provinces. That union had been brought about by Lord Sydenham who had surrounded himself with an administration the majority of whom were antagonistic to the views of Mr. Draper and those who acted with him. Notwithstanding the resignation of Mr. Baldwin, Mr. Draper continued to hold the office of Attorney-General and his place in the ministry hoping in the near future more harmony would prevail. This, however, was not the case, and before many months the whole ministry resigned.

By 1843 the Rebellion had been crushed out, and a totally new order of things was existing. Mr. Baldwin, for Upper Canada, and Mr. Lafontaine, for Lower Canada, had succeeded in securing the reins of power, and held office of chief advisers of the Governor from the union of 1841 onwards. In the same year the British Government thought proper to appoint Sir Charles Metcalfe Governor in the place of Sir Charles Bagot the successor of Lord Sydenham.

Sir Charles Metcalfe was essentially a Prerogative man, and nothing was more natural than that he should distrust the Baldwin-Lafontaine administration, which had entirely rejected Prerogative for Responsible Government; nothing more natural also than that he should take into his confidence an able, willing, and in every way true Prerogative minister. Such a minister he found in Mr. Draper.

During the whole season of 1844, Sir Charles, with the single aid of Mr. Draper, managed to carry on the executive business of the country.

Sir Charles had been in office in the East Indies, and had become enamored of despotic rule. Was he not Governor? Why should he be encumbered with a minister or ministers who had the confidence of the people? It was true that Mr. Baldwin and his confreres had a majority in Parliament. No matter, it was enough for the Governor that Mr. Baldwin and his friends did not enjoy *his* confidence. Sir Charles Metcalfe, in order to carry out his views, in the Autumn of 1844 brought about the resignation of the Baldwin-Lafontaine ministry, and threw himself into the arms of Mr. Draper. Mr. Draper a man of courage as well as ability was not at all appalled at the task of forming a new ministry, and he succeeded in the work of forming one to fill a gap. The new ministers were:

 James Smith, Attorney-General, East,
 William Henry Draper, Attorney-General, West,
 D. J. Papineau, Commissioner of Crown Lands,
 William Morris, Receiver-General,
 D. B. Viger, President of the Council,
 Dominick Daly, Provincial Secretary.

To form a ministry, is one thing, to get the people to accept that ministry, another.

New elections were ordered which came on late in the Autumn of 1844. It was a most exciting time in the Province, the issue being a direct one between the Governor and the people. Responsible Government in its new dress was on its trial. Mr. Draper affected to believe that now that the new system had been adopted, his ministry should possess the confidence of the people. He offered himself as a candidate for the City of London, told the constituency that he intended to carry on the Government on English principles, but at the same time in his address to the electors he adroitly asked the people to support the Governor, Sir Charles Metcalfe.

The electors of London returned Mr. Draper as their representative. It is alleged by those who were opposed to him that, having gained his seat, he forgot his pledges and the true principle of responsible government which required that a Minister, being defeated on a government measure by a majority of the House, should resign.

Mr. Draper stated at the beginning of the Session after the election that he would stand or fall by the University Bill, which he introduced into the House, but found that his supporters were not as favorable to the Bill as he expected. Many of his followers shirked the vote, and left the House. This rebellion in the ranks induced him to withdraw the Bill on the second reading; but the Minister did not resign. It may be that he thought a withdrawal of the Bill was not a defeat.

There was no man in the Parliaments of which Mr. Draper was a member, who could so readily enforce a dogma or turn a period as Mr. Draper. He was a most eloquent speaker, with a silver tongue and blandness of manner that had a mighty power in Parliament. A writer has said of him: "His tact and dexterity in passing measures through the House, were unrivalled." At the Bar he was considered one of the best of his class to influence the minds of a jury. His reasoning powers were of the first order, though perhaps technical : given any subject, he would first deal with it in all its aspects with the mind of a philosopher, and coming to a conclusion enforce it with the tongue of an orator. He acquired from some the soubriquet of "Sweet William,"—his mellifluous tones and winning manners may well have entitled him to the distinction. He was for some time a partner with Mr. Hagerman. The firm of Hagerman & Draper practised in Toronto, had a large business, and generally had the confidence of the public.

Mr. Draper's Parliamentary life after the arrival of Lord Elgin in the country as Governor, became irksome to him. Lord Elgin inclined to govern the country under Liberal auspices, which was distasteful to Mr. Draper. He had, before the advent of Lord Elgin, enjoyed the confidence of several Governors; he had represented two constituencies, Toronto and London, and could well afford to lay down the sceptre which he had for a long time wielded in Parliament for the more quiet seclusion of the Bench.

In 1847 Mr. Draper withdrew from Parliamentary life, and accepted a seat in the Queen's Bench, of which Court he was appointed a Puisne Judge on the 12th June, 1847. He was made a Companion of the Bath in 1854.

In the life of the Honorable Archibald McLean Chief Justice of the Queen's Bench, I have referred to the case of John Anderson which came before that Court in Michaelmas Term, 1860, on a habeas corpus issued at the instance of Anderson whose extradition was sought by the American Government. When the case came before the Court of Queen's Bench, after full argument, the Court was divided as to the legality of the proceedings. Mr. Justice McLean taking the ground that Anderson was in Canada on free soil, and was entitled to all its rights and privileges: that in escaping from the United States and the slavery to which he had been doomed he was justified "in using any necessary degree of force to prevent what to him must have proved a most fearful evil. He was committing no crime in endeavoring to escape and better his own condition, and the fact of his being a slave, can not in my humble judgment make that a crime which would not be so if he were a white man."

In the Queen's Bench Mr. Justice McLean was prepared to give effect to the technical objections to the warrant of commitment made out by the Justices in Brantford, before whom the prisoner had been brought and committed.

Anderson gained nothing by his motion in the Queen's Bench, was re-committed, and stood a good chance of being sent back into slavery. When the result of the decision became known the excitement was at fever heat in Toronto. He was a man, though a black one, and he excited a great deal of interest by his demeanor, and from the daring way in which he had effected his escape from slavery. It was fortunate for Anderson that he had as his counsel a most able and experienced counsel. Mr. S. B. Freeman, Q.C., had charge of his case from the beginning: the more he was baffled, the more strength he seemed to get: not daunted by the Queen's Bench declining to give Anderson his freedom, he brought the case before the Court of Common Pleas, in which Chief Justice Draper presided, on the same facts that had been brought before the Queen's Bench. I refer to the life of Chief Justice McLean for those facts. The following objections were taken to the warrant of commitment before Chief Justice Draper in the Common Pleas:

1st. That it was not issued in conformity with the statute, because—it did not contain a charge of murder, but merely of felonious homicide—whereas the treaty and the Canadian statute did not authorize a surrender, and consequently not a committal for the purpose of surrender for any homicide *not expressed to be murder.*

2nd. That it was not expressed to be for the purpose of surrender, but only until the prisoner should be discharged in due course of law, whereas the statute requires both.

3rd. That the Magistrate had no jurisdiction unless and until the prisoner had been charged with the crime in the foreign country where it was alleged to have been committed.

Chief Justice Draper, in giving judgment, stated that it had been argued by the prisoner's counsel that the Court had no inherent jurisdiction over offences committed in the United States: that the Court had no authority in the matter, except such as was given to them by the Canadian Extradition Act: that that Act did not give the Court power to do any one of the acts to effectuate the objects of the Extradition Treaty between England and the United States, and consequently that the *sole* power to act on the claim of extradition was the Executive

Government, which could if it chose, review the decision of the committing Magistrates.

It will be recollected that **the Court of Queen's Bench** had exercised the power of interfering, and had **made a rule re-committing** Anderson **to jail.** Chief Justice Draper, referring to this, said :

> The effect of **the** rule in question (Queen's Bench **rule**) **is** merely to remand the prisoner on the Magistrate's warrant, **or to** commit him by the authority of the Court alone. After a long and **most** anxious consideration, I have formed the opinion that the rule is not sustainable in either view. I have already given my reasons for thinking the warrant defective, and if the prisoner be remanded on that he must be discharged.

As to the other objections, the Chief Justice held the third objection good, that the Court had no jurisdiction till the prisoner had been charged with the crime in the foreign country.

Referring to the power of the Court of Common Pleas to interfere with the rule of the Queen's Bench he said :

> The rule of the Court of Queen's Bench is objected **to** as being beyond the power of the Court, and I enter somewhat **unwillingly** upon its consideration. We are in fact called upon **to reverse and** supersede the action of a Court of co-ordinate jurisdiction and not in any appellate, but in our ordinary character. But we have no alternative, for the prisoner *has a right* on this application to the benefit of our opinion if it should be in his favour.

The Chief Justice also held the warrant of **commitment** to be defective as it concluded by directing the jailer "him **(Anderson) safely to** keep until he should be discharged by due course of law," whereas to be in conformity with the statute it should have concluded, " him safely to keep until he should be discharged *in due course of law or until such surrender be made."*

The Chief Justice could not see a way of getting over the express words of the statute, not only in this particular but in another, viz., the warrant **of commitment** did not in express terms state that the prisoner had been charged with murder which in the opinion of the Chief Justice was essential.

30—L. J.

It was argued before the Court that the defects in the warrant might be cured by the evidence taken in the United States. To this the Chief Justice answered that he had referred to Bessett's Case, 6 Q. B. 481, who had been committed on the Imperial Act 6 and 7 Victoria, cap. 75, passed to carry into effect the Extradition Treaty between England and France, which was similar to the Canadian statute passed to give effect to the Treaty between England and the United States, and then said:

> It is true it does not appear in Ex parte Bessett that the depositions were before the Court, I infer they were not, but nevertheless the language used by the Judges clearly express to my mind their opinion that they had no authority to look at them for the purpose of supplying any defect in the warrant. The result is, that in my opinion the return to the writ of habeas corpus shews no sufficient ground for the prisoner's detention. He ought, therefore, to be discharged, and whatever conclusion I arrive at on the more general grounds on his behalf, the result must be the same.

The Chief Justice never did come to any conclusion on the general ground seized upon and so ably advocated by Mr. Justice McLean in the Queen's Bench, viz., that the prisoner had not committed murder in freeing himself from slavery. Nevertheless on the other grounds he adjudged the prisoner entitled to his liberty, the great aim and object of the motion for his discharge on habeas corpus.

The Chief Justice's subtle mind and strict interpretation of law proved a great boon to the swarthy son of Africa on this memorable occasion.

Mr. Justice Draper continued to perform his duties to the satisfaction of the public as Judge of the Court of Queen's Bench for nearly seven years after his appointment, and on the retirement of Sir James Macaulay from the Chiefship of the Common Pleas, he was appointed to the Chief Justiceship of that Court on the 6th February, 1856.

It is matter of Bar and Judicial history that his appointment to the Chiefship of this Court, over the head of his senior Judge McLean, gave grave offence in certain quarters. Judge McLean resigned his Judgeship of the Queen's Bench, which he had held for nearly twenty years, in consequence of what he considered a slight of the Minister of the day, but was induced by his friends to withdraw his resignation, accepting the same day the Senior Puisne Judgeship of the Queen's Bench. This accounts for the public records shewing two appointments of Judge McLean as Puisne Judge of the Queen's Bench, one in 1837, and the other on the 5th of February, 1856.

There is no doubt that Mr. Justice McLean aspired to a Chief Justiceship, and this he eventually reached in 1862, thus becoming the Chief Justice of the Senior Court before Mr. Draper, who was appointed its Chief in July, 1863. The Bar hailed with satisfaction his promotion to this office, regarding him as in every sense a lawyer who administered law for law's sake.

Chief Justice Draper was essentially a man of law. The great characteristic of his judicial life was, that in administering law he made it a point always to dissever law from fact in so plain a manner that he left it to a jury to determine fact, peculiarly within their province, always himself taking the law of the case into his own control, so that juries knew exactly what they had to do. There was no muddling of the matter with him, and so the jury never became muddled. He did not throw the case at their head, telling them to make the best of it; but clearly and distinctly enunciated the law, telling the jury with that they had nothing to do, and then clearly and critically called the jury's attention to the facts which they had to determine.

In Banc he always listened with the utmost attention to counsel, senior or junior, making no distinction, always aiming at getting at the justice of a case, within the rules of law applicable to the subject.

In 1869 he was appointed President of the Court of Appeal.

In concluding this memoir of his life I think I can do

no better than quote from the historical work of an author (Dent), who, as far as I know, did not hold the same political opinions as Chief Justice Draper before his appointment to the Bench, but who, in his "History of the last Forty Years," has truly said :

> Fortunately he has left a judicial record which all persons, of whatsoever shades of political opinion, must unite in admiring. For more than thirty years he adorned the judicial Bench of which his descendants may justly feel proud.

The Chief Justice died at his residence in Yorkville, on the 3rd November, 1877, and was buried in St. James's Cemetry, lamented by the members of a Bar of which he had been a most distinguished member, and by a Bench of which he had been an ornament.

XIX.

THE HONORABLE ROBERT BALDWIN SULLIVAN, JUDGE OF THE QUEEN'S BENCH AND COMMON PLEAS.

LORD BROUGHAM, in his treatise on the British Constitution, by way of introduction, said, that the Constitution had been likened to a pyramid with a broad base, supporting the whole, which was formed by the people; that the middle portion was the aristocracy of rank, property, talents, and acquirements; and on the narrow summit rested the Crown. The judicial power, pure and unsullied, calmly exercised by men independent of all the other orders, removed from all faction, and partaking neither its fury nor its delusions, formed a mighty zone which girded the fabric round about, connecting the loftier and narrower with the humbler and broader layers, binding the whole compactly together, repressing the encroachments, and smoothing the ruggedness of every part.

Robert Baldwin Sullivan was one of the builders of the Canadian Constitution of 1841. Besides being a Judge in the Province, he was the architect of his own fortune. To properly understand him it will be necessary to begin at the foundation, and trace him up till he reached that eminence which gives him a foremost place in Canadian history.

Mr. Sullivan was an Irish boy, born of Irish parents who lived at Bandon, near Cork, in Ireland. His father,

Daniel Sullivan, during the troubles of 1798, was engaged in trade, making money, if not a fortune, supplying the troops with necessaries during that remarkable period of Irish history.

Daniel Sullivan had been intended for the Church, was a student at Trinity College, carried off the Greek prize, and was otherwise well educated in Classical learning. He was a man of conscientious principles, as well as of conscientious scruples. When the full time came for his taking on himself the vows of the ministry, he quarrelled with the Thirty-nine Articles: rather than submit, he betook himself to trade. Hence he became dealer in merchandize rather than Church doctrines. He was a Protestant with all that name implied, but quailed before the Articles. He married Miss Baldwin, sister of Doctor Baldwin, whose name is so familiar to Canadians of the past, as well as of the present century. Daniel Sullivan had four sons, Daniel, Robert, Henry, and Augustus.

Robert was the second son, and was born at Bandon, on the 24th May, in the year 1802. He was from childhood a bright, intelligent boy, quick to learn, and what was better, able to retain in a remarkable degree, any knowledge he acquired. His early education was obtained at the principal private school of Bandon, supplemented by his father, who instructed him in the Classics and higher education.

In 1819, when he was but 17 years of age, Dr. Baldwin and others of the Baldwin family induced Robert Sullivan's father to emigrate, and make Canada his future home. Dr. Baldwin was then living in York, and had acquired a reputation in this new town in Canada, both as Doctor of Medicine and Lawyer. Dr. Baldwin was also at this time a member of the Legislature of the Province. Mr. Sullivan, in leaving Ireland to make a home in Canada, was not coming among strangers, his brother-in-law the Doctor having raised for himself a sure foundation in the new land. An incident of his travel has been told to me, which I would not if I could omit, as it serves to illustrate the estimate in which the Baldwins were held, even at places remote from the Capital. I believe I am correct in saying that the honesty and honest independence of the Baldwins has ever been proverbial in Canada.

Mr. Daniel Sullivan entered Canada at the port of Quebec; thence he and his family pursued the usual route from Quebec to Montreal by steamer; thence to Lachine by land, and onward up the St. Lawrence by batteaux.

It was customary in those days, when batteaux had to be dragged up the rapids and poled up the river, for passengers occasionally to land and visit settlers on the margin of the river. Mr. Sullivan landed at a place between the rapids and Kingston, and entered a farm house owned by Mrs. Strange. As was natural, Mrs. Strange enquired of Mr. Sullivan where he came, from and whither he was going: his dialect pretty well answered the former, but not the latter enquiry. On telling Mrs. Strange, however, that he was bound for York, she cautioned him to beware of the Lawyers in that town; that there was but one honest Lawyer in it, *and that was Dr. Baldwin*. We can well understand with what zest Mr. Sullivan enjoyed the joke, thus advised by a stranger in a strange land of this characteristic feature of his own brother-in-law. After that he had no reason to doubt that there was at least one person in Western Canada, who thought there was one honest Lawyer in the country, at any rate.

When Mr. Daniel Sullivan arrived in Toronto, acting on the advice of friends, he embarked in trade, and opened a general store, just east of where St. James's Church now stands, on King Street.

As was the custom in those days, the boys of the family were useful to him in shop work. This, however, did not long suit his son Robert. His mind was too well stored with knowledge, to make of the weighing and measuring of store goods a permanent employment. Doctor Baldwin his uncle, was engaged both in medical pursuits and in law. Robert Sullivan, in choosing for himself a profession, preferred the law. The education he had received in Ireland, now served him in good stead. Applying himself to his books he prepared himself to become a law student and was, as student, entered in the books of the Law Society, in Michaelmas Term, 4 George IV., 1823. On passing his examination he entered his uncle Doctor Baldwin's office, where he passed his five years of probation, and was called to the Bar in Michaelmas Term, 9 George IV., 1828.

During his studies in Doctor Baldwin's office, he was able to devote a portion of his time to another pursuit. Just then the Library of Parliament was in want of a Librarian. His knowledge of books and Dr. Baldwin's influence secured for him this office—it can hardly be termed an office—I should rather say it was an occupation.

As soon as Mr. Sullivan was called to the Bar, he determined to strike out for himself. Doctor Rolph, who had lived at Vittoria, in the County of Norfolk, had made up his mind to remove from that place. Mr. Sullivan thought that this offered an opening for him, to enter upon the practice of his profession at Vittoria; true, it was remote from the capital; but this did not signify to him— he was determined to exercise his talents at the beginning, in some place, where if success were to be his future, it would be based on his own merits; he never was a man to shine with borrowed light. He had been in Vittoria but a few years, when he was called upon by Dr. Morrison and his friends, to act as his counsel before the Legislative Assembly in his contest with Mr. (afterwards Chief Justice Sir) John Beverley Robinson, for the Parliamentary Seat of York. This was a spirited contest, not only out of, but in Parliament, and resulted in Mr. Robinson retaining his seat.

Mr. Sullivan acquitted himself so well before the Legislature in this trial of strength, that friends at once took him by the hand, and insisted on his coming to York, where he would receive their patronage and support. This was in the year 1830, when he was but 29 years of age. Mr. Sullivan could not but accept this flattering offer, and about this time moved from Vittoria to the Capital, where he became a junior partner in the office of his uncle.

When he had made his home in York, he soon rose into popular favor, as is evidenced by the fact that he had not been a resident of the place more than five years, when he was elected Mayor of Toronto, over William Lyon Mackenzie, who was his opponent for the mayoralty in 1835. Mr. Mackenzie was Mayor of Toronto the year previous, but was not able to hold the position the second year against Mr. Sullivan, who had been elected member of the council for St. David's ward.

William Lyon Mackenzie had brought himself into discredit with the majority of the Council of Toronto, (who at that day elected their Mayor,) by publicly approving a letter of Mr. Joseph Hume, a member of the British Parliament, addressed to Mr. Mackenzie, in which Mr. Hume referred in strong terms to the "baneful domination of the Mother country," and expressed a hope that the subsisting connection would terminate. Although Mr. Sullivan was supposed to have Reform views, from the fact that he was a partner in the office of Baldwin & Son, and that Dr. Baldwin and his son Robert, respectively uncle and cousin, had identified themselves with the Reform party, yet neither the Baldwins nor Mr. Sullivan held any such extreme views as those expressed by Mr. Hume, and endorsed by Mr. Mackenzie. That these gentlemen were Reformers is a well established fact of history; but they were conservative Reformers, not given to change for change sake, but seeking to build up a new country strictly on the lines of the Mother land.

Mr. Sullivan, being elected mayor, applied himself vigorously in advancing the progress of old York, now Toronto City and the Capital of the Province, in the matter of drainage and other works of necessary improvement.

It was during Mr. Sullivan's mayoralty that the citizens of Toronto had occasion to convey their thanks, through the Mayor, to the Lieutenant-Governor, as representing the Queen, for the liberality of the Crown in assisting them to complete the bridges across the Don, thought to be of the greatest importance, as leading to the peninsula opposite the town. The occasion of the presentation of this address might be said to be a great day, a white letter day, in the annals of the city. The formalities observed on the occasion were as follows: The civic authorities approached the new structure in procession; a barricade at the first bridge arrested their progress; a guard stationed there also forbade further advance; the officer in command (Captain Bonnycastle) appeared, and the Mayor (Mr. Sullivan) and corporation were informed that the two bridges were, by the command of the Lieutenant-Governor, presented to them as a free gift, for the benefit of the inhabitants, that they might in all time to come be enabled to enjoy the salubrious air of the peninsula. The Mayor, arrayed in an official robe of purple velvet lined with scarlet, read a reply to Captain Bonnycastle, expressing thanks to the Governor for the bounty of the Sovereign. He said, among other things:

> In the name of the Common Council and the citizens of Toronto, I beg you to convey to His Excellency the grateful feelings with which this new instance of the bounty of our Most Gracious Sovereign is received; and I take this occasion, on behalf of the city, to renew our assurances of loyalty and attachment to His Majesty's person and Government, and to pray, through His Excellency, a continuance of Royal favor towards this city.

After the Mayor had read the address, the band, which was stationed on the bridge, struck up "God save the King," during the performance of which the members of the council, followed by a large number of the inhabitants, passed uncovered over the bridge. After the usual cheers the ceremonies came to an end.

The City Council has kept in remembrance the second mayor by a portrait of Mr. Sullivan, which hangs on the walls of the Mayor's office at the City Hall.

Mr. Sullivan's term of office as Mayor having expired, he was not long in being sought after for further and higher employment. The early months of the year 1836 find Sir Francis Bond Head the Lieutenant-Governor of the Province.

Sir Francis Head, on assuming office, found himself surrounded by a Council of the old Tory school. These Councillors were Peter Robinson, Commissioner of Crown Lands; G. H. Markland, Inspector-General; and Lieutenant-Colonel Joseph Wells, Bursar of King's College. Either influenced by instructions from the Colonial Secretary, or from some other cause, Sir Francis determined to have a Council composed of the leaders of both parties, Tory and Reform. He first sought the advice of Robert Baldwin, and offered him a place in his Council. Mr. Baldwin would not accept a place in the Council, except on one condition, and that was, that he had the entire confidence of the Governor, and that Responsible Government should be established. Mr. Baldwin frankly told the Governor that he had no confidence in the other members of the Council. The Governor would not accept Mr. Baldwin's conditions, and Mr. Baldwin consequently declined to accept a place in the Council.

After a time had elapsed, Sir Francis sent again for Mr. Baldwin, and requested him to reconsider the matter, to state whom if any other new advisers than himself he would suggest to be called to the Council and that he, the Governor, would try to accommodate himself to his views. Mr. Baldwin to close the negotiations desired the Governor to call to the Council Doctor Rolph and Mr. Dunn. The Governor complied with this request and called these gentlemen to the Council. They had not long been members, however, when they found that his Excellency was making appointments on his own responsibility, without consulting his Council, and that they were kept in ignorance of administrative acts, for which, nevertheless, public opinion held them responsible. This was carrying on the business of the country in a way so entirely different from that which the Council had supposed the Governor would pursue, that they retired in a body, the old members as well as the new, and so the Governor was left without any Council. This was a sad state of affairs for him to be placed in, and likely to prove disastrous to the Province.

The Governor knowing, or having heard of the distinguished ability of Robert Sullivan, sent for him, and sought his advice.

In the general election of 1836, a House hostile to the existing state of things had been elected. Parliament was called to meet in November of that year. The Governor was certainly in a dilemma, and needed advice. Mr. Sullivan was a non-partizan man; he was just the kind of adviser the Governor required in such a crisis. He was selected as adviser more on account of his talents than his politics. He was not alone in entering the Council, others, viz., the Honorable William Allan, Captain (afterwards Admiral) Augustus Baldwin, uncle of Robert Baldwin, and John Elmsley, were called to the Council with Mr. Sullivan. Mr. Draper (afterwards Chief Justice Draper) was soon after added.

Mr. Sullivan has sometimes been called a Tory or Conservative, sometimes a Reformer; the fact is, he was *Mr. Sullivan* and that was all. He was not a party man in the strict sense. His partyism, if he had any, consisted in his desire to advance the interest of the Province under the Ægis of Great Britain—he was a Reformer, but not a Radical.

The Legislative Assembly, in the Session of 1836, as I have said, was hostile to the Governor. It is equally true that the Governor was hostile to the Assembly. In the view of the Assembly, an Executive Council without Robert Baldwin or Marshall S. Bidwell ought not to possess the confidence of the country. The Assembly, holding this view, passed a resolution of want of confidence in the new Councillors, and Mr. Sullivan had to go with the rest.

On 4th March, 1837, Sir Francis Bond Head thought proper to dissolve the House of Assembly. A most exciting election took place which resulted in the return of a House opposed to the introduction of Responsible Government.

When the Rebellion broke out in December, 1837, Mr. Sullivan buckled on his armour in defence of the Province. Both by precept and example he shewed his abhorrence of rebellion. With Doctor Baldwin and Robert Baldwin, he felt reform was necessary in the government of the country, but did not believe that armed revolt was the proper remedy for existing grievances.

In the Autum of 1837 Sir Francis Bond Head resigned his office of Lieutenant-Governor, but held office till the close of the Session, which took place on the 6th March, 1838.

Mr. Sullivan had the confidence of the Governor during his whole administration. At the close of the Session, on 6th March, 1838, Sir Francis Bond Head, K. C. B., Baronet, bade farewell to Canada in an address to Parliament, in which he reviewed all the events leading up to and during the Rebellion. It was a very lengthy address, which no one can read without concluding that sentiment more than judgment swayed His Excellency in his utterances. The concluding paragraphs of the address read as follows:

> As my successor is hourly expected here, I return to the Mother country as I left it, totally unconnected with party or politics, but in retirement I shall remember the lessons the people of Upper Canada have taught me; and I feel it my duty to declare that I leave the continent of America with my judgment perfectly convinced that the inhabitants of Europe, Asia, and Africa are right in their opinion *that all men are not by nature equal;* that the assertion of the contrary in America is a fallacy; and that talent, industry, and character must elevate individuals, as they do nations, in the gradual scale of society.
>
> May the resplendent genius of the British Constitution ever continue to illuminate this noble land, and animated by its influence, may its inhabitants continue to be distinguished for humility of demeanor, nobility of mind, fidelity to their allies, courage before the enemy, mercy in victory, integrity in commerce, reverence for their religion, and under all circumstances implicit obedience to their laws.
>
> Honorable Gentlemen and Gentlemen, Farewell!

Sir George Arthur succeeded Sir Francis Head as Lieutenant-Governor on 23rd March, 1838, and Mr. Sullivan was his most trusted Councillor. Sir George Arthur's Lieutenant-Governorship was, however, overshadowed by the advent to the Province of Lord Durham as Governor-General, which took place in the Autumn of 1839, and, on his return to England, by Mr. Poulett Thompson, (afterwards Lord Sydenham), who was sent out specially to build up a Union of the Provinces, founded on the report which Lord Durham made to the Imperial Government. The lesser light of the Lieutenant-Governorship, was dimmed by the greater light of the Governor General.

> "A substitute shines brightly as a King
> Until a King be by; and then his state
> Empties itself, as doth an inland brook
> Into the main of waters."

Lord Durham was in Toronto for one day, in July, 1838, and received an ovation from the citizens.

When Lord Sydenham came to Toronto in November, 1839, he took upon himself the management of affairs with the sole view of promoting the Union. He took up his residence at Beverley House, and from thence used all the means at his command to influence Parliament, which met in the early part of December, 1839. He found the Legislative Council composed of Honorable Members not likely to yield to his wishes, unless he could have the support of some trusted man of ability to advocate his views. He at once became impressed, not only with the oratorical powers of Mr. Sullivan, but with his aptitude to advance the work in hand. Mr. Sullivan was his principal adviser in all the negotiations entered into, and his spokesman when he wished his views conveyed through other channels than his own. In the Legislative Council he advocated the Union with all the eloquence at his command. He dealt with all the arguments advanced against the Union in a masterly manner. He assured the House that Her Majesty was determined to maintain the connection between the Colonies and the Mother Country. This was the foundation on which he raised a noble superstructure. After some introductory remarks in favour of the measure he said, as reported :

> The cry of discontent had come from loyal British subjects in Lower Canada. People had declared their willingness for a Union, but on what terms? The disfranchisement of the French Canadians. Such a plan of Union would be wholly unsupported in the British Parliament. England which had been pursuing steadily a course of emancipation from slavery, would never consent to establish a nation of serfs, without political rights, in any part of the British dominions. Honorable gentlemen had seen a rebellion amongst a people complaining of imaginary grievances ; but they would be rash to found their calculation from this poor experience, of what a rebellion would be amongst a people struggling against real oppression. It was true that by the disfranchisement of Lower Canadians they might banish sedition from the halls of legislation ; they might impose silence upon the discontented ; but would they make discontent less dangerous? Would there be a sword less to be drawn, or an arm less to wield it? Would the American emissary be less active or less successful amongst a nation of slaves? Would the dislike of Lower Canada to British be less active, or would not an effective and real regard be added to the natural prejudice with which they had to contend. He put it to Honorable Gentlemen, would they consent to be disfranchised for the sake of the few ? Would they live in quiet in a country, in which they and their race were branded with disgrace and excluded from common right ? or, if they consented to such exclusion, what man amongst them could so command his children ? Ask, he said, the rising youth of the country meekly to bow their necks to the chain, and be contented slaves in the country of their forefathers ! He had seen the experiment tried ; he had seen the energies of a noble and brave people exhausted in struggles ; he had seen guilt and murder prevail in a land, in which the attempt was made to exclude and disfranchise a people upon the grounds of difference in religion, or of natural origin ; and he could not but shudder at the prospect of introducing such a system into a British Province. He preferred to meet the cold and open declamations of the demagogue ; he preferred contending with him under the protection of law and within the walls of Parliament, to meeting his bitter, concealed but unextinguished hatred. On the one hand, truth, justice, intelligence, British principles, would, however severe the struggle, be at length triumphant. On the other, "The muffled rebel would steal forth in the dark," and night by night, add a brand to the pile which would consume the country.

Mr. Sullivan went on, and expatiated on the conditions which certain members wished to add to the terms of union : he concluded with a brilliant peroration as follows :

He had heard and read speculations upon the separation of these Colonies from England; but he must acknowledge that he did not possess the coolness and philosophy to consider the question with a view to consequences ulterior to such an event. He was certain the Honorable Gentlemen around him, so many of whom had spent their early lives in the service of that great Empire to which it was their pride to belong, would not, for light causes take from their children's inheritance the pride of England's glory. Those who had so often stood in the fast thinning ranks of British battle, would not readily give up, the trophies of the Peninsula or the medals of Waterloo, for the cotton bags of New Orleans or the much vaunted heroism of Chippawa. To them, and to him, the sound of the British drum which would beat the last retreat, would indeed be a funeral note; and the lowering the "meteor flag of England" in the country of their adoption would be a sad blow to England's prosperity, a blot upon the age in which it would happen, a disgrace to the rulers under which it would be permitted to take place. But he would turn from this distressing picture of the downfall of England's Colonial Empire, acquired with so much toil, defended with so much valour, and consecrated by so much British blood, to the more cheering and inspiring prospects opening before them. We have, he exclaimed, conquered our great enemies—indifference on the part of the Mother Country, and distrust of our attachment to her interests, and loyalty to our Sovereign. We have convinced British statesmen of the value of our country; we have shewn the true and loyal spirit of the inhabitants, we have obtained from our Queen that invaluable declaration that she will maintain the connection between these Colonies and the Empire. Let us then join heart and hand with her Government; let us cordially support measures intended for our safety and our welfare; let us not impair, by conditions implying distrust, the generous confidence we are invited to offer; but bestow it, readily and cheerfully, in the same spirit in which it is asked, looking forward with confidence to a bright future of rapidly advancing prosperity, secure in the powerful protection of the Empire.

This eloquent speech of Mr. Sullivan carried the House as it were by storm, and the Resolutions in favour of Union were carried by a good majority.

In February, 1839, Mr. Sullivan was appointed a Legislative Councillor, and in the Upper Chamber he had charge of many Bills, especially the Bills affecting Legal Matters, Property, and Civil Rights.

On the 3rd April, 1839, he gave notice that he would on the next day bring in a bill to amend the law for the alienation of the real estate of married women. This bill was crystalized into an Act of Parliament passed on the 11th May, 1839, and is chapter VI. of the Revised

Statutes of Upper Canada. The Act was considered a great boon at the time, as it not only confirmed titles which had been attacked by reason of certain technical defects in the certificates on the back of deeds of married women—providing against such defects in future—but it facilitated the barring of dower, by enabling married women to bar their dower by simply joining in the deed of their husbands, without acknowledging the same before any Court, Judge, or Justice of the Peace.

At a time when there were not so many Courts or Judges as now, and fewer Justices of the Peace, this provision of law was considered very beneficent legislation.

The Act of Union between the Provinces of Upper and Lower Canada, passed in 1840, was, by proclamation, declared to come into effect on 10th February, 1841.

In the life of Chief Justice Draper, I have shewn that Mr. Draper was a member of the first Executive Council formed after the Act of Union had been proclaimed. This Council was formed on the 13th February, 1841, and Mr. Sullivan was a member of that Council. His colleagues in that Council were Messrs. Baldwin, Daly, Dunn, Day, Draper, Harrison, and Ogden. This was clearly a Coalition Council, and did not prove a very happy family. The Honorable Robert Baldwin retired from this Ministry at the beginning of the Session of the Parliament of 1842. Mr. Sullivan continued to hold office until the formation of the first Baldwin-Lafontaine administration, which took place on September 16th, 1842.

Mr. Sullivan was again a member of the Baldwin-Lafontaine administration. From the period of the Union, up to the time of his resignation in 1843, he was the senior member of the Council and leader of the Government in the Legislative Council; while in the Assembly, although Mr. Harrison (the Honorable S. B. Harrison) conducted the business, Mr. Draper was in effect the leader. During the period from the Union in 1841 to the resignation of the Baldwin-Lafontaine administration, both Lord Sydenham and Sir Charles Bagot were in their turn Governors of the United Provinces.

Lord Sydenham met with an untimely death, the result of an accident, in September, 1841. He was succeeded by Sir Charles Bagot, who survived his appointment only about nineteen months, and died at Kingston on the 19th May, 1843. Sir Charles Metcalfe succeeded Sir Charles Bagot, and held office until November, 1845, when he was obliged to resign his position on account of ill-health.

The Baldwin-Lafontaine administration of which Mr. Sullivan was a member, had the entire confidence of Sir Charles Bagot. When, however, Sir Charles Metcalfe came out as Governor, he was not so ready to yield to the advice of his ministers as Sir Charles Bagot had been. Sir Charles Metcalfe had been Governor in the East Indies, and in a Crown Colony in the West Indies. He had no sympathy with the Baldwin-Lafontaine ministry, or their supporters in the House—they were altogether too liberally disposed to meet his views. Referring to the Conservative party, in one of his despatches to the Secretary of State, he wrote:

It is the only party in the Colony with which I can sympathise I have no sympathy with the Anti-British rancour of the French party, or the selfish indifference towards our country of the Republican party. Yet these are the parties with which I have to co-operate.

Such were Sir Charles Metcalfe's opinions of his constitutional advisers, enjoying at the time the confidence of an immense majority of the Canadian people. A pretty good idea of Sir Charles Metcalfe's views on the subject of Constitutional Goverment in Canada, is to be found in a letter addressed by him to Colonel Stokes, one of his India correspondents, which is as follows: "Fancy such a state of things in India, with a Mohammedan Council and a Mohammedan Assembly, and you will have some notion of my position."

Sir Charles Metcalfe, in himself a most excellent man, given to benevolence and good works, had no proper appreciation of Responsible Government as Mr. Sullivan understood, or as Lord Sydenham wished the people to understand it.

At the end of April or beginning of May, a rupture occurred between Sir Charles Metcalfe and the Baldwin-Lafontaine Cabinet. The Governor demanded to have the patronage of the Crown in appointments to office, while the Council held that the patronage was theirs to exercise so long as they had a parliamentary majority. On this question the Ministry resigned. Mr. Sullivan was no sooner out of office than he took up the pen to defend the administration and its principles.

Sir Charles Metcalfe had a doughty champion in Doctor Egerton Ryerson.

Mr. Sullivan wrote a series of letters in the *Examiner* newspaper, under the "nom de plume" of "Legion." I have these letters before me. Never before in Canada had more scathing letters on a political subject been written by any man. These letters are full of interest as to the principles of Responsible Government, enforced with logic and syllogism which had never been surpassed. Both the Reverend Doctor Ryerson and Mr. Sullivan are in their graves, and it will not be well therefore to exhume the controversy which was held by these two combatants, in which sarcasm as well as reasoning so much abounded.

I will content myself by making a quotation from Mr. Sullivan's first letter, which will show the power and force of his intellectual reasoning. Doctor Ryerson, in his letter signed "Leonidas," had said that Sir Charles Metcalfe "had spent forty years of public life in a colony, and has therefore all the habits and feelings of a colonist." Mr. Sullivan, in his reply, said: "That is to say, as applied to the real fact, Sir Charles Metcalfe has spent forty years in governing, or in connection with the government of a colony, and therefore—yes, therefore—he has all the feelings of a colonist. On the same syllogism, an overseer of a plantation must have all the feelings of the negro slave, the Judge must have all the feelings of the thief. 'He has spent all that time,' says Mr. Ryerson, 'not in the atmosphere of an exclusive hierarchy, but in a country where equal civil and religious rights are recognized, and has therefore all the feelings of religious equality, and adaptation of experience and views, for the government of Canada not possessed by any other statesman of his rank in the British Empire.'"

"In the name of common sense" says Mr. Sullivan, "does Mr. Ryerson speak of India, where widows mount the funeral pile and enjoy their religious rites in fire: where the Juggernaut rolls in his chariot over the crushed bodies of his adorers, under the politic eye of a Government which respects religion: where life, liberty, and property, are held by permission: where there are no political rights whatsoever, not even a 'shade of the views' of public opinion, to use the Doctor's own figure of speech: where the breath of freedom never was drawn: where justice, humanity, and human happiness, have been weighed against gold, and found as light as the Doctor's pen: where there is no bill of rights, no habeas corpus, no parliament, no freeholders, no representation: and so because Sir Charles Metcalfe helped to govern that country forty years, according to Doctor Ryerson, he has 'an adaptation of experience for the government of Canada, not possessed by any statesman of his rank in the British Empire.' If Doctor Ryerson hads aid, notwithstanding Sir Charles Metcalfe's residence in India he may yet be a good man, we would not deny his proposition; but to say that governing slaves for forty years gives a man experience in the government of free British subjects, is to tell the latter they are or should be slaves."

The Reverend Egerton Ryerson could and did wield a caustic pen as well as Mr. Sullivan. His nine letters before me show that the Reverend Doctor was actuated by the highest principles of devotion to his country's interest, but at the same time he took issue with Mr. Sullivan and the Reform Association on the question of appointments to the public service. Dr. Ryerson's views on this subject may be compressed in the single sentence of a speech by the Honorable Joseph Howe, quoted by the Doctor with approval: "The Sovereign is bound to bestow all offices for the general good, without reference to party."

When Mr. Sullivan left the Government he resumed the practice of the law in Toronto. He and Mr. Shuter Smith, of Port Hope, entered into partnership, and carried on their practice under the firm name of Sullivan & Smith, in Wellington street, Toronto.

I became more intimately acquainted with Mr. Sullivan at this time than before. I have been with him at the Assizes at Cobourg and Peterborough, where we were sometimes counsel on the same side and more frequently on opposite sides. In a case of a prisoner tried for murder at Peterborough, Mr. Sullivan was my senior counsel. He requested me to interview the prisoner in the jail, which I did, also to explore the premises where a murder had been committed, several miles from Peterborough, which I also did. The prisoner avowed his innocence, but there were certain expressions of his to me which failed to impress me with the same conviction on that subject. However, I got Mr. Sullivan interested in the case, which came on late in the afternoon before Judge Macaulay, and lasted well into the night. I have never heard a more powerful address to a jury than Mr. Sullivan made on that occasion. His speech was argumentative and most impressive; tears dropped from many eyes before he concluded his discourse. The jury acquitted the prisoner. At the Assizes in the following Spring, he was tried at the Hamilton Assizes for another offence, but did not meet with so good a fate, being convicted and sent to the Penitentiary for several years.

On another occasion, at Cobourg, I was opposed to Mr. Sullivan in a case about the boundary of land. I never can forget the amusement which it seemed to afford Mr. Sullivan when, on my calling two or three witnesses of sixty years of age to prove a blazed tree as indicating the true line, and then Mr. Sullivan calling a witness of seventy years of age whom he thought could settle the matter as to the original line and the older blazed tree, my client furnished me with a witness eighty years of age, going still further back. This caused Mr. Sullivan to cry, Enough! and with a smile bowing to the Court and saying, "respect for age would prevent his going further," he declined calling another witness, letting the old man of eighty settle the line and the blazed tree.

Mr. Sullivan took great interest in all public matters. In 1847 he delivered a most excellent address in the Mechanics' Music Hall, Toronto, on the subject of "Emigration and Colonization." This address was productive of much good in stimulating emigration, and shewing the capabilities and resources of Canada, as a field for the husbandmen of England and Ireland. Little was then known of the country to the west of Lake Superior. Mr. Sullivan related what he had heard from Mr. Angus Bethune and Mr. Ermatinger, then very lately from that country. I remember the address well, and how much I was struck with Mr. Sullivan's statement then made, that the Saskatchewan River ran from west to east fifteen hundred miles without obstruction! a truth we all know now, but which was then thought to be almost fabulous. Mr. Sullivan's whole address shewed the unbounded confidence he had in the possibilities of the future of Canada, so remarkably realized since his death.

Mr. Sullivan was not only a lecturer, but a lover of poetry, and often indulged his fancy in versification. Doctor Müllner, the great German dramatist, is said to have spent the hours of darkness with the ladies of Parnassus, and to have disturbed the whole neighborhood by the vehemence with which he declaimed his newly composed verses, and late in the morning retired to bed. I will not say Mr. Sullivan did all this; but that he did compose verses, and very excellent ones too, appears from verses on "The Emigrant Ship," published in Sibbald's Magazine, in January, 1833, under the nom de plume of

"Cinna." I transcribe the lines, expressive as they are of the tendency of the Irish heart, and descriptive of the emigrant leaving his native land. The lines are these:

THE EMIGRANT SHIP.

Our native hills are sinking fast
   Behind the troubled sea,
Farewell our cherished home, a last,—
   A fond farewell to thee.

Oh! darkly lour the angry skies,
   White break the billows foam;
And tears are sad which dim the eyes—
   That look their last on home.

Now driving clouds are all we view,
   Above the bounding main;
And for the landward streak of blue
   The eye is turned in vain.

Yet on its last receding trace,
   Our ling'ring glances hung;
And gloom is on the exile's face,
   And silence on his tongue!

Tell me, why sinks thy sturdy heart!
   Thou peasant hard of hand?
Methinks, 'twas well for thee to part
   From yon o'er crowded land.

The fields were green, the clime was fair,
   And fruitful was the soil;
But thou could'st look for nothing there,
   But thankless,—hopeless toil.

Yet cheer thee up! a home is found,
   With wealth and plenty strewn;
Where thou shalt till the teeming ground,—
   And it shall be thine own!

Thou mother hug thy laughing child,
   Not with that grasp of fear!
He seemed to know it, when he smiled,
   That pleasant days were near.

Thou hast a letter folded there?
   Thy laboring heart above!
That brings to him a father's care;
   To thee thy husband's love.

It tells thee of a woodland cot,—
    A sunny lake beside ;
That penury ne'er saw the spot
    In which thou shalt abide,

And oh ! not on thy bridal eve,
    A maiden bright and fair,
Didst thou a welcome home receive,
    More fond than waits thee there !

Then cheer thee up, the storm is kind,
    That hastens our career ;—
And He that raised the howling wind,
    The whispered prayer can hear !

And thou, oh man of wretched form
    And pallid wrinkled brow !
Why smilest thou midst wave and storm,—
    Who scarce e'er smiled till now ?

I know thee, 'twas thy wretched fate,
    The shuttles course to guide,
The costly robe to fabricate
    For luxury and pride :

Yet o'er the silken web to creep,
    And count thy sorrows o'er,—
When ceaseless labour could not keep
    Starvation from thy door.

Yes, smile upon the eager boys
    That cluster round thy knee ;
And tell them of their joys
    Within the forest free.

And who upon yon reeling deck,
    Steps with a chieftain's stride ?
There are no fears of storm or wreck,
    Within his heart of pride.

His arm he lifts as if his hand,
    Again a sword did yield ;
He dreams he cheers a gallant band,
    In some contested field.

A soldier once, and does he want
    The honours of the war ?
He bears them on his manly front,
    In many a dinted scar.

Yet midst the wealth by valour saved
　He drew his pittance scant,
And worse than all the foes he braved
　He found neglect and want!

The memory of the happy days.
　Alas! for ever gone—
When young ambitions beacon blaze,
　Through danger led him on,—

Came o'er him, and he seeks a grave,
　Where first in arms he stood;
And saw his countries banners wave,
　O'er many a field of blood.

But cheer thee soldier in that land,
　Thou shalt be happy yet,—
For many an old companion's hand,
　Whose hearts do not forget.

The coming of the brave will greet,
　And the wild woods will resound,
With friendships pledge, when the soldiers meet;
　And the rosy wine goes round.

And should again, stern wars abound,
　And the foeman's step be nigh,
A thousand youths will start to arms,
　At the veteran's battle cry.

But now breaks forth the setting sun,
　All glowing in the west,
The parted clouds he shines upon,
　And lights the billows crest.

May He, who gave the sun his light,
　To rule the glorious day,
Be with us through the gloomy night,
　Upon our trackless way!

York, 25th January, 1833.

The following lines published in the same magazine, and which were Mr. Sullivan's composition will shew that he had a tenderness not only for the emigrant, but an admiration for the weaker sex.

ON WOMAN.

(FROM MEMORY.)

Dame Nature's other works were done,
Just formed the stars, the golden sun,
    The blue ethereal skies;
And wide across earth's verdant lawn,
Arose young morning's orient dawn,
    And flowers began to rise—

And now in elegance arrayed,
Her last, her fairest work was made,
    Almost a seraph's frame;
To animate this form was given
A gentle spirit,—sent from Heaven;
    And Woman was her name.

Then on her softly smiling face,
Was lavished every winning grace,
    And every charm was there;
Upon her eye the violet's blue,
Upon her cheek the rose's hue—
    The lily, everywhere.

Yes, on that eye was seen to play
The lustre of the stellar ray,
    The diamond's humid glow!
She threw, to form her bosom's globe,
Life's tender flush, and beauty's robe
    On wreath's of virgin snow.

Then Woman's lips in smiles withdrew
Their veils of rich carnation hue,
    And pearls appeared beneath;
And blest Arabia seems to pour
The perfumes of its spicy store,
    To mingle with her breath.

Hark! hark she speaks, and silver strains
Melodious floating o'er the plains
    A nameless joy impart!
The Nightingale hath caught the tone,
And made that melting voice his own,
    That vibrates on the heart.

Fond Nature cast her glance around
The glowing sky, the flowery ground,
    The day diffusing sun;
On Woman last, her darling child,
She gazed, and said,—with accent mild,—
    "Creation's work is done."

In 1845 and 1846 there had taken place a correspondence between Mr. Draper, Attorney-General, West, and leader of the Draper-Daly Administration, which shews the weakness of the Administration, and the desire of Mr. Draper to strengthen it by the infusion of French Canadian Ministers, representing the French Canadian people of Lower Canada, it being alleged that Mr. Viger and Mr. Papineau, Mr. Draper's colleagues, had lost their confidence. This, which was called the Caron-Draper correspondence, was all made public by Mr. Lafontaine, then a member of the House, opposed to the Draper-Daly Administration.

As may be imagined Mr. Draper was accused of caballing with the opposition, attempting to undermine his own colleagues, a charge which Mr. Draper indignantly repudiated.

As is usual in such cases, there were charges and counter-charges made. Mr. Lafontaine was blamed by his political opponents for making public the correspondence; whereupon Mr. Baldwin made a lengthy speech in his defence. One honorable member prophesied the downfall of the Administration, and that Mr. Lafontaine would soon be in power. This all proved true. Lord Elgin arrived as Governor-General in the early part of 1847.

When Lord Elgin arrived he found the Draper-Daly Administration in power. As Lord Elgin had come out with instructions to form a ministry having the confidence of a majority of both the English and French members, he placed himself in the hands of Messrs. Baldwin and Lafontaine, who formed a ministry composed of French and English members, which commanded a majority of the House.

On the downfall of the Draper Administration, Mr. Draper accepted a seat on the Bench. The letters of "Legion" were now to bear fruit. Mr. Sullivan had so thoroughly argued the principles of responsible government with Dr. Ryerson, that Messrs. Baldwin and Lafontaine, on coming into power, were glad to avail themselves of his services in their ministry. He was again made a member of the Cabinet.

A vacancy occurred in the Queen's Bench by the death of Judge Jones, in 1848, and Mr. Sullivan was appointed to succeed him on, the 15th September, 1848, and was transferred to the Common Pleas, on the 21st January, 1850. As Judge of these Courts he held the Assizes in the various towns, and it was a real pleasure to the Bar to have him amongst them. He had a most generous heart, and could give or take a joke as well as the youngest.

At a trial at Woodstock about the warranty of a horse, one of the jurors was constantly interrupting the counsel in his address to the jury with questions which shewed that he was determined not to agree with the other jurors, and, sure enough, when the jury came into the Court room to deliver their verdict, he was not among them. "Mr. Sheriff," said the Judge, "where is the other juror!" "Please your Lordship," said the Sheriff, "he has escaped!" The incident and answer of the Sheriff so amused the Judge, that he was provoked to laughter. He was probably the most witty Judge that ever occupied a seat on the Bench in Osgoode Hall; his humor seemed to ooze out of him by uncontrollable pressure.

The judgments of Judge Sullivan while on the Bench were not numerous, and at this day the most of those he did deliver would, in consequence of the changes that have taken place in the administration of justice, be considered out of date. They will mostly be found in the first three volumes of the Common Pleas Reports. I will cite one of the cases decided, as it was an assertion of a principle since maintained. The case was Burney *vs.* Gorham, 1 C. P. Rep. 358, which decided that after a conviction by a magistrate, an action on the case would not lie against him, unless the acts complained of be proved to have been committed by him without any reasonable and probable cause and maliciously. And the question of malice must be left to the jury. In concluding his judgment he said :

The learned Judge at the Assizes fell into the error of supposing the mere fact of the fair claim of right to enter and take the poles being contended for before the Justice of the Peace, he should immediately have stopped the proceedings, and considered himself without jurisdiction. The case of The Queen *v.* Dodson, already cited, and Parrington *v.* Moore, 2 Exch. 223, prove incontestably that the Justice must pass his judgment on the fairness and reasonableness of the color of right set up; and in reviewing that decision in an action on the case against a Magistrate, the Judge at the Assizes should have pronounced as well upon the correctness of the decision of the Justice as upon the presence or want of reasonable and probable cause for a wrong decision, and then he should have left the question of malice to the jury. Instead of this, he treated the proceedings before the Justice as *coram non judice*, and the defendant as a trespasser. I think there was a misdirection in the charge; and that if this action can be maintained at all, it must be upon the ground of the defendant having convicted maliciously, and without a reasonable or probable cause.

I had the good fortune to be much in Judge Sullivan's company during the latter years of his practice at the Bar, on the circuit, and after he was promoted to the Bench. He was a most agreeable conversationalist, and was a scholar in every sense of the word, well acquainted with the prose and poetical writings of the past centuries as well as the present. He could read and translate French fluently, and frequently found use for that talent in a Government composed of English and French members.

A friend of mine who was intimately acquainted with Mr. Sullivan, and for a much longer period than I knew him, has thus expressed himself to me with regard to him, in language which I believe is a faithful portrayal of his character. He says: " He was brilliant in social life, beloved in his family circle, evinced wonderful power in rapidly writing; he would allow nothing to disturb him while writing—the young people around him could go on with their merriment, he would 'currente calamo' proceed with his composition, whether it were a Government despatch, or poetical effusion. His despatches to Downing Street elicited admiration from the Colonial Secretaries for their beauty of language and clearness of expression. It was not, even in the preparation of State papers, in prosaic orations, in the Legislative Council, or on the Bench, that his genius shone forth with the greatest splendor: it was rather when in the company of a friend or two, he soliloquisingly expressed himself on various subjects, such as on philosophy, in its highest sense; on politics, Canada present and future, or kindred subjects; his countenance would then brighten up, his language then betraying the deep thoughtfulness of his well-balanced mind."

From what I knew of Mr. Sullivan, I can well believe this. In walk and gait, if met on the street, he would be called a heavy man; but when occasion demanded, and his intellect roused, he was, truly, "fortiter in re."

Mr Sullivan was twice married: first to a daughter of Captain Matthews, who was a distinguished officer of artillery, and was with Sir John Moore in his retreat at Corunna. By his first marriage Mr. Sullivan had but one child, a daughter, who died in her infancy. His second wife was a daughter of Colonel DeLaitre, by whom he had several children.

Judge Falconbridge, of the Queen's Bench Division of the High Court of Justice, married one of his daughters: the late Chief Justice Thomas Moss also married one of his daughters, and Charles Moss, Q.C., another.

William Sullivan, Counsellor at Law, of Chicago, is his only surving son.

Judge Sullivan, of whom I have written but an imperfect sketch, will be remembered by all those who knew him as well as I did, with affection and regard. He died in Toronto, the seat of his triumphs, on the 14th April, 1853, at the comparatively early age of 51 years.

An obituary notice of him truly recorded that he was "Distinguished as a lawyer, statesman, and orator, that he won admiration and esteem by his splendid talents and the eminent services which he rendered to his adopted country in the Legislature and the Executive, during an eventful period of Canadian history, while in private he gained the affections of his associates and friends by the gentleness of his disposition and the generosity of his heart."

XX.

THE HONORABLE WILLIAM HUME BLAKE, CHANCELLOR OF UPPER CANADA.

THE Honorable William Hume Blake was of Irish parentage. He was the second son of the Reverend Dominick Edward Blake, a clergyman of the Church of England, Rector and Rural Dean of Kiltegan and Loughbrickland, County Wicklow, Ireland. His mother's name was Hume, daughter of William Hume, of Homewood, M. P., County Wicklow. The Blakes were a Protestant family, of the Blakes of Castlegrove, County Galway, who held a good place among the country gentry.

In the Rebellion of 1798, William Hume the maternal grandfather of the Honorable William Hume Blake sent his children to Dublin for safety, and himself took an active part in repressing the rebellion. He took personal command of a corps of yeomanry raised in his county. While in pursuit of some rebels he was shot near his own residence at Homewood, and thus fell a victim to the King's cause in Ireland. Lord Claremont in a published letter, alluded to this deplorable event "as the murder of Hume, the friend and favorite of his county," and characterized it as an "example of atrocity which excelled all that went before it."

It will thus be seen that the future Chancellor of Upper Canada was a man who could boast of a good ancestry, both civil and religious. His father, a Dean in the Church, and his maternal grandfather, a loyalist who fell in defence of his country, at a time when the flames of rebellion were burning with lurid light all over that Island, which has been, ever since, more or less, in a turbulent state.

William Hume Blake was born at the Rectory, Kiltegan, on the 10th March, 1809. He spent his early days at his native place, and on arriving at a suitable age was sent to Trinity College, Dublin, to finish his education. He was a ripe scholar on leaving Trinity. After completing his college course, he thought of choosing surgery for a profession, and for a time applied himself to the study of that noble science. Not being a roystering man, he was not able to keep pace with other Irish youths: the dissecting room, with its concomitants of human suffering and much levity on the part of those who were his companions in study, soon gave him a distaste for his profession. Giving up the study of surgery, he entered upon a course of theological study. His mind naturally turned in the direction of the Church, and had it not been that his elder brother Dominick had made up his mind to emigrate to Canada, it is possible that he would have become an ornament of the Pulpit in Ireland, instead of the Bench in Canada.

In the year 1832, Sir John Colborne was Governor of the Province of Upper Canada, and was constant in his endeavors to promote immigration to the Province. Several settlements of retired officers and gentry of Britain, owe their introduction to free life in Canada, to the inducements to emigrate held out by this old Waterloo officer.

Sir John Colborne was one of those Governors who took an active and personal interest in the progress of Upper Canada. There was a larger emigration of Irish to the Province in 1832, than in any previous year. The immigration was not confined to what has been termed "the poor Irish," but vast numbers of the better class, who stood higher in the scale of worldly goods and intelligence, responded to the call he made for a new population to come over, and make homes for themselves in a Colony which opened up a bright prospect for the overcrowded population of the old land.

William Hume Blake's elder brother had married a Miss Jones, the daughter of Major Jones, a retired officer who had held commission in the 37th, 49th, and 60th regiments, and had served in Canada during the war of 1812, and was at the battles of Lundy's Lane and Queenston Heights, so famed in Canadian history.

Major Jones, on his return to his native home, had influenced his son-in-law, Dominick Blake, with the great possibilities of Canada, as a field for his future success in life.

Dominick Blake had by this time become the Reverend Dominick Blake, well known in Canada as Rector in the Township of Adelaide, in the County of Middlesex, and afterwards for many years Rector of Thornhill, in the vicinity of Toronto.

The Reverend Dominick Blake was induced to emigrate, and not being disposed to come to a sparsely settled country where, at that time, bears and wolves more abounded than human beings—excepting wild Indians, he was glad to have the companionship of his brother. Not only did he succeed in attracting his brother to his venture, but also his mother, sisters, and several other relatives and friends.

To sum up the whole, in July, 1832, a regular family party was made up, consisting not only of the above, but also his brother-in-law the late Archdeacon Brough ; the late Mr. Justice Connor ; Dr. Robinson, father of Judge Robinson of Lambton, the Reverend Benjamin Cronyn, late Bishop of Huron ; and the Reverend Arthur Palmer, formerly Archdeacon of the Diocese of Toronto. This was a goodly party, and well equipped. The party did not come as ordinary emigrants, but chartered a vessel—the "Anne, of Halifax"—to carry them across the ocean. The voyage was not a pleasant one, one of the crew having died of cholera on the passage across, his body being committed to the deep. It was a question for a time whether the vessel should not be turned to the eastward, and the party, if they could escape the cholera, landed on the shores of the home which they had left. Other counsels prevailed, and they determined to make the port of Quebec. With such resolves, they battled with the wind and the waves, and arrived at Grosse Isle, after a six weeks voyage, late in August. They were there subjected to a long quarantine, and did not arrive at Quebec till September. Following the usual course of travel those days, from Quebec to the great lakes, partly by land and partly by water, they made their way to York. Here the party separated, some going north, and some west. The Reverend Dominick Blake, William Hume Blake, mother and sisters, chose the western country for their future home; Mr. Brough, Dr. Connor, and Dr. Robinson, going northward to the Township of Oro, on Lake Simcoe. The Blakes settled in the Township of Adelaide. William Hume Blake, like most of the new comers to the Province in that day, determined to take up land, and purchased a farm at Bear Creek, about seven miles from Adelaide, near where Strathroy now stands.

How many there are who, without experience in farming in the Old world, on coming to the New, imagine that if they only get land their fortunes are made. In nine cases out of ten, immigrants of this class learn by bitter experience, that the new land is really new land, and with that old trees, and that an immense deal of labor, as well as an immense deal of grubbing, has to be done before the land will produce a subsistence! A man like Mr. Blake, who had studied surgery, theology, and the dead languages, is destined soon to find that he is but little fitted for agricultural pursuits. In a wooded, wild country, such as the Township of Adelaide was at that time, the charm it possessed for a new comer was soon dissipated.

Mr. Blake was enabled to endure this kind of life for two years, when something told him that he was wasting his energies in fruitless toil. He was not afraid to work, and did work with his hands, but he must depend on his head to make his venture a success in Canada. He now thought he would try the study of the law.

Mr. Blake, with his young family, emerged from the woods of Adelaide, and bent his way to York. On arriving there he entered the office of Mr. Simon Washburn, a well known practitioner of York at that time. Mr. Blake's degrees at Trinity College were sufficient to enable him, without difficulty, to become a student. He was admitted to the Law Society in Hilary Term, 3 William IV., 1835, and was called to the Bar three years afterwards, in Easter Term, 1 Victoria, 1838.

At this time the Reverend Dominick Blake was still in Adelaide, actively engaged in the work of the Church.

William Hume Blake, after coming to York, used to be proud of relating some of his experiences in the country. Among others he used to tell how, on one occasion, he had walked to the blacksmith shop to obtain a supply of harrow pins, and finding them too heavy to carry home, fastened them to a chain which he put round his neck, and so dragged them home through the woods. I strongly suspect it was not long after this incident, that he began to think seriously that Hargrave would be better than harrow points: that, after all, the study of Blackstone was more fitted for him, than a journey to the blacksmith shop.

During the rebellion of 1837, Mr. Blake was in Toronto, and for a short time paymaster of a battalion. During his student life in Toronto, and for a short time after he was called to the Bar, his devoted wife, who was highly educated, occupied a portion of her time in giving instruction in the higher branches of learning to the daughters of the well-to-do citizens of the place.

Mr. Blake was too much of a student to care to cultivate society in Toronto, indeed he rather abstained from, than sought for the attention of the official society of those days. There was everything in his family connection, in his education, in the education and family of his handmaid, that should have made the ruling powers at the capital seek him, instead of his seeking them. Mr. Blake did not come to Toronto a rich man, but with a determination to achieve success, if not riches, by hard work and resolute will. He was a man eminently self-reliant, and if he had occasion to differ, as he often did, with the magnates of the day, either in politics or in law, he ever had the courage of his convictions, and was never afraid to express his opinions. In his opinion, there was too much arrogance and self-sufficiency, in the controlling powers of the country, then designated the "Family Compact." He adopted liberal views, in fact, was driven to adopt liberal views, by what he deemed superciliousness on the part of those who affected to manage public affairs. He determined to make for himself a name in Toronto, and he did it.

After being called to the Bar, he was not long in securing clients. It was soon ascertained that he possessed great powers of eloquence, and added to this untiring industry and a commanding presence; these were good qualifications for a successful Lawyer. It was not long before he had to meet at the Bar, such experienced and able counsel as William Henry Draper, afterwards Chief Justice; Robert Baldwin Sullivan, afterwards Judge; Henry John Boulton; John Hawkins Hagarty, afterwards and now Chief Justice; Robert Baldwin; Henry Eccles; and the Honorable John Hillyard Cameron. These names are all familiar to the old members of the Bar. It will be confessed by all, that they were all pre-eminent in their profession. William Hume Blake, when he had been but a few years at the Bar, was esteemed the equal, at least, of any of those named, who justly had a high reputation at the Bar. The difference between Mr. Blake and the others was in this: they, or most of them, were pure Common Law men, some had a special aptitude for particular branches of the profession, such as special pleading, Criminal Law, or Common Law, but Mr. Blake was great not only in these, but was looked upon as one of the best counsel of his day, in the Court of Chancery and all matters of Equity.

I can safely say that, of all men I have ever known at the Bar, I have never known one so thorough as William Hume Blake, late Chancellor. It was his mind that swayed the Court, in a case of embezzlement, which I have referred to in the life of Sir John Beverley Robinson, in which the prisoner had been committed before Judge Draper, at the Assizes at Toronto, and sentenced to seven years imprisonment, and who, on appeal, was set free by the arguments of Mr. Blake, as one of the Judges in Appeal, convincing Sir John Beverley Robinson, that the Court of Queen's Bench had erred in upholding the conviction. I can speak of Mr. Blake as counsel, as well as Judge, with confidence, having had him as my Senior at the Bar, and practised before him on the Bench. In a case where I gave him a brief at Hamilton, he at once impressed me with his great ability, when he so readily seized upon the points of the case which ultimately determined the result. In a case of Newton *vs.* Doran before him, in which I was counsel for the plaintiff, a witness was examined and cross-examined by counsel to establish a partnership, and as I thought exhaustively examined: the witness was doing what is called hedging—prevaricating. The Chancellor took a hand, questioned and cross-questioned him in such a way that the witness fairly quailed, and before the Chancellor concluded, became convinced himself that his scheme to deceive the Court and certain parties to the case was a failure. The Chancellor had excoriated him to such a degree, that he was glad to leave the Court, a disappointed and defeated man.

As an instance of Mr. Blake's power as an orator, I may instance the case of Kerby *vs.* Lewis, relating to the disturbance of the plaintiff's farm, at Fort Erie, in which Mr. Blake was counsel for the defendant. In this case, the Court held the law to be clearly with the plaintiff, and always charged against the defendant. The jury persistently found for the defendant, owing to the force with which Mr. Blake presented his case to their understanding. The case is reported in 1 Queen's Bench Reports, 66, and held that "where the jury in an action for disturbance of plaintiff, Kerby, found for defendant perversely, and clearly against law, and evidence, and the Judge's charge, the Court granted a new trial without costs."

After a practice of a few years, Mr. Blake formed a partnership with Joseph C. Morrison, afterwards Judge Morrison; subsequently Dr. Connor became member of the firm. The firm had a very large and lucrative practice. It got for itself the name of the "flourishing concern." It was during this time that the Markham Gang case came up, where a gang of men of the township entered into a conspiracy to steal horses, plunder, rob, and generally to destroy the property of farmers in the township. They were a desperate gang, and it took a long time to root them out. When finally ousted and brought to justice, they required the services of a most experienced counsel. Mr. Blake, in performance of his professional duties, was called upon to defend a number of them, and was but too successful in procuring their acquittal. It often falls to the lot of the best counsel to have to conduct the worst cases. The fault is not of the counsel, but of the cases.

Mr. Blake was Crown prosecutor, in the case of the Queen *vs.* McDermott and Grace Marks, in 1843, for the murder of Thomas Kinnear.

The murder of Kinnear was of a most revolting character. Mr. Kinnear was a gentleman who resided about a mile to the northward of Richmond Hill. He was a man of considerable means, and had a house-keeper, one Mary Montgomery, and two servants, James McDermott and a girl, Grace Marks, 16 years of age. These two, McDermott and Marks, became jealous of the position Mary Montgomery had, and determined to get her out of the way. Not satisfied with this fiendish desire, they resolved also to murder Mr. Kinnear, with the hope of possessing themselves of his money. At an unexpected moment, McDermott struck Mary Montgomery on the back of the head with an axe; stunned her, and then, with the help of Grace Marks, strangled her to death. On the same day McDermott shot Kinnear with a musket killing him on the spot. After this double murder, they both fled to Toronto, and the following morning took the boat for Lewiston, in the State of New York.

Mr. F. C. Capreol of Toronto, hearing of the murder and escape, chartered a boat in the afternoon of the same day, secured the services of the Chief Constable of Toronto, and the two proceeded on the chartered boat to Lewiston during the night, and before the next morning had the fugitives under arrest. They were brought back to Toronto, tried, convicted, and sentenced to death. McDermott underwent the extreme penalty of the law, but Grace Marks sentence was commuted to penitentiary for life. She afterwards feigned insanity, and was in the lunatic asylum for some years. The greater part of her life after the murder, was spent either in the penitentiary or asylum.

I need not quote other cases, but one referred to by Mr. Dent, where in a case of arson a witness was called to prove that India rubber would not burn. Mr. Blake's ingenuity soon confuted him by placing before his eyes several strips of old goloshes (India rubber). He then lit a candle, placed the strips before the candle light, burnt them up in his presence, and asked him if he thought he could be believed. The jury did not believe him, after seeing the rubber burn, and Mr. Blake won his case.

Mr. Blake was a dangerous antagonist to have in a case. His very appearance gave him weight with the jury. He could press a point before the Court, and to the Court, in such a forcible way, that it required great skill in his opponent to parry his blow.

It was not only before juries, however, that Mr. Blake was successful, or before the Common Law Courts.

He had in his time a large Equity practice as counsel, and, with Mr. Esten, was considered leader of the Equity Bar. In arguing cases before Jameson, V.C., it could easily be seen that the counsel had the better of the Judge. The result was shewn in the sequel, for in due time Mr. Blake was appointed Chancellor over the head of Vice-Chancellor Jameson.

Mr. Blake was a Liberal in politics, and so were all his partners in the firm of Blake, Morrison & Connor. He was a follower of the Honorable Robert Baldwin. In the early contests for Municipal Institutions, National Education, Law Reform, and all progressive measures, he took a prominent part.

The readers of Canadian Political History, know of the violent contest the Liberals had with Lord Metcalfe, on the question of Responsible Government and ministerial responsibility for official appointments.

In the Life of Judge Sullivan, I have gone so fully into the matter, that I need not repeat it. Suffice it to say that Mr. Blake was looked upon as a valuable coadjutor of Mr. Baldwin in these reforms. At the general election of 1844 he was the Reform candidate for the representation of the second Riding of York, now the County of Peel. He was opposed by George Duggan, afterwards Recorder of Toronto and Judge of the County Court, and was defeated. He was again, a little later on, defeated in his candidature for the County of Simcoe by the Honorable William B. Robinson. Mr. Robinson had in former years resided and carried on business at Newmarket, and had gained much influence in the county. Mr. Blake was not able to overcome this influence. I remember the election well, having been scrutineer for one of the candidates at the poll in Essa, and walking after dark, at the close of the election, six miles over a mud and corduroy road into Bond Head, to be the first to announce the result of the poll.

There were a good many men devoted to legal studies, who did not regret Mr. Blake's defeat at this election, on personal rather than on political grounds. Mr. Blake was Professor of Law in the University of Toronto. Young men studying for the profession, not members of the University, were admitted to his Law Lectures, which he delivered in one of the rooms in the east wing of the Parliament Buildings, on Front Street. He used to commence his lecture at eight o'clock in the morning. It was one of my greatest delights to attend and listen to these lectures. The matter and manner of the lectures so commended themselves to me, and those who attended the lectures with me, that there was not one who did not feel that they were under great obligations to the University authorities, in being permitted the advantages to be derived from their delivery. Each attendant generally had a book taking notes, which he would amplify at his leisure. The Lecturer never quailed before any decision, no matter by what Judge pronounced, English or Canadian. If he thought the judgment unsound reasoning, he did not hesitate to say so, and urge the students to examine for themselves. I well remember his impressing the students with the great value of the reports in Douglas. These were cases decided by Lord Mansfield, one of the greatest Judges of the English Bench. There are some living yet who attended those lectures: if I am not mistaken, Æmilius Irving, Q.C., and Mr. Lewis, the County Attorney of Huron.

Mr. Blake had not long to wait before obtaining a seat in Parliament. In the general election of 1847, while he was in England, he was returned for the East Riding of York in the Reform interest. The result of this general election was the defeat of the Conservative Government of Lord Metcalfe, and the advent to power of the Baldwin-Lafontaine Administration.

Mr. Blake was Solicitor-General in this Administration, and several notable events occurred during its existence. The principles under which Lord Elgin undertook to conduct the affairs of the Colony, as expressed by himself, were: that he should identify himself with no party, but make himself a mediator and moderator between the influential of all parties; that he should have no Ministers who did not enjoy the confidence of the Assembly, or, in the last resort, of the people; and that he should not refuse his consent to any measure proposed by his Ministry, unless it were of an extreme party character, such as the Assembly or the people would be sure to disapprove. These principles were the Colonial Secretary Earl Grey's views as recorded by himself in his "Colonial Policy." Lord Elgin arrived in Montreal, then the Seat of Government, early in the year 1847, and on the 30th January, 1847, was formally sworn into office.

It is singular what mistaken notions may exist as to the acts of administration, owing to ignorance of, or not rightly considering, the motive power impelling Ministers to a certain line of action. Never, perhaps, has this been more fully exemplified than in the act of this Government in passing the Rebellion Losses Bill, which passed both Houses, and received the assent of Lord Elgin on the 25th April, 1849. The Act is in the Statutes at large: 12 Victoria, cap. 58. This Act, which was assented to by Lord Elgin, and not reserved for Her Majesty, probably created more disturbance at the time, and was the cause of more disgraceful scenes (among others the burning of the Parliament Houses at Montreal), than any other Act that ever passed the Canadian Legislature; and yet this Act was but an outcome of a previous Act (9 Victoria cap. 65) entitled "An Act to provide for the payment of certain Rebellion Losses in Lower Canada, and to appropriate the proceeds of the Marriage License Fund," passed under a previous Governor and Tory Administration. The preamble of the Act partly gives the moving cause of the measure. It recites: "Whereas, on the 28th February, 1845, an humble address was unanimously adopted by the Legislative Assembly of this Province, and by them presented to the Right Honorable Charles Theophilus Metcalfe, the then Governor-General of the same, praying 'that His Excellency would be pleased to cause proper measures to be adopted, in order to insure to the inhabitants of that part of this Province formerly Lower Canada, indemnity for just losses by them sustained during the Rebellion of 1837 and 1838:' And whereas, on the 24th November, 1845, a Commission of five persons was, by His Excellency the said Governor-General, duly appointed to enquire into such losses arising from or growing out of the said Rebellion : And whereas, to redeem the pledge given to the sufferers of such losses, as well by the said address of the said Legislative Assembly, and the appointment of the said Commission, as by the letter addressed by the Honorable the Secretary of the Province, by order of the Right Honorable Charles Murray, Earl Cathcart, the then Administrator of the Government of the same, to the said Commissioners, on the 27th February, 1846, it is necessary and just that the particulars of such losses, not yet paid and satisfied, should form the subject of more minute enquiry under Legislative authority ; and that the same, so far only as they may have arisen from the total or partial, unjust, unnecessary, or wanton destruction of the dwellings, buildings, property, and effects of the said inhabitants, and from the seizure, taking, or carrying away of their property and effects should be paid and satisfied."

After this recital the Act goes on to authorize the issue of £100,000 of debentures, to pay such losses, which by clause ix., should also "include the sum of £9,986:7:2, raised by debentures under the said Act, hereinbefore mentioned." (9 Victoria cap. 65).

The Act of 1849 was an enlargement of the Rebellion Losses Bill of 1846. (9 Victoria cap. 65).

Sir Francis Hincks, in his Reminiscences, has thrown more light on this measure and the reasons of Lord Elgin's assent to it, than any previous writer. Quoting Lord Elgin's biographer as follows :

> Such was the measure, so clearly inevitable in its direction, so modest in its proportions, which falling on an inflamed state of the public mind in Canada, and misunderstood in England, was the occasion of a riot and

nearly a rebellion in the Province, and exposed the Governor-General, who sanctioned it, to severe censure on the part of many whose opinions he most valued at home.

Lord Elgin himself, in a confidential letter to Lord Grey, dated 1st March, 1846, thus wrote:

A good deal of excitement and feeling has been stirred up in the Province, by the introduction of a measure by the ministry, for the payment of certain rebellion losses in Lower Canada. I think that it will soon subside, and that no enduring mischief will ensue from it; but the opposition leader has taken advantage of the circumstances to work upon the feelings of old loyalists, as opposed to rebels, of British as opposed to French, and of Upper Canadians as opposed to Lower, and thus to provoke from various parts of the Province, the expression of not very temperate or measured discontent. I am occasionally rated in not very courteous language, and peremptorily required to dissolve the Parliament elected only one year ago, under the auspices of this same clamorous opposition who were then in power. The measure itself is not free from objection, and I very much regret that an addition should be made to our debt, for such an object, at this time. Nevertheless, I must say I do not see how my present Government could have taken any other course in this matter than that which they have followed. Their predecessors had already gone half way in the same direction, though they stopped short, and now tell us that they never intended to go further. If the ministry had failed to complete the work of alleged justice to Lower Canada, which had been commenced by the former administration, Mr. Papineau would most assuredly have availed himself of the plea to undermine their influence in his section of the Province. The debates in Parliament on the question have been acrimonious and lengthy, but Mr. Lafontaine's resolutions were finally passed by a majority of 50 to 20.

A fortnight later, Lord Elgin again wrote to Earl Grey:

The Tory party are doing what they can by menace, intimidation, and appeals to passion to drive me to a "coup d'etat." And yet the very measure which is at this moment the occasion of so loud an outcry is nothing more than a strict logical carrying out of their own acts. It is difficult to conceive what the address on the subject of the rebellion losses in Lower Canada, unanimously voted by the House of Assembly, while Lord Metcalfe was Governor and Mr. Draper Minister, could have been meant to lead to, if not to such a measure as the present Government have introduced.

Lord Elgin, on another occasion, gave his reasons for not reserving the Bill for the signification of Her Majesty's pleasure. His reasons were as follows:

There are objections, too, to reserving the Bill which I think I shall consider insurmountable, whatever obloquy I may, for the time being, entail on myself by declining to lend myself, even to this extent, to the plans of those who wish to bring about a change of administration. In the first place, the Bill for the relief of a corresponding class of persons in Upper Canada, which was couched in terms very nearly similar, was not reserved, and it is difficult to find a sufficient reason in so far as the representative of the Crown is concerned, for dealing with one measure differently from the other ; and in the second place, by reserving the Bill I should only throw on Her Majesty's Government, or (as it would appear to the popular eye here) on Her Majesty herself, a responsibility which rests, and I think ought to rest, on my shoulders. If I pass the Bill, whatever mischief ensues may probably be repaired, if the worst come to the worst, by the sacrifice of me ; whereas, if the case be referred to England, it is not impossible that Her Majesty may only have before her the alternative of preventing a rebellion in Lower Canada by refusing her assent to a measure chiefly affecting the interest of the *habitans*, and thus throwing the whole population into Papineau's hands, or of wounding the susceptibilities of some of the best subjects she has in the Province ; for among the objectors to this Bill are undoubtedly to be found not a few who belong to this class ; men who are worked upon by others more selfish and designing, to whom the principles of Constitutional Government are unfathomable mysteries, and who still regard the representation of royalty and, in a more remote sense, the Crown and Government of England, if not as the objects of a very romantic loyalty, at least as the butts of a most intense and unrelenting indignation, if political affairs be not administered in entire accordance with their sense of what is right.

It is deplorable that these noble sentiments of Lord Elgin could not have been published to the Canadian public during his lifetime. The seal of secrecy was, however, imposed by official etiquette. When the veil is thrown aside we can see how truly conscientiously Lord Elgin acted ; even to the extent of offering himself a sacrifice on the altar of Constitutional Government.

This was one of the acts of the Lafontaine-Baldwin administration with which Mr. Blake was connected, of which he, as well as the Government, had in his lifetime to bear the odium, but of which subsequent events have shewn the injustice, as directed towards the parties responsible for the Act.

Mr. Blake's appointment as Solicitor-General was on the 22nd April, 1848, so that he, as well as the rest, were subjected to much unmerited abuse.

There was another Act passed during the time the Lafontaine-Baldwin administration of 1847 was in power, of the very greatest importance, which gained for Mr. Blake a great deal of undeserved obloquy. That was "An Act for the more effectual administration of justice in the Court of Chancery of the Province of Upper Canada." This Act is the foundation and charter of the present Court of Chancery, as it existed before the Judicature Act, and was passed on the 30th May, 1849. It is the Act, 12 Victoria cap. 64.

The Court of Chancery, under the old system, with no perceptible Chancellor, but only a Vice-Chancellor, in the person of Jameson, V C., had got into great disfavor. The delays were terrible. The whole administration of the Court seemed to have got into an unrecognizable mass of stale Equity.

The history of the Chancery Act is this: Five years before the Act was passed a Commission had been issued under the Great Seal of the Province, whereby the Chief Justice of the Queen's Bench, the senior Judge of the Queen's Bench, Henry John Boulton, Robert Easton Burns, William Hume Blake, and James C. Palmer Esten, Esquires, were appointed Commissioners, with authority to make diligent enquiry whether and what alterations could be made in the practice established in the Court of Chancery for the Province of Upper Canada, or in the offices of that Court, in the different stages of the proceedings therein, from the commencement to the termination thereof, by which the expenses attending such proceedings and the time during which they depend in Court, might be lessened and abridged usefully and beneficially to the suitors of the Court, and the ends of justice be promoted.

The names of the Commissioners are a sufficient evidence that it was not a political Commission. The members of it were Judges or leading Barristers, and the Commission was named at a time when Mr. Blake was not in Parliament, was pursuing his practice, and that a large practice, in his profession, and so far as known, had not at the time any idea of entering Parliament. The head of the Commission was Sir John Robinson, the head of the Common Law Court of Queen's Bench, and with him was the senior Judge of that Court. This Commission recommended certain alterations to be made in the pleadings and practice of the Court, of a cardinal nature.

When Mr. Blake became Solicitor-General in 1849, in the Lafontaine-Baldwin Administration, he had to deal with the report which the Commission had made, and take measures to reform the Court. It was quite evident to his mind, as it was to all those who practised in the Court, that the whole construction of the Court required changing. More than this, he thought, and so did all the profession, that the time had come for doing away with the old Court of Appeals, which consisted of the Lieutenant-Governor or Chief Justice of the Province, and two or more members of the Executive Council, and substituting a Court composed of experienced Judges, leaving out Executive Councillors, who under the new order of things were likely to be, if not necessarily, politicians and heads of political Governmental departments. What would be thought now, if the Court of Appeal of the Province was composed of the Governor and his Executive Council?

Entertaining, as Mr. Blake did, the view that the administration of pure justice required a change, not only in the Court of Chancery, but in the Court of Appeal, he on the 13th March. 1849, (see Journals), obtained leave to bring in a Bill to make further provision for the administration of justice, by the establishment of a Superior Court of Common Law and also a Court of Error and Appeal in Upper Canada, and for other purposes. This resolution, which was subsequently passed by the House is the ground work of all the beneficial legislation of that Session, tending to the due administration of justice. It led to the passing of the following Acts : (1) The Court of Chancery Act, 12 Victoria cap. 64, with its far reaching consequences. (2) "An Act to make further provision for the Administration of Justice by the establishment of an additional Superior Court of Common Law, and also a Court of Error and Appeal in Upper Canada, and for other purposes." 12 Victoria cap. 63. Under the last named Act was constituted two new Courts ; the Court of Common Pleas, and the Court of Error and Appeal which was composed of the Judges of the Court of Queen's Bench, the Judges of the Court of Common Pleas, and the Judges of the Court of Chancery, which latter Court, under the new system, was made to consist of a Chancellor and two Vice-Chancellors.

Mr. Blake, during the same Session, brought in and carried "An Act to improve the Law of Evidence in Upper Canada (12 Victoria cap. 70), under which witnesses were not to be excluded from giving evidence by reason of interest, in any Civil or Criminal Court. This was a most beneficial measure, in every way tending to the elucidation of truth, by the admission of evidence theretofore totally excluded. If objections were to be made, the scheme of the Act was that such objections should apply to the credibility, and not to the admissibility, of the evidence.

The old practitioners have a very lively remembrance of how much of the time of the Courts was taken up, in deciding whether a witness should be excluded on this ground of interest or not, the nature and extent of such interest, &c. Many an injustice had been done by this exclusion of evidence: Mr. Blake's Act was to remedy the evil, and did it most effectually.

There were other legal Acts passed during the Session of a most beneficial character, promoted by the Attorney-General, the Honorable Robert Baldwin ; and the Solicitor-General, the Honorable W. H. Blake.

Sufficient has been written to shew the interest Mr. Blake took in legal Legislation. I do not think it would be going too far, to say that he was the greatest Law Reformer that had been in public life, from the early history of the Province till his time.

It was not only in Law matters that Mr. Blake proved himself a devoted son of Canada ; but in Educational matters also he was to the front. During the Administration of Lafontaine and Baldwin, the Attorney-General Baldwin, on the 3rd April, 1849, obtained leave to bring in a Bill to amend the Charter of the University of King's College. This resolution, the object of which was to put the University on a more liberal basis, was violently opposed in the House by the Tory party, but was finally carried on 18th May, 1849—forty-three members voting for the resolution, and only ten against. Mr. Blake constantly supported the resolution, voting against every amendment offered to delay the measure. The resolution became crystallized into "An Act to amend the Charter of the University establised at Toronto by His late Majesty King George the Fourth, to provide for the more satisfactory government of the said University, and for other purposes connected with the same, and with the College and Grammar School forming an appendage thereof: 12 Victoria cap. 82."

What inestimable benefit has the country gained by that Act. Graduates of the University of Toronto have, by its degrees, been given a passport to any and every place, on or off the continent of America, where education is prized for its own sake.

Mr. Blake was the first Chancellor of the new Court of Chancery. He was appointed on the 29th September, 1849, and had well earned the distinction. His appointment received the approbation of the Bar generally. Some political confreres took exception because of his having been the author of the Chancery Act, a frivolous objection, unworthy of those who made it. The Act was one which the country demanded, and who was so well qualified to administer the Act as the Chancellor, skilled as he was in the doctrines of Equity, who had held the Professorship of Law in the University. Time, the ofttime curer of misconceptions, and allayer of political virulence, has in this, as in many other cases, with many other persons, proved that the best men are often the targets at which men of little minds are willing to aim their harmless shots.

36—L. J.

As Chancellor of the Court, the Honorable William Hume Blake laboured diligently to give the Court a reputation second to none; a reputation which it has ever since borne. His judgments were lucid, always shewing that independence of mind which distinguished him as an advocate, and never failed him as a Judge. His chief characteristic was a disregard of case law, where case law came in conflict with principle. A reading of the numerous cases decided by him in the Chancery Court, shews that he appreciated the difference between an old land and new country. Wherever the English law, adapted as it might be to England and her condition, failed to impress him with its justice as applied to the state of things existing in Canada, he threw aside old precedents, to establish Canadian rights.

As an illustration, the Chancellor, in Chisholm vs. Sheldon (1 Chancery 318), threw out the suggestion, whether the doctrine applicable in England between termor and reversioner in respect to felling timber, ought to prevail as to an estate in Canada, the beneficial enjoyment of which is ordinarily obtained only through the destruction of the growing timber; and whether the doctrine of the Common Law as to growing timber, can be applied in all its extent to forest land. The Chancellor would have decided that the English law was not applicable; but the law did not require a decision on the question. The suggestion of the Chancellor bore fruit in subsequent cases. Even the Common Law Courts have adopted the doctrine. In Drake vs. Wigle (24 C. P. 409), the Court held "that it was not waste, in a tenant for life, to cut down timber on wild land for the sole purpose of bringing it into cultivation, provided the inheritance be not damaged thereby, and it is done in conformity with the rules of good husbandry." This decision was founded not only on Chancellor Blake's suggestion, but upon subsequent cases, both English and American, confirming his view. Galt, J., said, in giving judgment:

> When we bear in mind the natural state of lands in this Province, and that they are almost invariably useless for agricultural purposes until they have been cleared and cultivated, it appears to me that it would be highly inexpedient and unjust, if we were to hold that a tenant by the courtesy could not bring the lands under cultivation, by clearing and cultivating them; inexpedient, because it is for the interest of the public that the lands should be cultivated, and unjust, because it would leave the tenant, or, at all events, the land, subject to the taxes, and so far from a tenant by the courtesy deriving a benefit from the lands of his deceased wife, he would be subject to a loss.

I need not more than quote Chief Justice Hagarty in the same case, where he says:

> When the state of England, in the old time, more resembled that of our comparatively new country, I do not see anything in the authorities to have prevented the allowance to a life-tenant of the right to resort to the only method by which any benefit whatever could be derived from a piece of original forest, namely, the clearance of a moderate part for cultivation, by removal of the trees.

The Chief Justice quoted also Mr. Leith's Blackstone in favor of this view, and held, with Judge Galt, that it was not waste to cut trees from uncleared land, in order to cultivate the same.

I need not refer to other decisions or dicta of the Chancellor. Grant's Chancery Reports abound with his decisions, the reading of which would be profitable to the lay as well as legal reader.

Mr. Blake continued to hold the Chancellorship from 30th September, 1849, to the 18th March, 1862. Afflicted with gout, he sought relief in a milder climate. Failing health compelled him to retire from the Chancellorship in December, 1850. He subsequently, in March, 1864, accepted a position as one of the Judges of Appeal. He had not long to enjoy this position; his health became completely shattered, and he died at Toronto, on the 17th November, 1870, leaving surviving his widow, his two sons (the Honorable Edward and the Honorable Samuel Hume Blake), and two daughters. He had always been a member of the Church of England, in which faith he died, and was buried in St. James's Cemetery.

XXI.

The Honorable James C. Palmer Esten, Vice-Chancellor of Upper Canada.

THE Honorable James C. P. Esten was the son of the Honorable John C. Esten, Chief Justice of Bermuda. His father, the Chief Justice was of English Birth, and was sent out to that Crown Colony about the year 1805.

The Vice-Chancellor was born in Bermuda, in the early part of the present century. His father was Chief Justice at the time of his birth. Mr. Esten's early life was spent in Bermuda, and in Virginia, near Harper's Ferry, where he had numerous relations. Those of us who remember the Vice-Chancellor know that, though short and solid, of English breed, he nevertheless shewed in his face the effects of a southern climate. He had not the ruddy complexion of an Englishman, but the paleness begotten of a southern climate. His father, following in the footsteps of most of the emigrants from England to Bermuda, determined that his son should have an English education. He was sent to England at an early age, and received an English education at the Charter House, London, which has attained celebrity from the fact that some of the best novelists and writers of England have been educated at that institution. We call to mind names which have added lustre to the English nation: Addison, Steele, Thackeray, and a host of others who have earned renown, were educated at the Charter House.

Mr. Esten was also a pupil of Dr. Crombie, the author of "Crombie's Gymnasium."

Mr. Esten was called to the English Bar after completing his scholastic studies, and practised his profession for a short time in London and in Exeter, England. He read in the Chambers of S. B. Harrison, in London. Mr. Harrison, as is well known, in due time became a Colonist, making Canada his home till the time of his death. Mr. Harrison had gained a reputation in England before coming to Canada as a Compiler and Reporter. Those ponderous volumes on the shelves of the Law Library, Harrison's Digest, were the work of his hands. Harrison and Wallaston's Reports also serve to keep his name in mind with the Canadian Lawyer. Mr. Harrison was a member of Parliament, in this Province, in 1841, and a member of the Draper Government, holding the office of Provincial Secretary at the time of the Union of the Provinces. He was also Judge of the County Court of the County of York, for a number of years, and was much beloved by the Profession. Being possessed of equable disposition and unobtrusive manners, he earned the respect of all who knew him.

I mention these characteristics of Mr. Harrison, because it would almost seem that Mr. Esten had the same qualities which he derived from his quondam master, Mr. Harrison.

Vice-Chancellor Esten was of a quiet, undemonstrative manner, which in his early professional career, was the distinguishing characteristic of those who chose the branch of the profession in which he was educated.

In England, conveyancers are generally Barristers, and in most instances, of the Equity Bar. Mr. Esten applied himself to the practice mostly of a conveyancer, the very essence of which is careful investigation and profound thought. In the year 1836 he was induced by Captain Truscott, the senior partner in the firm of Truscott & Green, who carried on business in Toronto, to come to Canada. Captain Truscott had been a Post Captain in the navy, and was a relative of Mr. Esten by marriage, and thought he could advance his interest, by giving him a clerkship in his banking house. The banking business did not prove a success, however, and Mr. Esten instead of being advanced was thrown backward in his prospects. With the collapse of the bank, he was thrown on his own resources, and determined to become a member of the Canadian Bar. He was not an Attorney or Solicitor, either in England or Canada. It was a venturesome thing for an English Barrister, with no clientele in Canada, to undertake the business of counsel alone. Mr. Esten, however, with true English pluck, felt that with a stout heart and perseverance he might accomplish his purpose.

As a member of the Bar of England, he was entitled to be called to the Bar in Upper Canada, without going through a course of study here. He accordingly applied, and was admitted Student and Barrister on the same day, in Trinity Term, 1 & 2 Victoria, 1838.

Mr. Esten had not been a silent observer of events after his arrival in Canada in 1836, till the time of his call to the Bar. On his arrival in Toronto he took up his residence at Holland House, on Wellington Street, now the Reform Club.

When the Rebellion broke out in 1837, Mr. Esten had very little knowledge of the politics of the country. It was sufficient for him, that the din of battle and war's alarm were shaking the foundations of society. He volunteered to take up arms, for the defence of the Province. When the troops and militia moved from Toronto to the attack on the insurgents, who were coming down Yonge street to seize and sack Toronto, he served as a volunteer in the attacking party. He was present at the skirmish with Mackenzie's force at Montgomery's; shouldering his musket on behalf of the Loyalists, who were engaged in putting down the Rebellion. Referring to muskets, Mr. Esten's musket was almost too much for him: he was short in stature, but the musket was long and bulky. The muskets of those days were not like the rifles of to-day; both in latitude and longitude they far exceeded the present arms. Mr. Esten's musket almost got the better of him: he, however, was enabled, with much fatigue, to carry it to and from the scene of action; but when the Rebellion was suppressed, he had a weapon made, somewhat shorter and less bulky than the old musket, to use in case of emergency.

I well remember, on the breaking out of the Rebellion, that many of the boys at Upper Canada College applied to Sir Francis Head for arms to put down the Rebellion, and were told by the Governor to go home, as the arms were too heavy for the would-be bearers.

As Mr. Esten, was not a boy, but had grown to man's estate, he was accepted as volunteer, and, as I have said, marched up Yonge Street with the men collected to put down the Rebellion, and was at what has been called the "Battle of Gallows Hill," or as it might more fitly be styled the "Skirmish of Montgomery's Farm."

I will give a description of that affair as given by an eye-witness, a stranger in the city. He said:

Being a stranger in the city, I had not then (6th December, 1837,) formally volunteered, but took upon myself to accompany the advancing force, on the chance of finding something to do, either as a volunteer or a newspaper correspondent, should any opening occur.

The main body, led by Sir Francis himself, with Colonels Fitzgibbon and McNabb as Adjutants, marched by Yonge Street and consisted of six hundred men, with two guns; while two other bodies, of two hundred and a hundred and twenty men respectively, headed by Colonels W. Chisholm and S. P. Jarvis, advanced by by-roads and fields on the east and on the west of Yonge Street.

Nothing was seen of enemy till within half-a-mile of Montgomery's tavern. The road was there bordered on the west side by pine woods, from whence dropping rifle shots began to be heard, which were answered by the louder muskets of the militia. Presently the artillery opened their hoarse throats, and the woods rang with strong reverberations. Splinters were dashed from the trees, threatening, and I believe causing more mischief than the shots themselves. It is said that this kind of skirmishing continued for half-an-hour, to me it seemed but a few minutes. As the militia advanced their opponents melted away. Parties of volunteers dashed over the fences and into the woods, shouting and firing as they ran. Two or three men of both parties were lifted tenderly into carts, and sent off to the city to be placed in hospital. Others lay bleeding by the road side—rebels by their rustic clothing; their wounds were bound up, and they were removed in their turn.

Soon a movement was visible through the smoke, on the hill fronting the tavern, where some tall pines were then standing. I could see there two or three hundred men, now firing irregularly at the advancing loyalists; now swaying to and fro without any apparent design. Some horsemen were among them, who seemed to act more as scouts than as leaders.

We had by this time arrived within cannon shot of the tavern itself. Two or three balls were seen to strike and pass through it. A crowd of men rushed from the doors and scattered wildly in a northern direction. Those on the hill wavered, receded under shelter of the undulating land, and then fled like their fellows. Their horsemen took the side road to the westward, and were pursued, but not in time to prevent their escape. Had our right and left wings kept pace with the main body, the whole insurgent force must have been captured.

Sir Francis halted his men opposite the tavern, and gave the word to demolish the building, by way of a severe lesson to the disaffected. This was promptly done by firing the furniture in the lower rooms, and presently thick clouds of smoke and flames burst from doors and windows.

The battallion next moved on to perform the same service at Gibson's house, several miles further north.

Many prisoners were taken in the pursuit, all of whom Sir Francis released, after admonishing them to be better subjects in future.

The march back to Toronto was very leisurely executed, several of the mounted officers carrying dead pigs and geese slung across their saddle-bows as trophies of victory.

These pages may meet the eye of some old college boys, if they do I would recall to their recollection the loot that some of the boarding-house boys brought home, taken by one of themselves at Montgomery's. This loot was in the shape of preserves which had been carefully put up by the Montgomery's for the season. Alas! for the fate of war, the pots of preserves were seized upon by the boys, brought to the college boarding-house where the boys in residence enjoyed a rich feast of preserves, as loyal young subjects feeding on the "Spolia opima" of their enemies.

I had a conversation, a few days ago, with an old coloured man, ninety-eight years old, living in St. John's Ward. He told me: "Yes, sah! I was at the Battle of Gallows Hill, in Colonel Jarvis's Coloured Corps! Yes, sah! and we came off victors!" And so they did: the troops returned with flags flying and drums beating: the city was saved.

When absolute peace was again restored to the Province Mr. Esten went to work in the practice of his profession as Barrister, Counsel, and Conveyancer. He soon gained the reputation of being skilful as a Conveyancer and Special Pleader. Several firms of Solicitors often availed themselves of his services as Special Pleader, and finally as supporting his pleading in Court. Thus he went on, from step to step, till he obtained a good practice as Counsel in cases in Equity.

I have known him, when the late Chancellor Blake was at the Bar, to be engaged as Counsel in opposition to him in the old Court of Chancery. Frequently Mr. Blake gave him briefs as Counsel with him, in cases before the Court. Mr. Blake had a great deal of confidence in him, for the faithful attention he would give to a case.

Mr. Esten's is a singular, and one of the very few, instances where an English Barrister has come out here, not being a Solicitor, but Counsel only, who has successfully undertaken the profession here, and attained to a seat on the Bench. In his case he had only been practising eleven years when, on the 29th September, 1849, he was appointed Vice-Chancellor.

While at the Bar he had taken no special interest in politics. If anything, his sympathies were with the Reform party. He had taken no active part, however, in political contests. His success was entirely attributable to a conscientious discharge of duty on his part, which gained for him favorable notice and attention from those with whom rested preferment in the profession. He received his promotion to the Bench from the second Lafontaine-Baldwin Government.

During the time Mr. Esten was on the Bench, many reforms were introduced in the Court of Chancery. He was on a commission appointed by the Crown to introduce reforms in the practice of the Court. The system of Circuits for hearing of causes was established in his time, and other reforms of an equally useful nature.

Mr. Esten was regarded as a Judge the soundness of whose decisions were seldom challenged by the Bar. This was specially the case in all matters relating to real estate.

37—L. J.

One of the earliest cases decided by Mr. Esten is the case of Newton *vs*. Doran, 1 Grant's Reports 473-490, with the circumstances of which I was familiar, having been Counsel in the case with Mr. Mowat. In that case the majority of partners, combining with their general manager Towns, had excluded the plaintiffs from their due control of the business. The plaintiffs, on default of answer to the bill, had obtained a injunction restraining Towns from receiving debts due the partnership, and that he might make discovery of the facts set forth in the bill, and for general relief. The defendants afterwards answered, denying all fraud and collusion, and moved to dissolve the injunction: 1st. Because Wilson, one of the partners not made a defendant, was a necessary party (Wilson was made a party defendant in the morning, before the sitting of the Court); 2nd No equity for relief prayed; no relief prayed against Towns except an account. It was the second ground that was mostly urged for dissolution of the injunction. During the argument, Mr. Turner, Counsel for defendants, argued, as to his second objection: "This is not relief, but discovery; and a plaintiff is not at liberty to file a bill for discovery as against one defendant." Esten, V. C., said: "I do not recollect any instance of such a bill." However, when he came to give judgment he demolished the objection, saying:

> This bill must be treated as one for relief against Towns; it prays that *he* may make a discovery; and be restrained from proceeding at law; and there is a prayer for further relief. He is not bound to make any discovery: an account, however, may be obtained under the general prayer, and an injunction may of course be obtained if proper. Then, is this proper to be conjoined with the other purposes of the suit? We think this objection cannot govern.

The case has always been kept green in my memory from the circumstance that Mr. Turner, a very experienced Counsel and Solicitor, well versed in the practice of the Court, felt convinced that it was improper to have joined Towns the manager, as a co-defendant with the partners: that as to Towns the matters were the subject of a separate suit. Not so, however—Towns was charged with fraudulent collusion. When Mr. Esten. V. C., came to consider the case he readily disposed of the objection. The case was afterwards heard by Chancellor Blake (1 Grant, 496,) and the plaintiffs granted relief.

This is the case which I have referred to in the life of Chancellor Blake, in which he gave the defendant Towns in the witness box such a dressing that he was glad to leave the Court, a sadder, but a wiser man.

The case Chisholm *vs.* Sheldon (1 Grant 319), was an important case, and was thought to involve the question, whether the principle of law which settled the rights of termor and reversioner in relation to growing timber, would have been regarded in England as applicable to an estate of this kind, as to which the beneficial enjoyment of the land is ordinarily obtained and can only be attained through the destruction of the growing timber: and also, whether the doctrines of the Common Law, as to growing timber, could be applied in all their extent to forest lands in this country. The Court did not think the case called for a decision on these points: the real point to be decided was, whether a mortgagor of a term of years could restrain his mortgagee, being in possession, from felling timber, although he may have obtained the consent of the reversioner to it, and on this point Vice-Chancellor Esten held he should be restrained. He said, in giving judgment:

> There is no doubt that, as an abstract principle, the owner of a term of years who has mortgaged it may restrain his mortgagee, being in possession, from felling timber, although he may have obtained the consent of the reversioner to it. If the plaintiffs (the termors and mortgagors) have not only a right of enjoyment as to the timber, but also power to fell it and convert it to their own use, their title to an injunction is stronger, but not clear or decided. This question it is not necessary to decide upon the present occasion; for, admitting that the plaintiffs, as the absolute owners of a term of one thousand years, have, as against the reversion, a right to fell forest trees the original growth of the country, the defendants, as mortgagees, could not claim this right as against the plaintiffs until foreclosure.

Fuller *vs.* Richmond (2 Grant, 24,) is another case in which Mr. Esten, as Vice-Chancellor, gave an important decision on a point much debated at the time; and that was, whether a manufacturer of logs under an agreement for advances, when it had been agreed also that when the logs were manufactured they should be marked with the initials of the party so making advances, could give a title to a third party after such marking had taken place, as against the party making advances; as to which the Vice-Chancellor decided in favor of the plaintiff—the party making advances—and granted an injunction against the transferee of the manufacturer. He said:

> The sale and delivery by the defendants Richmond & Case (the manufacturers) was undoubtedly an abuse of their power and a breach of trust as agents. It could confer no legal title on Redmond, for Richmond & Case had no legal title to give, and the plaintiff had not acted in any manner which would make their disposition effectual for this purpose, for he had simply intrusted his goods to his agents that they might be conveyed to the mouth of the river (the place named in agreement for their delivery).

The case is well worth referring to also as discussing, though not deciding, the question of the transfer in equity of unmanufactured goods, so as to give an equitable title or lien to the transferee, and as to parol agreements collateral to the main agreement in writing.

I will cite only one other decision of Vice-Chancellor Esten, though I might cite a great many, all of which shew the close attention he gave to the facts and application of the law. It was a question whether the Court, at the instance of a first voluntary grantee of land, would use its power and set aside a second voluntary conveyance to another party. The point came up in Houlding *vs.* Poole (2 Grant, 685,) when the Vice-Chancellor held that where there are two voluntary settlements the Court will, at the suit of those interested under the first, set aside the subsequently executed settlement, and it is no objection to relief in such cases, that the Courts of Law would give effect to the first against the second.

Vice-Chancellor Esten was on the Bench fifteen years. If I were asked to give the chief characteristics of the Vice-Chancellor I would say it was conscientiousness. He was regarded by the Bar as possessed of sterling honesty of purpose, and faithful in the discharge of his official duties. He was a reserved man, not given to ostentation or show. He was always ready at the call of duty.

I remember when a war was threatened with the United States, in the matter of the Oregon boundary, a corps of rifles was formed in Toronto. Volunteers were called for, and Mr. Esten, though a Judge, enrolled himself with the Victoria Rifles, of which I was a member. We used to meet nightly in the St. Lawrence Hall for drill purposes. Mr. Esten was always there, and was my right hand man. We had some difficulty in forming fours, but ultimately succeeded. Just about this time, the matter in dispute was settled between Great Britain and the United States, and drill ceased. Good came out of it, however, as the Victoria Rifles merged into that crack corps the Queen's Own, which has a Dominion reputation.

In the year 1861 the Vice-Chancellor was seized with a lingering and painful illness, ending ultimately in death, which took place at Toronto, on the 24th day of October, 1864.

He left surviving one son and three daughters. Mr. Esten, the Secretary of the Law Society, is his only surviving son.

XXII.

THE HONORABLE ROBERT EASTON BURNS,
JUDGE OF THE QUEEN'S BENCH.

OBERT EASTON BURNS was the son of the Reverend John Burns, a Presbyterian minister, who emigrated from Scotland in 1803; and, on his arrival in Canada, settled at Niagara. Robert Easton Burns was born at Niagara on the 26th December, 1805; and was educated by his father, who was then Master of the Grammar School, and from whom he received a liberal education. He was a diligent student, acquiring by industry and perseverance (his permanent characteristics through life), knowledge and learning, which fitted him to fill the position of Principal of the Grammar School in his native town, at a very early age. When sixteen years of age he determined to obtain a legal education, and, in Easter Term, 3 George IV., 1822, was admitted as a student of the laws.

Mr. Burns commenced his studies for the Bar with John Breakenridge, who was at this period practising as a Barrister and Attorney in Niagara.

So far as I have been able to ascertain, Mr. Burns completed his whole course with Mr. Breakenridge.

Miles O'Reilly, Q.C., of Hamilton, and at one time Judge of the County Court of Wentworth, (Hamilton) was a fellow student of Mr. Burns, in the office of John Breakenridge. Mr. Burns was called to the Bar in Hilary

Term, 7 George IV., 1827, after which he practised his profession for some years in Niagara, St. Catharines, and Hamilton, with considerable success. He had been at the Bar only ten years, when, on the 16th July, 1836, he was appointed Judge of the Niagara District. The routine of the duties of a District Court Judgeship did not suit Mr. Burns's active and ambitious mind. In the Spring of 1838, he resigned his office, and removed from Niagara to Toronto, when he entered into partnership with Christopher Alexander Hagerman, then Attorney-General. The Attorney-General had a large and extended business, and required a partner to conduct the ordinary business of his office, while he was engaged in the performance of public duties. Mr. Burns had acquired such a reputation for steady, plodding work, that Mr. Hagerman had no difficulty in choosing him for a partner. Mr. Burns had other qualifications which fitted him to fill the place of partner with Mr. Hagerman. He did not aim at brilliancy, so much as honesty and fidelity, in the performance of any work he undertook.

When the seat of Government was removed from Toronto to Kingston in 1841, the Court of Chancery, in which Mr. Burns had, in addition to other work, begun to practise, was removed with the Government. The Court of Chancery was young at this time; still the amount of work involved was very great, owing to the system then in vogue. Bills and answers, interrogatories and cross-interrogatories, entailing much more labor than afflicts the practitioner of the present day. Mr. Burns's untiring industry and determination to succeed, induced, if it did not compel him to give the utmost attention to business.

When the seat of Government was removed from Kingston to Montreal in 1844, the Court of Chancery was again removed to Toronto, compelling Mr. Burns to change his residence from Kingston to Toronto, the seat of the Court.

On his return to Toronto, Mr. Burns formed a partnership with Mr. Oliver Mowat, the present Attorney-General of the Province, and Philip M. Vankoughnet, who afterwards became Chancellor. The firm name was Burns, Mowat, & Vankoughnet. The business of that firm was very large, probably the most extensive of any in Toronto. They had their office on the south side of King Street, at or near the place where the Romain Buildings now stand. Mr. Burns did not continue long in this partnership, as shortly after his removal to Toronto, he was offered and accepted the appointment of Judge of the Home District.

In 1844, he received two appointments from Government, one, that of Bankrupt Commissioner, on the 24th February of that year; and the other, the Judgeship of the Home District, on 19th August, 1844, which office he held till 1848. In 1848, he received a Commission of Enquiry to investigate the management of the Provincial Penitentiary.

Mr. Burns held the appointment of Judge of the Home District till 1848, when he resigned. and formed a partnership with the late John Duggan, Q.C. The partnership name was Duggan & Burns.

In 1850, a vacancy occurring in the Queen's Bench, Mr. Burns was appointed Judge of that Court. As a Judge he was painstaking, and gave general satisfaction. He was an unobtrusive man. On the Bench he was patient and careful in consideration of points presented for his adjudication. In charging juries, he was not as careful as some other Judges in dissevering the law from the facts, making an express ruling, but rather submitted the whole case to the jury. I have practised before him in both Courts, the District and Queen's Bench Courts. The experience he had in the District Court stood him in good stead in the Queen's Bench.

Judge Burns was very much esteemed for his integrity while at the Bar, and for his unassuming worth on the Bench. He was very unostentatious in his manner; and ready at all times to receive the Bar in a manner which made them feel that it was pleasant to come before him.

He was ever liberal in his dealings with his fellow man. He was of a generous disposition, and fully illustrated the adage, that a friend in need is a friend indeed. In his declining years he had to stint himself, by reason of his having come to the rescue of friends in financial straits. In personal intercourse he was most agreeable. Few men enjoyed a joke better than he: he had what might be called a laughing face, and whenever the risible faculties were agitated, his hearty response shewed itself in his face with wonderful quickness, so that bystanders could not but join in the laugh. His intercourse with the Bar was of the most friendly character: he always acted with them as an elder brother. He was much beloved by the Students, who shewed their appreciation of his urbanity and condescension by year after year electing him President of the Osgoode Club. His popularity was further evinced by his election to the Chancellorship of the University of Toronto, during the time that he held the position of Judge. His decisions as a Judge were much respected, from the fact that he was always most painstaking, and never adjudged a case till he had mastered all the facts.

Judge Burns was never in political life, hence the incidents of his existence may not possess the attractions which belong to those who make a study of politics, and obtain power and place through political agencies. He was eminently a self-made man, of plodding habits and honesty of purpose, which obtained favorable recognition from all who knew him.

There are those still living who practised before him on the Bench, though few who knew him as I did, practising at the Bar. He was not considered a brilliant man at the Bar; but his slow, but honest, utterances often commanded more respect, and had more weight, than the oratorical displays of the most rhetorical of the Bar of his time. He was a living instance of success from honesty, rather than from forensic eloquence, or from what is sometimes called "genius," the handmaid of the "heaven-born" lawyer.

Mr. Burns was twice married. His first wife was Miss Anne Taylor, by whom he had four sons. His second wife was Miss Nanton, a sister of the late Edward Nanton, of Toronto.

In the early part of 1863, Judge Burns was stricken down with an illness which terminated fatally. He died in Toronto on the 12th January, 1863.

XXIII.

THE HONORABLE JOHN GODFREY SPRAGGE, CHANCELLOR OF ONTARIO, AND CHIEF JUSTICE OF ONTARIO.

THE Honorable John Godfrey Spragge was an Englishman. He belonged to a Dorchester family, but was himself born at New Cross, one of the Surrey suburbs of London, in 1806. The family came to Canada in the year 1820, in a Government ship, as appears by a letter from the Admiralty, in answer to a letter written them with the object of their coming out to Canada :

NAVY OFFICE, *28th April, 1820.*

SIR,—In reference to your letter of the 22nd ulto., we acquaint you, for the information of Earl Bathurst, that Mr. Joseph Spragge, his wife, three sons and two daughters, and his mother-in-law, may embark on board the Huddart, at Deptford, about the 7th May, for passage to Quebec.

I have a copy of this letter in my possession.

Mr. Spragge's father was by profession a tutor. He was tutor in the Central School of York, now Toronto, in the years immediately following his coming to the country. He lived to a good old age, and died about the year 1848. I remember well being at his funeral, which took place from the family residence, in or in the vicinity of York street, between King and Wellington streets.

Mr. Spragge (the Chancellor's father) was not willing that his son should be entirely educated by himself, and so, in due time, trusted the completion of his education to Doctor, afterwards Bishop, Strachan, at the Royal Grammar school; or, as it was usually called, the Home District school.

These schools, the Home District and Central, had a high reputation in the early days of York. They were both situated in a large six acre field, just to the north of the plot on which St. James's Church now stands. The Central School was kept by Mr. Spragge's father, who had enjoyed the advantage of a regular training in England as an instructor of the young. Doctor Scadding has given us a description of him in his "Toronto of Old." He says of him: "Though not in holy orders, his air and costume were those of the dignified clergyman." Referring to the Central School, and to the fact that the Chancellor was educated at it, he says: "Of the Central School, the words of Shenstone, spoken of a kindred establishment, become in one point, at all events, true to the letter:

> E'en now sagacious foresight points to shew
> A little bench of bishops here
> And there, a chancellor in embryo
> Or bard sublime."

To form a proper estimate of the Home District School, the school at which the Chancellor completed his education, as also a reminder of the boys of those days, I transcribe the order of examination at that school on Wednesday, 11th August, 1819, First Examination day.

FIRST DAY.—The Latin and Greek classes. Euclid and Trignometry.

Thursday 12th August. SECOND DAY.—To commence at 10 o'clock. Prologue by Robert Baldwin.

READING CLASS—

George Strachan—*The Excellence of the Bible.*
Thomas Ridout—*The Man of Ross.*
James McDonell—*Liberty and Slavery.*
St. George Baldwin—*The Sword.*
William McMurray—*Soliloquy on Sleep.*

ARITHMETIC CLASS—
  James Smith—*The Sporting Clergyman.*
  William Boulton, Jr.—*The Poet's New Year's Gift.*
  Richard Oates—*Ode to Apollo.*
  Orville Cassel—*The Rose.*

BOOK KEEPING—
  William Myers—*My Mother.*
  Francis Heward—*My Father.*
  George Dawson—*Lapland.*

FIRST GRAMMAR CLASS.   SECOND GRAMMAR CLASS.
  Debate on the Slave Trade.

  FOR THE ABOLITION—Francis Ridout, John Fitzgerald, William Allan, George Boulton, Henry Heward, William Baldwin, John Ridout, John Doyle, James Strachan.

  AGAINST THE ABOLITION—Abraham Nelles, James Baby, James Doyle, Charles Heward, Allan McDonell, James Myers, Charles Ridout, William Boulton, Walker Smith.

FIRST GEOGRAPHY CLASS.   SECOND GEOGRAPHY CLASS.
  James Dawson—*The Boy that Told Lies.*
  James Bigelow—*The Vagrant.*
  Thomas Glassco—*The Parish Workman.*
  Edward Glennon—*The Apothecary.*

NATURAL HISTORY—
        Debate by the Young Boys.
  Sir William Strickland—Charles Heward.
  Lord Morpeth—John Owens.
  Lord Hervey—John Ridout.
  Mr. Plomer—Raymond Baby.
  Sir William Yonge—John Fitzgerald.
  Sir William Windham—John Boulton.
  Mr. Henry Pelham—Henry Heward.
  Mr. Bernard—George Strachan.
  Mr. Noel—William Baldwin.
  Mr. Shippen—James Baby.
  Sir Robert Walpole—S. Givins and James Doyle.
  Mr. Horace Walpole—James Myers.
  Mr. Pulteney—Charles Baby.

CIVIL HISTORY—
  William Boulton—*The Patriot.*
  Francis Ridout—*The Grave of Sir John Moore.*
  Saltern Givins—*Great Britain.*
  John Boulton—*Eulogy on Mr. Pitt.*
  Warren Claus—*The Indian Warrior.*
  Charles Heward—*The Soldier's Dream.*
  William Boulton—*The Heroes of Waterloo.*

CATECHISM—

Debate on the College at Calcutta.

SPEAKERS:—

Mr. *Canning*—Robert Baldwin.
Sir *Francis Burney*—John Doyle.
Mr. *Wainwright*—Mark Burnham.
Mr. *Thornton*—John Knott.
Sir *D. Scott*—William Boulton.
Lord *Eldon*—Warren Claus.
Sir *S. Laurence*—Allan Macaulay.
Lord *Hawkesbury*—Abraham Nelles.
Lord *Bathurst*—James McGill Strachan.
Sir *Thomas Metcalf*—Walker Smith.
Lord *Teignmouth*—Horace Ridout.

RELIGIOUS QUESTIONS AND LECTURES—

James McGill Strachan—*Anniversary of York and Montreal Colleges, anticipated for January 1st, 1822.*

Epilogue by Horace Ridout.

Not half a dozen of the boys who took part in that examination are now living. The names of most of them are household words in Canada. Robert Baldwin, afterwards the Honorable Robert Baldwin, Attorney-General and Premier of the Province, on this occasion delivered the prologue. In it the administration of Hastings, in India, is eulogized thus :

> Her powerful Viceroy, Hastings, leads the way
> For radiant truth to gain Imperial sway,
> The arts and sciences for ages lost,
> Roused at his call, revisit Brahma's coast.

A school with such a bill of fare as was presented on this occasion was no mean school. There has perhaps never been in the schools of Canada a better educated set of boys than Dr. Strachan's. In 1833, the Doctor had presented to him an address, accompanying a piece of plate. Among the forty-two subscribers to the address were the names of four gentlemen, all pupils of his, who had then, or afterwards, attained to a position of Judge of the Queen's Bench. These names were, the Honorable Sir John Beverley Robinson, Chief Justice; the Honorable Archibald McLean, Chief Justice; the Honorable James

Buchanan Macaulay, Chief Justice; and the Honorable Jonas Jones, Puisne Judge.

I have written the lives of all these Judges, and now add to the list another distinguished Judge, Chancellor Spragge.

On leaving this School (Home District), Mr. Spragge was equipped for a start in life, and chose the law for his profession. He was entered on the books of the Law Society as a Student, in Michaelmas Term, 4 George IV., 1823. He first was articled to Sir James B. Macaulay, then plain Mr. Macaulay, and afterwards to Honorable Robert Baldwin, with whom he finished his studies. We have seen that both Mr. Macaulay and Mr. Baldwin had been pupils of Doctor Strachan, at the same Home District School at which Mr. Spragge was educated.

Mr. Spragge was admitted to the Bar in Michaelmas Term, 9 George IV., 1828. On being admitted to the Bar he commenced the practice of his profession in York. He secured for himself a good practice, and when the late Honorable J. H. Cameron was called to the Bar in 1838, Mr. Spragge admitted him to a partnership, which lasted for some years, the firm name being Spragge & Cameron.

While at the Bar, Mr. Spragge had a large business. He had a large agency coupled with a good local business. When Mr. Cameron joined him in business, the new blood brought new business. Mr. Cameron soon gained a reputation as Special Pleader. He was at one time Reporter for the Queen's Bench, and by that time had got into a large Counsel business.

Mr. Spragge was more of an office than Court-man. He was the ablest Equity Draftsman of his day practising in the Courts. He never engaged in politics, having no taste for the excitements of political life. He was a steady, industrious, painstaking counsel. English born, he from boyhood retained an affection for the ways of the English. He was fond of the English game of cricket, was an excellent player, and was often to be seen with his fellow cricketers giving play to physical exercise, to the relief of mental strain. In his youthful days, there was a large English emigration to the Province, officers and sons of officers, besides many civilians of the higher class.

Cricketing, in England, is not confined to the higher classes. It is the peoples' popular game, cultivated in all the schools. In Canada, other games in the field have largely taken the place of the English pastime. The Chancellor, even to the latest period of his life, retained his interest in the game, and did not consider it beneath his dignity, while a Judge, to give countenance and support to friendly matches of cricketers in their strife for mastery.

Mr. Spragge was elected Bencher of the Law Society in 1835; was at one time Surrogate Judge of the Home District, having received his appointment to that office in 1836; he continued to retain the office till the re-union of the Provinces of Upper and Lower Canada in 1841.

Upon the establishment of the Court of Chancery, by the Chancery Act of 1837, Mr. Spragge was appointed Master in Chancery—the first in the Province. His appointment was made on the 20th June, 1837. He held this office for a longer time than any Master that has succeeded him, with the exception of Mr. Buel. He was a most able and efficient Master. The profession universally gave him credit for the manner in which he performed his new and important duties. The business of the Master's office in Chancery is always very onerous and exacting—never more so than when the office was filled by Mr. Spragge. On the establishment of the Court, rules had to be framed to regulate the procedure therein. Mr. Jameson, the first Vice-Chancellor of the Court, had not had a very extensive experience, consequently Mr. Spragge felt the responsibility thrown on him in inaugurating the new Court. He undertook the task with vigor, and hence was evolved a set of rules which were of the greatest value in the transaction of the business of his department.

On the removal of the Seat of Government to Kingston, just after the Union of 1841, the Court of Chancery and its Master had to follow the Government. It was one of the duties of the Master, during his incumbency of office, to attend the Legislative Council in that capacity.

The Seat of Government was not destined to favor Kingston with its presence for a long period of time, and was removed from Kingston to Montreal in 1844. When this took place, the Court of Chancery returned to its old grounds in Toronto. It was a sad day for Kingston, losing the Governor and the Government officials; how much sadder was it to lose the Court of Chancery, the very fountain of justice as administered in a Court of Equity. There had surrounded this Court a certain halo, which seemed to permeate the whole atmosphere. The gentlemen practising in that Court were mostly real old, or real young, English gentlemen. There was a Turner, a Maddock, an Esten, and others who, as it were, gave tone and dignity to the Court. The removal of the Court gave occasion to the effusion of some lines by Mr. John Ramsey, an English Barrister, which are worth recording. Here are the lines :

> Dreary and sad was Frontenac,
> Thy Duke ne'er made a clearer sack
> Than when the edict to be gone,
> Issued from the Vice-regal Throne.
> *Exeunt omnes*, helter skelter,
> To Little York again for shelter,
> Little no longer : York the New,
> Of imports such, can boast but few,
> A goodly freight, without all brag,
> When comes 'mongst other Master Spragge,
> And skilful Turner, versed in pleading,
> The Kingston exiles gently leading.

To the lines was appended a note, written no doubt, in order that there should be no mistake of the names mentioned in the poetical effusion. The note is as follows :

J. G. Spragge, Esq., the present very highly esteemed and respected Master of the Court of Chancery ; R. J. Turner, Esq., a skilful Equity Draftsman and Solicitor in Chancery.

Mr. Turner will be remembered as the senior member of the firm of Turner & Bacon, in Toronto ; and as being afterwards Referee of Titles, with his office in Osgoode Hall.

Mr. Spragge was not only Master, but was at one time Registrar of the Court of Chancery. He was appointed to this office on the 13th July, 1844.

From what has been written, it will be seen, that in the various offices held by Mr. Spragge, he had splendid opportunities for becoming familiar with all the duties appertaining to officers of that Court.

I have mentioned before that Mr. Spragge was not a politician, and had no taste for politics: his sympathies, and I believe, the voting power he possessed were, however, with the Conservative party.

In the year 1850 and beginning of 1851, the second Baldwin-Lafontaine Reform administration was in power. Mr. Baldwin had always a most conscientious regard for law and its due administration. The Court of Chancery with its Chancellor and two Vice-Chancellors, was indeed his and Mr. Blake's creation. When afterwards, an attempt was made in Parliament to abolish the Court which he thought so essential for the country, he resigned his place in the ministry, rather than submit to such an insult. The attempt was considered by him like an attempt to strangle one's own child. When it came to the appointment of a second Vice-Chancellor, under his and Mr. Blake's Bill, he had no difficulty in offering Mr. Spragge the position, which Mr. Spragge accepted, and thus became Vice-Chancellor of the Court in which he had held the minor offices for thirteen years. He was appointed Vice-Chancellor on the 27th December, 1850, and on the same day Andrew Norton Buel was appointed Master of the Court.

In 1869, Vice-Chancellor Spragge was promoted to the Chancellorship of the Court, in succession to the Honorable Philip VanKoughnet.

There were many cases before him as Vice-Chancellor, which he disposed of to the satisfaction of the profession.

He was always ready to hear a case through, not coming to sudden or erroneous conclusions. His experience as Master had paved the way for a successful Judge. I need not cite any of the cases adjudged by him while Vice-Chancellor, but will only refer to some cases in which he gave judgment as Chancellor and head of the Court of Appeal, of which Court he was created Chief Justice on the 2nd May, 1881.

Archer *vs.* Scott, 17 Grant 247, was a case decided by the Chancellor shortly after his promotion to the Chancellorship, and is important as bearing on the Statute of Frauds. The plaintiff brought suit to set aside a conveyance, which the plaintiff had been induced to execute, and for relief against the second clause in a will, under the following circumstances: The defendants, Scott & Erritt, had acted as solicitor and agent, respectively, to one Mrs. Hill. Erritt was employed by her to get her will drawn. She was on her death bed at the time, and was anxious to leave whatever she had to her niece, the plaintiff. He procured a will to be drawn by a solicitor (not Mr. Scott), and left it with her for execution, expressing a wish not to be a witness. She was an intelligent person, and competent to make a will; and having read the instrument, she executed it in the presence of two female friends. By the first clause, all her real and personal property were given to the plaintiff. The second clause was as follows:

> Having sold and agreed to convey unto W. H. Scott, Esquire, of Peterborough, aforesaid, Barrister, the following parcels of real estate, namely, the south half of lot number nine, in the fourth concession of the Township of Ennismere, in the County of Peterborough, containing one hundred acres more or less; also, the residence and one acre of land in the Township of Monaghan, adjoining the said Town of Peterborough; I hereby devise the said two parcels, sold to Mr. Scott, unto the said Sophia Archer in fee simple: and I hereby direct her to convey the same to said Scott; and I hereby devise and bequeath unto the said Sophia Archer along with all my other property the purchase money to be paid in respect of said parcels to be her own property for her own use and benefit absolutely.

A few days after executing the will the testatrix died, and Erritt induced the plaintiff, who was under age, to execute to the defendant Scott, a conveyance of the property mentioned in the will, without his paying or providing for the consideration. There was no evidence of any bargain with Scott for the two lots, as stated in the will. There was a written bargain with Scott as to one of the lots, and Erritt said there was a verbal bargain to sell to Erritt the other lot mentioned in the will; but he did not set up any writing to that effect, or any part performance of the alleged bargain.

It was argued before the Chancellor that the admission, in the second clause of the will, of the sale was sufficient to sustain the transaction. The Chancellor, however, held differently, saying:

> I do not see how the Statute of Frauds is to be got over. There was no contract in writing between Mrs. Hill and Erritt, and assuming her will to be a sufficient note in writing within the Statute, as I think it would be if it contained all that is necessary to constitute a contract, there is this difficulty, that it does not contain all that is necessary in a contract for the sale of land; the price is an essential element. The will speaks of the purchase money, and I suppose it is to be inferred that the amount of purchase money had been agreed upon, but the difficulty remains that there is no note or memorandum in writing of the person to be charged upon the contract, of that essential element of a contract.

Mills vs. Cottle, 17 Grant 335, was an interesting case, involving the right of a party making advances to a trustee for the purposes of a trust, but taking the trustee's personal bond for repayment, the money advanced having been applied to the purposes of the trustee, to stand in the place of the trustee to the extent of the advance, against the trust estate. The Chancellor held that the party advancing the money had such right. He said:

> The plaintiff's equity is, that he advanced money to the defendants as trustees taking their personal bond for repayment, and that the money so advanced was applied to the purposes of the trust, and he claims to stand *pro tanto* in the place of the trustees as against the trust estate. It is not disputed that money was so advanced by the plaintiff and that it was so applied by the trustees. I think the plaintiff has the equity which he claims by his bill.

The cases so far quoted may be considered by some, not all of much importance, they do, however, involve principles, the elucidation of which is useful for the instruction of the popular if not the legal mind.

We come now to consider a case, which has perhaps been the subject of more controversy, than almost any other case that has ever occurred in Ontario. The misfortune is, that the case has been the subject of controversy not only in the Courts, but in the Councils of two Governments, the Dominion Government and Ontario Government, and has been the subject of special Local Legislation. I do not propose to deal with the political questions involved, but only with the legal and equitable issues. In these, I think, the Chancellor stands out pre-eminent. The question presented for his consideration, and that of his brothers of the Ontario Court of Appeal Bench, was a simple one in itself, but in the principle involved of far reaching consequences, nothing more or less than the blocking up a stream against parties desiring to float their logs and timber down that stream, to or towards the market where the logs or timber were to be sold.

The case I refer to is McLaren *vs.* Caldwell, reported in 6 Ontario Appeal Reports, page 472, *et seq.* The plaintiff, a lumber merchant, on the stream in question, had made improvements on the stream, had acquired a title to twelve parcels of land on the margin of the stream, and in some, if not in all the cases, including the bed of the stream ; the stream itself was about two hundred miles long, and during time of freshets was capable of floating down its course timber, rafts, and crafts. The plaintiff's bill was filed for the purpose of obtaining an injunction against Caldwell, the defendant, a rival timber merchant, higher up the stream, to prevent his floating his timber down the stream to market.

By the Act of 11 Victoria, cap. 87, sec. 5, embodied in secs. 15 and 16 of the Consolidated Statutes of Upper Canada, it was enacted :

> That it shall be lawful for all persons to float saw-logs, and other timber, rafts, and craft, down all streams in Upper Canada during the Spring, Summer, and Autumn freshets, and no person shall by felling trees or placing any other obstruction in or across any such stream, prevent the passage thereof.

Now, singular as it may appear, leaving out surplusage of words, the real point was, whether "all," in the section quoted, meant what it said, or only meant "some" streams, instead of all streams. It had been decided by the Court of Common Pleas in Boale *vs.* Dickson, 13 C. P. 337, that that section did not apply to the case of any stream when improvements were necessary to be made to render the stream floatable : that the clause did not alter the character of the private streams, and that the owner of the land over which the stream flowed had a right to prevent an intrusion upon it. On the case going before Proudfoot, V.C., in the Court of Chancery, he granted the injunction, in the law applicable to the case following Boale *vs.* Dickson. His conclusion, as well as the correctness of the decision in Boale *vs.* Dickson, was challenged by the defendant, who appealed to the Ontario Court of Appeal. The case was most ably argued by counsel for both sides, and the judgment of the majority of the Court given on the 8th July, 1881.

Chancellor Spragge gave a judgment, in which he held the decision in Boale *vs.* Dickson not to be conformable to the Statute : in effect holding that the defendant Caldwell had a right to float his timber down the stream. Two others of the Judges of the Court of Appeal concurred in his conclusion, one of them, Mr. Justice Patterson, giving a lengthy, well reasoned judgment. As I have only to deal with the Chancellor, I will only give the important parts of his judgment, which I may be permitted to say is clear, non-diffusive, striking the point without circumlocution, and giving effect to the Statute as it was, and not legislating to a conclusion. He said, in his judgment :

> Upon the appeal to this Court it is contended that the construction placed upon the Statute in Boale *vs.* Dickson was not correct. It becomes, our duty, therefore, to consider and determine that question.

It is obvious from a perusal of the Acts (which are consolidated in cap. 48 of the Consolidated Statutes of Upper Canada) that it was the policy of the Legislature to encourage the lumber trade of the Province, and to preserve the fish in the streams. The Act of 1828 (9 George IV. cap. 4), recites: "Whereas it is expedient and found necessary to afford facility to the inhabitants of this Province, engaged in the lumber trade, in conveying their rafts to market, as well as for the ascent of fish, in various streams now obstructed by mill dams." The same policy is evidenced by 12 Victoria, cap. 87, the 1st section of which supplies what may be taken to have been omitted in the Act of 1828, viz., that aprons or slides to mill dams should be so constructed as to afford sufficient depth of water for the passage of saw logs, lumber and timber, a provision embodied in section 4 of the Consolidated Act. Then in section 5 of the same Act we find enacted what is embodied in sections 15 and 16 of the Consolidated Act. The first clause of section 5 is in the same terms as section 15, beginning thus: "And be it enacted, that it shall be lawful for all persons to float saw logs, &c., and other timber, rafts and craft down all streams in Upper Canada during the spring, summer, and autumn freshets; and that no person shall, by felling trees, or placing any other obstruction in or across any such stream, prevent the passage thereof." In Boale *vs.* Dickson the opinion is expressed "that this right so given extends only to such streams as, in their natural state, will, without improvements, during freshets, permit saw logs, timber, &c., to be floated down them;" to streams of a different class to those mentioned in the 3rd section, "down which lumber is usually brought."

No such qualification of right is to be found in the Act, nor in any of the previous Acts thereby consolidated. There is nothing in the contexts of any of these Acts shewing, or tending to shew, that such qualification was intended; and we know, from what we find in the evidence taken in this cause, that, confining the right given by section 15 to such streams as are described in the passage I have quoted from Boale *vs.* Dickson, would go far to defeat the avowed policy of the Legislature.

* * * * * *

To adopt the construction put upon the Act in Boale *vs.* Dickson, we must read "all streams" as meaning "some streams," and we look in vain in the Act for any class of streams defined as they are defined in Boale *vs.* Dickson. If what is supposed in that case to have been intended by the Legislature had really been intended, section 15 should have run thus: "All persons may float saw logs and other timber during the spring, summer, and autumn freshets, down," not "all streams," but "such streams as in their natural state will, without improvements, permit saw logs, timber, &c., to be floated down them."

Is it too much to say that such an alteration of the Act is not construction, but legislation. I am unable to concur in the construction put upon section 15 of the Act in Boale *vs.* Dickson. There being no context, nor indeed anything whatever in any of the Acts on this subject, to control the ordinary grammatical meaning of the words used, we must read them in their ordinary grammatical sense, and should therefore construe section

15 as giving the privilege to all persons to float saw logs and other timber down *all* streams in Upper Canada, during the spring, summer, and autumn freshets.

Notwithstanding this plainly expressed judgment the Supreme Court of the Dominion, at Ottawa, reversed the decision of the Chancellor and Ontario Court of Appeal, holding that the decision of Boale *vs*, Dickson was good law. See McLaren *vs*. Caldwell, 8 Supreme Court Reports, 435. But, on appeal to the Privy Council, in England, the decision of the Chancellor was sustained, and the Supreme Court reversed: 9 Appeal Cases, 392.

The parties to this suit expended as much as $20,000 in costs, before the final conclusion was reached. It seems a large sum to expend in unravelling the question involved, but Judges, as well as Doctors, will differ, and when that occurs, a reference to the Court of final resort must be made, in order to a final and conclusive settlement of the controversy.

The case of Regina *vs*. Hodge, 7 Appeal Reports, is another case in which the judgment of the Chancellor was sustained by the Privy Council. The question was, whether the Ontario Legislature could delegate its powers in regard to shop, saloon, tavern, auctioneer, or other licenses, to a Board of License Commissioners. In the particular case, Hodge, a licensed tavern keeper, in the City of Toronto, had been convicted by the Police Magistrate for allowing a billiard table to be used in his tavern after the hour of seven o'clock at night, in contravention of a resolution and enactment of the Board of License Commissioners of the City. The Court of Queen's Bench held the conviction to be bad, holding that the Legislature could not delegate its powers to the Board of License Commissioners. The Chancellor held that the Legislature had such power. He said:

My conclusion is, that it cannot be correctly laid down as a proposition of law, that a Legislature cannot delegate its powers to other bodies, or to boards of officers created by itself, in order to the carrying out its legislation upon particular subjects. It is not necessary to go further.

It has been the course of legislation to do this in England and in Canada, and also in the neighbouring republic, and it is manifest that a contrary doctrine would cripple legislation to a very serious extent.

I need not refer to any more decisions of the Chancellor, but will add that he was a Judge of sound judgment and great experience.

The Chancellor was a devoted son of the Church of England, and was frequently a delegate to the Synod of the Church. He married a daughter of Doctor Alexander Thom, Staff Surgeon and Medical Superintendent of the military settlements on the Rideau. He died at his residence, in Toronto, on the 20th day of April, 1884, leaving him surviving two sons and two daughters. One of his sons is a practising physican in Toronto, and another a clergyman of the Church of England, stationed at Newmarket, in the County of York. The widow of the Chancellor only survived him four days, she having died on the 24th April, 1884.

The memory of the Chancellor and his wife is perpetuated by a tombstone inscription in St. James's Cemetery, which reads as follows:

IN

LOVING REMEMBRANCE

OF

JOHN GODFREY SPRAGGE,

CHIEF JUSTICE OF ONTARIO,

BORN SEPTEMBER 16TH, 1806,

DIED APRIL 20TH, 1884,

AND

CATHERINE SPRAGGE,

BORN JANUARY 26TH, 1815,

DIED APRIL 24TH, 1884.

———

IN DEATH NOT DIVIDED.

"Make them to be numbered with Thy Saints in Glory Everlasting."

ERECTED BY THEIR CHILDREN.

XXIV.

THE HONORABLE PHILIP MICHAEL MATTHEW SCOTT VANKOUGHNET, CHANCELLOR OF UPPER CANADA AND OF ONTARIO.

THE Honorable Philip VanKoughnet was second Chancellor of Upper Canada. I omit the Michael Matthew Scott here, and, as he was generally known as Philip VanKoughnet before he reached a seat on the Bench, I could not, if I would, call him by any other name. The pleasures of memory call me back very many years, to the time I first made the acquaintance of Philip VanKoughnet. I think it was in the year 1839, or 1840, when I met him, a guest at the hospitable table of Robert Hervey, of Brockville. I was then a Law Student in the office of George Sherwood, who was afterwards Judge of the County Court of Hastings, and was invited to Mrs. Hervey's, where, as I have said, I first met Mr. VanKoughnet and a friend, Doctor Dickenson, of Cornwall. I had an idea then, which I have since learned was a mistaken one, that Mr. VanKoughnet was two or three years older than myself. He presented to my mind a young man of manly qualities, and of sociable disposition. He was most agreeable in conversation, referring with engaging vivacity to the life of a soldier, which he had led during the Rebellion of 1837. He had "turned out," as it was termed, in defence of the Province, and was an officer in the Incorporated Militia. All I knew of him then was, that he was the son of Colonel VanKoughnet, of Cornwall, who had for many years, some time before then, represented respectively the counties of Stormont and Dundas, in the Upper Canada Assembly. Colonel VanKoughnet, the father of Philip VanKoughnet, was a man who had earned the respect of his contemporaries, for his sterling qualities and honest patriotism. He had all the stubbornness of a German, with the patriotism of a Briton.

In the early part of the eighteenth century, the ancestors of Philip VanKoughnet, or, according to the orginal spelling VonGoughnet, emigrated from Colman in Alsace, to the British Colonies in America, and the family remained there till the close of the Revolutionary War. During the American struggle for Independence, the VanKoughnets espoused the cause of the Royalists, adhering to England's Crown and King. At the close of the war, they found, like many others, that it was all but impossible to live among a people, who, puffed up with their success in the revolution, were ready and willing to drive from the country those who preferred King George to George Washington.

In the year 1783, the family left the United States and settled in the neighbourhood of Cornwall. It is a tradition in the family, that the Americans had become so incensed at him on account of his loyalty that they set a price on his head, hoping to force him into submission to the new Government. In this, however, they were unsuccessful.

Philip VanKoughnet, (the future Chancellor,) was born at Cornwall on the 26th January, 1823. He received his education there under Doctor Urquhart, who was district school master at Cornwall, the school being held in the same building in which Doctor Strachan educated so many of our Judges. Doctor Urquhart was recognized as one of the best scholars in the eastern part of the Province. Doctor Urquhart had a very high opinion of the capacity of his young pupil, and prophesied for him a future successful career in whatever profession he might adopt. Mr. VanKoughnet's mother was most desirous that he should become a clergyman, and directed his earlier education to that end. The rebellion breaking out, the sound of martial music was too much for Doctor Urquhart's pupil, and his experience in these days, diverted his attention from theological studies in another direction. Hearing Mr. Hagerman, when Solicitor-General in 1837 or 1838, make a brilliant speech, he determined to abandon the idea of entering the Church, hardly perhaps his own, and take up law as a profession. He had no sooner resolved than he acted. Presenting himself before the Benchers of the Law Society, he was entered on the books as Student, in Michaelmas Term, 2 Victoria, 1838, and at once entered upon his studies in the office of George Jarvis, Esquire, of Cornwall, afterwards Judge of the County Court there.

Philip VanKoughnet had very much of the soldier in him; to retain soldierly qualities, and at the same time devote himself to law, he could not have done better than become a student of Mr. Jarvis, who had performed distinguished service for his country in the war of 1812. After being in the office of Mr. Jarvis for a time, his ambition caused him to seek out an office in the capital, Toronto, where he might complete his course of studies. Messrs. Smith & Crooks of Toronto, then had a very large and growing business, and were glad to admit Mr. VanKoughnet to their office, where he proved to be a most studious and painstaking student. Philip VanKoughnet was one of those men, who, without seeming to be, was really in his Student and early Bar days, the most industrious of his class. He could apply himself to the routine work of an office all day, and apply himself to the study of law books nearly all night, and not feel the worse for his labour. In his early days he had an iron constitution, which gave him an advantage over most of his fellows. When he was in the office of Smith & Crooks, he was recognized by them as their best and most diligent student. He took the lead in the office, and retained it till the expiry of his articles in 1843. He was called to the Bar in Hilary Term, 7 Victoria, 1843, and soon afterwards formed a partnership with Robert Easton Burns, afterwards Judge of the Queen's Bench, and with Oliver Mowat, the present Premier and Attorney-General of the Province of Ontario.

At this time, the Act prohibiting County and District Court Judges practising, had not yet been passed. As soon, however, as the Act making such prohibition was passed, Mr. Burns withdrew from the firm, which then became the firm of Mowat and VanKoughnet. During the time he was in these firms he was not only a day worker, but a night worker also; he and Mr. Mowat frequently giving a good part of the night, as well as the whole day, to the business of their clients. The practice of these firms was largely Equity; and in those days of long, voluminous bills, and equally long, voluminous answers, with interrogatories and cross-interrogatories, now happily abolished, those who wished to practise their profession successfully, had necessarily to devote their whole time to work. It must be remembered, too, that these were not the days of either stenographers or typewriters, consequently the manual labor of an office was much greater than it is now.

Mr. Mowat and Mr. VanKoughnet were in partnership for a considerable time, their office being a little above what are now the Romain Buildings, on King street. As I boarded at McDonald's Hotel, then located on the spot where the Romain Buildings stand, as did also Mr. Mowat, I had a knowledge of the retirement of Mr. Mowat from hotel to office, to do night work there, which seemed to occupy him as much as his day's labours.

On the termination of Mr. VanKoughnet's partnership with Mr. Mowat, his brother, Matthew R. VanKoughnet, joined him, and they carried on business together for some time. He had by this time got a very prominent position at the Bar, and was much sought after as Counsel to conduct important cases. He had great natural ability, which, added to his legal knowledge and eloquence, made him a very successful nisi prius Advocate, as well as Counsel in Term. I have been frequently with him at the Cobourg Assizes, and witnessed the large number of briefs which fell into his hands, and the ability and successful manner in which he conducted cases in the Courts.

During the latter years of his practice at the Bar, Mr. VanKoughnet gave the most of his attention to Equity. His contemporaries practising in that Court, were Mr. Mowat, afterwards Vice-Chancellor; Mr. Strong, afterwards Vice-Chancellor, and now Judge of the Supreme Court; William Roaf, and other prominent Chancery Barristers.

Mr. VanKoughnet was one of the few men who practised both in the Common Law Courts and in Chancery. His rivals of these days were all men of ability. I don't think any of them claimed superiority over, if equality with, Mr. VanKoughnet. He was for some time Professor of Equity Jurisprudence in Trinity University. It was his custom to lecture orally, which is no doubt the best mode for impressing the hearers; of more value than reading from notes. His lectures were instructive, and much appreciated by those who heard them.

Mr. VanKoughnet had naturally a large and expansive mind. He preferred the wide paths of Equity to the narrow limits of the Common Law.

Mr. VanKoughnet was appointed Queen's Counsel by the Baldwin-Lafontaine Government in 1850, though he had been only seven years at the Bar, and was only twenty-seven years of age. As he was a political opponent of that Government, it was considered at that time a tribute to his ability and standing at the Bar.

We now come to Mr. VanKoughnet's Parliamentary career. Up to 1856 the Legislative Council had been nominative. In 1856, by the Act 19 & 20 Victoria, cap. 140, the Council was made elective. The Act provided that thereafter the Council should be composed of the then present nominated members, and of forty eight members to be elected for eight years, and to that end the Province should be divided into forty-eight electoral divisions, twenty four in Upper Canada and twenty four in Lower Canada. This Act received Her Majesty the Queen's assent on the 24th June, 1856, and proclamation thereof was made by His Excellency, Sir Edmund Walker Head, Governor-General, in the Canada Gazette of the 14th July, 1856. By the 8th section of the Act, the Governor was directed on or before the first day of the following September, to issue writs for the election of twelve Legislative Councillors to represent the twelve electoral divisions. In 1856, Sir John Macdonald induced Mr. VanKoughnet to enter the Government of the day. He was very reluctant to enter politics. I was with him half an hour before he accepted office, and know how unwilling he was to enter the Ministry. Personal friendship for Sir John Macdonald, however, prevailed with him, and he became a Cabinet Minister, as President of the Council. The choice had to be confirmed by an electoral constituency, and Mr. VanKoughnet became a candidate for the Rideau division, to represent that District in the Legislative Council. He was a comparative stranger to the constituency, but by vigorous action, and the aid of influential friends, he was elected for the division by a handsome majority. He was Commissioner of Crown Lands in the Macdonald-Cartier Government, formed in 1857, on the retirement from the Government of Mr. Taché.

The day after the formation of the Macdonald-Cartier Government Parliament was dissolved, and the parties went to the hustings, the "Clear Grits," as the extreme Radicals had got to be known, with the cry of "non-sectarian schools," and "representation by population."

By the Union Act of 1841, the Representatives from each Province were equal, although at that time Lower Canada had the larger population. The Clear Grits now contended that, as Upper Canada had outgrown the Lower

Province, and had considerable preponderance of population, she should have more members than the sister Province—in other words, should have a preponderance of power. However popular such a cry might be in Upper Canada, it gained no assent from the Lower Canadians, who always contended that the Union was forced upon them. In the contest which took place on this issue, the Ministry lost three of their members, viz., Messrs. Cayley, Spence, and Morrison. The Lower Canada electors returned an overwhelming body of Ministerialists.

The new Parliament assembled in February, 1858. When the House met, they were informed that Ottawa had been selected as the Seat of Government, on the recommendation of Mr. Macdonald, leader of the Government. The announcement to the House had a very disturbing effect. The opposition in the House moved a resolution, and several amendments, to the Address proposed by the Government, disapproving of Her Majesty's choice of Ottawa as a Capital. After an animated discussion, Mr. Piché moved, that in the opinion of the House, " Ottawa ought not to be the Seat of Government for the Province," which was carried by a majority of sixty-four to fifty. This was a clear defeat of the Government, and the Government resigned. Mr. Macdonald treated the defeat as disrespect shewn by the House to the Queen's decision. The Government had a majority in the House on other questions, but on this exceptional matter they were not able to command a majority.

The Opposition, however, were eager for office, and in face of the fact that they were in a minority, except on that sole question, on being applied to by the Governor for counsel and advice, formed a Government under the leadership of the Honorable George Brown for Upper Canada, and the Honorable A. A. Dorion for Lower Canada, ever since known as the Brown-Dorion Government.

Mr. VanKoughnet, on the fall of the Macdonald-Cartier Government, fell with it. The fall, however, was not to be of long duration, for after an existence of but two days the Brown-Dorion Government suffered a defeat in the House. Not more than eight days had elapsed before a new Government was formed, composed of nearly all the old members of the Macdonald-Cartier Government, the exceptions consisting in Messrs. Galt and George Sherwood taking the places of Messrs. Cayley and Loranger, who were left out of the new arrangement. The new Ministry was called the Cartier-Macdonald Ministry, and was formed on 8th August, 1858. Mr. Macdonald was, however, the real leader, as before.

During the Session of 1857, an Act relating to the Independence of Parliament was passed, the 7th section of which provided that:

> Whenever any person holding the office of Receiver-General, Inspector-General, Secretary of the Province, Commissioner of Crown Lands, Attorney-General, Solicitor-General, Commissioner of Public Works, Speaker of the Legislative Council, President of the Committees of the Executive Council, Minister of Agriculture, or Postmaster-General, and being at the same time a member of the Legislative Assembly, or an elected member of the Legislative Council, shall resign his office, and within one month after his resignation, accept any other of the said offices he shall not thereby vacate his seat in the said Assembly or Council.

As the old Macdonald-Cartier Ministry had not been out of office a month, the new Cartier-Macdonald Ministry could, giving a strict interpretation to this Act, avail themselves of it, and, by merely changing places, retain office without going back to the people for re-election. This they did. Mr. VanKoughnet, from being Minister of Agriculture in the Macdonald-Cartier Government, becoming Commissioner of Crown Lands in the new Government. The other Ministers were:—for Upper Canada: Honorable John A. Macdonald, Attorney-General, Upper Canada; Honorable John Ross, President of the Council; Honorable Sidney Smith, Postmaster-General; Honorable George Sherwood, Receiver-General. For Canada East: Honorable George E. Cartier, Premier and Attorney-General; Honorable A. T. Galt, Inspector-

41—L. J.

General; Honorable L. V. Sicotte, Minister of Public Works; Honorable N. F. Belleau; Honorable Charles Alleyn. Some of the Ministers made a double change of office; hence this rearrangement was called, "The Double Shuffle."

It was fortunate for the Ministry that the Act to secure the Independence of Parliament, 20 Victoria, cap. 22, was on the Statute Book, for it saved them a great deal of trouble and inconvenience. They were not disposed to go back for re-election so soon after a general election. They insisted that they had never, as a Government, lost the confidence of Parliament; that though defeated as an old Government, on the question of the locality of the Seat of Government, they were quite justified, as a new Government, in taking the benefit of the Independence of Parliament Act.

This is a grave Constitutional question, which for the purpose of writing the life of Mr. VanKoughnet, need not be discussed. As a question of law, the Ministry were sustained in the interpretation they had placed on the Act.

To test the question, two actions were instituted, one in the Court of Queen's Bench, and the other in the Court of Common Pleas. The cases were Macdonell *vs.* Smith, 17 Q. B. 310; and Macdonell *vs.* Macdonald, 8 C. P. 479. In the pleading in those cases, it was stated that the Ministry of which the defendant, as Postmaster-General, was a member, all resigned office on the 29th July, and on the 2nd August were succeeded by the Opposition, who resigned on the following day: that, on the 6th, the old Ministers were re-appointed, but took different offices from those which they before held, and on the 7th, resigned again and were re-appointed to their old places; and it was alleged that the appointment to a different office was colorable, and made only to enable defendant to resume his original appointment, without going back for re-election.

The Court, after full investigation and considering the whole case, held, that although such a proceeding was probably not contemplated by the Act, it was allowed by it: that the Court could not look at the motives of Ministers, or strain the construction of the Statute so as to impose a penalty; and that, whether the course taken was or was not consistent with the system of political government established in this Province, was a question which they could not take into consideration.

It will thus be seen, that the Court did not undertake to decide as to the propriety of the step taken by Ministers, to sustain themselves in office. It is enough to say they had the right, they claimed it, and were within the law. The precedent was certainly not a good one, and if ever attempted to be repeated, would probably be the cause of much constitutional inquiry.

The writer of the "Life and Times of Sir John A. Macdonald," has cited two instances in which, as he says, similar proceedings in relation to the holding of office were resorted to in England. One case, in 1839, by Lord Melborne, and another in 1873, when the Liberal Government found themselves defeated on their Irish University Bill. Mr. Gladstone resigned, and by his advice the Queen invited Mr. Disraeli to form a Ministry. Mr. Disraeli thought the situation over, and concluded not to try his luck in the Commons as constituted; whereupon Her Majesty again sent for Mr. Gladstone, who, with the other Ministers, resumed their places. There was no re-election in either case, as the writer thinks. He says, in reference to the Canadian case:

> The case here differed somewhat, but not so as to change the constitutional principle involved in the English cases. There was a slight legal barrier in the way in Canada, and it was avoided by taking advantage of the letter of the law.

So far as Mr. VanKoughnet was concerned, he was probably in a better position than any of the other Ministers, as he had but recently been returned to the House to hold his place as Legislative Councillor for eight years. Had he been a nominative member, instead of an elective, he would have had no cause to consider the question of re-election. In his various offices of Minister of Agriculture and Commissioner of Crown Lands, he gave great satisfaction, inaugurating reforms in the departments which were of permanent use. From the time of his election to the Legislative Council he was leader of the Government in that body. His conciliatory manner disarmed opposition in the Council, he was smooth and ready in debate, and could always be depended upon to do justice to any subject left in his charge.

Mr. VanKoughnet was sent as a delegate to England, to confer with the Imperial authorities on the subject of the Intercolonial Railway, the purpose of which was to unite the Maritime Provinces by an iron bond, and afford a ready means of access to the capital, not only for the colonists, but for emigrants coming to the country, as also a ready means of transport for troops if required from England for defence of the country.

Mr. VanKoughnet was appointed Chancellor of Upper Canada, on the 18th March, 1862. On taking his seat on the Bench, he found the duties onerous, requiring all his skill in the performance of judicial work. Owing to the long illness of his predecessor, Chancellor Blake, and the vacancy subsequent to his resignation, there were large arrears to be brought up. The new Chancellor had been some years out of practice. Notwithstanding that, by assiduity and attention, he soon had the Court and all its offices in good working order. It was soon apparent to the profession and to the public that he was the man for the place. He had great quickness of perception, and grasped the points of a case readily. In most of the cases argued before him he gave judgment at the close of the argument, and was seldom reversed by a higher Court. It was he who introduced the present practice of hearing the argument of a case immediately on the close of the evidence. Before that, the evidence was first taken and the case subsequently argued at Toronto, whether the Court had been held in the country or in Toronto. His courtesy and consideration made him highly esteemed by the Bar. He introduced many reforms in the practice of the Court, which were of great value to the practitioners and to suitors.

The cases heard before him are reported in volumes ten to sixteen of Grant's Reports. His decisions will all be found to the point, without undue prolixity. I remember many such cases, but need only refer to one, regarding the novelty of an invention. He decided the case in favor of the plaintiff, and that the patent, which was for an improvement in the method of making the fluted iron rollers used in the construction of grain-crushing or chopping mills. The case is Summers *vs.* Abell, 15 Grant's Chancery Reports, 532. It went to a re-hearing, and the Chancellor's judgment was sustained. The plaintiff was a poor man, the defendant a wealthy manufacturer at Woodbridge. The plaintiff claimed that the defendant had obtained a knowledge of the plaintiff's machine, and that he was manufacturing machines the same in form and principle, in violation of the plaintiff's right as first inventor and patentee thereof. The defendant denied that Summers, the plaintiff, was the first inventor; he also alleged that the machine had been used for the same, and like purposes, long before the plaintiff applied for his patent. Mr. J. A. Boyd, the present Chancellor, was of counsel for the plaintiff; and Mr. Maclennan for defendant. As may be supposed, with such counsel, the case was vigorously contested. The defendant, among other objections to the patent, alleged that the machine was so simple that it could not be the subject of a patent; but the Chancellor, in giving judgment, said:

> Upon the evidence, I find that the invention of the inclined plane, or perhaps the form and position of the inclined plane, employed by the plaintiff as a means, or appliance, for directing the tool cutter, or the roller upon the tool cutter, so as to produce spiral or curved grooves in the roller, was and is a novelty, first introduced and discovered by plaintiff; and that his invention is of great utility in reducing the labor and cost formerly incurred in preparing such grooves. Its simplicity is no

objection, but is its greater recommendation. Many of the most valuable contrivances, when produced, are remarkably simple in character, and therefore of the greater benefit and advantage. One may be astonished that everyone did not before adopt so simple a plan; but the merit of it belongs to him who first suggested and brought it into use. This inclined plane is, I think, the novelty in the plaintiff's cutting machine. That the plaintiff has combined with it, for the purpose of working the machine, other things—not new—cannot detract from the value of this invention, else no machine could be patented, as boards, nails, screws, bolts, &c., necessary to its construction are not new in character. The cutting of straight grooves in solid, or hollow, rollers, or cylinders, by machinery appears not to have been new; and so the cutting of spiral grooves by hand, or chipping, was well known; and perhaps other means have been used: but it does not appear to have occurred to any one but the plaintiff to produce spiral grooves by giving the plane, on the edge of which the turning or index wheel works, an incline, the necessary effect of which is to give the grooves more or less curvature, according to the dip or steep of the incline—very simple, true—when it is pointed out to you; and yet, introduced into practice, how valuable.

I will not pursue the Chancellor any further in the matter of judgments—they were generally terse, not too diffusive, and, reading them, readily understood.

The Chancellor was an intimate and life-long friend of mine. While at the Bar, I had much companionship with him. Always pleasant and agreeable: with a great sense of humour, which lent a charm to his conversation his society was always welcome.

> "A merrier man,
> Within the limit of becoming mirth,
> I never spent an hour's talk withal."

In his political life, I had the means of knowing his sentiments and opinions. He was a man very firm of purpose; of a most generous disposition; unostentatious, and ever ready to help a friend. He was naturally of a vivacious temperament, and had hosts of friends. He married the daughter of Colonel Turner, an officer of one of the regiments of the line. He had two sons born of the marriage—Philip and Edmund. The latter is now a Commander in the Navy: he earned distinction with Lord Charles Beresford in his brilliant achievements in Egypt.

The Honorable Philip VanKoughnet died at Toronto, on the 7th November, 1869, after a short illness.

At the time of his death the Honorable Mr. Mowat was one of the Vice-Chancellors of his Court. He was at that time holding the Court at Cobourg. On receiving intelligence of the death of the Chancellor, he pronounced the following eulogy, which, coming from one who had known him at the Bar, was his partner in business, and colleague of the Bench, has especial value. Vice-Chancellor Mowat said :

> As a Judge he was most conscientious, he had a profound love of justice, and an exalted sense of judicial duty. In the discharge of his office he acted without fear, favor, or affection, if any Judge ever did. He was from the first prompt in deciding, and that he was generally accurate as well as prompt is shewn by the fact that his decrees were generally (I believe) as seldom appealed from as those of any Judge we ever had. Whatever those opposed to him, politically, may have thought of the measures or proceedings of the Government of which he formed part, nobody doubted the purity of his motives or the soundness of his patriotism. He loved this Canada of ours, which was the land of his birth, and he earnestly desired to promote its interests.

Mr. Mowat had not been of the same political party as the Chancellor, had indeed often found occasion to differ with him on political subjects. The estimate he formed and expressed of him as a Judge, was but voicing the opinion of the opinion of the whole Bar, and of the public. His too early death was a great loss to the Bench. He was not 47 years of age when he died. If it had pleased providence to prolong his life, there was open for him a career of great usefulness. Personally, he was to me one of my most special friends, and it was with pain and sorrow that I joined the cortege which followed him to his last resting place in St. James's Cemetery.

> " Friend after friend departs,
>   Who has not lost a friend ?
> There is no union here of hearts,
>   That finds not here an end."

XXV.

The Honorable George Skeffington Connor, Judge of the Queen's Bench.

HE Honorable George Skeffington Connor was Irish to the manner born. He was the son of a successful Irish Lawyer, who practised in Dublin.

George Skeffington Connor, better known in Canada as Doctor Skeffington Connor, was born in the City of Dublin. He was an out and out Dublin man, and took his D. L. Degree at Trinity College. Doctor Connor was an accomplished and highly educated man. Before coming to Canada he had been called to the Irish Bar, not with the intention of practising however, as he had expectations of a good income from other sources than the Bar—he only went to the Bar "causa honoris." It was the custom of Irish gentlemen who were men of wealth, or expected to come into a fortune, to take a Degree at the University and attach themselves to the Bar as an honorable and liberal profession. Doctor Connor came to Canada with William Hume Blake, afterwards Chancellor Blake, in 1832. In July of that year a number of young Irish gentlemen formed themselves into an emigration society, determined to leave their native land and make their future home in a new country, where with prospects of fortune from tilling the soil, they could at the same time satisfy the love for adventure so congenial to the Irish heart. The company was a goodly one; it consisted of William Hume Blake; the Reverend Dominick E. Blake; their mother and sisters; the late Archdeacon Brough; Doctor Robinson; the Reverend Benjamin Cronyn, late Bishop of Huron; the Reverend Mr. Palmer, afterwards Archdeacon Palmer; and Doctor Skeffington Connor.

It must not be supposed that these emigrants had the titles of honor or dignity, which I have ascribed to them, when they left Ireland. These were all, or nearly all, of Canadian growth. They did not come out as ordinary emigrants, but chartered a vessel, the "Ann of Halifax," to carry them across the Atlantic. When only three days out, one of the crew was seized with cholera, and before morning his body was thrown overboard. Owing to the prophylactic measures of Doctor Robinson, the plague was stayed.

There was after this an inclination in the hearts of the emigrants to return to Ireland; but taking courage they persevered in their undertaking and after a six weeks' voyage, arrived in the St. Lawrence. They were subjected to a long quarantine at Grosse Isle. The cholera was epidemic in Canada this year (1832), and the emigrants were not allowed to proceed on their journey till September; they then took up their course for York (Toronto), where they arrived unattacked by the dreadful disease which in that year carried off so many native Canadians and emigrants. The party separated in York: Mr. Brough, Doctor Robinson, and Doctor Connor going northwards, to the Township of Oro, on Lake Simcoe, and the remainder going west, to the Township of Adelaide, of which the Reverend Dominick E. Blake had been appointed Rector, by Sir John Colborne, then Governor of the Province.

Doctor Connor settled in Oro, and tried his hand at farming. It is hardly to be supposed that a Trinity College man, whose life had been devoted to study and polite literature, would be a perfect success in extracting stumps in the back woods of the Township of Oro. He bought land in the neighborhood of Orillia, but after being there a few years, he left Canada, and spent some years on the continent, and then returned to Canada.

I first heard of him on going to the County of Simcoe, on the occasion of the contest for representation of Simcoe in Parliament, between William Robinson and William Hume Blake, in 1846. I took some part in that election, having been scrutineer at the poll in the Township of Essa, in the interest of Mr. Robinson. I recollect hearing of a gentleman named Connor, who had been speaking in different parts of the county on behalf of Mr. Blake. He was represented as an Irishman, fluent of speech and weighty in argument, doing yeoman service for Mr. Blake in his candidature for representation of the county. I did not expect then that at some future time I would meet Doctor Connor at the Bar, and know him as the cultured gentleman he was, and as a member of the Canadian Bar.

As I look back and ponder over the events of those days, I find I have to acknowledge that Doctor Connor, at the time of the election, was really a member of the Canadian Bar, without my being aware of it, for I find him entered on the books of the Law Society, as an admitted student, in Easter Term, 5 Victoria (1842), and called to the Bar the same day. Having a degree, he was entitled to be called to the Bar without service in Canada. I think he must have come down from Oro, taken his call to the Bar, and then returned again north, where he was found on the occasion of the election to which I have referred.

Some time after being called to the Bar, Doctor Connor became a partner with Mr. Blake (William Hume Blake), and Mr. Joseph Morrison, under the firm name of Blake, Morrison, and Connor. This firm had their office in what had been the old Toronto Club Building, on the corner of King and Bay streets, where the Mail Building now stands. The firm did a large business. Mr. Morrison had attached himself very much to the people of Toronto, and had established for himself a good mercantile business. Mr. Blake, as head of the firm, had gained a great reputation as Counsel, and also in conducting the Equity department of the office. Doctor Connor came in to give his services in the development of their large business. I remember Doctor Connor as member of that firm. He did not, while with them, do much outside business; but was generally to be seen at his desk drawing pleadings, or in consultation with clients. His appearance was remarkable. He had become prematurely grey, or rather white, for both his countenance and hair were as white and delicate as that of any lady who had passed the meridian of life ; and yet he was a young man, he was active and vivacious, and in every move shewed the Irish gentleman. He had more the appearance of a poet, or a man of literature, than one who had ungergone the hard life of one of the back townships of his adopted country.

After being several years a member of this firm he withdrew, and formed a partnership with George Boomer, who afterwards became Police Magistrate. The firm was Connor & Boomer, and had their office on the corner of Church and King streets. He did the counsel business of that firm, and held outside briefs for a goodly number of clients. He was a Queen's Counsel, and one of the Commissioners for Consolidating the Statutes of Canada and Upper Canada in 1858. On that Commission he made it a specialty to consolidate and revise the Real Property Acts.

In politics the Doctor was a **Reformer**. He commenced his active political life in 1859, when he was elected member for Oxford, and sat for that constituency for that year and until 1862.

Shortly after he entered Parliament, the House and the country were much excited over a matter of much moment in the administration of justice. It arose out of what was alleged to be a sale of the office of Sheriff of the County of Norfolk, by the incumbent Sheriff Rapelje to Laurence W. Mercer, for a money consideration and an annuity. Politics ran high at this time, and inasmuch as Mercer, who was to be the successor of Rapelje, would receive his appointment from the Government of the day, it was thought by those opposed to the Government, that it afforded a good weapon for the probable demolition of the Government. The Attorney-General was compelled to take notice of the matter, as there were complicating opinions as to the legality of the transaction. Mercer contending that he had not bought or negotiated for the purchase of the office, but only, that through political influence, Rapelje was to resign and he was to be appointed in his place. Mercer, before taking the step he did, had advised with counsel, and Doctor Connor was one of the counsel he consulted. The result was, that the transaction was consummated, so far as an agreement in writing could consummate it. The Attorney-General filed an information in the Queen's Bench against Mercer, claiming penalties, that the transaction was illegal, and contrary to the policy of the law. The Court decided that the agreement was void, and that by entering into it Mercer had subjected himself to penalties, which involved disability to hold the office. The judgment was forfeiture of office and the penalties.

From the Court the matter got into Parliament. On 17th February, 1859, Laurence W. Mercer petitioned the House to be relieved from the penalty of disqualification of office. Leave was given to bring in a Bill to remove the disqualification. The Bill was read the first time on 16th April, 1859, when Mr. Simpson moved, seconded by Mr. McMicken, that the Bill be read a second time. Mr. Rymal moved in amendment, that the Bill be read that day three months. The question did not come to a vote till the 23rd April, 1859 when the House divided, and twenty-five members voted for the amendment and fifty-one against On the main question being put, that the Bill should pass the second reading, was carried, fifty-one voting aye, and twenty-five nay.

There was another division of the House on 25th April, when Mr. Dunkin, from the Private Bills Committee, reported the Bill with amendments, and the Honorable George Brown moved in amendment, "that the House would resolve itself into a committee to consider the same that day six months." Mr. Brown's motion was lost, twenty-two voting for the motion, and thirty-three against. The Bill was reported to the House, and on the 26th April, 1859, on the motion of Mr. Simpson, seconded by Mr. McMicken, was read a third time, and on the 29th April, 1859, passed the Legislative Council. The Act as it now appears on the Statute Book is 22 Victoria, cap. 128, entitled "An Act to relieve Laurence William Mercer from a penal disability." By the Act the disability was removed, and Mercer "restored to his competency to take and hold any office in the gift of the Crown in this Province, in as full, ample, and beneficial a manner as if he had never incurred the penalty of such disability and disqualification."

Doctor Connor, who was a man having high regard for professional honour, did not vote on any of the motions in Parliament relating to the question. Party pressure was brought on him, to get him to vote for the motion to disqualify Mercer, but no amount of pressure made him swerve from his purpose not to vote at all, inasmuch as he had been one of the counsel consulted. It is due from me to make this statement, knowing, as I do, that obloquy was attempted to be thrown on him, in certain quarters, for abstaining from voting on one side or the other. His view was, that political considerations should not allow him to sully his professional honour, and vote to disqualify an officer, who had in the privacy of professional intercourse held consultation with him on the question. He was very sensitive on the subject, and I do not doubt that this matter somewhat embittered his after life.

On the 26th March, 1860, the Opposition, of which Doctor Connor was a member, made a desperate attempt to secure a vote of the House to dethrone the Cartier-Macdonald Administration. The House was moved to declare that the Administration did not possess the confidence of a majority of the representatives of Upper Canada, but retained power through a Lower Canada majority. Two amendments were made, the last of which was, that:

> This House is of opinion that the conduct of the Administration in governing continually and systematically one section of the Province, in opposition to the wishes of that section, often expressed in this House by its representatives, is fraught with danger to the well-being of this Province.

This amendment was lost, forty-four members voting for the motion and sixty-eight against. Doctor Connor voted with the minority. On the other amendment, which was:

> That the present Administration possesses the confidence of the House and of the country;

the vote of the House was seventy yeas and forty-three nays. Doctor Connor voted with the nays.

During this Session, a question was presented to the House which caused a great deal of excited discussion. A member returned to the House,—George Byron Fellowes,—and two others, Martin Casselman and John Sexton Casselman, had been committed to the Toronto jail for the conspiring to obtain the election of George Byron Fellowes. A motion was made in the House that an humble address be presented to His Excellency the Governor-General, praying that he would be pleased to remit the sentence of these three individuals, inasmuch as the law had been sufficiently vindicated by their conviction, and the imprisonment they had suffered. The motion was carried in the House by a majority of twenty-four. Doctor Connor voted with the minority.

Doctor Connor was very fastidious in all professional matters, either of honor or etiquette. No party political consideration would make him deviate from the path of rectitude.

On the 2nd August, 1858, Doctor Connor was appointed Solicitor-General. In that capacity he performed his duties ably and well. I have frequently been present when he conducted the Crown business. He always acted in a gentlemanly, professional way. He, while pressing for a conviction in all serious cases of violation of the criminal law, would not endeavor to twist or distort the evidence for the mere purpose of getting a conviction. He did not glory in a conviction for the conviction's sake, but only as a vindication of the law and principles of justice.

Doctor Connor was, in 1848, Lecturer in Law in the University of Toronto. He lectured with care, and instructed the students in a manner as agreeable to them as it was elegant and useful. He had a pleasant manner, with a refined Irish accent: these two attributes gave zest and point to his lectures.

I remember him as an accomplished gentleman; if anything, more fond of literature than law. He was a good French scholar; could read and speak French fluently: he was fond of music and flowers: in social life he was agreeable and refined. Whether as host or guest, he was always a perfect gentleman. His political life was not in every way a success. In one of his contests to gain his seat for South Oxford, he had a very narrow escape from defeat, being elected by a majority of but one vote, and, it was said by his opponents, that majority of one was a mistake, the free and independent elector, in his excitement, having his vote recorded for Connor, when he really merely named Connor, with an objurgation. However this may be, Doctor Connor's generous disposition fitted him better for private life, than the exacting duties of Parliament. He had not a strong constitution; such as it was, it was undermined by electoral contests in the country, and the wear and tear of political warfare.

In the beginning of the year 1863, Mr. Connor was offered and accepted a seat as Pusine Judge of the Court of Queen's Bench. He was appointed Judge on the 31st January, 1863. He had been but a few months on the Bench, when the seeds of the disease he had contracted while in Parliament, began to shew themselves with increase. He survived his appointment to the Bench but a few months, when he died at his residence on Peter Street, in Toronto, on the 29th April, 1863, at the age of fifty-three, and was buried in St. James's Cemetery.

His wife, who was the sister of Judge Charles Robinson, of Sarnia, survived him.

Doctor Connor left no family to perpetuate his name; his widow since his decease has followed him to the grave.

XXVI.

THE HONORABLE JOHN WILSON, JUDGE OF THE COURT OF COMMON PLEAS.

IT is to be regretted that there exists no written record of the life of this excellent Judge.
That elegant writer, the late W. J. Rattray, B.A., in his "Scot in British North America," alludes to this want in his reference to Chief Justice Sir Thomas Galt. Referring to him he says:

> Mr. Galt was in 1858, appointed Queen's Counsel, and in 1869, on the death of Judge John Wilson—a Scot of whom unhappily we have no record—was elevated to the Bench, as a Justice of the Court of Common Pleas.

As I knew Judge John Wilson from my early boyhood, when he resided in the Bathurst District, and I, with my family, in the Johnstown District, I have felt it a duty to endeavour to rescue from oblivion the memory of a Judge, who was a man of noble instincts, and a Judge of irreproachable integrity.

Judge John Wilson was a Scotchman, son of Ebenezer Wilson, and was born at Paisley, in November, 1809. He was only fourteen years of age when his father determined to emigrate to Canada. The determination was put into execution, and soon John's father and family found themselves settled on a farm in the County of Lanark, about twenty miles from Perth. The names of Paisley, Lanark, and Perth, will bring home to the reader the fact that there must have been a good deal of Scotch in Canada even at that period; and so there was. Many North Britain men had left their homes in the old world to hew out for themselves homes in the new. Ebenezer Wilson was one of this class.

Ebenezer Wilson, John's father, was a highly intelligent person. He had a large family of children, and John was the oldest. Settled on the farm, John had to work hard, as did his father and mother. They were able to purchase a farm, but the working it was another matter. The early settlers in Canada had all to endure great hardships if engaged in farming, and the Wilsons were not an exception to the general rule. Clearing land, felling large trees, summer fallowing, and all the usual labour of the first settlers is difficult work for the most experienced in such matters. It may be well understood, therefore, that a Scot from Paisley, entering upon such an enterprise, would have his hands full.

In his latter years, John Wilson used to tell of his having carried the first bag of potatoes raised on the farm to Perth, the nearest market, twenty miles, and bare footed. It so happened that the road was part swamp, part morass, and part stone, so that the young man may be said, in some part at least, to have had a hard road to travel.

The father, mother, and whole family suffered great hardship. After paying for the farm, they had but scanty means, and were often obliged to exercise great self-denial. As Scotchmen are proverbial for their thrift, so it was with them. John had received something of an education in Paisley, before leaving Scotland. His aspirations were something higher than a farm life in the woods, he therefore bethought himself that he might not only better his own condition, but relieve his father somewhat by completing his education in Perth. John Stewart, (familiarly known as four-eyes Stewart, from the fact that he wore spectacles), at this time kept school in Perth, and Master Wilson became a pupil of his. John Stewart afterwards became a Lawyer, and practised in Stratford. I knew him well—a highly educated man, something after the style of Doctor Dunlop. The polish was about the same, and not much at that. Mr. Stewart, however, was Irish, while Doctor Dunlop was Scotch.

John Stewart was capable of giving, and did give, John Wilson a good education : so good that in his turn he was engaged to teach the children, or some of the children, of the late Honorable William Morris. The Honorable Alexander Morris, of Toronto, was a pupil of his.

About this time the late Honorable Malcolm Cameron was a resident of Perth, carrying on a mercantile business. John Wilson wrote some verses which had found their way to a house in town, where Mr. Cameron saw them, and pronounced them so good that he expressed the opinion that the writer ought to be a lawyer. On inquiry, he found the writer to be John Wilson, and at once took him into his friendship, which stood young Wilson in good stead, and they were ever after friends, so long as life lasted. They were not of the same politics ; but that never in the least interfered with their bond of friendship. While in Perth, by his teaching and otherwise, John was able to shew his filial gratitude to his kind mother ; not forgetting to furnish her with some little luxuries, which could not be obtained on a newly cleared (or in process of being cleared) farm, twenty miles from Perth. To her he could say, or sing :

> "Oh ! be it it mine, with sweet and pious care,
>   To calm thy bosom in the hour of grief ;
> With soothing tenderness to chase the tear,
>   With fond endearments to impart relief :
> With dexterous love, in thy declining hours,
> My filial hand shall strew unfading flowers."

The hopes and prognostications of Mr. Malcolm Cameron were soon fulfilled. Mr. Wilson, by thrift and industry, was soon enabled to present himself to the Benchers of the Law Society, and to be admitted a Student of the Law. He was entered on the Rolls of the Society, as Student, in Easter Term, 11 George IV., 1830. As soon as admitted, he entered the office of James Boulton, then practising at Perth, studied his term with him, and was called to the Bar in Easter Term, 5 William IV., 1835. He had so much the confidence of Mr. Boulton, that he was no sooner admitted to the Bar than he intrusted him with the conduct of a branch of his office at Niagara, to which town Mr. Boulton himself in a short time removed, leaving a large and lucrative practice in the County Town of Lanark. Niagara at this time was a flourishing town, carrying on a successful business with houses in Montreal, shipping goods westward, to be portaged to Chippewa, at the foot of Lake Erie.

I remember Niagara in 1836, as a most business-like place, They still affected to believe there that it was the Capital, though it had been long since supplanted by Toronto. The place was not wanting in lawyers, for there were several there at that time. I call to recollection James Boulton, Miller and Boomer, Charles Hall, and several others, whose names I have forgotten. It was not an unusual thing to have upwards of one hundred records entered for trial at the Assizes.

In 1835, Mr. Wilson left Niagara, and settled in London, to practise his profession in that town. He soon here gained a wide-spread reputation. He was not only a good, but a reliable lawyer, just and reliable in all his dealings. He was a man who was free from all those blemishes that defaced the credit of the sharp-practice lawyer. Blunt, but honest, he earned the respect of all who knew him. He soon gained the soubriquet of "Honest John Wilson." His practice was not confined to London alone, but to the whole Western District. He used to hold briefs at Chatham, St. Thomas, Sandwich, and in Woodstock, where his brother-in-law, Mr. now Judge Hughes, was practising. I have often met him at the Bar of that town. From meeting him there frequently, I had opportunity of judging of his measure. He was intimately acquainted with all the ways and wants of the country people: he could easily adapt himself, therefore, to their comprehension, and so had great weight with juries. He only formed one partnership when at the Bar, and that was with Mr. Hughes, his brother-in-law. As a man, he was never forgetful of old friends. He had known my brother in Chatham, and others of my relations in the eastern part of the Province, which always earned for me a fatherly regard from him.

Mr. Wilson was a soldier as well as a Lawyer. When the Rebellion broke out in 1837, he was one of those men of London who did honor to his town, by at once turning out to repress the insurrection. There were no regular troops then in London, and therefore the more necessity that the loyal should, at whatever cost, by precept and example, encourage the loyal to stand by their guns; this Mr. Wilson did in a marked manner, which gained for him the confidence and esteem of the whole people.

The insurrectionists had assembled in large numbers in Gosfield. Mr. Wilson, as Captain, mustered all the volunteers he could gather, and in mid-winter started from London to march twenty miles a day, with the object of putting down the revolt. Both he and the men suffered much; the winter storms, coupled with scant clothing of himself and men, made them suffer great hardships on the route. Both in London and on the march, Mr. Wilson shewed his courage and devotion to his country's interests and his comrades wants.

After the Rebellion, the 85th Regiment was stationed at London. A case occurred at this time which enabled Mr. Wilson to exercise not only his legal but his military skill. The Colonel of the 85th Regiment laid some twenty odd charges against the Major of the Regiment. This caused a Court Martial to be assembled. The Major was tried on the charges, Mr. Wilson acting as counsel for the prosecutor, the Colonel; while John Prince, Q.C., acted for the Major. The Court sat for three weeks, while the charges were investigated. A number of the charges being sustained, the Major was permitted to retire from the Regiment. Mr. Wilson, from his manner of conducting the case, was awarded great credit by the military authorities in Canada and in England.

I should not omit to mention here that James Shanly, Master in Chancery at London, was a Student of Mr. Wilson at this time, and acted as his amanuensis at the Court Martial. He has a great affection for the memory of the deceased Judge, and says in a letter which conveys information as to this Court Martial :

> When I came as a law student to the office of my good and kind old friend and master, he had been a good many years in practice, and I was his sixth or seventh student, and when called to the Bar had been for a year before the senior and managing student of his office. He had a kind and generous disposition, an earnest love of truth and justice, and singular originality in the mode and management of nisi prius matters, and in his tact before juries.

The following complimentary reference to Mr. Wilson on his retiring from the Colonelcy of the 2nd Batallion, Sedentary Militia, was published in the Canada Gazette:

> Lieutenant-Colonel the Honorable John Wilson is permitted to retire, retaining his rank.
> His Excellency, the Commander-in-Chief, cannot permit Lieutenant-Colonel Wilson to retire without expressing the sense he entertains of the value of Lieutenant-Colonel Wilson's services in the Militia of the Province for the last five and twenty years.

Mr. Wilson was twice returned as representative for London in Parliament, on the first occasion in 1847, by a large majority of the electors, and on the second occasion at the general election of 1854, unanimously.

After his election, in 1847, he sat until the dissolution of the Parliament, but was defeated in 1851, and after his election in 1854, sat in the House from his return till 1857. In 1863, he was elected Legislative Councillor for the St. Clair Division, but did not take his seat, as he was shortly after appointed to the Bench.

He was a Conservative in politics; but not such a bigoted partizan as to cause him to believe there was no virtue in his opponents. He was not so strong a party man as to condone any act, however outrageous it might be, if committed by his own party. This trait in his character was most conspicuous on the occasion of the passing of the Rebellion Losses Bill, and burning of the Parliament Buildings, in Montreal, in 1849. It is matter of history that, on account of giving his sanction to that Bill, Lord Elgin was mobbed and hooted by a mob in Montreal—something more offensive than sugar balls was thrown at him while returning in his carriage, from the Parliament House after assenting to the Bill, and the Parliament Buildings set on fire and burned, by persons who were said to be supporters of the Opposition in Parliament, of which Opposition Mr. Wilson was a member.

After the burning of the Parliament Buildings, and the assembling of the members in another place, the conduct of the incendiaries was subjected to much Parliamentary hostile criticism. Some of the members of the Opposition, without justifying, sought to excuse the act. This gave an opportunity to Mr. Wilson to express his views, which he did in an independent, non-party, patriotic way: he condemned the burning of the Parliament Buildings as most fiendish, and claimed that every member of Parliament, no matter of what party, should condemn such lawlessness: as a Conservative, he repudiated the idea that his party should be held responsible for the acts of misguided men; that there was not only no justice in, but no excuse for such conduct.

The mob riots in Montreal, on the occasion of the passing of the Rebellion Losses Bill, nearly equalled, and in some respects eclipsed, the Lord George Gordon Riots, in London and Westminster, on the occasion of the passage of the Catholic Relief Bill. The mob on that occasion did not burn the Houses of Parliament, though they did burn the house of Lord Mansfield, in Bloomsbury Square.

Mr. Wilson was a countryman of Lord Mansfield, and, following the example of the noble Lord, he denounced the outrages committed, although he did not suffer so much inconvenience and loss. Lord Mansfield, by the burning of his house, was deprived of a splendid library, consumed in the conflagration. In London, troops were called out to put down the riots: in Montreal, the Parliament Houses were burnt before the troops could be called out. Some people thought that Lord Mansfield, by the loss of his books, would lose his law also. This was not so, however, as when the right to call out the troops was questioned in the House of Lords, he said:

> I hold that His Majesty, in the orders issued by the advice of his Ministers, acted perfectly and strictly according to the common law of the land, and the principles of the constitution; and I will give you my reasons within as short a compass as possible: I have not consulted books; *indeed, I have no books to consult.*

After arguing at length, and giving his reasons why, for the repression of those riots, it was not necessary to have martial law proclaimed, but that the common law was sufficient to meet the case, Lord Mansfield concluded thus:

> Upon the whole, my Lords, while I deeply regret the cause which rendered it indispensably necessary to call out the military, and to order them to act in the suppression of the late disturbances, I am clearly of opinion that no steps have been taken for that purpose which were not strictly legal, as well as fully justifiable in point of policy. Certainly the civil power, whether through native imbecility, through neglect, or the very formidable force they would have to contend with, were unequal to the task of putting an end to the insurrection. When the rabble had augmented their numbers, by breaking open the prisons and setting the felons at liberty, they had become too formidable to be opposed by the staff of a constable. If the military had not acted at last, none of your Lordships can hesitate to agree with me that the conflagrations would have spread over the whole capital, and in a few hours it would have been a heap of rubbish. The King's extraordinary prerogative to proclaim martial law (whatever that may be), is clearly out of the question. His Majesty, and those who have advised him (I repeat it), have acted in strict conformity to the common law. The military have been called in, and very wisely called in—not as *soldiers*, but as *citizens*. No matter whether their coats be red or brown, they were employed, not to subvert, but to preserve, the laws and Constitution which we all prize so highly.

I make no apology for giving this opinion of Lord Mansfield from his place in the House of Lords, as there is in some places great misconception as to the extent to which military power may be used to put down dangerous riots without the proclaiming of Martial Law. Besides this, the outburst of public feeling in London on the occasion of the passing of the Catholic Relief Bill, was not unlike the outburst in Montreal, on the occasion of passing the Rebellion Losses Bill.

Mr. Wilson's opinion on the subject of the riots in Montreal, as expressed in the House, shew that he had a true conception of the duties of the situation, as expounded by Lord Mansfield.

I need not say more of Mr. Wilson's Parliamentary career than to add that he evinced the same manly independent spirit in the House as out of it : he had an honest desire to advance the best interests of the couutry, and voted and acted accordingly.

Mr. Wilson was made a Queen's Counsel in 1856, and promoted to the Bench as a Pusine Judge of the Common Pleas on 22nd July, 1863. The Chief Justice of the Common Pleas, while he occupied a seat on the Bench, was the Honorable Sir William B. Richards, afterwards Chief Justice of the Supreme Court, and his associate Judge was the Honorable Sir Adam Wilson, lately retired from the Chief Justiceship of the Queen's Bench Division of the High Court of Justice. As a Judge, the Honorable John Wilson enjoyed the confidence of the Bar and the Bench.

After the Fenian Raid in 1866, it fell to his lot to be obliged to try many of the Fenian prisoners. The atmosphere of the Toronto Court House, never of the best, was particularly bad at this time. The labour imposed on the Judge, with the foul air of this much-condemned Court House, seriously impaired his health. It is believed that the poisonous air of the Court House hastened his end. He died on the 3rd day of June, 1869, and was buried in the Cemetery at London, the place in which he had lived so many years. His widow, who is the sister of Judge Hughes of St. Thomas, still survives him, and has her residence with a married daughter in Toronto.

XXVII.

The Honorable Joseph Curran Morrison, Judge of the Court of Appeal.

THE Honorable Joseph Curran Morrison, as his name would seem to indicate, was not altogether Irish, though Irish born. His father, Hugh Morrison, was a native of Sutherlandshire, Scotland, which was also the native county of Sir John Alexander Macdonald, and may in some measure account for the friendship which existed between these two (the Judge and the Premier), for a good part of the life of Mr. Morrison.

Mr. Morrison, (the Judge) was born in the south of Ireland, on the 20th August, 1816. His father had removed from his native Scotland to the south of Ireland before this period, had married, and for the time being, made the south of Ireland his dwelling place.

During Mr. Morrison's life time he claimed his Scotch descent, and was a member of St. Andrew's Society. He did not at the same time disclaim his native Ireland, and would often boast that he had received his early education at the Royal Belfast Institution.

Mr. Morrison had not yet passed his boyhood, when his father removed to York, Upper Canada, now Toronto. Mr. Morrison on arriving in York, was enabled to avail himself of the advantages afforded the youth of that time in receiving further education within the walls of Upper

Canada College. After leaving Upper Canada College his ambition led him to adopt the study of the law. In order to the gratification of his desire he entered the office of Mr. Simon Washburn, a local practitioner of note in those days.

In the life of Chancellor Blake I have mentioned the fact that Mr. Blake was a student of Mr. Washburn. He and Mr. Morrison were students in this office at the same time. This must have been about the year 1835 or 1836, as Mr. Morrison was admitted a Student by the Law Society in Hilary Term, 4 William IV., 1834, while Mr. Blake was admitted just a year afterwards. Mr. Blake being a University man, was admitted to the Bar a year before Mr. Morrison. He was admitted, as the books shew, in Easter Term, 1 Victoria, 1838, and Mr. Morrison in Easter Term, 2 Victoria, 1839. They were fellow students part, if not the whole of the time of their probation, became fast friends, and on being called to the Bar, formed a partnership which continued until Mr. Blake's elevation to the Bench in 1846. Doctor Connor joined the partnership at some period of these ten years, after which the firm was known as Blake, Morrison & Connor, and had a large and extensive practice. Mr. Morrison had a great many friends in Toronto and surrounding Townships, and was thus enabled to bring to the firm a large number of valuable clients. He confined himself more to the routine of the office, while Mr. Blake's well known ability secured to the firm a counsel and advocate with a reputation second to none in the Province. Mr. Blake in his advocacy was not in the habit of going regular circuit, confining himself to local business and special retainers in outside counties.

In 1843, Mr. Morrison became Clerk of the Executive Council ; not so much for the ordinary business of the Council, but to perform the duties of Clerk of the old Court of Error and Appeal, composed of the Lieutenant-Governor and members of the Council.

Mr. Morrison and Mr. Blake were Reformers of the School of Reform as it existed at that time, and were warm admirers of the Honorable Robert Baldwin, the then recognized leader of the Reform party. Mr. Morrison's activity and energy, displayed on all occasions when Reform principles were to be battled for in the struggle of parties in 1848, secured for him the nomination in the Reform interest, as candidate for the representation in Parliament of the west riding of York.

Lord Elgin had arrived in the Province as Governor-General: the election of 1848 was the first general election after his assuming the Governor-Generalship of the Province. Mr. Morrison was returned as a supporter of Mr. Baldwin and the Baldwin-Lafontaine Administration which came into power in March, 1848.

The supporters of Mr. Baldwin were generally called Baldwin Reformers, as distinguished from the more radical wing of the party. Mr. Baldwin, while demanding Constitutional Reform, had never sided with those of revolutionary tendencies. His great object was, to weld the two Provinces of Upper and Lower Canada together in one homogeneous whole. Mr. Morrison was of his school, and gave him loyal support in the third Parliament after the Union, elected under Lord Elgin's auspices.

Mr. Morrison sat in Parliament from the beginning to the close of the third Parliament, in 1851. Mr. Hincks (Sir Francis Hincks) had at this time gained great prominence in Parliament.

Mr. Baldwin retired from the Ministry at the close of the session of 1851, and it then became the office of Lord Elgin to secure a new administration, on such principles as would likely secure the confidence of a new Parliament. There were many difficulties to overcome, as Mr. Lafontaine had expressed his resolve to retire from public life. Mr. Hincks, who had been a member of the Baldwin-Lafontaine Administration, was entrusted by His Excellency with the formation of a new Ministry for the next Parliament. Mr. Hincks called to his aid other gentlemen, representative men of the different sections of the Reform party, which, after the retirement of Mr. Baldwin, had become considerably disorganized. Among the gentlemen selected was Mr. Morrison. On the 28th October, 1851, Mr. Hincks was enabled to announce his administration as fully organized. Mr. Morin became leader of the Lower Canada section of the new administration, which sailed into power under the name of the Hincks-Morin Administration. The administration was all Reform; some members of it, notably Dr. Rolph and Mr. Malcolm Cameron, being of the advanced wing of the party. The programme of the administration, as told by Sir Francis Hincks in his Reminiscences, was, the secularization of the clergy reserves, the increase of the representation, the extension of the franchise, the abolition of the seignorial tenure, the extension of the principle of election to the Legislative Council, and the encouragement of railway enterprises.

In this administration, with this large bill of fare, Mr. Morrison was allotted the office of Solicitor-General for Upper Canada, on the 22nd June, 1853, having gained his seat for Niagara at the general election in the previous year. On assuming office, he was obliged to obtain the consent of his constituents to his acceptance of office, which they cordially gave him, by again returning him as their representative in 1854. Mr. Morrison was always a staunch friend of Mr. Hincks—none more so—and as such he was recognized by Mr. Hincks.

In order to justly appreciate Mr. Morrison, it is necessary to refer to Mr. Hincks, as being leader of the administration. He was generally charged with making exposition of its principles and, so far as possible, enforcing them in the House. Mr. Morrison was not a silent member, nor was he an obtrusive one. It was sufficient for him, in Council and out of Council, to lend Mr. Hincks his support.

There were members of the House, Reformers, not pleased with the formation of the administration. Among these were Mr. Brown and Mr. McKenzie. So objectionable had their opposition become that, in the spring of

1854, Mr. Hincks advised a dissolution of the House. As regards the measures proposed to the House, and passed by that body, prior to the dissolution, they were large and beneficial to the country; though not all that had been placed in the programme at the formation of the Ministry.

Mr. Hincks was obliged to postpone the Clergy Reserve and Abolition of Seignorial Tenure Bill, which gave umbrage, or seeming umbrage, to his more advanced supporters. Mr. Hincks, on September 8th, 1854, tendered his resignation in the Ministry to His Excellency the Governor-General. His colleague from Lower Canada, Mr. Morin, did the same. On the same day Mr. Hincks made his explanation to the House, giving reasons for his resignation, which without giving in full I will quote. Addressing the Speaker, he said:

> I shall not, Sir, go back--for I deem it unnecessary to do so—to any matters connected with the formation of the administration that preceded the present one, and of which I had the honor of being a member. But I shall content myself with stating, that after that administration had been some time in office, after we had carried, by very considerable majorities, measures which have been received, I believe, with very great satisfaction by the country at large—measures that we shall always be proud to have our names identified with, and to which, as they are recorded on the Statute Book of the country, I do not think it necessary to refer more particularly at present. During the Session of 1851 we had such evidence of the disorganization of the party in Upper Canada, by whose support and confidence we had been enabled to conduct the affairs of the Province, that at a late period of that Session, my honorable and learned friend the then Attorney-General of Upper Canada (Mr. Baldwin) was under the necessity of tendering his resignation.

The bulky Statute Books of 1851, 1852, and 1853, shew with how much truth Mr. Hincks could justly say: "That measures had been passed under his administration which were received with very great satisfaction by the country at large."

I do not find, on going over the old Statutes of Canada, that there had ever been passed in the same period of time, as many or as important Acts as during this period,

(1851, 1852, 1853). In the passing of these measures Mr. Morrison lent his aid and assistance to Mr. Hincks.

In 1855, Sir Edmund Head succeeded Lord Elgin as Governor-General. With the advent of a new Governor-General there was installed a new administration. The Taché-Macdonald administration was formed to to succeed the Hincks-Morin Government. On the 24th May, 1856, Mr. Morrison became Receiver-General in that Government, and a member of the Board of Railway Commissioners. In August, 1856, his constituents of Niagara again returned him to Parliament to represent that Town, thus confirming his appointment as Receiver-General.

By this time the Baldwin Reformers, of whom Mr. Morrison was one, had become largely merged with the Conservative party, owing to their divirgence from the "Clear Grits" or advanced wing of the Liberal party. Hence we find Mr. Morrison, whilom Reformer, a member of the Tory Macdonald-Taché administration.

Mr. Morrison not only gave his support to that administration, but he held office in the Macdonald-Cartier administration which succeeded it.

In 1856, he was appointed one of the Commissioners on the Commission for revising the Statutes of Upper Canada, of which I had the honor of being member as well as Secretary. I will not speak of the work of that Commission, the work speaks for itself in the bound volume of the Consolidated Statutes.

Mr. Morrison's parliamentary duties admitted of his only giving occasional assistance to the Commission. In the Consolidation of the Municipal Acts, which were then engaging the attention of Parliament, his experience gave strength to the work, which also derived great advantage from the assistance of the Honorable Oliver Mowat, also a member of the Commission.

The period during which Mr. Morrison held office in the several administrations was peculiarly a Railway period. Sir Francis Hincks had justly concluded that the building of railways was absolutely essential to build up the country. Mr. Morrison was his faithful lieutenant, He took great interest in the promotion of the old Ontario, Simcoe and Huron, now the Northern Railway. The first sod of this new highway to the north was turned by Lady Elgin, on the 15th October, 1851. This was an important event for Toronto—a great deal of her subsequent prosperity is ascribed to the building of this railway.

Those of us who look back to the time, and know of the difficulties which had to be overcome, can well appreciate the fidelity to the enterprize shewn by the late F. C. Capreol and Mr. Morrison. I remember meetings being held when the cabmen and carters were almost in armed rebellion because of the work; they argued if a railway was built their occupation would be gone.

Mr. Morrison was a constant advocate for the building of the road, and was for several years President of the first Board of Directors, succeeding the Honorable Henry John Boulton in that office. Against much opposition and overwhelming difficulties the road became a reality. In May, 1853, the road was opened to Aurora, and in 1855, to Collingwood, in which year Toronto obtained direct railway communication with Hamilton by the Toronto and Hamilton Railway, and with Montreal by the Grand Trunk road. The latter line was extended westward to Guelph in the early part of the following year, and soon after to Sarnia.

Mr. Morrison's residence, Woodlawn, was in Yorkville, and though a long way from the railway offices and the business part of the city, he gave special attention to the railway interest, attending faithfully the meetings of the Board of Directors with whom rested the responsibility of the work. Woodlawn was a house which its owner occupied in no selfish spirit. The hospitality of Mr. Morrison was proverbial among his many guests who always received a warm welcome within its walls. The grounds, laid out with taste, were not far from the residence of Sir David Macpherson.

45—L. J.

Mr. Morrison was a lover of art, and did not fail to adorn his house with pictures of the best masters, which lent a charm to the hospitalities of his house. In his travels on the Continent he had secured not only most valuable pictures, but statuary and other works of art, with which he graced the interior line of his well furnished house.

Mr. Morrison had a taste for horticulture and floriculture. His conservatory was as good, if not better, than any other in Toronto. He used often to carry off prizes at the horticultural show of fruits and flowers at the Horticultural Gardens, in Toronto. A well established rivalry was kept up between him and the late Henry Eccles, Q.C., and others who, like him, revelled in the delight afforded by the fairest flowers.

Mr. Morrison retained the office of Receiver-General till the expiration of the fifth Parliament after the Union. At the general election of 1857, he presented himself as a candidate to the electors of South Ontario, but suffered defeat. In 1858, he sought election for North Oxford, and was defeated by the Honorable William Macdougall. The star of the "Clear Grits," as it were, was in the ascendant, and the Parliamentary life of the Honorable Joseph C. Morrison, Baldwin Reformer, was rapidly drawing to a close.

In 1859, he was appointed Registrar of the City of Toronto, which had been separated from the County of York as a distinct registration district. In 1860 (February), having resigned as Registrar, he essayed politics again, and was appointed Solicitor-General by the Cartier-Macdonald Government. The appointment was not a popular one, and was rather the individual act of friendship of Sir John A. Macdonald. Mr. Morrison sought a constituency in the County of Grey, and was defeated. He tendered his resignation to the Government, which they refused to accept. He retained the office of Solicitor-General for two years without a seat in the House, which was the subject of much unfavorable comment. In 1862,

Mr. Notman moved a vote of censure in the House, because of Mr. Morrison's retention of office; but the motion was defeated.

During all his political life Mr. Morrison made no enemies and many friends. He was a man so equable in his disposition, and possessed of such sound good sense, that it was impossible to quarrel with him, however much one might differ from him in opinion. He was not possessed of a large fortune, and the fortune he had was much diminished by his heavy election expenses. He never wanted friends, however, some of the warmest of whom were those opposed to him in politics. Even during his Parliamentary life, he was not altogether removed from association with the Bar, having, during that time, conducted many criminal prosecutions for the Crown. Among others, he prosecuted James Brown, in 1860, for the murder of John Sheridan Hogan, M. P. He also conducted the trial of James Greenwood, convicted of murder; and of the Fenian prisoners, taken at Fort Erie in 1866.

Mr. Morrison took great interest in educational matters. He was for twenty-eight years a member of the Council of Public Instruction for Upper Canada. He was always a friend of the University of Toronto, and was for twenty-five years a member of the Senate of that institution., and fourteen years Chancellor of the University.

On the 19th March, 1862, he was appointed a Puisne Judge of the Common Pleas; and on the 24th August. 1863, was transferred to the Queen's Bench, as a Puisne Judge. Entering on his judicial duties, Judge Morrison found himself surrounded by a Bar which held him in high esteem. On the Bench he was always complaisant, and never got ruffled in the performance of duty. Firm in his rulings at Nisi Prius, he was always ready to reconsider his decisions in Banc, directing his mind to the attainment of justice conformable to the principles of law.

Judge Morrison, sitting as vacation Judge, after Easter Term, 1887, gave a decision which was very much canvassed at the Bar, and which was pronounced by very eminent counsel as a wrong decision, but which has since received the support of the Chancery Division of the High Court of Justice, in England, in another case, but on the same point. The case in Ontario is the case of Allan *vs.* McTavish, 41 U. C. Q. B. Rep. 567. The action was on a mortgage, bearing date on or about the 24th November, 1856, in which the mortgagee covenanted to pay one Arnold, or his assignee, the sum of £30:5s, and interest, in four annual instalments, the first instalment whereof became due and was payable on or before the 24th November, 1857. Arnold assigned the mortgage to the plaintiff in the action, who brought suit on the covenant for the recovery of the money. The defendant pleaded that the plaintiff's claim was for a sum of money secured by way of mortgage on lands in Ontario, and that the alleged cause of action did not accrue within ten years before commencement of the suit.

The plaintiff demurred to this plea, on the ground, that the action was an action of debt arising upon a covenant contained in a deed, and that the plaintiff was entitled to bring his action at any time within the period of twenty years after the cause of action arose.

Under the Upper Canada Statute of Limitations of 7 William IV., cap. 3 sec. 3, (Consolidated Statutes of Upper Canada, page 807), it had been enacted that:

"Actions of covenant or debt upon a bond or other specialty should be commenced within twenty years after the cause of such action arose. But the Ontario Act of 38 Victoria, cap. 16. (A.D. 1874), entitled 'An Act for the further Limitation of Actions and Suits relating to Real Property,' had by section 11 declared that 'no action or suit or other proceedings shall be brought to recover any sum of money secured by any mortgage, judgment, or lien, or otherwise charged upon or payable out of any land or rent, at law or in equity, or any legacy, but within ten.

years next after the present right to receive the same shall have accrued to some person capable of giving a discharge for, or release of the same.'"

Judge Morrison held that the action was barred at the end of the ten years, and that the words in Consolidated Statutes referred to "actions of covenant or debt upon a bond or other specialty," extended as well to actions on covenant contained in mortgages as to covenants contained in other deeds.

In the minds of many, the provisions of the Ontario Act, 38 Victoria cap. 16, were confined to actions directly affecting the land, to liens and other remedies against the the land, the title of the Act, and general scope of the Act relating to realty gave colour to this construction of the Act.

By Judge Morrison's decision many people who had been delaying taking their actions for debts on mortgages over ten years due, were suddenly awakened to the prospect of losing their claims or part of them, where the land itself was not a sufficient security. They were refreshed, however, by the decision of the Court of Appeal in the same case, reversing Mr. Justice Morrison's decision (Allan *vs.* McTavish, 2 Appeal Reports, 278).

Not long after the decision of Allan *vs.* McTavish in appeal, however, the legal barometer fell, and Judge Morrison's decision was in effect, though in another case, upheld by the Court of Appeal in England. Sutton *vs.* Sutton, (December 12, 1882,) 22 Chancery Division, 511, brought up the same question as was decided by Mr. Justice Morrison, and the Judges, Sir George Jessel, the Master of the Rolls, and Lord Justice Bowen, were of the same opinion as had been expressed by Judge Morrison. Fearnside *vs.* Flint, 22 Chancery Division, 579, followed Sutton *vs.* Sutton, and even apparently went further, as it held to the ten years limitation on a bond collateral to the mortgage. I say apparently, but still it did not go further. In Lindsell *vs.* Philips, 30 Chancery Division, 291, it was held that the ten years limit does not apply to any covenant which does not immediately affect the land. Referring to Sutton *vs.* Sutton and Fearnside *vs.* Flint, the Court said :

> But these cases decide only that the remedy on the covenant or bond is barred when the remedy against the land is barred, and in the present case the remedy against the land is not barred.

The eminent Judges of our Court of Appeal, who overruled Judge Morrison, fortified their decision by a reference to many cases to sustain their view. I find scarcely any of them referred to in Sutton *vs.* Sutton. The case of Hunter *vs.* Nockolds, 1 Macnaughton & Gordon 640, cited in Allan *vs.* McTavish, is referred to, but not many of the cases cited. In this state of the decisions, it is difficult to say what the law really is, or will be declared to be when the point is presented to the Privy Council.

In the mean time, in McDonald *vs.* McDonald, 11 Ontario Reports, Mr. Justice Proudfoot had the point before him in the Chancery Division of the High Court and there determined to follow the decision of the Court of Appeal, without expressing any opinion of his own. He there said :

> The case of Allan *vs.* McTavish also answers the other ground of appeal that not more than ten years arrears should have been given. It is true that the Court of Appeal in England has taken a different view of the effect of the reduction of the limitation, and held that it applied to the covenant as well as the land, Sutton *vs.* Sutton, 22 Ch. D. 511. But Allan *vs.* McTavish is the decision of the highest appellate tribunal in the Province to which an appeal lies from me. The Court of Appeal in England is not the Court of ultimate appeal for the Province. And therefore whatever my own view might be, I feel constrained to decide according to the opinion of our Court of Appeal. The appeal is therefore dismissed, with costs.

I have thought it right to refer to the decision of Allan *vs.* McTavish, as in that case Judge Morrison decided a new point on a Statute which is open to different constructions, in which interpretation he has been sustained by eminent Judges in England, though the Judges of the Ontario Court of Appeal came to a different conclusion. Mr. Justice Proudfoot's decision was on the appeal from the Master's report only. Until the Supreme Court, or Privy Council, have the point before them, the decisions are not satisfactory.

On the 30th November, 1877, Judge Morrison was appointed Judge of the Court of Appeal.

There is another case in our reports of great commercial importance, in which Mr. Justice Morrison gave judgment on a totally new point, with no English or American decisions to direct, and he was sustained in his conclusion by the Superior Court. The case is Cosgrave vs. Boyle, 5 Appeal Reports 458. In that case one Purdy had given a promissory note to the plaintiff Cosgrave, endorsed by a man named Stewart. Plaintiff had the note discounted at a bank, and not being paid by the maker at maturity, the bank protested the note for non-payment, addressing the notice of non-payment to the address of Stewart at Toronto, *i.e.*, to Stewart by name, Toronto, Toronto being the place of date of the note. As a matter of fact Stewart was at that time dead, and had left a will which had been proved by his executors. The plaintiff paid the note to the bank and then sued Boyle the endorser. Two questions arose : 1st, Was the notice sufficient as given by the bank, the holder of the note at maturity ? 2nd, If sufficient, did it enure to the benefit of the plaintiff who knew of the endorser's death when they paid the note.

By the Statute 37 Victoria, cap. 47 D., it is recited and enacted :

> Whereas it is desirable that the law relating to bills of exchange and promissory notes should be amended in the particulars in this Act mentioned. Therefore, &c. Notice of the protest or dishonor of any bill of exchange or promissory note, payable in Canada, shall be sufficiently given if addressed in due time, to any party to such bill or note, entitled to such notice at the place where such bill or note is dated, unless any such party has, under his signature, on such bill or note, designated another place when such notice shall be sufficiently given, if addressed to him, in due time at such other place ; and such notice so addressed should be sufficient, although the place of residence of such party be other than either of such before mentioned places.

Judge Morrison was of opinion that the judgment of the Queen's Bench, which decided that the defendant was discharged by reason of insufficiency of notice, no notice having been sent to the executors of the endorser either by the bank or the plaintiff, was erroneous. Judge Armour in the Queen's Bench, had dissented from this holding. The plaintiff appealed to the Ontario Court of Appeal, which was equally divided. Judge Morrison was of opinion that by virtue of the Statute the notice addressed to the endorser at the place of the date of the note was perfectly good, although the endorser was dead when the note matured. Judge Galt was of the same opinion. The Court being equally divided, the appeal was dismissed. On further appeal to the Supreme Court the judgment of the Court of Appeal was reversed, the Supreme Court holding :

> That the holder of the note sued upon when it matured, not knowing of S's death, and having sent him a notice in pursuance of sec. 1 cap. 47, 37 Victoria gave good and sufficient notice to bind the defendant, and that the notice so given enured to the benefit of the appellants, the plaintiffs.

Vogel *vs.* The Grand Trunk Railway Company, 10 App. Rep. 162, in which Mr. Justice Morrison gave judgment, is an important case on the subject of liability of railway companies for negligence. The plaintiff had shipped by the defendant's railway a number of horses, to be carried by the railway from Belleville to Prescott. It was alleged that through the negligence of the servants of the defendants, the trains on which these consignments were being carried, collided with other trains, and some of the horses were killed, and all of them more or less injured. In the shipping note signed by the consignor under the heading " No. of packages and species of goods," there was written, " 1 car horses, O. risk "; meaning, owner's risk. Amongst the general notices and conditions of carriage endorsed on the shipping note in each case was the following :

The owner of animals undertakes all risks of loss, injury, damage, and other contingencies in loading, unloading, transportation, conveyance, or otherwise howsoever, no matter how caused.

On the back it was (amongst other things) declared that live stock :

Is taken entirely at the owner's risk of loss, injury or damage, * * whether in loading, and unloading, conveyance, or otherwise * * all live stock shall be carried by special contract only, &c.

When free passes are given to those in charge, it is on condition that the company are not responsible for any negligence, default, or misconduct of any kind as to the injury of the person using the pass. A receipt for the animals was given by the defendants in the same form and conditions. The animals were killed or lost by the defendants' negligence. It was admitted that, but for these special conditions, the company would be liable. The plaintiff urged that, by statute, the conditions could not avail where there was actual negligence. To this the defendants replied, that their company was not bound by any such statutable provision; and secondly, that even if so bound, the law did not prohibit their making a special contract for the carriage of the goods. The case was tried at Belleville, before Wilson, C. J. The jury found in substance that the horses were not carried under the special contract, and that the plaintiff did not know what the terms on the back of the shipping bills were, but that he supposed the terms were of the like nature as those upon the other papers he had signed for the carriage of horses by the Grand Trunk. The jury assessed the damages at $725. The Chief Justice (Wilson) entered the verdict for the defendants. The plaintiff moved in term in the Queen's Bench to set aside this verdict, and to have a verdict entered for him, because the damage having been occasioned by defendants' negligence, they were liable, notwithstanding the conditions of the contract, under the Consolidated Railway Act, 1879, Revised Statutes of Canada, cap. 109, sec. 104, sub-secs. 1, 2, 3.

46—L. J.

> Passengers and goods shall be taken, transported to and from, and discharged at such places (places to which the goods were to be transported) on the due payment of the toll, freight, or fare lawfully payable therefor.
>
> Every person aggrieved by any neglect or refusal in the premises shall have an action therefor against the company; from which action the company shall not be relieved by any notice, condition, or declaration, if the damage arises from any negligence or omission of the company or of its servants.

The Court of Queen's Bench held that the defendants could not escape liability by their conditions, for their liability was expressly provided for by the above clause of the Railway Act.

On the same question being presented to the Court of Appeal, that Court was equally divided, Justice Burton holding that the company was not precluded by the terms of the Act of Parliament, from making a special contract, exempting themselves from liability even in case of negligence on their part; and Burton, J., and Patterson, J., holding that the transaction was not within the Statute, being, in fact, the hiring of a car, and not a neglect or refusal to perform any other obligations cast upon them by the Statute. Justices Morrison and Osler held that the company could not, by any special contract, relieve themselves from liability or negligence. The case was carried to the Supreme Court, where the opinions of Justices Osler and Morrison were affirmed, that Court holding that, "the company could not avail themselves of the stipulation (on shipping note) that they should not be responsible for the negligence of themselves or their servants." In the Court of Appeal, Mr. Justice Morrison, concurring with Mr. Justice Osler in his conclusion, said in his judgment:

> The defendant railway is subject to the sections of the Statutes referred to, which deprive the company of defence in an action like this, where the loss has been occasioned by the negligence of the company or their servants, and I am of opinion, with my brother Osler, that it was the intention of the Legislature so to deprive them.

Mr. Justice Morrison was not in the habit of delivering

long judgments except in cases where the whole responsibility was thrown upon himself alone. In other cases he often adopted the opinion of other Judges, giving his conclusions, as in this case. The point raised was a new one on a new statute, and, as will be seen, Mr. Justice Morrison was sustained by the Supreme Court. I will not cite any further judgments of Mr. Justice Morrison.

Before Judge Morrison was promoted to the Bench I knew him well as a practitioner. While engaged in politics I did not see much of him, but know that he was a favourite with all the members with whom he was associated. He had good judgment in political affairs. He was not brilliant, but a well balanced mind enabled him to give a dispassionate and trustworthy opinion on public questions. He was, I may say, better in council than out of council. To serve his friend Mr. John A. Macdonald, he held office for a year in the Government without a seat in the House. During this time he was much abused by the political press, but it was not known how much he desired to resign his position. He was induced by Mr. Macdonald to believe that public exigency required him to retain his office, even though a victim of public displeasure. In this he sacrificed himself to serve a friend.

I believe I know more of Judge Morrison after he reached the Bench than before. Being on circuit with him often enabled me to know him well. Off the Bench he was most agreeable, unostentatious, and companionable. On one occasion, after the close of the Picton Assizes, there being a day to spare, he, a couple of friends, and myself took a carriage and paid a visit to the sand banks near Wellington, on the Lake Shore. I had spent part of the time of my professional studies in Belleville, and had often visited Picton, but never the sand banks. These huge banks of white sand some distance from the margin of the lake, form a curious contrast with the waters of the lake and with the country round. Here we have a fine agricultural Township, with good alluvial soil largely covered with mountains of shifting sand, which extend miles longitudinally and latitudinally across the country. It is not land sand either. The theory is, that the sand mounds are formed by drift sand thrown up from the bed of the lake during great storms. I know not if this be the case, but there is much to prove this conclusion. Be that as it may, we were all delighted with our visit to the sand banks, and whiled away a few hours gazing at a hot sun shedding its rays not only over Ontario's waters, but over a bit of country, even though of sand, as interesting as would be the sand regions in the vicinity of Berlin, the great German capital, or the northern part of Germany.

At the time of my writing Judge Morrison has been dead but a little over two years. He was not in good health for a few years before his death. He died at his residence Woodlawn, on 6th December, 1885, and was followed to the grave through the avenue of that beautiful country seat by many mourning friends.

XXVIII.

THE HONORABLE ROBERT ALEXANDER HARRISON, CHIEF JUSTICE OF ONTARIO.

THE feeling which possessed me when reading Thomas Carlyle's "French Revolution," possesses me in writing of Robert A. Harrison— a feeling of wonder and amazement at the amount of work some men undertake for the accomplishment of a purpose. Thomas Carlyle set out in life with a determination to make himself a great man by unceasing labor: his works shew how completely he succeeded in the attainment of the prize. Thomas Carlyle was the architect of his own future in literature. Chief Justice the Honorable Robert A. Harrison was the architect of his own future in law.

I do not wish my readers to understand that, in associating the name of Carlyle with that of a Chief Justice in Canada, I do so for the purpose of making a comparison of men: it is rather with a view of illustrating the value of work, and perseverance in work, in the accomplishment of any object in any walk of life. All philosophers are not lawyers, nor are all lawyers philosophers; yet there is so much of philosophy in law that there is, after all, a kind of kinship—an association of ideas. John Locke, perhaps the greatest, but certainly the most characteristic of English philosophers, has given us instruction on "association of ideas." He is indeed said to have been the first author to use the expression, "association of ideas." "Some ideas, indeed, have," he says "a national correspondence; but others, that 'in themselves are not at all of kin,' come to be so united in some men's minds that one no sooner at any time comes into the understanding than the whole gang, always inseparable, shew themselves together."

Robert Alexander Harrison was the eldest son of Richard Harrison, formerly of Skegarvey, in the County of Monaghan, Ireland, by his marriage with Miss Frances Hall, daughter of the Reverend Alexander Hall, Vicar of Newton-Butler, in the County of Fermanagh. Mr. Richard Harrison, when he first came to this country, remained for a time in Montreal. It was there Robert A., the Chief Justice, was born, on 3rd August, 1833. As soon as he was able, however, he removed from Montreal to Upper Canada, and took up his residence in Markham, in the vicinity of York. This removal took place a few months after Robert was born. Not long afterwards, Mr. Harrison again made a removal : this time into the City of Toronto from the outlying township.

I became acquainted with Mr. Richard Harrison soon after I came to reside in Toronto, in 1844. He was clerk of the market, and was highly esteemed by every one who knew him, for his honesty and uprightness of character; withal he had an Irish heart, which overflowed with liberality and benevolence. He resided in Queen street. His house was a little west of Spadina avenue, near the residence of the Honorable John Hillyard Cameron.

Robert, on arriving at a proper age, was sent by his father to Upper Canada College, where his industry enabled him to make his mark, carrying off many prizes from his competitors. Not satisfied with a mere College course, his ambition led him to become a graduate of a university.

At a very early period of the University of Trinity College history, Robert A. Harrison took his degree from that institutuion. He acquired the distinction of Bachelor of Civil Law in 1855, and Doctor of Civil Law, about four years afterwards.

It will not be out of place here to record that Trinity College is a University, situated on a property, which in the early days of York, had a certain celebrity, from the fact that Captain S. Smith, while once President of the Province, selected this property as his residence, and that "Gore Vale," so named in honor of Governor Gore, runs through the property. Doctor Scadding, in his "Toronto of Old," is quite enthusiastic in his description of the College and grounds. Referring to the Smith lot, he says:

> The sonthern half of this lot now forms the site and grounds of the University of Trinity College. Its brooklet will hereafter be famous in scholastic song. It will be regarded as the Cephissus of a Canadian Academus, the Cherwell of an infant Christ Church. The elmy dale which gives such agreeable variety to the park of Trinity College, and which renders so charming the view from the Provost's Lodge, is irrigated by it. The cupola and tower of the principal entrance to Trinity College will pleasantly, in however humble a degree, recall to the minds of Oxford men the Tom gate of Christ Church.

Mr. Harrison became a Student of the Law Society in Hilary Term, 1850. As soon as he was admitted he entered upon his studies in the office of Messrs. Robinson & Allan. Mr., now Sir Lukin Robinson was the senior member of that firm, and Reporter of the Queen's Bench. Mr. Harrison was a diligent student, ready for any kind of hard work in the line of the law. He had only been two years in the office, and was but eighteen years of age, when he conceived the idea of publishing a digest of all the cases in the Queen's Bench and Practice Courts in Upper Canada, from 1823 to 1851. He undertook the work under the supervision of Mr. Robinson. The book came out under the name of "Harrison & Robinson's Digest," and was published in 1852. This Digest was a very valuable hand-maid to practitioners of large practice, placing in their hands a ready reference to all decisions during a period of nearly thirty years.

During Mr. Harrison's student days, he was a prominent member of the Literary and Debating Society and Osgoode Club. This Society affords to Students at Law a good opportunity for developing their nascent legal intellects, and improving their debating powers. Much of Mr. Harrison's education tending towards making him a successful counsel at the Bar, was gained within the doors of the Society. In 1853, he made a change of office, going from Robinson & Allan to the office of Hagarty & Crawford, of which Mr. Hagarty, afterwards Chief Justice of the Queen's Bench, and now President of the Court of Appeal, was the senior member.

In 1854, Mr. Harrison received the appointment of Chief Clerk in the office of the Attorney-General. The Honorable John Ross was Attorney-General at this time. On the Honorable John A. Macdonald succeeding to the Attorney-Generalship in the McNab-Morin administration in 1854, he retained Mr. Harrison as his Chief Clerk. This caused him to follow the Government to Quebec. He was there not less inclined to the gay pleasures of society than the many government officials of that gay capital, and it was not to his disadvantage that in the following year the Government was removed to Toronto, where he had the less frivolous society of his old friends and relatives. In Toronto he had all the comforts of a home, presided over by a good father and fond mother.

Mr. Harrison was called to the Bar in Michaelmas Term, 1855. He was called with honours. He was, indeed, the first called to the Bar with honours, under the new system inaugurated by the Law Society a short time before his call. The Honorable Robert Baldwin was at the time Treasurer of the Society, and congratulated Mr. Harrison on being the first to gain the distinction of being called with honours.

Mr. Harrison had no sooner been called to the Bar than he shewed a disposition to mix in politics. He had been a pupil of the Honorable John A. Macdonald, and was tinged with his ideas of political life. He was of the Tory school, and had it not been for restraining influences he would have been deeply engaged, too early in life, in political agitation. He frequently contributed to the *Colonist* newspaper, the Conservative organ of the day in Toronto, articles in espousal of the Conservative doctrines and principles as he understood them. He soon, however, ceased this occupation in order to confine himself more exclusively to his profession. He was fond of writing. When he gave up writing political articles, he applied himself to writing on subjects appertaining to law, probably more profitable and less delusive than political controversy. In 1857 he published "The Statutes of Practical Utility in the Civil Administration of Justice in Upper Canada, Chronologically arranged." This work is more of a compilation than original matter. It required, however, a discriminating mind. This book, as well as his book containing the "Rules, Orders, and Regulations as to Practice and Pleading in the County Courts, with Notes," was well received by the profession, and obtained a large sale.

Mr. Harrison, in 1857, was still in the Attorney-General's office, connected with the Crown Law Department. It was during this year that a great excitement existed in the County of Haldimand, on account of depredations and crimes committed by one Townshend, alias McHenry. Townshend was arrested and tried at Cayuga, before Mr. Justice McLean and a jury. There never has been a case in Canada where such extraordinary evidence has been given as to the identity of a prisoner. There was not one trial only, but several trials of the case, and several weeks were taken up in endeavoring to solve the question presented. I have referred to the case more fully in the life of Mr. Justice McLean, and need not repeat what I have already said about this Canadian Tichborne case. Suffice it to say, it was the most important case of the period, and was conducted for the Crown by R. A. Harrison, and defended by that able and experienced Counsel, the late S. B. Freeman, Q.C., of

47—L. J.

Hamilton. This was the first trial of great importance in which Mr. Harrison was engaged. It required great endurance and skilful management, and was conducted in a manner satisfactory to the Attorney-General.

Mr. Harrison, notwithstanding his employment as Counsel for the Crown at this time, was devoting a considerable portion of time to the execution of a most important work, which he undertook, "Harrison's Common Law Procedure Act, and County Courts Procedure Acts." This valuable contribution to legal literature was, as the title page expresses, dedicated :

> To the Honorable John Alexander Macdonald, Attorney-General of Upper Canada, to whose ability as a Lawyer and influence as a Statesman the Profession are indebted for the Acts here annotated, this work is inscribed, by the Editor.

In the preface to the work, Mr. Harrison gave his reasons for entering on its performance, and bringing it to a successful termination. He said :

> The law, and the administration of the law, are two things essentially different. By the former we understand the great body of legal rights and liabilities which teach that justice should render to every man his due ; by the latter we understand the practice of the Courts, or the machinery used for dispensing justice. All laws are designed either to prevent a mischief ; to remedy it, if committed ; or to compensate the sufferer, if no other remedy can be applied. The proper application of the remedy is thus of vital importance to the due dispensation of justice. The spirit of modern legislation is to make the remedy coextensive with the mischief intended to be prevented or redressed. For this the Courts have at all times struggled ; for this the Legislature have labored ; and for this has the Common Law Procedure Act, 1854, been passed.

These were very good reasons for the undertaking. Slovenliness in practice is as prejudicial as unsound law ; any work worth performing is worthy of being well performed. Mr. Harrison always kept this in view, and acted upon it as a cardinal principle. The work was got out specially to instruct the profession in procedure.

Mr. Harrison's Common Law Procedure Act will always endure as a lasting monument to his memory, and evidence of his work. It was first published in 1858, and received great commendation, not only in Canada, but in England, and in whatever country it reached. The London legal press placed Mr. Harrison in the front rank of those commentators who had undertaken to edit the Acts embodied in the work. "The Jurist," in reviewing the work, said :

> These are the Acts which have revolutionized the law of Upper Canada, after their progenitors had exercised a like radical influence in the Old Country. They are, in effect, an amalgamation of our Procedure Acts of 1852-1854, together with an Act applying them, in a great measure, to the County Courts of Canada. The work is, therefore, almost as useful to the English as to the Canadian lawyers ; and is not only the most recent, but by far the most complete edition which we have seen of the most important Acts of Parliament. The editor has not been content with industriously collecting the numerous decisions which are now scattered through our Reports upon these Statutes, but has displayed both skill and judgment in their arrangement, and in deducing, wherever it was possible, the principles of which the decisions are either suggestive or illustrative.

Notwithstanding a large practice which he had succeeded in getting, Mr. Harrison still devoted a part of his time to writing. In 1859 he brought out "The Municipal Manual for Upper Canada," containg notes on decided cases, and a full analytical index. This work was very conducive to his success in gaining a name for diligence and usefulness, not only to the profession at large but to the whole public. He was, after this, the constant adviser in municipal matters in a large number of the municipal questions constantly arising in the Province. His Municipal Manual was largely sought after in outside counties, yielding him not only a good income but making him known in the various counties in the Province. Perhaps nothing tended more to build up his general reputation than this work.

In 1859 he formed a partnership with James Patterson, who had a good connection in the Counties of York and Peel. He was considered one of the best office men and special pleaders of his day. He and Mr. Harrison together had a large and remunerative business.

The firm of Patterson & Harrison was afterwards augumented by adding to it Mr. Hodgins, the present Master of the Supreme Court of Judicature for Ontario, and John Bain, Q.C. Mr. Moss, afterwards Chief Justice Moss, was at one time a partner of Mr. Harrison.

In 1859 Mr. Harrison was employed by the Crown to prosecute in the celebrated case of The Queen *vs.* Mercer. It arose out of an agreement entered into between Sheriff Rapelje of the County of Norfolk and Lawrence William Mercer, by which the former agreed to surrender his office, on doing which he was to receive from Mr. Mercer £500, and an annuity of £300 a year. This transaction was no doubt based on the assumption that Mercer would, on the resignation of Rapelje, get the appointment of Sheriff of the County. An information was filed by the Attorney-General against Mercer, for a misdemeanor, and as being a transaction involving the sale of an office, and contrary to the provisions of the English Statute 5 & 6 Edward VI., extended to Upper Canada by 49 George III. cap. 126. It was held by the Court of Queen's Bench, that the transaction was not only illegal under the Statute, but at Common Law, and that the ignorance of the Government as to the illegal agreement was immaterial. The Crown obtained judgment, and Mr. Mercer lost his office. The case will be found reported in 17 U. C. Q. B. Rep. 602.

Mr. Harrison was for several years editor of the Upper Canada Law Journal, and frequently contributed editorial articles which were well received. During his partnership with Mr. Patterson his business much increased. His early connection with the Law Department of the Government had secured him the confidence of Mr John A. Macdonald, who was of great assistance to him in his profession. Through him his firm received all the Upper Canada revenue business of the Government.

About this time there had been a great deal of smuggling and infringement on the Custom's laws. A great many suits had to be brought for penalties and forfeitures.

These suits were intrusted to him on the part of the Crown, and were conducted with diligence and success.

He was of counsel for the Crown in the case of the Attorney-General *vs.* Sherman Smith Halliday, 26 U. C. Q. B. Rep. 397, which deserves mention. It was an information filed by the Attorney-General against the defendant, who was a distiller carrying on business in Maitland, in the County of Grenville. He had gained a wide celebrity in that county for his hospitality, and because of his large business, which brought money to the farmers, who sold grain to him for his distillery business. He was growing affluent; but in some way the Revenue Department were not satisfied that he made correct returns to them of all the whiskey which he distilled. On investigation, they ascertained that it was more than probable there were upwards of 2,000 gallons short in his returns, the duty on which, if paid into the treasury, would have amounted to a large sum; which large sum they had not received. The suit for penalties and duty was tried at Toronto, in 1847, and resulted in a verdict for the Crown for $47,999.00, being the duty on 159,608 gallons of manufactured whiskey not returned.

J. H. Cameron, Q. C., moved a rule nisi in term to set aside the verdict on many grounds. Galt, Q. C., Anderson and Robert A. Harrison shewed cause. S. Richards, Q. C., supported the rule.

The case was very hotly contested. Mr. Halliday held a prominent position in the county, and if it should be decided against him, his reputation would be injured, and his future prospects blasted, on account of crookedness of dealing. Chief Justice Draper gave the judgment of the Court of Queen's Bench, and discharged the rule. The principal question decided was on the onus of proof. The Crown proving that the defendant had sold to customers more than he returned, was it for the Crown to prove the quantity manufactured, or was it for the defendant to establish that he had paid duty on all manufactured by him. It was held: (1) That the defendant was liable to pay duty upon all spirits manufactured by him, not merely on such as had been measured and ascertained in the manner prescribed by 27 and 28 Victoria, cap. 3. (2) It was proved by an agent of the defendant that he sold, as agent for the defendant, at Montreal, between the days mentioned in the information, 159,608 gallons more than appeared on the credit side of the defendant's stock books, and on which duties had been paid; and a number of invoices of these sales, which were produced, represented the spirits to be 50 more than proof. Moreover, the agent said that large quantities of spirits had been consigned to him direct; and it was to be gathered from the evidence that deliveries had been made to the purchasers direct from the conveyance by which they had been sent by the defendant. Held, that from this evidence, unanswered in any way, the jury was warranted in finding against the defendant for the duty on that quantity. Held also, that sub-sec. 2, of sec. 14, of 29 Victoria, cap. 3, throwing the payment of duty on the defendant, was properly treated as applicable, though passed after the period for which duties were claimed, for it related to matter of evidence and procedure.

I have written of this case because it not only involved a much argued legal question as to onus of proof, but from the fact that so many counsel whose names are familiar, not only to the Bar, but to the Bench and public, were counsel in the case, viz., Galt, Q. C., now Sir Thomas Galt, Chief Justice of the Common Pleas Division of the High Court; Harrison, afterwards Chief Justice of the Queen's Bench; and M. C. Cameron, afterwards Sir M. C. Cameron, Chief Justice of the Common Pleas Division of the High Court of Justice; besides S. Richards, Q. C.; J. H. Cameron, Q. C.; and Mr. Anderson, all able counsel, but who never occupied seats on the Bench.

Mr. Harrison was also Counsel for the Crown in the John Anderson case, referred to fully in the life of Chief Justice McLean. Anderson was an escaped slave, whom it was sought to get back into the United States on a charge of murder, committed when he was endeavoring to escape from slavery. The attempt to have him sent back to the United States failed, he was discharged from custody on habeas corpus, and given his full liberty.

Mr. Harrison was created a Queen's Counsel in 1867, and elected a Bencher of the Law Society in 1871. He was for some time an Alderman in the City Council of Toronto. He found time to perform the duties of a director of the Life Association of Scotland while at the Bar. He interested himself in some degree in Church matters and identified himself with the Church Associations of the Diocese of Toronto. He was evangelical in his views, and liberally disposed towards all denominations of Christians.

Mr Harrison had resolved, when about to matriculate at Trinity College, to proceed to study for the Church Ministry in case he attained a certain scholarship in his examination. In this he failed, and turned his attention to the study of law. Whether rightly or wrongly, he looked upon the failure as the finger of God directing his energies to be employed elsewhere. He continued, however, to take great interest in the Church, and did "yeoman's service" among its laymen. Brought up among the associations of Trinity East and St. James's Cathedral, he was evangelical in his views. As soon as he ascertained that his youngest brother had determined on entering the profession of their maternal grandfather, from which he had felt himself providentially deviated, he never ceased to help and encourage him, though the latter had refused a partnership in the famous firm of "Patterson and Harrison" more than once in the course of his academical career. No difference of theological taste (if such existed) prevented the Chief Justice from giving material and other support, whenever required, to this younger brother, in the various projects of Church work—whether at St. Alban's, Beverley, in the backwoods, or at St. Matthias's, Toronto, under the shadow of their common Alma Mater. He sympathized with good work everywhere.

Mr. Harrison first entered Parliament in 1867, when he defeated Mr. John Macdonald, now a member of the Dominion Senate, who contested one of the divisions of Toronto with him. His strong Conservative opinions gained him the support of the Conservative party in his candidature for Parliament. He continued to represent the constituency till 1872. He was not altogether a success in Parliament. Parliamentary life was not to his taste. Involving, as it did, a great departure from his professional pursuits, the occupation became irksome to him. At the general election of 1872, he declined to contest the seat, and frankly told his constituents, in an address which he published, that he was glad to be relieved of duties that entailed not only a loss of time, but of money, without adding to his prestige, as he viewed political life. While in Parliament, he was for two Sessions Chairman of the Miscellaneous and Private Bills Committee. As a member of the House, he was connected with some important measures. Amendment of the laws as to stamping promissory notes and bills of exchange, and Bills relating to the Criminal law, received his attention. After his retirement from Parliament, he resumed his active practice at the Bar, when his business grew to large dimensions.

On the 8th of October, 1875, Mr. Harrison was, quite unexpectedly to himself, appointed Chief Justice of the Queen's Bench, under the title of Chief Justice of Ontario, succeeding Chief Justice Richards, who was promoted to the Supreme Court.

On the Bench the Chief Justice continued the same unremitting labor he had performed at the Bar. The profession appreciated the energy he displayed in his duties There were arrears to be cleared off, which he soon caused to disappear. Accustomed to hard work, and with a good constitution, he had no difficulty in fulfilling the expectations that had been formed of him, that his untiring industry as Chief of the Court would enable him to keep up with the business of the country. He was called upon to decide many important cases. I will not pretend to give more than a few, as, though but a short time on the Bench, he disposed of so much legal business that it would require more time than I can command to make full report of it. He was called upon to decide the case of McIntyre *vs.* McCracken, which, being a semi-commercial case, may be referred to as evidencing the soundness of his decision. In that case, which is reported at 37 Upper Canada Queen's Bench, 422, and was decided by him but a few years after he was promoted to the Bench, he was called upon to decide an equitable question under an equitable plea, though his practice at the Bar had been almost exclusively in the Common Law. In substance the principal question was, whether a person having in good faith and for a valuable consideration, without notice, purchased shares in a joint stock company, incorporated by the Government of Ontario, under 27 and 28 Victoria, cap. 23, on the representation by the seller that they were fully paid up shares, and having, before he purchased, had the representation confirmed by the proper officer of the company, could afterwards, at the instance of a creditor of the company who discovered that in truth the shares were not fully paid up, be sued by the creditor.

Chief Justice Harrison held, that the defendant, before he purchased, made all the enquiry he was bound to make. He said :

> He had a perfect right to believe the statement of the accredited officer of the company; that he was under no obligation to discredit it, and search the books of the company to prove its falsity; and, under the circumstances, he was a bonâ fide purchaser for value.

Morrison, J., and Wilson, J., concurred in the judgment of the Chief Justice. Nevertheless, the case was carried to the Ontario Court of Appeal, which overruled his decision, but the Supreme Court, on appeal, confirmed his judgment.

Regina *vs.* Wilkinson—Re Brown, 41 U. C. Q. B., is a case which ought not to be passed over in writing of Chief

Justice Harrison's judicial life. As is well known, the Honorable George Brown was a journalist who had control of the *Globe* newspaper, published in Toronto. In the Daily *Globe* of 8th July, 1876, and in the Weekly *Globe* of 14th July, 1876, there appeared an article written by him, wherein there was a description, argument, or comment, not only scandalizing the Court, but also scandalizing Wilkinson, the defendant in a libel suit. Wilkinson applied to the Court of Queen's Bench, and obtained a Rule calling on Mr. Brown to shew cause why he should not be committed for contempt of Court for these articles. Mr. Brown, in person, shewed cause to the Rule. The main points decided by the Chief Justice were: 1st That when *leave to file* a criminal information had been given, there was a pending litigation, though such information had not in fact been filed, and that such publication was a contempt of Court. 2nd That a Judge sitting out of Term under the Administration of Justice Act, did not represent the full Court, so as to enable him to punish for contempt of Court. 3rd That the article complained of was a contempt of Court. There were other points on which Morrison, J., sitting with the Chief Justice, differed; but they both agreed on the main question, that a contempt of Court had been committed. There are some remarks of the Chief Justice which I think it right to quote, as shewing the privilege of the press, and the duty of, as well as protection afforded to the Court against newspaper assailants. The Chief Justice said :

All that now remains of the cause shewn to the Rule is the contention that Mr. Brown, in publishing these articles, did no more than his duty as a public journalist, and so is privileged. I have already expressed my views as to the real and supposed liberty of the press. I have no wish to repeat these expressions. They exclude all idea of privilege on the present occasion. The argument is, that, considering the notoriety of what is called the Big Push Letter, and the prominent position of the writer of it in one of the political parties of the country, that it was for the public interest that the articles in question should be written, although severely reflecting on one of the Judges of a Superior Court of Law, in respect of a judgment delivered by him in Court. But it is not for the public interest that any part of our Judiciary, who, Mr. Brown admits, are worthy of the highest admiration, should be recklessly assailed in the public press. There is no privilege for any man in Canada, under the pretext of the public good, rashly to assail in the public press any of our Judges for his conduct on the Bench, and to impute to the Judge assailed, conduct so wicked and corrupt as to render him unfit to occupy the distinguished and responsible position of a seat on the Bench. The remedy for such a state of things, if ever it should unfortunately arise in our country, is wholly different. But whatever may happen, the Judges must be kept high above the struggles of party warfare and party rancour. Judges have no political bias. They know nothing, as Judges, of political parties, or political contests, except when forced on their attention in controverted election trials. They are neither Reformers nor Conservatives. It is a matter of no interest whatever to them which of the political parties for the time being is in office. The moment a man consents to accept a seat on the Bench, his mere party predilections are left behind, and should, if possible, be for ever abandoned. He must henceforward do justice to all men, and so to both political parties. He cannot do so if he has a leaning to either; and his usefulness as a Judge must be impaired, more or less, if either political party entertain the belief, well or ill founded, that he is a prejudiced or unjust Judge. The office of a Judge of the Superior Courts, either at Law or Equity, in this Province is an arduous one. Judges, of all men, in the discharge of their high and arduous duties, need not only the protection of the law, but the genuine sympathy of all the honestly disposed classes of the people. One of the greatest blessings which can be conferred upon an intelligent people is an able and independent Judiciary: one of the greatest curses would be the belief on the part of the people, or any considerable portion of the people, that the Judiciary is either weak or corrupt. The labors of the Judge permeate all ranks of society. They ascend to the occupants of the palace, and descend to the hearth of the humblest cotter in the land. All men and all parties stand before the majesty of the law on an equal plane. All have, in the eye of the law, equal rights. All have property, reputation, or life demanding protection. All have the right to the protection of the blessings conferred upon them. And for the safety of society, all must feel that all their rights will be protected by the judiciary. It would not, in my opinion, be in the public interest that the author of the publications now before us should go altogether unpunished. Individually I bear him no ill-will; I admit his talents; socially I respect him; I respect his position as a public journalist, a prominent public man, and a Senator of the Dominion. But the higher the station of the offender, the greater the necessity for his being made to bend and submit to the law. I am sincerely sorry to see Mr. Brown in the position where he has voluntarily placed himself, and from which, although ample opportunity was offered him, he refused to extricate himself. If I were to consult only my own feelings as an individual, I would forbear to punish. But when I consult my duty as presiding Judge of this Court, the line of my duty appears to be so clear that I cannot refuse to see and follow it. It is not because a line of duty is disagreeable that a Judge is to shrink from following it to all its consequences. In my opinion the rule should be absolute.

This case was remarkable for the alleged virulence of Mr. Brown in the remarks made by him in open Court, in argument of the Rule. I heard Mr. Brown argue the Rule on his own behalf, and witnessed the expressive energy which he gave to the discourse. I do not think he used language stronger than that used by him in his affidavit in answer to the Rule; which on reference to it will be seen to be quite strong enough. The spectacle presented in the Court of a journalist not only being guilty of contempt in writing articles reflecting scandalously on the Court, but also before the Judges all but repeating the scandal, was not an edifying one, and it is hoped will never be repeated.

In this particular case, owing to the difference of opinion in the Court on minor questions the Rule, commitment or attachment, was refused.

The Chief Justice heard Mr. Brown through a long and vituperative address with much patience, knowing that not being a barrister, he could not know all the courtesies of professional decorum. He argued his own case, although he had two counsel with him. I think for further guidance the judgment of the Chief Justice is valuable as shewing the duty of journalists in criticising the acts of a Court, and the duty of the Court in dealing with such questions when presented.

Having quoted cases in which the Chief Justice was engaged at the Bar, and his decisions on the Bench, I may proceed to shew what manner of man he was. At the beginning of his Bar life he evinced a determination to overcome all obstacles. Whether addressing the Court or jury, he had about him what some would call a pompousness of manner. When analysed, however, it will be found that it might more properly be called pride of place than pompousness of manner. He was conscious of his own ability and endurance to give full play to a case even if it took days, where with others, hours might have finished the business. He was as cool a man as ever I have met at the Bar. Nothing seemed to disturb him, when other men would be ruffled he would smile at the most sarcastic and caustic remarks of counsel at the Bar levelled at him. He may have felt the arrows as they pierced his side, but he never flinched at the stroke, going right on with his work as if a shaft had not been shot from the bow.

He was a portly man, and in conducting cases at nisi prius, threw all his ponderous weight upon the attention of the jury. I have known him to be opposed by counsel more skilful in ethics and not less skilful in law, and yet he held his own. If opposed by the Court he submitted kindly, bundled up his papers, put papers and brief in his bag, and left the Court with a determination to seek redress in full Court in Term, which often heard of cases again in which he had been engaged.

In addressing juries he in plain, but not polished language, with well arrayed arguments, sought with much force to lead them to a conclusion favourable to his client's side of the cause.

Doctor Hugh Blair, in one of his lectures, draws a contrast between eloquence of the Bar and popular assemblies. Mr. Harrison was more of a success at the Bar than with popular assemblies, and was proud to have that distinction.

Blair wrote :

> The difference between eloquence of the Bar and of popular assemblies is this : In the first place, the ends of speaking at the Bar and in popular assemblies are entirely different. In popular assemblies the great object is persuasion ; the orator aims at determining to some choice or conduct as good, fit, or useful. For accomplishing this end it is incumbent on him to apply himself to all the principles of action in our nature ; to the passions and to the heart ; as well as to the understanding. But, at the Bar *conviction* is the great object. There it is not the speaker's business to persuade the Judges to what is good or useful, but to shew them what is *just* and *true,* and of course it is chiefly or solely to the understanding

that his eloquence is addressed. This is a characteristic difference which ought ever to be kept in view.

Young men just budding will, no doubt, read this with attention, and, I hope, with profit. Some neophytes at the Bar are apt to think that flowery eloquence is enough to ensure them attention and success in their profession. It is not so in the least degree. Sounding brass may be very good for a town church bell, but is of only momentary value to a Lawyer, it has no enduring effect. I have often heard men at the Bar talk, indulge in rhetoric in vast proportions, be eloquent indeed in words, without one seeming word of thought. Beware of such men, my friends. Read Hamlet's advice to the players, it is as applicable to the barrister as to the actor :

"But if you mouth it as many of the players do * * Nor do not saw the air too much with your hand, * * Be not too tame neither, but let your own discretion be your tutor : suit the action to the word, the word to the action ; with this special observance, that you o'erstep not the modesty of nature."

Chief Justice Harrison, after his promotion to the Bench, did not forget his old friends at the Bar. He was in the habit of entertaining liberally at his fine, large, roomy residence and grounds of his Spadina Avenue residence, Englefield.

His constant work out of vacation gave him the right, indeed it was necessary for his health to have some recreation during vacation. He then would meet members of the Bar on his well ordered grounds in friendly matches of lawn tennis or bowls, and enjoy the change from mental exercise to healthy amusement.

He was an excellent host, and had at his table at convenient times guests, whether their homes were in Toronto or abroad on a visit to the capital and seat of the Courts. He was not exclusive, but extended his invitations to different professions. The Archbishop of the Roman Catholic Church, and the Bishop of the Protestant Anglican Church alike enjoyed his hospitality. He was an admirer of Doctor Potts of the Methodist Church, both as a preacher and as a man; he frequently used to attend to hear him preach at the Metropolitan Church, and not unfrequently had him as a guest at his house.

In 1877 the Chief Justice was appointed one of the arbitrators on the question of the northerly and westerly boundaries of Ontario. His associate arbitrators were Sir Francis Hincks and Sir Edward Thornton, the British Minister at Washington. The arbitrators examined all treaties, orders in Council, Acts of Parliament, and other documents which would enable them to make a lasting and binding award. Their work of investigation being completed, they, on the 3rd August, 1878, published their award as follows :

> To all to whom these presents shall come:
> The undersigned having been appointed by the Governments of Canada and Ontario, as arbitrators to determine the northerly and westerly boundaries of Ontario, do hereby determine and decide that the following are and shall be such boundaries, that is to say :
> Commencing at a point on the southern shore of Hudson's Bay, commonly called James's Bay, where a line produced due north from the head of Lake Temiscaming would strike the said south shore; thence, along the said south shore, westerly to the mouth of the Albany River; thence, up the middle of the said Albany River and of the lakes thereon, to the source of the said river at the head of Lake Joseph; thence, by the nearest line, to the easterly end of Lac Seul, being the head waters of the English River; thence westerly, through the middle of Lac Seul and the said English River, to a point where the same will be intersected by a true meridianal line drawn northerly from the International monuments placed to mark the most north-westerly angle of the Lake of the Woods, by the recent boundary commission; and thence due south, following the said meridianal line, to the said International monument; thence southerly and easterly, following on the International boundary line between the British Possessions and the United States of America, into Lake Superior.
> But if a true meridianal line drawn northerly from the said International boundary, at the said north-westerly angle of the Lake of the Woods, shall be found to pass to the west of where the English River empties into the Winnipeg River, then, in such case, the northerly boundary of Ontario shall continue down the middle of the said English River, to where the same empties into the Winnipeg River, and shall continue on a line drawn due west from the confluence of the said English River with the Winnipeg River, until the same will intersect the meridian above described; and thence due south, following the said meridianal line, to the said International monument; thence southerly and easterly,

following upon the International boundary line between the British Possessions and the United States of America, into Lake Superior.

Given under our hands at Ottawa, in the Province of Ontario, this third day of August, 1878.

ROBERT A. HARRISON.
EDWD. THORNTON.
F. HINCKS.

Never did three men charged with public duties, enter upon the performance of them, and accomplish their work with more zeal and fidelity, than did the three arbitrators who made this award, an award which after full examination into its merits by the Privy Council, has been sustained by that Court, and by Her Majesty, the Queen. The award did not give Ontario as much as was claimed for the Province, but much more than the Dominion Government was willing to allow, hence the appeal to the Privy Council.

Notwithstanding the high reputation of the arbitrators, and the conviction in the minds of those who took the trouble to examine into the matter for themselves, there were not wanting objectors and politicians who set about criticising the award, condemning all, great and small, connected with it. All this did not disturb the equanimity of Chief Justice Harrison. Sir Francis Hincks, however, who had not so impassive a nature as the Chief Justice, being invited to Toronto to deliver a lecture, complied with the request, and on the 6th May, 1881, in the theatre of the Normal School, discussed the whole subject of the award, in a manner which brought conviction to the minds of all those present, that the arbitrators had acted on the highest principles of justice and true interpretation of documents forming the basis of their award, and that the reasons for the award, which were then for the first time given to the public, were incontrovertible in defence of the conclusion of the arbitrators.

Sir Francis, after explaining that the arbitrators had been governed in making their award by Acts of Parliament, Official Records, and Treaties, and not by Commissions to Governors, that some contended they should have regarded, said :

I shall offer no apology for citing a few extracts from letters of the late Chief Justice Harrison, addressed to me in August, 1878, on the subject of the criticisms made on the award: "I feel satisfied that you can give an answer to all and sundry who attack the award. I believe there never was an award made in a matter of such importance that is so little open to honest criticism * * Singular to say, since the award was made, I have received from Judge McDonald, of Guelph, an old lithographed map without name or date, but evidently made long before the Constitutional Act of 1791, which indicates the northern boundary of Upper Canada to be the precise line where we have placed it." * * Our duty was judicial, we had little or nothing to do with questions of policy. By the light of the evidence adduced, and the arguments propounded, we unanimously decided upon certain boundaries, for the north and west of the Province. Whether the land thus given to the Province was full of diamonds, or only of worthless rocks, was no business of ours. The surveyor who finds the boundaries of two lots of land is never influenced by the consideration that one piece of it is intrinsically more valuable than the other. None of the able counsel who addressed us ventured so far to take leave of his senses as to attempt to take such untenable ground.

The excessive labor which the Chief Justice bestowed upon this Boundary Award matter, added to his other judicial work, was no doubt largely the cause of the impairment of his health. He accomplished an enormous amount of work in a very short time, so short, indeed, that in the minds of some the value of the work was lessened, because, as viewed by some, it was an utter impossibility for him to have considered the whole question. Such people did not know Chief Justice Harrison; if they had, they would have known that it was not his habit to turn out any work only half finished. The results have shewn that his work was as solid as it was complete.

In 1878 the Chief Justice went to Ottawa on business connected with the arbitration. His health, which before this had been somewhat shattered, was not improved by his trip to the Dominion Capital. On his return to Toronto, his health being bad partially incapacitated him for judicial duty. The usual expedient of an over-worked man was resorted to, in the hope that he might recover. He undertook travel as a specific. All, however, was to no purpose. The doctors pronounced that he had dilatation of the heart, which must prove fatal; and so it did. He died at his residence, Englefield, on the 1st November, 1878, at the early age of forty-five, much regretted by the Bar and his many friends.

Mr. Harrison was twice married. His first wife was Anna, daughter of Mr. J. M. Mickle, formerly a merchant of Quebec. She died in 1866. His second wife, and now widow, was Kennethina Johanna MacKay Scobie, only daughter of Hugh Scobie, formerly of Toronto, and proprietor of the *British Colonist* newspaper.

There was issue of the first marriage only one daughter and no sons, and of the second marriage one daughter. The Reverend Richard Harrison, of Toronto, is a brother of the deceased Chief Justice.

XXIX.

THE HONORABLE THOMAS MOSS, CHIEF JUSTICE OF ONTARIO.

WHEN I look back upon the sands of time as they have distributed themselves over the past, burying so many of high and low degree, I feel a poignant sorrow for the loss of so many friends. The old and the young alike, have been cut down by the relentless scythe of the old man, Time, shewing how unstable are the things of this world; how slippery the paths we tread. It is not, however, within the compass of the work I have in hand to compose an elegy. Even if I had the ability to make elegiac verse or poetic measure, I would not indulge the sentiment. This is a prosaic, not a poetic age. It is well to conform to the condition of things as we find them.

The drama of life is made up of so many incidents, that without indulging in the humours of poetry, one may interest himself, and perhaps others, in describing in plain and understandable language, the goodness, and I may add, the greatness of a man so endowed with nature's best gifts as the Honorable Thomas Moss. To award praise where no praise is due, is no praise at all; but to acknowledge the commanding ability of a man who was so much beloved as he of whom I am now writing, is only making a confession which is begotten of appreciation of true worth and high respect.

The Honorable Thomas Moss was the son of John

Moss, formerly of Cobourg, in the County of Northumberland, Ontario, and was born in that town on the 20th August, 1836. Mr. John Moss subsequently removed to Toronto, where I first knew him. He lived on Queen Street west, near to Bathurst Street. Mr. Moss's place of business was on Queen Street also, further west. Whether or not his son Thomas, as by inheritance acquired from his father the spirit of industry, which his father undoubtedly had, I do not know, but this I can say, that Mr. John Moss was a man who gave attention to business early and late, frequently passing my house for his office at six o'clock in the morning.

I am a great believer in heredity, and so I feel called upon to mention this quality in Mr. Moss père, some of which I would fain believe his son Thomas inherited, or otherwise I could not account for his rapid and brilliant career in life. That he was, as a child, precocious and in advance of most children of his own age I know. I also know that as he grew in years, he grew in knowledge at a quicker rate than most of his fellows. Still I am not prepared to acknowledge that, without industry accompanying talent, he would have had all the successes which were his portion in this life.

Thomas Moss, when a boy, attended the public or common school, where he acquired the rudiments of learning, and a tolerable proficiency in such subjects as were taught at the public school. He had, in addition to this, the advantage of the instruction of his paternal grandfather, who resided with the family; and still further, of one McLachlin, who taught a school for some time in Toronto, on the corner of Duke and Berkeley streets. Mr. McLachlin was a Trinity College, Dublin, man, and no doubt took particular pains with Thomas, as the son of a fellow-countryman, who might give lustre to the Irish name. The Irish schoolmaster, as well as Thomas's grandfather, found in their pupil a diligent student—not as a groveller in school books only, but as a student of general literature.

Thomas read a great deal, and is said to have had a capacious and retentive memory. He had, indeed, a remarkable memory: he had only to read a book, when all the principal incidents that had engaged his thoughts and reading seemed photographed on his memory: added to this a gift of language surprisingly chaste and beautiful, he could at any moment give to listeners a treat more delicious than nectar, and more invigorating than the prairie breeze.

At ten years of age, Thomas Moss was intellectually as old as most boys of fourteen or fifteen years of age. At this period of his life he also had great physical vigor, and keenly enjoyed the ordinary sports and amusements of boyhood. He was fond of athletic sports, and was known as an enthusiastic and expert cricketer. What more manly recreation is there for boys than cricket? The very rules of the game were founded in honor, integrity, and principles of right. No undue advantage is allowed to be taken of a man in cricket; if such a thing were attempted, the culprit would bring down on him the disfavor of the whole club.

Cricket is truly the gentlemen's game—gentlemen, not in the sense necessarily of birth, but of men of every degree associated together in an exercise of a most healthful nature, imparting vigor both to mind and body to a degree scarcely equalled by any other pastime.

Upper Canada College has been the nursery of cricket in Upper Canada. Thomas Moss was an instance of the good results flowing from the noble game, combined with diligence in storing the mind with choice morsels of classical and cognate literature.

The biographer of Sir Walter Scott has said that as he grew, entered the classes of the college, and began his legal studies, first as apprentice to his father, and then in the law classes of the university, he became noticeable to all his friends for his gigantic memory, the rich stores of romantic material with which it was loaded, his giant feats of industry in accomplishing any cherished purpose, his delight in all athletic enterprises. This description given of the great Scotch writer is quite applicable to Mr. Moss.

Mr. Moss, senior, and family removed from Cobourg to to Toronto in 1846. Shortly after arrival in Toronto Thomas was entered a student of Gale's Institute, which subsequently developed into Knox College. When about twelve years of age he left Gale's, and became a student in Upper Canada College, and was admitted to the fourth form. His progress through the College was rapid and brilliant, he carried off many of the prizes which the College awarded to deserving and proficient students, amongst others, the Principal's prize, and seventh form prize, and the Governor General's prize.

In 1854 he matriculated at the University of Toronto. His previous training, his unwearied industry, coupled with his material talents of the highest order, soon enabled him to make his presence felt within the scholastic bounds of the University. He was a prominent member of the Literary and Debating Society, that "imperium in imperio" of this seat of learning which had served to develope the intellect of the students, giving them place among the best men of the day. In this Society Mr. Moss was a prominent member, his speeches there are said to have been marked by a purity of thought and chasteness of diction, which are not often associated with a young man of the early years of the future Chief Justice.

When he graduated at the University in 1858, he took Triple First Class Honors and won the gold medals in Classics, Mathematics, and Modern Languages. In 1859 he took his Degree of Master of Arts and wrote the prize Essay for the year. He had now gained a status in the educational world second to none in the Province. He had gained a Provincial reputation He was known far and wide as one of the most brilliant young men of the country, and all those who knew him foreshadowed that he was destined to make his mark, to fill a high position in whatever calling he might adopt.

In 1860 he had the high honor of being presented to H. R. H. the Prince of Wales, on the occasion of his visit to Toronto, as the most distinguished Alumnus of the University. The honors bestowed on Mr. Thomas Moss never caused any jealousy in the bosoms of his competitors; they were so well deserved that not one could say "nay." Besides this, his was such an amiable, lovable disposition that he endeared himself to all who knew him. With his intimates, there was not one, who in case he was attacked, would not have thrown himself into the breach, and warded off every blow. But he had no enemies. There was no necessity for the knights of the University to champion his cause.

Mr. Moss's talent eminently fitted him for the profession of the law. Immediately after taking his Bachelor of Arts Degree at the University, and before his advancement to the higher Degree of Master of Arts, viz., in Michaelmas Term, 1858, he was entered a Student of Law at Osgoode Hall, due effect being given to the Degree which he had taken at the Provincial University. He immediately entered the office of Adam Crooks, then a practising Barrister in Toronto, afterwards the Honorable Adam Crooks, member of the Ontario Government and Minister of Education. He remained with Mr. Crooks as his student for two years. At this time the firm was Crooks & Cameron, Mr. Hector Cameron, Q.C., being a member of the firm. On the dissolution of the firm of Crooks & Cameron, Mr. Moss's articles were assigned to Mr. Cameron, and with him he completed his term of study.

He was called to the Bar in Michaelmas Term, 1861, (25 Victoria), and soon afterward formed a partnership with Mr. Hector Cameron. Several years later, he formed a partnership with the Honorable James Patton, who, after running the gauntlet of political life and being made a member of the Government, accepted the office of Collector of Customs at Toronto, which position he filled till his sudden death. Mr. Featherstone Osler, Justice of the Court of Appeal, was a partner with Mr. Patton, and when Mr. Moss joined them the firm was known as Patton, Osler, and Moss, and had their office in the Exchange Building, on Wellington street, in Toronto. All the members of the firm were men of great integrity. The firm soon acquired a good name and extensive business, the outcome of a good name and business capacity.

At the Bar, Mr. Moss's career was an exceptionally brilliant one, as it had been at the University. From the time he was given his first brief, it was evident to the entire profession that the sanguine expectations formed of him would be fully realized. Early in his professional career he was appointed Equity Lecturer of the Law Society, at Osgoode Hall, and also Registrar of the University of Toronto.

It was in Equity that Mr. Moss more especially distinguished himself. His critical examination of this branch of jurisprudence had led his mind to favor the expansiveness of Equity, as compared with the contraction of Common Law. He was familiar with all the Equity writers, and had given diligent attention to the decisions of Equity Judges. He was, in the time of his first three partnerships, viz., of Patton, Osler, and Moss; Osler and Moss; and Osler, Moss, and Foster, nisi prius counsel of these firms: when Mr. R. A. Harrison became a partner of his firm, the jury part of the business fell to him.

Mr. Moss, however, preferred the quiet of the Equity Courts to the confusion of the Common Law Courts. No man could give an argument on Equity law, before the Equity Judges, with more skill and ability than Mr. Moss. His manner was quiet, but impressive, and usually carried great weight with the Court.

His partnership with Mr. Osler and Mr. Harrison, the firm name of which was Harrison, Osler, and Moss, was a successful and lucrative one: all the partners deriving a large income from the business.

In 1871, Mr. Moss was elected a Bencher of the Law Society. He had no sooner become a Bencher than he applied himself to the educational department of the Bench, so dear to his heart. The project of the founding of a Law School, for the advancement of legal education, was one in which he took great interest ; and in November, 1871, then being Chairman of the Committee on Legal Education, he brought in a report formulating a scheme which, after mature consideration, was adopted by Convocation on the 6th of December, 1872 ; and on the 3rd of February, 1873, the School was formally inaugurated, an opening address being delivered by the Honorable John Hillyard Cameron, Q. C., the then Treasurer of the Law Society.

Mr. Moss was created a Queen's Counsel in 1872.

Early in 1875 he was appointed a member of the Law Reform Commission, an evidence of the esteem in which he was held by the Attorney-General. This Commission was created for the purpose of inquiring into the expediency of amalgamating the Courts of Common Law and Equity, and it was on the report of this Commission that the Legislature acted afterwards, in amalgamating the Courts and the passage of the Judicature Act. No higher benefit could have been conferred on the country than this legal reform. Suitors bandied about from one Court to another, had begun to think that there was no abiding place in law.

It is thought by some that the arrangement of the Courts has increased the expenses of the luxury of law to the litigant. When it is considered, however, that as the law now stands, both the equitable as well as the legal aspect of every question has to be considered in all matters of controversy, and besides this, that all matters of controversy between suitors may be determined in one suit, the objection of expense is overcome and deserves no further consideration. "*Interest reipublicæ ut sit finis litium.*"

The work done by Mr. Moss on the Commission as well

as his standing at the Bar, entitled him to recognition. He was offered a Vice-Chancellorship, which he declined.

In the Autumn of 1873, upon the fall of Sir John A. Macdonald's Government, Mr. Moss, for the first time, entered the field of politics. He had always had an inclination to Reform principles, although his father had been a Conservative, and generally voted with that party.

Political principle is often formed from professional and social association, it is not always hereditary, nor in this age should it be. I think we should always judge, not by what our fathers were, but what they would have been if they had lived to witness the changes in men, manners, and all that tend to enhance the progressiveness of the time. There is no reason because our ancestors in breaking up the soil, used wooden ploughs, that we should adhere to those primitive implements of husbandry. If our forefathers wore blue coats with brass buttons, there is no necessity for our absolutely clothing ourselves in the same cut of raiment. This is an advancing and progressive world, and it is necessary to watch the events of the times, and act for the best interests of our country.

This was Mr. Moss's idea, and led him to adopt principles, as he conceived, leading to reform and progress. He was an especial friend of the Honorable Edward Blake, an association which did not in the least degree tend to lessen his Reform principles—principles which Mr. Blake had inherited, and of which he was an able exponent.

The Reformers of Toronto now selected Mr. Moss as of their party, not only most deserving, but if he could but be elected, one in every way able to advocate their cause on the floor of Parliament. He contested the constituency of West Toronto with Mr. E. O. Bickford, and was elected by a triumphant majority. This election took place in consequence of the constituency of West Toronto being thrown open by the appointment of Honorable John Crawford to the Lieutenant-Governorship of Ontario. Soon after, the General Election took place, when Mr. Moss again stood for the constituency and was elected, defeating the Honorable John Beverley Robinson by a handsome majority. The constituency was one in which he had lived the greater part of his life. It was no small honor to him to be returned for that constituency, and equally an honor to the constituency to have returned such a member. On his taking his seat in the House he made a speech which has been characterized as one of the most brilliant and masterly efforts ever heard within the walls of the Canadian Parliament. He continued to sit for West Toronto till October, 1875, when he was appointed a Justice of the Court of Appeal.

In 1874, the year before his appointment to the Bench, he had been appointed Vice-Chancellor of the University of Toronto, his Alma Mater. He was twice elected to this honorable position in the University, and continued to hold the office till 1878. His graciousness as Vice-Chancellor of the University secured him the confidence and support of all connected with this seat of learning. I am not at all sure that he did not prize the position of Vice-Chancellor of the University of Toronto, more than the Judgeship in the Court of Appeal.

A writer, in discussing the characteristics of Mr. Moss—his brilliancy and worthiness of elevation to the Bench—has written of him thus:

> It might be thought that all the brilliancy and solid attainment, the capacity and industry, implied by a career of such unvarying success, implied an ambition more eagle-like in its instincts than one which could content itself with a prosperous professional career, and an early elevation to the Bench—a most honorable position, but one, nevertheless, in which men of strong political instincts and large capacities put on, and are properly bound to put on, ermine manacles, and bury one of the choicest privileges of free citizenship in the marble tomb of dignity; or perhaps the case might be more fully stated, by saying that the Judges have to make great sacrifices on the altar of public usefulness.

The writer's conclusion is true enough; but he is not quite right in saying, or insinuating, that Mr Moss was a man of strong political instincts, for this he was not; and as to his accepting a position on the Bench, I know that he had great reluctance to take the position, however honorable it might be. I know with what unwillingness he accepted the Judgeship. It was more the advice of friends than his own judgment which led him to give up professional and political life for the assumption of the Ermine.

Mr. Justice Moss, as Judge in Appeal, gave great satisfaction to the Bar and the public; his clear judgment was also highly appreciated by his brother Judges. In Council of the Judges he was argumentative, in decision prompt, in expression lucid.

On the death of Chief Justice Draper, in 1877, he was promoted from a Judgeship to be Chief Justice of the Court of Appeal. He was then only forty-one years of age. He was the first who ever attained that position at so early an age. Becoming Chief Justice, he applied himself most diligently to the work—too diligently for his health. The onerous duties of his office, with the steady labour which it entails, left him but little time for recreation. His judgments were remarkable for their lucidity and beauty of diction. A proper conception of his value as Chief Justice may best be formed by referring to and quoting some of his decisions. I will, however, cite one judgment of his, which was indeed the judgment of the Court, while he was yet the Junior Judge of the Court, and which was concurred in by the whole Court of Appeal, overruling the Chancellor. The case I refer to is, Gilleland *vs.* Wadsworth, 1 Appeal Reports, 82. Stripped of all verbiage and technicalities, the case was this: A. owns a lot of land, which he mortgages to B., a solicitor; and B. assigns the mortgage to C., and covenants with C. for payment of the mortgage money; C. registers the assignment, and should imagine that he was all safe in his security; a year after the making of the mortgage, A. assigns the equity of redemption to D.; D. owns another lot of land unincumbered; he and A. enter into a bargain to exchange lots; A., in getting D.'s lot, with the consent of A.'s mortgagee C., who both parties thought still held the mortgage of A., was to satisfy C., not by payment of the mortgage money in the terms of the mortgage, but by giving him a new or substantial mortgage on the lot he was to get from D. This was all carried out, or apparently carried out, by both parties, and the assignee of the mortgagee going to the solicitor to have the deeds drawn up and transaction perfected, the mortgagor (A.) and D. each bearing half the expense of the conveyancing. Neither A. nor D. called upon the solicitor to produce title deeds, or the mortgage which A. had made to B., and which B. had assigned to C. The solicitor did not make known to D. that he had assigned the mortgage to C. The transaction between A. and D. was carried out; the solicitor becoming mortgagee of the incumbered lot of D., as a substitute for the mortgage on the other lot, which he knew he had assigned to C. C. died, leaving a personal representative; D. died intestate, leaving a widow and infant children. The personal representative of C. filed a bill against the widow and infant children of D. for foreclosure of the mortgage. Several questions arose:

1st. Had the mortgage been paid by the substitutional mortgage made by D. to B.?

2nd. Could the representative of C. avail himself of the mortgage against the representatives, widow and heirs of D. D., having taken the title of the lot A. had mortgaged, he, D., at the time not having actual notice of the assignment, B. to C., by reason of the fact that the assignment was registered when he completed the transaction of exchange.

3rd. Must not D. be taken to have had constructive notice of the assignment of the mortgage, B. to C., inasmuch as B., the mortgagee, was a solicitor, and his solicitor in carrying out the exchange drew deeds &c., and took his mortgage in exchange for the first mortgage.

4th. Was not D. guilty of negligence in not enquiring for the first mortgage, and getting it discharged before giving his new or substitutional mortgage?

According to the judgment of the Chancellor, the plaintiffs, (representatives of C.), were not in a position to foreclose the mortgage, that in fact the mortgage must be considered to have been discharged by the transaction of exchange and substitutional mortgage given to B. (the solicitor), and that the security could not be enforced against the land.

Mr. Justice Moss combated all the positions taken in the Court below against the plaintiffs rights to enforce the mortgage, with great ability, and held :

1st. That the registration of the assignment of the mortgage was notice to D., under the Registry Act, that the mortgage had been assigned and hence the settlement with the solicitor and mortgagee was no settlement of the mortgage as against C. or his representatives.

2nd. That it was not necessary for the plaintiff to have stated the registration in the Bill, one of the reasons given by the Court below for not giving effect to the registration as notice.

3rd. That from the position the solicitor and mortgagee occupied, acting for both parties in the transaction of exchange, notice to him, was constructive notice to his client D., and to his representatives.

4th. That D. was not guilty of negligence in not searching the registry, and in not seeing that the mortgage on the land he was acquiring was discharged.

On these points I refer to Mr. Justice Moss's own language, as being perspicuous and elucidating his opinion in an expressive manner, omitting the names of the parties and using alphabetical letters, as I have done in describing the facts. Mr. Justice Moss, inter alia, said :

There is no controversy between the parties as to the facts established by the evidence. A bargain was made between A. and D. for an even exchange of properties, A. undertaking to get the mortgage he had given on his lot discharged, so that D. should have a clear title (states the transaction with the solicitor and mortgagor as I have described it). Neither of the parties made enquiry for the mortgage A. to B. D. lived for nine years after the mortgage was made, and does not appear to have ever asked B. for the mortgage. Supposing, as he did, that it had been discharged in the usual way, it is probable that he never thought of the propriety of having possession of the **instrument itself.** A. not having received any notice from C., and also **believing that the** old mortgage had been discharged, paid the new mortgage before it became due, and **some** time afterwards obtained a regular discharge from B. **It seems to me clear that** the question for adjudication is, **whether the law will impute notice of** the assignment. If neither A. nor D. is **chargeable with notice, I think** that the giving **of** the mortgage (the **substituted mortgage) may well** be treated as a satisfaction of the original mortgage. The essence of the transaction would be that A., without notice of any assignment, applied to his mortgagee to accept something else in lieu of the mortgage. I see no **reason why** this should **not fall** within the **rule** which protects payments **made to the** mortgagee before he has any notice of the transfer.

* * * * * *

Upon the question of notice, the learned Judge went on to say :

Now I think that if C. is entitled to rely upon the fact that he had registered his assignment, notice must be attributed to D. The registration of the assignment would not be notice to A., because a mortgagor paying off his mortgage, does not come within the class of persons to whom registration constitutes notice. But D. was expressly within the terms of the Statute, for he **was a person claiming an interest in the land** subsequent to the registry of the assignment. He became a purchaser of this land while an assignment of the mortgage **stood registered.**

Upon the question of constructive notice, Mr. Justice Moss said :

I think, upon principles too well established, D would be held to have had constructive notice. His failure to make *any* inquiries for **the mortgage deed would itself** suffice. The essence of the transaction in which he was engaged was a purchase of the mortgaged land. He was to get an unincumbered title. The concurrence of two persons, viz., **the mortgagee and the morgagor, was necessary to** carry out **the bargain.** * * * The law upon this point has been summarized by Sir George Turner, in the well known case of Hewit *vs.* Looseman, 9 Ha. 458.

His conclusion was :

That in transactions of sale and mortgage of estates, if there be no inquiry as to the title deeds which constitute the title to such property, the Court is justified in assuming that the purchaser or mortgagee has abstained from making an inquiry from a suspicion that his title would be affected if it was made, and is therefore *bound* to impute to him the knowledge which the inquiry, if made, would have imparted.

I need not cite further. The case is a most interesting one, involving as it does so many questions, such as actual notice, constructive notice, registration, payment, and negligence. The result of the judgment of the Court of Appeal, Mr. Justice Moss giving the judgment, carries out the principles of justice within the well established rules of Equity and the plaintiff did not lose his security.

When Mr. Justice Moss had been promoted to the Chief Justiceship, he had brought before him for decision a question which had previously engaged the attention of the Courts of this country in Buchanan *vs.* Brooke, 24 Grant 585, but had not yet been considered by a Court of Appeal. The question was one of equitable execution, to what extent, in whose favor, and what equitable interests would herein attach under a judgment and execution at law, and how far such judgment and execution could be made to operate on equitable interests by the machinery of the Court of Chancery. The case was that Daniel Brooke, the elder, deceased, had, by his last will and testament, inter alia, bequeathed to his son, John Edmund Brooke, and his wife, Betsey Johnston Brooke certain real and personal estate, upon the following trusts:

> In the first place, to and for the support and maintenance of himself and his wife in a fit and suitable manner, according to their rank and station, during their joint lives and during the life of the survivor of them; secondly, for the support, education, and maintenance of the children of the said John Edmund Brooke and Betsey Johnston Brooke, now living, according to their rank and station in life, and at the discretion of John Edmund Brooke and Betsey Johnston Brooke.

Power was given to the defendant and his wife jointly, during their lives, and to him if he was the survivor, but not to her if she was the survivor, to sell the lands, mortgages, and all other securities, and to stand possessed of the proceeds upon the same trusts. Power was also given to them jointly, and to the survivor of them to divide the real and personal estate, or the proceeds thereof, or so much thereof as remained unexpended and unappropriated, in carrying out the trusts, between the children and their said heirs, if any, in such manner and in such proportion as to them might seem fit ; or to exclude any of them entirely from any benefit or portion thereof if they should see fit to do so, or to convey or make over to any of them, by way of advancement, any portion of the same, to become theirs absolutely.

Chief Justice Moss, in which his brother Judges concurred, held, that the gift was for the benefit of the defendant, John Edmund Brooke and his wife jointly, and that his interest could not be attached by an execution creditor. He held also, that the defendant had no estate in the land corresponding to an estate at law ; at most he had but a charge upon an income arising out of a mixed fund, the amount of which was in the discretion of the trustees.

After expressing the opinion that the interest of John Edmund Brooke under the will was not such an interest as could be attached in Equity, and that the case of Gilbert *vs.* Jarvis settled that point, the Chief Justice said:

> But the argument before us was conducted upon a line of cases which were not discussed in Gilbert *vs.* Jarvis. These are the decisions in which assignees in bankruptcy have been entitled to the benefit of a trust for the maintenance and support of the bankrupt. Assuming for the present that these cases are authorities where the plaintiff is only a judgment creditor seeking to enforce the remedies, which are available in equity by virtue of his execution, it is far from clear that they establish the plaintiff's position. The trust here is in the following words (the trust quoted above set out, also the power). I agree with Mr. Boyd's argument, that as large rights ought to be accorded to the plaintiff as if the trustees were not the debtor and his wife, but two wholly independent persons. It appears to me, however, that the intention of the testator was that Brooke and his wife should receive sufficient for their maintenance. I cannot bring myself to the conclusion that the language of the will imports the existence of any right in the husband to file a bill against the trustees for payment of a separate annual sum for his maintenance, while he and his wife were living together. The testator did not contemplate anything resembling a divorce or separation of their interests, and if not, the authorities do not, in my opinion, force us to the conclusion that, upon bankruptcy, any interest in the estate would pass to the assignee.

I think I need not refer specifically to any other cases decided by the Chief Justice. A number were collected by the editor of the Law Journal, and cited in that valuable legal periodical in the number of February 1st, 1881, in an obituary notice of the Chief Justice, in which, after giving the substance of the judgments, the writer said :

> We have referred to these judgments, commending them to the special notice of the profession, because they abundantly illustrate our previous remarks upon the Chief Justice's peculiar merits as a Judge. To read them with care and attention is to form a high estimate of the judicial qualities of our departed friend.

There is this specialty about the judgments of Chief Justice Moss: the words chosen to express his ideas are in the choicest language. I have often read Chief Justice Storey's Equity Jurisprudence with pleasure and satisfaction. There is no dryness about it; everything is expressed in familiar and readable phrases. There is no attempt at stilting; the sense is made easy to the understanding. There would seem to have been no effort in writing this great legal work, and as little effort in comprehending the principles of Equity which it enforces. I can only compare Chief Justice Moss's judgments to the writings of Chief Justice Storey; nor do I think they suffer by the comparison.

In the spring of 1880, the Chief Justice had a severe illness, from which he never quite rallied. In the autumn of the year, by the advice of his physician, he went to France, in the hope and expectation that a change of climate would benefit his health, and ultimately lead to his recovery. This, however, was not to be; the hand of death was upon him. He died at Nice, on the 4th day of January, 1881.

Truly the Bench and Bar lost in him a Judge who, had he lived, would have been an ever increasing strength to the Bench; and an able exponent of those great principles of Equity which, while softening the regime of Common Law, add immeasurably to the attainment of complete and absolute justice.

On the day following the news of the death of the Chief Justice, his colleague and very particular friend, Mr.

Justice Burton, sitting in the Court over which the Chief Justice had presided, paid the following touching tribute to his memory, as elegantly expressed as it was heart-felt and appropriate :

My colleagues agree with me that it is not fitting to proceed with the ordinary duties of the day without some allusion to the loss the profession, the public, and especially the members of this Court, have sustained by the death of the eminent Judge, who but a few short days since filled the position of President of this Court and Chief Justice of Ontario.

It is, perhaps, a singular coincidence that within a few weeks death has robbed this and the Mother country of two of their most distinguished judges, both of them men in the prime of life, to whom there appeared to be opening a brilliant future, and as to each of whom I may say, I think without exaggeration, a national loss has been sustained. Each of them, however, has left an imperishable monument of his learning and ability in the reports of their published judgments, which may well be referred to as models of judicial style.

Many of those who hear me, have listened with pleasure and admiration to the oral judgments delivered from where I am now sitting, by the distinguished Judge whose death we are now deploring, and must have been struck with the simplicity, ease, and grace of manner, combined with depth of thought and elegance of diction, with which those utterances were delivered ; but few beyond his intimate acquaintainces, were aware of the untiring energy with which he investigated the cases requiring more careful preparation, or that the rising sun has occasionally found him still engaged in examining and verifying the authorities on which he proposed to base his decisions.

His loss is too recent, and my appreciation of it too keen, to permit me to make more than a passing reference to his personal and social qualities. " To know him was to love him." My heart is too full for me to venture to say more.

We may, one and all of us, whether on the Bench, at the Bar, or the youngest student entering for the first time the portals of the profession, safely adopt him as our model, combining as he did in his own person, the kind and courteous gentleman, the brilliant and able advocate, the upright and impartial Judge. I wish I had the command of language to do justice to his many virtues and his great intellectual gifts, but I yield to none of his numerous friends in admiration of his character, and in tender and affectionate regard for his memory.

XXX.

THE HONORABLE SIR MATTHEW CROOKS CAMERON, CHIEF JUSTICE OF THE COMMON PLEAS DIVISION OF THE HIGH COURT OF JUSTICE.

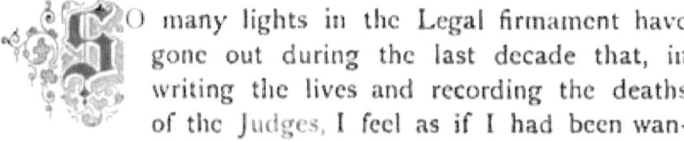O many lights in the Legal firmament have gone out during the last decade that, in writing the lives and recording the deaths of the Judges, I feel as if I had been wandering among the tombs. As I draw near the close of the catalogue, and record the fact that within the last year two of our Judges have passed away, I recognize the futility of human ambition, and the uncertainty of human hopes.

Little did I think in the spring of last year, when everything seemed bright and joyous, that only a few months would pass before the grave should claim the mortal remains of that most excellent citizen, and most upright Judge, the Honorable Sir Matthew Crooks Cameron. He was one of the boys of Upper Canada College when I was there, a boy myself. He was my constant friend during life; in his death I mourned not for a friend only, but for a country's loss.

The Honorable Sir Matthew Crooks Cameron was no ordinary man: he was a man among men. Canada has produced no more worthy son. He was of Scotch extraction, and possessed all the magnanimity of a Scottish Chief. Descended as he was from the old and illustrious family of Fassifein, he added additional lustre to the Cameron name, which had already gained renown in the walks of literature, science, and the military art. He was the son of John McAlpine Cameron, who emigrated from Invernessshire, Scotland, to Upper Canada, in 1819, and settled at Dundas, in the County of Wentworth, where he engaged in commercial pursuits : there he continued till 1826, when he removed from Dundas to Hamilton, and became Deputy Clerk of the Crown for the Gore District. Subsequently he entered the service of the Canada Company, and removed to Toronto, where he died at an advanced age in 1866. I remember him as a man short in stature, much Canadianized by his long residence in Canada, but retaining his Scotch accent in sufficient force to make him distinguishable from the native-born Canadian. He had several sons, all of whom I knew. They were: Duncan, born in Scotland; John, born in Scotland; and Matthew Crooks, the Chief Justice, who was the youngest, and born in Canada, at Dundas, on the 2nd October, 1822. Duncan and John were both lawyers. John, in his early professional career, practised in Hamilton ; but, on the County of Brant being set off as a separate county, removed to Brantford, the county town of that county, where he practised his profession for many years.

I knew both of Matthew Crooks Cameron's brothers: they were both generous hearted men, but had neither the staid demeanor nor habits of their younger brother. The mother of the Camerons was English. Her maiden name was Miss Nancy Foy, and she was a native of the County of Northumberland. She died many years ago.

Matthew was named Matthew Crooks after Mr. Matthew Crooks, of Ancaster, brother of the Honorable James Crooks and uncle of Adam Crooks, Q. C., formerly Minister of Education for Ontario. When the father of Matthew Crooks Cameron removed from Dundas to Hamilton, Matthew Crooks Cameron was but four years of age. The first school he attended after going to Hamilton was presided over by a Mr. Randall. On the removal of his father to Toronto, he was placed at the Home District Grammar School, on the corner of New street (now Adelaide street) and Nelson street (now Jarvis street). I have, in a previous page so fully described this school, that I need say no more than that many boys, subsequently distinguished, received their early training at the Home District Grammar School.

After leaving this school, in 1838, Matthew Crooks Cameron entered Upper Canada College, where he remained nearly two years. It was at Upper Canada College I first knew him. He was a day scholar: I was in residence; or, as we used in those days to call ourselves, a boarder.

When I first entered Upper Canada College as a student, Dr. Harris was Principal, and Mrs. Fenwick kept the boarding house. Dr. McCaul succeeded Dr. Harris as Principal, and Mr. Cozens succeeded Mrs. Fenwick in charge of the boarding house. Everything was built on the model of the English schools, even in the matter of plain food and corporal punishment. If the boys of the present day were subjected to the same discipline and senna tea, I question if the college would be as popular as I am glad to say it is. Cameron was a day boy. We boarders often, in a measure, envied the day boys, as they had more liberty, and had their single room and comfortable homes to go to after college hours; whereas we boarders were packed in rooms with a dozen beds, for a dozen sleepers.

Perhaps, after all, the liberty which Matthew Crooks Cameron as a day boy enjoyed, was the cause of the accident which befel him and which caused him to be lame all his life. As a boy he was naturally of a lively, sociable disposition, fond of amusement and the society of other boys. He was not before the accident, to which I have alluded, what might be called a studious boy; he was rather fond of out-door life. One of the things he dearly prized was a gun, and an opportunity of using it in shooting ducks, plover, and other game which was abundant in the vicinity of Toronto when he was a College boy.

In 1840, while he was still at College, he and a companion, a school-fellow, went up the Don on a shooting expedition, which ended most disastrously. His companion, by the purest accident, in firing off his gun, made a mis-shot, and the shot took effect in his schoolfellow's ankle, part of the joint of which was completely blown away. Matthew was conveyed home, and was confined to his room for several months. I well remember the day of the accident, and how much sorrow for the occurrence overcame the boys of the College, day boys and boarders. Cameron was a general favorite. College boys, if they read this, will understand the feeling of grief which affects a fellow student when a favorite meets with an accident like this.

The injury to the leg was so serious that it had to be amputated, and from that time Cameron had to wear an artificial leg. He suffered more or less all through life from the effects of the accident.

The accident caused the withdrawal of Matthew from College, and probably changed the whole of his after life. There was to be no more shooting for him, he could not indulge in the sports of boyhood, or the pastimes of youth. Companionship seemed to have no further charm for him, and he became of a serious turn of mind, contemplating life from an entirely different standpoint than that from which he had been accustomed to consider it.

When he became sufficiently well enough to get about, he determined to follow the example of his elder brothers, and make the law his profession. The education he had received at College and his own diligence in study at home, enabled him to pass the examination of the Benchers of the Law Society. He was admitted a Student of that Society in Easter Term, 6 Victoria, 1843, and on his admission immediately entered the law office of Messrs. Gamble & Boulton, who had their office on

Church street. He served the whole term of his articles with Gamble & Boulton. He was a diligent student, and soon rose to a prominent position in the office, taking the lead in the routine work of the office, constant in his attendance and giving evidence of intellectual strength which was sure to lead him on to success in his chosen profession.

When I was called to the Bar in 1845, I had my office in the same building, and it used to be a surprise to me to see with what ease Matthew Cameron, notwithstanding his lameness, was able to perform all his duties of clerkship. He had the entire confidence of the heads of the firm, which he repaid by assiduity and faithfulness.

He was called to the Bar in Hilary Term, 12 Victoria, 1849. As soon as he was called to the Bar he began to go on circuit, and soon gained a name in his profession which procured for him many briefs, and brought him corresponding fees. I used often to meet him in Court combats, and had therefore the best opportunity, in the early period of his professional career, of forming an opinion of his power and his worth.

Mr. Cameron had acquired a very complete knowledge of his profession. He had subtle powers of analysing evidence. In cross-examination of witnesses he had few, if any, superiors. He had ready command of language, an impressive utterance and delivery, and besides an open, candid manner which carried great weight with juries.

He had not been many years at the Bar, when he had gained a reputation which secured for him briefs in causes where he used to be opposed by the most eminent counsel of the day; such men as John Hillyard Cameron, Q.C., Henry Eccles, Q.C., P. M. VanKoughnet, Q.C., and Mr. Hagarty, the present head of the Court of Appeal. Those were all doughty champions of their client's rights. It is not too much to say that Matthew Crooks Cameron was well up in the race with these his contemporaries.

Mr. Cameron was generally very successful with juries; in criminal cases, where the result so much depends on their verdict, he was "facile princeps." He had so large a practice in criminal cases, that he familiarized himself with medical jurisprudence, and understood as well the principles governing the dissection of a subject as the rules for dissecting a case. I do not know of any at the Bar who was his superior in this branch of the profession, unless it was John Hillyard Cameron.

In the early part of Mr. Cameron's career he was more frequent in attendance at the Hamilton Assizes than elsewhere; his brother John, who was practising in Hamilton, used to give him briefs; when John removed to Brantford, he extended his criminal business to that county. He and I used often to meet on opposite sides in cases at Brantford, Simcoe, and Berlin, in the old Oxford Circuit. Thomas Galt, now Chief Justice Sir Thomas Galt, used to go on that circuit. I think we three were the only Toronto men who attended the Assizes in these counties. S. B. Freeman, of Hamilton, used often to be with us.

My readers will excuse my referring to myself; as I write, the associations of those days present themselves so vividly to my mind that my pen seems to run along without regard to any obstacle.

But to return—Mr. Cameron, like so many others in his profession, did not always carry on business alone. He had not been long at the Bar when he formed a partnership with William Henry Boulton, after the dissolution of the firm of Gamble and Boulton. Several years later he entered into partnership with the Honorable William Cayley, who held the port-folio of Minister of Finance in the Government formed under the auspices of Sir Allan Napier MacNab, in 1854.

Mr. Cameron, in politics, was a Tory of Tories; William Henry Boulton will be remembered as of that party, and at one time Mayor and Representative of Toronto in Parliament.

The names of Sir Allan MacNab, and Mr. Cayley, are well known as representative men, of what may be termed the old regime of toryism, in days now past and gone.

It will not be out of place here to mention that the year 1854 was a memorable one for two things ; one, the Reciprocity Treaty between Canada and the United States; the other, the downfall of the Hincks-Morin Ministry, brought about by a Coalition between extreme Toryism and extreme Radicalism, the Tories led by Sir Allan MacNab and Mr. John A. Macdonald, and the Radicals by Mr. George Brown. A mixture of interests in this, as in many other cases, seemd to have brought about a mixture of parties, for a time at all events.

We will find, further on, that Matthew Crooks Cameron a recognized Tory of the highest order, who had not at this time taken much active part in politics, did, when the necessity of the case presented itself, enter into a coalition, not, however, with the extreme Radical, but with the moderate reforming of the party, under the leadership of John Sandfield McDonald.

With this diversion brought about by the figures of Sir Allan MacNab and Mr. Cayley crossing my vision, bringing up recollections of political incidents of the past, I must return to Mr. Cameron, in his legal and political capacity. In the year 1856, Daniel McMichael, better known as Dr. McMichael, became a partner with Mr. Cameron and Mr. Cayley, and the firm was then known as Cayley, Cameron & McMichael. This firm had a very large business ; Mr. Cameron was its leading spirit. With two such men in the firm, as Mr. Cameron and Mr. McMichael, it is not surprising that they gained for themselves as large a business as any firm in Toronto. Looking back to the time I call to mind of what great value Dr. McMichael was to the firm in the pleading and general management of the business of the office. He had not yet reached the high position of counsel which he afterwards attained. Mr. Cameron continued to do the principal outside business as counsel, while Dr. McMichael, skilled in pleading, of much more importance in those days than now, used to exercise his refined reasoning powers in challenging opponents to a set-to in demurring or arrest of judgment.

During the first ten years of Mr. Cameron's legal career he devoted his whole time to his profession. Indeed, the calls made upon him for his services as counsel, from all parts of the Province, made it necessary for him to give his undivided attention to legal work.

In 1859, he was induced to take part in municipal affairs, and was returned as Alderman to represent St. James's Ward, in the Municipal Council of Toronto. A good many of his friends were anxious for him to contest the Mayoralty in 1860. I was one of those friends, and suggested that he should walk up Queen street (St. Patrick's Ward) with me, when I would introduce him to municipal electors there of influence, who would be of service to him in promoting his election. I had represented that ward myself in the council, and municipally I knew the electors better than Mr. Cameron.

Mr. Cameron consented to my proposal, and walked with me a short distance up the street. Meeting several influential electors, I introduced him as Mr. Cameron, who intended to run for Mayor. The electors, as was natural and polite, shook hands with him on being introduced. After this had occurred a few times, he said to me: "Read, must I shake hands in this way? Is it necessary in a candidate for the mayoralty?" I said: "Yes, certainly, the electors like to greet their candidate." "Then," said he, "if that is so, I must not run for the mayoralty," turned on his heel, walked away, and abandoned the candidature.

Mr. Cameron was just that kind of man. He was manly, open, generous, a lover of men; but he could not bear to have it supposed that he would solicit support from any quarter—if hand-shaking meant soliciting support, he would have none of it. I never knew a man like him in regard to the high sense of honor and independence, which were marked traits of his character. He was very tenacious of his opinion when he had formed one. He had a decided opinion that a representative should be sought out by the electors, not that the representative should seek the electors: anything that seemed to have even the appearance of solicitation was abhorrent to his nature.

In 1861, he was induced to be a candidate for the mayoralty, this time he ran the gauntlet of an election, with a candidate opposed to him not so sensitive of municipal ways as he was, and it is not surprising that he was defeated.

Although defeated in his candidature, Mr. Cameron scored a greater success the same year in being returned to represent the County of North Ontario in Parliament. He was elected as a Conservative, and continued to represent the county till 1863, when presenting himself to his constitutents for re-election he was defeated. I have been told of an incident that occurred during this contest, which, I dare say, had much to do with his defeat. Mr. Cameron was a man very jealous of his honor, thoroughly opposed to unfair dealing of any kind or shape, he would, in a political contest, see in acts, innocent in themselves, cause for exception, and repudiation. On the occasion of this election a friend of his offered to drive him from Whitby around to the different villages in the county, as the candidate of the party, and did drive him to a village or two. His friend was a kind, good-hearted man, and seeing some men working at a bridge, he went to them and gave them some small sum of money, twenty-five or fifty cents, to regale themselves with. Mr. Cameron found this out, immediately dismissed his friend from further escort, and engaged another party to drive him round. Mr. Cameron thought that the presentation to the men savored of solicitation for votes, if not more, and at once repudiated the act and the man performing it. The man returned to Whitby not well pleased that his candidate shewed himself possessed of so high a sensitiveness in the matter of the rights and privileges of elections. The result of the contest at this election was that he was defeated. But in 1864, a vacancy occurring in the representation of the constituency, he again offered himself as a candidate and was elected, defeating the Honorable William Macdougall, who had accepted office. He continued to represent the county till the Confederation of the Provinces, in 1867. He was a regular supporter of the Cartier-Macdonald Government, his name appears in the minority on the second reading of the Militia Bill. He opposed the Macdonald-Sicotte Government while in Parliament. Through the debate on Confederation Mr. Cameron voted with the minority, because he thought that justice was not secured under it to the Province of Upper Canada. As soon as the Union was consummated he gracefully bowed to the decision of Parliament.

On the Honorable Sandfield McDonald being entrusted with the formation of a Government for the Province of Ontario, he chose Mr. Cameron as a colleague, and he accepted office, and held a portfolio in the first Administration formed in the Confederated Province of Ontario. This Administration, of which the Honorable Sandfield McDonald was leader, was a coalition Administration : Mr. Cameron and Mr. Carling representing the Conservative interest in the Government. He was Provincial Secretary and Registrar from 1867 to 1871, (25th July), when he became Commissioner of Crown Lands ; this latter office he held until the fall of the Government in the following December, in consequence of the adverse vote of the House on the Railroad Subsidy question.

Upon the formation of a new Government under the leadership of the Honorable Edward Blake, Mr. Cameron became leader of the Opposition, and so continued for four years. His parliamentary career was marked by sterling honour and integrity, and constant and infallible devotion to his party ; he was never open to even a suspicion of corruption, jobbery, or political dishonesty of any kind. While Cabinet Minister he performed all his duties, and, at the same time, when Parliament was not in Session he attended to briefs and other professional duties.

His physical endurance was of the most extraordinary nature. He thought nothing of being in Court all day in the Eastern part of the Province, and taking the night train, he would arrive in the West in time to conduct a case the next day. If he happened to be at Cobourg or Belleville, and retained to be in a case the next day at Brantford, the attorney in the case could be sure that he would appear in Brantford the next morning in time for his case ; he rarely failed in his appointments.

The late Mr. Rattray, in his " Scot in British North America," truly wrote of him :

> His intellect was eminently a logical one, and had been trained in the legal school. He knew nothing of compromises, and was given to the blunt expression of his honest views. There was little pliability in his disposition, and the necessary shifts and expedients resorted to in active political warfare were distasteful to him. As a speaker, he has always been clear and incisive, going straight to the point, as well balanced minds are wont to do.

I take pleasure in making this extract from Mr. Rattray's excellent work, because of Mr. Rattray's well known correctness of description, as well as elegance of expression. No word of mine could better express the real bent of Mr. Cameron's mind and his general character. He was a most truthful man ; if he said he would do a thing, one could rely with certainty that it would be done. He believed in the truth of the lines—

> Dare to be true, nothing can need a lie,
> A fault which needs it most grows two thereby.

Mr. Cameron had not only the confidence of political friends, but of those with whom he differed in politics.

In 1852 he was appointed by the Hincks-Morin Administration, jointly with the late Col. Coffin, to inquire into the frequent accidents which had then recently occurred on the Great Western Railway. He took an interest in many public matters outside of his profession. He was one of the early promoters and directors of the

Dominion Telegraph Company, and of several prominent insurance companies. He was a member of several societies, charitable and national associations, including the St. Andrews and Caledonian Societies.

His prominence at the Bar entitled him to a seat on the Bench. He was appointed a Puisne Judge of the Queen's Bench on the 15th November, 1878. His appointment was a very popular one with the profession. There was no man in the Province in whom the public had more confidence. He was very reluctant to accept the appointment; when he had accepted he regretted that he had done so. After a while, however, he became reconciled to the position, and settled down to the judicial work with all the energy and ability which had distinguished him through life. In the Queen's Bench he gave his utmost attention to all the various and difficult questions which engaged the attention of that Court. On the 13th May, 1884, he was appointed to the Chief Juticeship of the Common Pleas Division of the High Court of Justice.

I might refer to many decisions of Chief Justice Cameron, both in the Common Pleas Division, and in the Queen's Bench while he was a Puisne Judge, which shew that he took especial pains to master every point that a case presented, always aiming at justice being the result of his decisions. He soon found that the duties of a Judge required not only the principles of abstract law to be regarded, but a fulfilment of the maxim, "Justitia fiat, ruat cælum." While at the Bar, there was no man more astute inadvancing his arguments, always in a clear and comprehensive manner. On the Bench, while he retained a share of that adhesiveness to pre-conceived opinions that he generally displayed, he not only listened to all arguments presented by counsel, but fully considered them, and adjudged in the interest of right.

During the time Judge Cameron was in the Court of Queen's Bench, that Court was presided over by Chief Justice Hagarty, and the Senior Puisne Judge was Judge Armour, the present Chief Justice of the Queen's Bench

Division. There probably has never been a period in the history of the Queen's Bench when three such brilliant jurists were found at the one time on the Bench in that Court. It was not at all surprising then to find that the sittings of that Court were always looked forward to with the keenest interest by the Bar. The meetings of the Court were always full of interest, and any case that came before these Judges was pretty thoroughly investigated before it left the hands of the Court. They were not always unanimous, and when differences of opinion arose between the two Puisne Judges, neither hesitated to express his opinion in good set terms. These varying opinions provoked frequent sallies of wit from either end of the Bench, while the central guardian of the Court not infrequently added his toll to the humor which floated so rapidly through the Court.

The method of hearing causes was decidedly Socratic in those days. The principal occupation of counsel was, to endeavor to evade or solve propositions of law or fact originated by the Bench, and the life of a counsel in a doubtful case was at least exciting. Prosing was unheard of, or, at least, vigorously suppressed in that Court, and the consequent mental friction undoubtedly did much to elevate the intellectual style of counsel practising in this Court. They rapidly learnt to abandon roundabout ways of argument, and found that if they wished to be heard in that Court, the surest way was to come to the point, and endeavor to stay there.

In these sessions of the Court Judge Cameron bore no idle part; and his rather raspy voice was frequently heard asking questions, making keen or sarcastic comments, and throwing light on intricacies.

At nisi prius the Chief Justice preserved his vigorous style of addressing juries, and brought his keen insight into men and their motives to bear with penetration. A witness who shuffled or prevaricated before him had indeed a hard experience. The Chief Justice generally reclined backwards in his chair; but if anything of that sort took place, he raised himself forward, eyed the witness keenly, and presently, in his deliberate incisive tone, put a question which frequently had the effect of causing that witness to wish the witness box had an automatic drop floor, and that he could be comfortably dropped to the basement of the Court House.

Those who practised before him sometimes complained that the Chief Justice was too emphatic in his charges; and, I have no doubt, many a counsel who had convinced himself that his cause was just, and hoped he had converted a doubtful jury, regretted that the presiding Chief Justice had the last word with the jury. Many an ingenious argument was demolished, and many a theory destroyed in these charges.

The Chief Justice generally formed a pronounced view of the truth or falsity of a statement of fact; and, while he always exerted great self-control in the expression of his views, his strong opinions frequently unconsciously shewed themselves. Fortunately his judgment was very accurate, and no miscarriage of justice could be complained of being brought about by his charges to the juries.

After he had become Chief Justice of the Common Pleas Division, he felt that he had taken on himself additional responsibility, and guided himself accordingly. His associates on the Bench—Mr. Justice Galt, and Mr. Justice Rose—recognized his ability, and conscientious performance of the requirements of his high office, and would almost have wished that he had spared himself more in the excessive labor he undertook in the exercise of his office.

There were some cases decided by him and his Court which presented new points and have historical importance, and it is only those I will give in speaking of his judgments.

One of those cases is Stuart *vs.* McKim, reported in 8 Ontario Reports 739. The facts presented in that case were these. The defendant, a member of the Legislative

53—L. J.

Assembly, received a sum of money as an inducement, or bribe, to influence him in his course in the Assembly, which he handed to the Speaker of the Assembly, to wait the action of the House with regard to the alleged bribery. The plaintiffs, judgment creditors of the defendant, issued an order attaching all debts due from the Speaker to the defendant, claiming that the money so handed to him became a debt payable to the defendant.

The plaintiffs then applied to the Common Pleas Division of the High Court, for an order under the Ontario Judicature Act, on Charles Clarke, Esquire, Speaker of the Legislative Assembly of Ontario, to try the right of the defendant to a sum of money delivered by him to the Speaker, on the 17th March, 1884.

It was not necessary on the motion to determine whether or not the creditors of McKim could garnish the money in the hands of the Speaker, but only whether the Court should now make a summary order on the Speaker to pay over the money to McKim's judgment creditors, or whether the question as to such creditors' right to the money should be tried in any manner. Chief Justice Cameron, in disposing of the motion, said :

> The garnishee (the Speaker) contends that there is no garnishable debt or liability on his part to the defendant in respect of the said money, which he holds, not in his individual capacity, but as Speaker of the Legislative Assembly.
>
> I am of opinion, the plaintiff desiring it, and not wishing to leave the matter with the Court to dispose of on the material before it, is entitled to have an issue tried under Rule 373 of the Ontario Judicature Act.
>
> The right of an issue is not absolute, but I think the question ought not to be disposed of on a summary application without pleadings or evidence taken in the ordinary way, against the desire of the plaintiff; and, therefore, without intending in so doing, in any manner to intimate to the plaintiff, that I have formed any opinion in favour of the merits on the law or facts being with him, but solely because I think he ought not to be denied the right of having the question tried, and that an order for that purpose should be made.
>
> The issue to be tried will be whether, at the date of the attaching order there was any debt due or accruing due from the garnishee to the defendant.

It goes wtihout saying that the attempt to bribe a Member of Parliament was, in itself, detestable. To Chief Justice Cameron's mind it was a crime of the highest magnitude. Yet it will be seen he avoids expressing any opinion on the merits, simply deciding that a jury should determine who had a right to the money. The Chief Justice's judicial character and his judicial fairness present themselves here in a strong and favorable light.

The singular result of this matter was, that neither McKim nor his judgment creditors got the money, but the Ontario Legislature by an Act of the Assemby, 48 Victoria, cap. 5, declared that the money was forfeited to Her Majesty, for the public use of the Province, and to have been so forfeited from the time of being delivered to the Speaker. Many people wish that the name of Her Majesty had not been used in connection with this matter. The recital of the Act reads :

> That certain sums of money (the money in question in Stuart *vs.* McKim being one of them) were delivered during the Session of the Legislative Assembly held in the 47th year of Her Majesty's reign, by a certain person, to two persons of said Legislative Assembly for the purpose and under the hope of thereby influencing their votes as members of the Legislative Assembly, to wit : the sum of $1,000 to the one member, and the sum of $800 to the other. And whereas the said members at once delivered the said sums of money to the Speaker of said Legislative Assembly to be by him produced to the said Legislative Assembly : and whereas, afterwards and during the said Session the said Speaker produced the said sums of money to said Legislative Assembly, and thereupon and during the the said Session the said Legislative Assembly, ordered the said Speaker to impound and keep the said sums of money on behalf of the said Legislative Assembly, to be dealt with as the said Legislative Assembly should thereafter decide.

If I understand the recital, it means to convey the impression that though the money was paid to influence the members of the Assembly, that nevertheless the members repudiated the action and at once handed over the money to the Speaker. The Legislature, in other words, must have considered that although the money was bribery money, and paid as such, that the State should become possessed of it for public uses, because the members refused to be bribed, and therefore there should be a forfeiture so far as the payer was concerned. Logically, it would seem to be the right thing to deprive the payer of the money and to in effect declare that the same never vested in McKim, and therefore the creditors could have no claim to it. Nevertheless in the opinion of many Her Majesty's name ought not to have been used in connection with the vile money, paid for such a purpose. The Act by its first clause enacts: "The said sums of $1,000 and $800 are hereby declared to be forfeited to Her Majesty for the public use of the Province."

The case of Williams *vs.* McNeely, 9 Ontario Reports 728, is a case in which the Chief Justice was, in his own Court, overruled by his brother Judges, but was sustained in the Court of Appeal: S. C., 13 Ontario Appeal Reports 324. In that case the vexed question as to how far the Courts will go in admitting verbal evidence to explain written instruments arose. The plaintiffs sued for breach of contract to furnish scows and deliver stone to the plaintiffs at the Omemee bridge, which the plaintiffs were building under contract for the County of Peterborough. The defendants wrote the plaintiffs as follows :

> We will furnish scows, and deliver all the stone required for the Omemee bridge as fast as you require them, for the sum of seventy-five cents per cubic yard.

To which the defendants replied :

> We accept the above offer, at the price and conditions named.

The majority of the Court, the Chief Justice dissenting, held that parol evidence was admissible to shew that the carriage was to be by lake and river navigation, and was only to take place provided the water along the route remained of a named height, sufficient to enable the defendants to use their steamers in towing the scows.

The Court of Appeal was unanimous in overruling the Common Pleas Division, and sustained the ruling of Chief Justice Cameron that the evidence offered to qualify or limit the contract was not receivable. Mr. Justice Burton, after giving his reasons for his conclusion, said:

> I am of opinion, therefore, with the learned Chief Justice of the Common Pleas, that the parol evidence was improperly received, and that the appeal should be allowed, and the rule made absolute for a new trial.

Mr. Justice Osler, after giving his reasons, said:

> For the foregoing reasons, and for those stated in the able judgment of Chief Justice Cameron, the appeal should be allowed, and the rule made absolute for a new trial, if the parties cannot agree upon the damages.

This case has often been referred to since the decision of the Court of Appeal, as a leading case on the question of the admission of parol evidence.

Todd *vs.* Dun, Wiman & Co., 12 Ontario Reports 791, is a very important mercantile case decided by his Court, in which the Court of Appeal has differed from the Common Pleas Division, overruling and reversing the judgment in that case. The Common Pleas Division of the High Court held, that a letter of the defendants, the proprietors of a mercantile agency, was libellous. The letter was to the defendant, and requested him to advise them confidentially of the plaintiff's standing and responsibility for credit, stating that the plaintiff "claimed that his premises had been burglarized, that he had lost from $1,200 to $1,600;" asking, if this were so, for full particulars, and whether there was not something wrong. The defendant replied: "I have made enquiry, and find that the general opinion is, that he was not robbed at all, and what has been done he has done himself; at all events, if he was robbed, it is not of more than $100 or $200. Circumstances are against him; still I cannot say." The defendants Dun, Wiman & Co. subsequently issued a printed circular, or notification sheet, on which, after the plaintiff's name, were the words: "if interested, inquire at the office." This was published and circulated amongst the defendants' customers, some 800 in Canada and the United States. The circular also contained the following: "The words, 'if interested, inquire at the office,' do not imply that the information we have is unfavorable. On the contrary, it may not unfrequently happen that our last report is of a favorable character; but subscribers are referred to our office because, in justice to them, the parties reported, and to ourselves, the information can only be properly conveyed to those entitled to receive it by the full report, as we have it in our records."

The question to be decided was, were the words used in the letter privileged. The judgment of the Common Pleas was pronounced by Mr. Justice Galt, now Chief Justice and Chief Justice Cameron's successor, Chief Justice Cameron concurring in the judgment. The Court of Appeal, since his death, has given judgment on the appeal to them reversing the judgment below, and ordering a new trial.

I will cite but one other case decided by Chief Justice Cameron: I select this case from many of his decisions as it so immediately concerns a branch of the law of daily application in towns and cites. It is what may be termed a party wall case. The case is James et al. vs. Clement, 13 Ontario Report 115. The plaintiffs claimed that the wall between their and the defendants' buildings was a party wall, that the defendants had, without the plaintiffs' consent, raised it a foot above the plaintiffs' premises, and altered the roof from a flat to a slanting one, whereby water was discharged on the plaintiffs' premises and injured them, for which they claimed damages, and also asked for a declaration that the wall was a party wall that the defendants should be restrained from preventing plaintiffs from using the wall together with the new part thereof, on payment by plaintiffs of half the cost thereof, and also from allowing the water to be discharged on the plaintiffs' premises. The wall was proved to be wholly on the defendants' land. The part constituting the cellar foundation projected some seven inches, upon which the plaintiffs had rested the joists of their building in the cellar, the joists of the upper floors being let into the wall. The jury found that the wall was a party wall, and that the plaintiffs had sustained $35 damages. Judgment was entered for the plaintiffs, and a decree made as asked. On motion to the Divisional Court Chief Justice Cameron held, and his brother Judges concurred, " That the wall was not a party wall, nor was there any evidence from which a grant of the right to use a part thereof, could be presumed. That it was a misdirection in the learned Judge who heard the cause to tell the jury that the user of the wall for the said purposes for over twenty years constituted it a party wall, for at most it would merely give an easement for such purpose. Held, also that the case being one in which before the Judicature Act it would have been in the sole jurisdiction of the Court of Chancery to grant the relief asked, the Divisional Court could act without the intervention of a second jury, and the evidence failing to establish the plaintiffs' right to the relief asked for, the decree was set aside.

I think I need not quote any more decisions of Chief Justice Cameron: they will be found in the Ontario Reports from volumes 6 to 13 inclusive. In the 13th volume the reader will see he is styled Knight. A very short time before he died he was honored by Her Majesty with the title of K. C. B., which he thought proper to accept.

In 1841, he married Miss Charlotte Ross Wedd, who died on the 14th January, 1868. The Chief Justice survived his wife nearly twenty years. He never married again. By his wife he had three sons and three daughters. Doctor Irving Cameron, of Toronto, is one of his sons. The Chief Justice had for some time before his death been suffering from a carbuncle, and had partially recovered from this, but a week before his death, his system being run down, he took an unfortunate turn which caused his death on 25th June, 1887. He will long be remembered as one of the most distinguished in the roll of Canadian Judges.

In his private life Chief Justice Cameron was distinguished by the amiable kindness of his disposition. No one could know him and fail to be impressed by the warm hearted tenderness of his character, which was rendered all the more striking by the keenness of his wit. His acute penetration led him to quickly detect any sham or imposture, and his naturally vigorous style of conversation made him sometimes appear severe. But under this was ever present the warmest humanitarian, the heartiest feeling of active benevolence. To be his friend once was to be his friend always. Loyalty in every detail of life was one of his most prominent characteristics. His private charities were numberless. To the poor, the afflicted, the unfortunate, he was ever the prompt Samaritan, and many an unfortunate had cause to lament the untimely death of the Chief Justice, whose heart and purse had always been open for their necessities.

His devotion to duty undoubtedly hastened his death. During the last days in which he sat in Court he suffered greatly from the malady he endured with such fortitude, and it was only at the earnest solicitation of his brother Judges that he ceased from the labor he was utterly unfit for. Up to the last it was hoped that his iron constitution would overcome the ravages of disease ; but, weakened by the sufferings of years, caused by the loss of his leg, he at last laid down that life which he had spent in untiring labor and inexhaustible good works.

XXXI.

THE HONORABLE JOHN O'CONNOR, JUDGE OF THE QUEEN'S BENCH DIVISION OF THE HIGH COURT OF JUSTICE.

HE Honorable John O'Connor was of Irish descent. His parents emigrated from the County Kerry, Ireland, to Boston, Massachusetts, in 1823.

John O'Connor was born at Boston, in January, 1824. When four years old his parents removed to Upper Canada, and settled in the Township of Maidstone, in the County of Essex. It was in this township that the future Judge spent his infancy and early boyhood: it was in this township that he spent part of his school days and received such an education as a country place afforded. Before going to the law he had further advantage in schooling with Mr. Gordon in Windsor.

The family residence was fourteen miles from the Town of Sandwich, the road being a mere cart-road cut through the wood. It used to occupy two days, with an ox-team and cart, going to Sandwich, and two more to return. It was not a very inviting place to live in, but the settlers were nearly all Roman Catholics. The O'Connors being Catholics had the satisfaction of being among their co-religionists, even though without a Church, for the first Church built in the township was erected in 1839 or 1840, at a place called Maidstone Cross, hard by the Willow

Swamp. Up to the time of the building of this Church, which was nothing but a log building, the O'Connors and other settlers were visited by clergymen from Detroit and Sandwich every second Sunday.

As an instance of the privations of the settlers, the Honorable John O'Connor used to refer to a family from Kilkenny, named Kavanagh, consisting of the father, mother, three sons, and two daughters. The father, the sons, and the daughters set to work clearing up the land, and tilling it from year to year. While they were thus employed, the mother, forty-five years of age, supplied them with provisions, which for two years, she carried on her back from Sandwich, a distance of thirteen miles, frequently bringing a hundred-weight of flour, while at every step she was almost knee deep in mud and water. But what will not an Irish man or woman do and endure for a fellow countryman and co-religionist.

After young O'Connor had received a tolerable education under difficulties, he removed to Sandwich, and entered a law office in that old town. He became a student-at-law, having been admitted a student by the Law Society, in Easter Term, 11 and 12 Victoria (1848). As soon as admitted, he entered the law office of W. D. Baby. He studied with him for a time, and then was articled to Mr. Vidal, with whom he completed his studies. He was called to the Bar in Hilary Term, 17 Victoria (1854). He settled down, immediately after his call, at Windsor, where he practised his profession successfully for some years. In the early part of his career he was in partnership with Mr. Charles Baby. He was not long in gaining a good education: not a little assisted by his capacity for forensic speaking—a qualification indigenous to the Irish, as well when transplanted on a colonial or foreign soil as when at home.

His business at Sandwich was a profitable one. Besides this, he soon acquired a good deal of local influence, political and otherwise. He was for a considerable time Reeve of Windsor. He was Warden of the County of

Essex for three years, having been twice elected to that office by the unanimous vote of the County Council. For twelve years he performed the duties of Chairman of the Board of Education of Windsor. These various appointments shew that he was no ordinary man, and that his influence was great in the place where he resided and carried on his business. He was a man of iron will, of great determination, and secured the friendship of the majority of his fellow citizens. Not satisfied with being a member of the Canadian Bar, he procured his admission to the Bar of the adjoining State of Michigan.

In his practice at the Bar he shewed considerable ability, and seldom accepted the services of other counsel in the prosecution of his business. He had the highest reputation at his own local Bar, and seldom went abroad in prosecution of professional work.

He had not been long at the Bar, about seven years, when, in 1861, he was thought to be an available candidate for the representation of the County of Essex in Parliament. He contested the county in 1861, with Mr. Arthur Rankin, but was defeated. In 1863, however, he succeeded in unseating Mr. Rankin, and in obtaining a new election. He was on this occasion returned as member for the county, and sat in Parliament until the dissolution of the House in May of that year. He again contested the county in 1863, when a special return was made to the House by the returning officer. Both candidates petitioned the House of Assembly to be declared entitled to the seat. Mr. Rankin, his opponent, succeeded in obtaining the seat, and so Mr. O'Connor was again left without a seat in Parliament.

At the first general election after Confederation, he was returned to the House of Commons; again in 1872, he succeeded in his candidature, and was returned to represent the county as their representative in Parliament.

On the 2nd of July, 1872, he was sworn in of the Privy Council, and thenceforward was President of that body until 4th March, 1873, when he became Minister of Inland

Revenue. On the 1st of July he was transferred to the position of Postmaster-General, which office he retained until the fall of the Ministry in the following November.

At the General Election of 1874, he again presented himself to his constituents in the County of Essex for re-election, but was defeated by Mr. William McGregor by a large majority. He was out of Parliament the next four years, and opened an office in Ottawa, where he soon built up a good practice.

At the General Election of 17th September, 1878, he was returned for the County of Russell, and upon the formation of Sir John A. Macdonald's Government in October of that year, he accepted office in it as President of the Council, which office he retained till January, 1880, when he again became Postmaster-General. Before the next Session of the House he was transferred from President of the Council to Secretary of State, which office he retained till he left the Government.

It will thus be seen that Mr. O'Connor had a long and varied political career. He was regarded as a representative Roman Catholic. It was as such that he held his position in the Government. He was a Conservative in politics, and an ally and suporter of Sir John A. Macdonald. His ability in the House was not so conspicuous for oratory as for sound and lucid argument. Before accepting office in 1872, he was made a Queen's Counsel.

In the management of the Department of which he was the head he performed the duties to the satisfaction of his colleagues. He was always accessible to those who required his advice or assistance, and to all who had business to transact with his Department at the seat of Government. He strongly opposed the introduction of Fenianism into Canada, and in 1870 wrote a pamphlet, which he addressed to the Governor-General, strongly deprecating the introduction of old country issues into Canada, where his fellow-countrymen and co-religionists had prospered so well, under the protecting ægis of the British flag.

I have appended these letters of the Honorable John O'Connor at the end of the volume.

Judge O'Connor was loyal to the Crown throughout life; he did not recognize a difference between Catholics and Protestants in the code of allegiance. In private and public life he had as many warm friends who were Protestant as he had of his own creed.

He at one time, during one of the periods during which he was relieved of the attendance in Parliament by the electors of Essex, opened an office in Toronto, formed a partnership with Mr. John Blevins, now Clerk of the City Council, and transacted law business at the seat of the Courts, in addition to retaining a connection with his business in Windsor or Sandwich. The partnership name was O'Connor & Blevins, and continued through the years 1863, 1864, and 1865.

While in Toronto, no such thing as differences of dogma or faith was allowed to influence him or those who knew him in any way. I will presently shew that any difference of this kind did not prevent his appointment to the Bench.

When the Honorable John O'Connor left the Government he was engaged in the double work of examining into the question of the disputed boundary between Ontario and Manitoba, and on the Commission for Consolidating the Statutes of the Dominion and certain other Statutes which were passed by the several Legistatures of the Provinces of Canada before they respectively became a part thereof. The work done by Mr. O'Connor was confirmed by Parliament and crystallized into an Act, entitled. " An Act respecting the Revised Statutes of Canada " cap. 4, A.D. 1886, which recites :

Whereas it has been found expedient to revise, classify, and consolidate the public general Statutes passed by the Parliament of the Dominion of Canada and also certain public general Statutes which were passed by the several Legislatures of the Provinces of Canada before they respectively became a part thereof, and which are still in force, and relate to matters within the Legislative authority of the Province of Canada ; and whereas, such revision, classification, and consolidation have been made accordingly ; and whereas, it is expedient to provide for the incorporation therewith of the public general Statutes passed during the present Session, and for giving the force of law to the body of the Revised Statutes to result from such incorporation : Therefore Her Majesty etc., etc., enacts.

These Acts now form the volumes which make up the Revised Statutes of Canada published in 1886, and which under a proclamation of Lord Lansdowne, the Governor General, dated at Government House at Ottawa, on the 24th day of January, 1887, were, on the advice of the Privy Council declared to come into force and have effect as law from and after the 1st day of March, 1887.

The Honorable John O'Connor was appointed Judge of the Queen's Bench on the 11th September, 1884. So far as I knew, he is the first Roman Catholic appointed to a Judgeship of a Superior Court in Upper Canada, or Ontario. When his appointment was gazetted there were not wanting some who cavilled at the appointment, because of his being a Roman Catholic. It was well that it should have been made known by his promotion, that faith or creed is no bar in Canada to advancement in any profession, above all, in that of the law. Before his appointment to the Bench he had been out of practice, and had had no experience in the fusion of law and equity under the Judicature Act. As soon as he was appointed he sat down to work, and to the mastery of the Judicature Act, and was not long in qualifying himself for active work on the Bench.

Judge O'Connor soon developed into a painstaking Judge, and thus gradually obtained from the Bar a confidence in his rulings, which his independence and desire to secure absolute justice well deserved.

Judge O'Connor was an unostentatious, unpretending man ; but he had a great deal of that uncommon commodity called sound common sense, which stood him in good stead in all his dealings with questions of law or fact.

It is hardly necessary to refer to any cases decided by Judge O'Connor, as his judgments are so recent, and besides, were in many cases concurring judgments. However, in Warren *vs.* Grover, 8 Ontario Reports, he differed from the Chief Justice of the Queen's Bench Division of the High Court, throwing in his judicial lot with Mr. Justice Armour. In an action by a tenant against his landlord, for refusing to give him possession of demised premises, O'Connor and Armour, JJ., (Wilson, C. J., dissenting), held, that the proper measure of damages in such case is the difference between what the tenant agreed to pay for the premises and what they were really worth. But it is not open to the tenant to shew that he rented the premises for the purpose of there carrying on a certain business, of which the landlord was aware, that he could not procure other premises, and to claim the profits which he might have made in such business, if he had been let into possession.

There is another case reported, heard before Mr. Justice O'Connor sitting alone, and in which he gave judgment, which I will quote from, as it has general application in the matter of natural justice, and shews that the Judge would not allow any tyrranical abuse of legal process · it will also be of interest to Justices of the Peace in the performance of their duties. The case is Regina *vs.* Eli, 10 Ontario Reports, 727. In that case the complainant was steward of a "social club" in Walkerton. The members were elected by ballot, and, on paying an entrance fee of $1 and a subscription of $25 per month, were entitled to use the club room, and buy from the steward spirituous liquors. The members were not responsible for goods ordered, or for any general expenses. An information was laid against the defendant on 10th September, 1885, for an offence against the second part of the Canada Temperance Act, 1878; and on the 21st September, 1885, he was, about 4 P.M., served with a summons to apppear, at 8:30 A.M. next day, before two Magistrates. On the 22nd day of September, informations were, in two other cases, laid against him for similar offences, and he was in each, at 8:15 A.M., served with a summons to appear before a Magistrate at 9 A.M. that day. When the Magistrates Court met the cases were partially gone into, and before it was closed the prosecution asked the Magistrates to take up the second and third cases. The defendant stated that he had not understood what the summonses meant, and, by advice of counsel, he refused to plead. The Magistrates entered a plea in each case of not guilty, and went on with both cases. The evidence in both cases shewed that the offence charged in each case occurred on dates different from those laid in the informations. The Magistrates amended the dates in the informations. The defendant and his counsel were in Court all the time, awaiting completion of the evidence in the first, but refused in any way to plead or take part in the second or third cases, or to ask adjournment thereof. The Magistrates, after taking all the evidence therein, at the request of the defendant, adjourned the first case, and in the second and third cases convicted the defendant of the offences, as charged in the amended informations. It was shewn by affidavits that the Magistrates were willing in these cases, had the defendant pleaded, to adjourn after taking the evidence of the witnesses present. There were also affidavits shewing that the Magistrates had been, before the "Scott Act," interested in promoting Prohibition.

On the above state of facts, Mr. Justice O'Connor, in giving judgment, said:

> To say that these cases were tried is simply preposterous. The proceedings of the morning of the 22nd September, the taking of the information and the issuing of the summonses apparently before breakfast, and the service on the defendant immediately after that meal, the short time allowed for appearance thereon at the town hall, allowing neither time for digestion nor reflection, and the sham trial which followed so soon, appear dramatic, and irresistibly suggest the notion of a farce. Three cases tried concurrently; a witness in one, a witness in another, and still a witness in the third case, sworn and examined alternately or concurrently, as suited the prosecuting counsel, while the defendant, defending in the first case, is compelled to listen to evidence in the other cases in which he, after objecting, had refused to plead or take any part, although only fifteen minutes had elapsed between the

service on him that morning and the time for appearing at the town hall to answer the first summons, and no time had been allowed him to prepare his defence in these last two cases, was actually a display of injustice and a wanton mockery of justice not to be expected in a civilized country. I trust that such exhibitions are of rare occurrence in this country. The defendant had a substantial and apparently a bonâ fide defence to offer; a defence which, however, required a reasonable time to formulate it, and which would present grave matters of law for consideration—matters of law which ought not to be, and which cannot be, treated in Dogberry's style. In the first place, he produced the constitution of the club. He denies some of the facts alleged against him, explains others, and denies that he is guilty. He has a right to a full hearing and a fair trial. In these two cases he has had no trial. To allow the convictions to stand would, under the circumstances, be contrary to natural justice, and to the principles of our laws; and practically the cases fall within the principle of Re Holland, 37 Upper Canada Reports, 214. The order nisi will be made absolute, with costs against the complainant, upon the grounds stated in the orders, having reference to the material facts above stated.

The cases I have stated are sufficient to shew that Mr. Justice O'Connor had a just appreciation of natural justice, and was desirous to see it carried out.

The Judge, from early manhood, had an infirmity which, in some degree, affected his whole life. He was obliged to walk with a cane and a wooden leg. He lost his leg from an accident while cutting down a tree in the woods in Maidstone. In some way the tree fell across him, on a cold winter's day, breaking his leg and imbedding it as it were in a vice. When he found himself thus pinned he took his knife, cut the laces of his shoes, and then, with the knife or an axe, dug the snow and earth away from under his leg, and so managed to extricate himself: he then started to crawl home, but was met by some one who carried him, where his leg was amputated by Dr. Donnelly. This is a true relation of this incident of his life, which received much exaggeration from hearsay evidence. It was said that he had cut off his own leg: the almost impossibility of such a thing would bear its own contradiction.

The Judge was a tall, well formed man, and in his walk on the street, or elsewhere, could be noticed as having an erect, manly appearance.

55—L. J.

In 1849, he married Miss Mary Barrett, eldest daughter of Richard Barrett, formerly of Killarney, Ireland.

He was in his usual health when called upon to take the Cobourg Assizes, in November, 1887. While at Cobourg, holding the Assizes, he burst a blood vessel, lingered on for a couple of days, when death put an end to his sufferings, on Thursday, November 3rd, 1887.

Before his death he received the rites of his church. His body was brought to Toronto for burial, which took place from his residence on Gerrard street, on the 7th day of November.

He left a widow and five children to mourn his loss.

XXXII.

The Law Society and Osgoode Hall.

HE writers of letters, when they have forgotten something they desired to communicate to a friend, generally add a postscript, to indicate they have something more to say.

In launching the "Lives of the Judges," I remember that I have neglected to write of the cradle in which most, if not all, of the Judges were nurtured, and therefore proceed to add a postscript chapter, in order to bring to the recollection of readers the past of that Society of which not only the Judges, but Barristers who have gone to their rest unclothed with judicial dignity, have been members. The professional reader will at once discover that I refer to the Law Society.

Eighty years is not a long period in the history of a nation; but when, as in the case of Ontario, that period comprises the whole, or nearly the whole, of the legal history of a Province, the period has more significance. The infancy of a nation is of interest to every citizen; the infancy of law ought to possess an interest with the whole community, but is of especial interest to those engaged in legal pursuits.

The student of law does not care so much to examine into the origin of the law, as to travel on in beaten paths; the paths that lead to emolument, or future fame in his calling. It is well, however, that he should be reminded of the early years of the profession on which he has entered.

The Bar of Ontario is, in some respects, the offspring of the Bar of Quebec, as it existed prior to the division of the old Province of Quebec into the two separate Provinces of Lower Canada and Upper Canada, which took place in 1791, the thirty-first year of the reign of His Majesty King George the Third.

In the year 1785, the twenty-fifth year of the reign of King George the Third, there was enacted in the Province an Ordinance entitled, "An Ordinance concerning Advocates, Attorneys, Solicitors, and Notaries, and for the more easy Collection of His Majesty's Revenue." This Ordinance enacted that:

> No person shall be commissioned, appointed, or permitted to practise as Barrister, Advocate, Solicitor, or Proctor, unless articled for five years to some Advocate or Attorney duly admitted and practising in the Province, or some part of His Majesty's dominion, unless such person shall have been already called to the Bar, or entitled so to be, and in practice as an Advocate or Attorney in some Court of civil jurisdiction within some part of His Majesty's dominion.

The ordinance further provided:

> That no person should be commissioned unless examined by some one of the first or most able Barristers, in the presence of the Chief Justice or two Justices of the Court of Common Pleas, and found of fit capacity.

It was under this Ordinance that causes were advocated in the Old Province of Quebec, comprising the Provinces of Upper and Lower Canada. In 1791, the thirty-first year of the reign of King George the Third, the Imperial Parliament passed a law giving to each of the Provinces a Legislative Council and Assembly; and the Upper Canada Parliament, at its first Session in the following year, 1792, passed an Act enacting:

> That thereafter, in all matters of controversy or civil rights, resort should be had to the laws of England as the rule for the decision of the same.

Up to the passing of this Act, the laws which had been in force in regard to property and civil rights were the laws of Canada—the French law. It was soon found, after the passing of this enactment, that it was necessary to have Advocates in the Province of Upper Canada, skilled in the English law, and to that end the Legislature, on the 9th July, 1794, thirty-fourth of His Majesty's reign, passed an Act entitled, "An Act to authorize the Governor or Lieutenant-Governor to license Practitioners in the Law," by which it is enacted that the Ordinance of Quebec, to which I have previously referred, should be suspended; and—

> That it should be lawful for the Governor, Lieutenant-Governor, or person administering the Government of this Province, to authorize by license under his hand and seal, such and so many of His Majesty's liege subjects, not exceeding sixteen in number, as he shall deem from their probity, education, and condition in life best qualified to act as Advocates and Attorneys in the conduct of all legal proceeding in this Province.

The 14th section of the Act provided:

> That nothing therein contained should prevent any person, duly qualified according to the provisions in the said Act or Ordinance (Ordinance of Quebec) contained, from being admitted to the exercise of the practice of the law conformably to the said Act.

In 1803, several gentlemen—William Dickson, D'Arcy Boulton, John Powell, William Elliott, William Warren Baldwin—were admitted to the Bar by license of Lieutenant-Governor Peter Hunter, made in pursuance of an Act of the Province entitled, "An Act to authorize the Governor, Lieutenant-Governor, or person administering the Government of this Province, to license Practitioners in the Law." The license is set forth *in extenso* in the record, and states that the gentlemen had been examined by Henry Allcock, Esquire, Chief Justice, and found fit.

Why these gentlemen availed themselves of this Act, instead of passing the Law Society, does not appear. Six years before their admission, on the 17th July, 1797, a meeting of Barristers took place at Newark, now Niagara, for the formation of a Law Society. The following is an extract from the books of the Law Society in Osgoode Hall :

NEWARK, *July 17, 1797.*

In obedience to the direction of an Act passed this Session in the Parliament of the said Province, the following gentlemen assembled in Wilson's Hotel, at eleven o'clock in the forenoon of the above day :

John White, A. G.	Robert D. Gray, S. G.
Angus Macdonell.	James Clark.
Christopher Robinson.	Allan McLean.
William D. Powell.	Alexander Stewart.
Nicholas Hagerman.	R. C. Beardsley.

The subject of the meeting, being taken into consideration, it was moved by the Attorney-General that the Act of Parliament of the Province be read, and it was read accordingly by Mr. Beardsley, the junior.

The subject of the meeting referred to was the carrying out of the Act, read by Mr. Beardsley, 37 George III., cap. 13, passed 9th July, 1797, entitled, "An Act for the better regulating the practice of the law," by which the persons theretofore admitted to practise in the law, and practising at the Bar of any of Her Majesty's Courts in the Province were authorized to form themselves into a Society, to be called the Law Society of Upper Canada, "as well for the purpose of establishing of order among themselves as for the purpose of securing to the Province and the profession of a learned and honorable body to assist their fellow-students as occasion may require, and to support and maintain the constitution of the said Province."

These records from the books of the Law Society, and the Acts of Parliament mentioned, are valuable to be referred to as shewing :

1st. That after the division of the Province of Quebec into the two Provinces of Upper and Lower Canada the Legislature of Upper Canada very soon saw the necessity of retaining and giving effect to the Ordinance of Quebec relative to Attorneys and Advocates, thus at once giving license to trained practitioners in the law : not only those who had been called in the Province of Quebec, but, as the Ordinance expressed it, "those who had been called to the Bar, or entitled so to be, and in practice as an Advocate or Attorney in some Court of civil jurisdiction within some part of His Majesty's dominions."

2nd. That the further necessity existed of having called to the Bar gentlemen licensed by the Lieutenant-Governor of Upper Canada, after examination as to fitness by the Chief Justice of the Province, as one skilled in English law.

3rd. To crown all, the formation of a Society, " For the purpose of securing to the Province and the profession of a *learned* and *honoraile* body to assist their fellow subjects as occasion might require, and to support and maintain the *Constitution* of the said Province."

The young law students of this day hardly realize the fact that fourteen years had not passed after the Treaty of Peace was signed declaring the independence of the United States, before the Legislature of the Province of Upper Canada had set to work, by legislation in the direction of providing that gentlemen of education and probity should be those privileged to conduct legal proceedings for their fellow subjects in the Province. There were no Inns of Court in Canada in 1797, yet, nevertheless, the gentlemen of that day had not forgotten the origin of some, at least, of the English Inns of Court, for they met in Wilson's Tavern or Inn, at Newark, to transact their business. Cunningham, in his " Inns of Court," published in 1780, thus writes of settled places for students of the law, called Inns of Court and Chancery. He says : " So that Inns of Court (*i. e.*, after Edward I. had appointed John de Metingham Chief Justice of the Common Pleas, and that the other Judges should supply to every Court Attorneys and Lawyers to do service in the Court), though we have no memorandum of the direct time or absolute certainty of the places, we may safely conclude that they settled in certain *hostels* or *Inns*, which were henceforth called Inns of Court, because the students in them did there not only study the laws, but such other exercises as might make them the more serviceable to the King's Court; as Sir John Ferguson, in the forty-ninth chapter of his book, *De Laudibus Legum Angliæ*, observes, when he says: " *That the students in the University of the Laws* (for so he calleth the *Houses of Court and Chancery*) *did not only study the laws, to serve the Courts of Justice and profit their country, but further learn to dance, to sing, to play on instruments on the ferial days, and to study Divinity on the festival, using such exercises as they did who were brought up in the King's Court.*"

Whether or not the Lawyers who met in Wilson's Tavern at Newark, on the 17th July, 1797, to discuss matters appertaining to their profession, did dance, or sing, or study Divinity, there is no record. But if they did they were not without precedent, one of the dearest things to a lawyer's existence.

The names of those who attended the meeting of the 17th July, 1797, as well as those who were called to the Bar, by the license of the Lieutenant-Governor in 1803, after due examination as to fitness by the Chief Justice, are familiar to all those acquainted with our Canadian legal history.

So far as can be ascertained from the records in Osgoode Hall, members were first admitted to the Bar under the new order of things, following the passing of the Acts for regulating the practice of the law, passed 9th July, 1797, in Trinity Term, 1797, when the following gentlemen were admitted to the Bar :

1. John White,
2. Robert Isaac Dey Gray,
3. Walter Roe,
4. Angus Macdonell,
5. James Clark,
6. Christopher Robinson,
7. Allan McLean,
8. John McKay,
9. Alexander Stewart,
10. Nicholas Hagerman,

11. Bartholomew Crannel Beardsley,
12. Timothy Thompson,
13. Jacob Farrand,
14. Samuel Sherwood,
15. William Dummer Powell, jr.

Who was the first admitted to the Roll of Barristers of the gentlemen above named, or if any others were called to the Bar before them can not be ascertained, as the first Barristers' Roll is not among the parchments in the archives of the Court. The first Roll there begins with the names of gentlemen admitted to the Bar in 1808. The information as to those admitted in Trinity Term, 1797, is not obtained from the original Rolls, but from the Journals of the Law Society. As the Roll of 1808 is still preserved, what has become of the Rolls from 1797 to 1808? Were they burned or destroyed by the incendiary hand of the invaders in 1813?

Doctor Scadding, in "Toronto of Old," in referring to the site of the first House of Parliament thus writes:

> It was nearly on the site of this rather hard-featured building (an old house near the Don) that the first House of Parliament of Upper Canada stood, humble but commodious structures of wood built before the close of the eighteenth century, and destroyed by the incendiary hand of the invader in 1813. They consisted, as a contemporary document sets forth, of two elegant halls, with convenient offices for the accommodation of the Legislature *and the Courts of Justice*. The library, and all the papers and records belonging *to these institutions* were consumed.

The Parchment Roll of 1808 bears a very mottled appearance, and it is not impossible it was saved while its ancestor perished in the flames.

The Law Society shortly after their organization saw the necessity of having a head, or Treasurer, as he was called, (following the English precedent), to their body, and appointed John White to that office in 1797. He was the first appointed Treasurer of the Society. Angus Macdonell was appointed Treasurer in the 43rd year of the reign of King George the Third, A. D. 1803. He was an uncle to John Macdonell, whose name figures prominently and holds high place in both the legal and military history of Canada. John Macdonell was admitted a Student of the Law on the 6th April, 1803, and called to the Bar in Easter Term, 1808. He rose rapidly in his profession, and became Attorney-General, which office he filled to the time he was killed in the engagement on Queenston Heights, while in attendance on General Brock as Provincial Aide-de-Camp. Alex. Macdonell of Osgoode Hall is a collateral relative of Angus Macdonell.

In the same Trinity Term, 1808, that John Macdonnell had been called to the Bar, three other gentlemen, afterwards distinguished in Canadian annals as Judges, whose names are familiar to the public and the Bar, were admitted as Students of the Law. I refer to the name of Archibald McLean, who became Chief Justice, and to the names of Jonas Jones and Christopher Alexander Hagerman, Judges of the Court of Queen's Bench.

The second Treasurer of the same Society was Robert Isaac Dey Gray, appointed to that office at the Chambers of the Attorney-General, Trinity Term, 1798.

William Warren Baldwin was at one time Treasurer, and appointed in Michaelmas Term, 52 George III., 1812. There was no Convocation of Benchers from this time down to Michaelmas Term, 56 George III., 25th February, 1815. This hiatus of three years was, doubtless, occasioned by the war, which during that period raged with the United States, familiarly known as the war of 1812. An incident occurred at the meeting on the 28th of February, 1815, which is not likely to occur again in the annals of the Canadian Bar. A member of the Society, who had been admitted as a Student in 48 George III., was on this day, 25th February, 1815, made a Barrister, Solicitor-General, and Bencher. This may be called pretty rapid promotion at the Bar. The incident proves in what esteem John Beverley Robinson, afterwards Sir John Beverley Robinson and Chief Justice, must have been held when he was called upon in one day to fill the three important offices.

The record in the Journal of the Law Society stands thus :

The next meeting after Michaelmas Term, 52 George III., (1812), was not held till Hilary Term, 1815, D'Arcy Boulton, Attorney-General, presided, and John Beverley Robinson called to the Bar.

Present

D'Arcy Boulton, Attorney-General,
John Beverley Robinson, Solicitor-General,
Timothy Thompson,
Allen McLean,   } Esquires.
Wm. W. Baldwin,

I owe it to the students, before completing my postscript to the "Lives of the Judges," to make some reference to them as a body. They belong to a class to which all the Barristers, except those licensed in 1797, have belonged, and we must not despise the day of small things. Down to the year 1825 the curriculum for law students was not very severe. In the Law Society's Journals, under date of July 1st, 1825, is this entry:

Whereas no small injury may be done to the education of that portion of the youth of the country intended for the profession of the law by confining the examinations to Cicero's Orations, and it is advisable further to promote the object of the sixteenth Rule of this Society, passed and approved of in Hilary Term, 60 George III., it is unanimously resolved that in future the student, on his examination, will be expected to exhibit a general knowledge of English, Grecian, and Roman history, a becoming acquaintance with one of the ancient Latin poets, as Virgil, Horace, or Juvenal, and the like acquaintance with some of the celebrated prose works of the ancients, such as Sallust or Cicero, *De Officiis* as well as his orations, or any author of equal celebrity which may be adopted as the standard books of the several district schools; and it is also expected that the student will shew the Society that he has had some reasonable portion of mathematical instruction.

Even with this amended curriculum, the student of the present day may well exclaim, "*O, Fortunate Puer!*"

The curriculum is now based on the University model, and woe betide the student that loiters by the way!—let him scrutinize the seal of the Law Society, and he will there find a column surmounted by the figure of a little animal, whose example he must follow if he wishes to succeed.

The seal of the Law Society has more significance and has given birth to much more deliberation than it ordinarily gets credit for. In the Journals of the Law Society, to which I have so frequently to refer, under date of the 13th November, 1823, there is this record :

<blockquote>
At a Convocation of the Law Society at the Chambers of the Treasurer, the Attorney-General procured, at the request of the Society, a seal upon the shield whereof are engraved the following arms and motto : —In the centre of the shield is a Doric column, modestly indicating the state of the legal erudition of the Society in its first establishment and at the time of its incorporation, ready to receive at a future day its embellishment from the finished models of the ancient and learned societies in England ; surmounted by a beaver, always occupying a compartment in the armorial bearings of Canada, and forming an appropriate emblem in the seal, descriptive of the industry of the profession. On the dexter side of the shield is represented the figure of Hercules, and on the sinister side the figure of Justice, with the scales in her right hand and a sword in her left, and are intended to place in a prominent view that spirit of justice and fortitude which constituted the character of its members. The words, " Magna Charta Angliæ," inscribed upon the ribbon floating round the column, indicate the foundation upon which Canadian liberty is established. Upon the exterior circle is inscribed the words, " Incorporated 1822," which seal is unanimously adopted and declared to be the seal of the Law Society of Upper Canada.
</blockquote>

The Law Society of the olden time used to hold their Convocation at divers places—if not Justices in Eyre, they were at least Benchers in 'Eyre,' now cropping out in the Parliamentary Library, now at the Attorney-General's office, then at the Court House, or at the Treasurer's private office—they had no abiding place. The necessity of a permanent house came to be felt, but how to obtain it was the question.

At a meeting of Benchers of the Law Society of Upper Canada, held at the Chambers of the Treasurer, on the first day of Michaelmas Term, in the first year of the reign of George IV., it was "resolved that the Society do apply a sum not exceeding £500 in the erection of a building for the use of the Society, to be called 'Osgoode Hall,' on the site opposite to the church lately purchased by them."

I confess to having had some difficulty in ascertaining

what site was here referred to. It is so contrary to the generally received notion that lawyers would locate their hall directly opposite to a church that one would hardly believe it. Besides, the resolution in its terms does not make it very clear, whether it was a site for a hall or the church which was purchased.

After consulting Dr. Scadding, I have come to the conclusion that the site intended was on the then vacant square to the south of King Street opposite to St. James's Church ; and it is probable that site would have been selected for the Lawyers Hall had not the Attorney-General stepped in and offered to sell to the society the plot of ground on which Osgoode Hall now stands.

Dr. Scadding, in "Toronto of Old," describing Osgoode Hall thus writes :

OSGOODE HALL.

The east wing of the existing edifice was the original Osgoode Hall, erected under the eye of Dr. W. W. Baldwin, at the time Treasurer of the Society. It was a plain, square, matter-of-fact brick building, two stories and a half in height. In 1844-46 a corresponding structure was erected to the west, and the two were united by a building between, surmounted by a low dome. In 1857-60 the whole edifice underwent a renovation, the dome was removed, a very handsome facade of cut stone, reminding one of the interior of a Genoese or Roman palace, was added, with the Court rooms, Library and other appurtenances, on a scale of dignity and in a style of architectural beauty surpassed only by the new Law Courts in London, &c., &c.

The edifice, called by Dr. Scadding the *original* "Osgoode Hall," must be the east wing of the present Osgoode Hall, at the head of York street ; this being so, the original resolution before referred to as passed 1 George IV., 1820, was not carried out, as the site there spoken of was evidently the site opposite St. James's Church, whereas the present Osgoode Hall is on the land purchased of Sir John Robinson in 1828, or about that time, for £1,000, as shewn by the resolutions of Easter Term, 2nd May 1828, which I set forth below as transcribed from the Law Society Journals.

The subject of acquiring a site and erecting a permanent hall seems to have first occupied the attention of Benchers in 1825 and down to 1828, when the present site was purchased. There seems to have been a contest raging in the Convocation of Benchers as to whether the site should be obtained from the Government on the square which had been occupied by the Public Buildings near the Don, or in the west near the Government House. The west seems to have carried the day, as the following series of resolutions shew, and which I think, even at the expense of being pronounced tedious, is a matter of interest to all Barristers, if not to the general reader

CONVOCATION, *18th day of November, 1825.*

The subject of inquiry for a site for a Hall and the erection of suitable buildings having been taken into consideration, the former minutes read, and the matter discussed.

It was unanimously resolved that the Treasurer do draw up a brief statement of the intention of the Society immediately to appropriate its funds towards the erection of a Hall, and its disposition to accommodate the Court of King's Bench, with all necessary apartments, according with the importance and dignity of its functions, if the funds of the Society could be aided by a reasonable grant of money on the part of the Province, and that the Government and Judges should approve of such a measure of inviting funds in order not only to secure more immediate and ample accommodation, but also to erect a building worthy of the Province and its seat of Government. And such statement be presented to the Judges as soon as practicable; and that the Treasurer may assure them of the willingness of the Society to pledge themselves to the extent of £2,000 towards this desirable object.

W. W. BALDWIN,
Treasurer.

The statement having been accordingly drawn up by the Treasurer and shewn to the Judges in Court and approved by them, was presented to the Judges on the Bench.

Easter Term, 7 George IV. On motion of the Attorney-General, it was unanimously resolved: That the Treasurer do prepare a draft of a memorial to His Excellency Sir Peregrine Maitland, Lieutenant-Governor, and representing on the part of the Society, the great disadvantage they labor under by the want of buildings wherein to transact business, collect and deposit a library, and to accommodate the youth studying the profession. That learning from public report that the new buildings for the contemplated Parliament House are to be built on Simcoe Place, they hope His Excellency will not consider them unreasonable in soliciting a grant of a portion of the old site of the Public Buildings now abandoned, and that in the event of his favorable reply to their memorial, the Society would lose no time in commencing such a building as would be ornamental to the town, as well as convenient to themselves.

W. W. BALDWIN,
Treasurer.

Michaelmas Term, 7 George IV. The Treasurer submitted a plan of the elevation of a building as a hall for the use of the Society, upon which he was requested to proceed with the plan, and procure an estimate of the left wing.

Hilary Term, 7 George IV. Mr. Ridout and Mr. Macaulay examined the Treasurer's accounts, by which examination it appeared that the funds of the Society immediately available amount to £1,839 10s. 1½d.

The Attorney-General
Jonas Jones, Esquire
Archibald McLean, Esquire
John Rolph, Esquire
} Benchers entered and took their seats.

Whereupon, General Convocation having met pursuant to the resolution of Tuesday, the 2nd instant, and the Treasurer having laid before the Society the above general statement of its funds, the Society discussed the subject of the application to the use of the Society. Wherefore, after consideration, upon the motion of the Attorney-General, it was unanimously resolved :

That the Society is very grateful for the grant of six acres of land which they are informed the Honorable the Executive Council have recommended to be made for the purposes of the Society, but as in their application no definite opinion was expressed as to the quantity which would enable the Society to carry their object into effect, and as they have been given to understand that the most favorable disposition existed to comply with their wishes, it is expedient that the Treasurer should, on behalf of the Society, represent to His Excellency that if the grant could be extended to any convenient tract between fifteen and twenty acres, it would be much more suitable to the purposes contemplated.

The Treasurer then laid before the Society the plan prepared and executed by him, agreeably to the request made of him last Michaelmas Term, but without an estimate, which could not be obtained at present, sufficient time not having been had for that part of said request.

The plan having been inspected and considered, it was unanimously resolved :

That William W. Baldwin, Esquire, the President and Treasurer, do obtain an estimate of the expense of building the south wing of the plan submitted by him ; this estimate to be separate from the portico and vestibule in one amount, and for the hall, library, &c., in the second amount. That he do submit the plan to His Excellency the Lieutenant-Governor, and also to the Honorable the Judges of the King's Bench, for their consideration as to the accommodation proposed for the Court and offices appendant in the north wing; and it is further resolved that in case the Honorable the **Judges** of **the** King's Bench and the Executive Government give any assurance **on their part that the** plan, **so** far **as** regards the Court of King's Bench, will **be pursued** with effect on their part, the said Treasurer shall **lay the estimate** to be obtained before the Society in the next Term, for their final approbation, before contract be entered into. It **is also further resolved** that a further estimate be made and procured of the expense **of building the** Court and **range** of Chambers between the wings, as in **the design.**

Easter Term, **8 George IV. The** Treasurer having laid **before the Society a diagram of the** Surveyor-General of the plot **of land wherein His Excellency has been pleased** to recommend the grant **of this site for the use of the Society, and the** Society having inspected the **same, and selected that part** therein the most suited to their purpose, directed **the Treasurer to communicate** such their selection to the Honorable **the Executive Council, and** request their acquiescence **in the** same.

W. W. BALDWIN,
Treasurer

Michaelmas Term, 8 George IV., November, 1827. The Treasurer reported that he had as yet received **no definite answer** from the Executive Council relative to the application of the **Society, for** the selected **part** of the land described in the diagram alluded to in the proceedings of the Convocation held the 23rd day of April last, upon which, after some deliberation, it was deemed most prudent to suspend that application for the present, and that in the meantime the Attorney-General be requested to inquire how far the application for a site in Russell Square might be acceptable to the Government.

Hilary Term, 8 George IV., 11th January, 1828, Criminal Court **House. The Society directs** the Treasurer to request the Attorney-General **in their name to renew the application for the portion of ground at the site of the old Government buildings.**

W. W BALDWIN,
Treasurer.

Trinity Term, 9 George IV. A site for erection of a hall was described **and inquiry as to value of those offered** by Mr. Mercer and the Attorney-General was recommended.

Trinity Term, 2nd May, 1828. It was unanimously Resolved, that the **purchase of** six acres of land from the Attorney-General in front of his **Park lot be carried** into effect without delay, the sum agreed for by the **Society** with him being £1,000. Resolved also, that the Attorney General, the Solicitor-General, Doctor Baldwin, Mr. Ridout, and Mr. Macaulay be a committee of management for approving a plan, making contracts, and superintending the erection of a building.

W. W. BALDWIN,
Treasurer.

THE LAW SOCIETY.

Trinity Term, 9 George IV. At Convocation held on 26th day of June, 1828. Present :

William W. Baldwin, Treasurer.
John B. Robinson, Esquire, **Attorney-General.**
Henry John Boulton, Esquire, Solicitor-General.
John Rolph, Esquire.

The necessity of building a hall and chambers for the use of the Society was discussed.

The Attorney-General proposed that a hall and buildings sufficient for the present purposes of the Society, not to exceed £3,000 in expense, and to form the central edifice of future buildings, to be extended laterally as the increase of the Society may hereafter require, should be undertaken.

The Solicitor-General proposed a smaller building, which might cost about £700, to be built near to the street, for the present purpose of the Society, and at a future day answering some other subordinate use of the Society.

The proposal of the Attorney-General was approved, and a plan to that extent for that purpose was desired to be obtained.

The result of this resolution was, the building of Osgoode Hall which was carried on under the superintendence of the Treasurer. This was the beginning of that handsome pile, now the seat of the Superior Courts and the headquarters of the Society whose small beginning I have described, which now has its hundreds of members, where it then had tens.

XXXIII.

THE ADVOCATES SOCIETY.

HE old Barristers were not unmindful of the Students. I find that even before the Incorporation of the Law Society, they had created a Society called the Advocates Society, which was a kind of mock Court where legal questions were discussed after the manner of Parliamentary debates in procedure, and judicial solemnity in practice. Sir Adam Wilson, late Chief Justice, has recently presented to the Law Society a manuscript book from which I make extracts, as they will be found of interest not only to the professional but to the lay reader. I give the proceedings of the Advocates Society which are on record in the book to which I refer:

MONDAY, 20th January, 1823.

The Society met. The Journals were read. The Bencher made the following report from the Legal Sitting : On this day three several cases were argued, (1) A demurrer in an action on a bail bond. (2) Case—verdict subject to opinion of the Court in an action for slander. (3) Practice case as to service of process. The conclusion of the last case is, "After hearing counsel, held, the Rule be discharged.

A. CHEWETT, *Bencher.*

The Counsel engaged in the above cases were Robert Baldwin, Mr. Notman, and Mr. Richardson (of Messrs. Smith & Richardson).

Mr. Taylor reported that the Committee had elected Mr. Alexander Chewett, Bencher, and Mr. Richard C. Robison, Vice-Bencher.

Ordered, That the Report be received and Messieurs Chewett and Robison respectively elected Bencher and Vice-Bencher.

Mr. Baldwin, seconded by Mr. Robison, moves for leave to bring in a Rule to add ordinances to the Constitutions of St. Michael.

Several notices of motions on internal economy made.

TUESDAY, 30th January.

Mr. Baldwin, seconded by Mr. Notman, moves that Messieurs Henry Baldwin and Campbell be a Committee to wait on Mr. Bencher and request a copy of his address from the Bench. Committee report address procured, and that the Committee was directed to submit the same to the Society.

ADDRESS.

GENTLEMEN,—Mr. Dawes in his address to the Students of the Law makes the following observations: "Of all the liberal Professions there is not any so difficult to study as that of the Law. Those young gentlemen who are intended for it, after they have quitted an University or Academy, are either impeded in their researches for want of a proper instructor or they are affrighted from them by the glowing appearance of a black-lettered folio. Resolution and industry may have overcome many disadvantages, and time with perseverance may have produced good lawyers, but the greater number of Students feel their weakness and forbear a profession in which with the assistance of a tutor they might have shone with lustre and gained honor and emolument. Many men who have travelled the wilds of law without a guide to direct them, have been called to the Bar in the hope of business, and there experienced that serious truth that few of them are chosen. What they have acquired is perhaps undigested and without system. They have either accustomed themselves to use less oratory and become speakers of infinite nothing, or they have turned over the pages of an experienced commentator before they have read an elementary writer, and lost in the mazes of legal knowledge, they have raised a barrier against it, which ever after they are unable to pass; while on the contrary, had they trodden the paths which a preceptor would have marked out for them they might have come forward and made themselves useful."

So true is this, that at our own Bar we see young men, whose talents and acquirements led themselves and their friends to hope for every thing excellent in them as lawyers, but who for want of the advantages mentioned by Mr. Dawes, are neither good orators nor sound lawyers, who have acquired an inveterate hatred of "Case hunting" and a petulant and illiteral spirit arising from their own ignorance when arguing at the Bar that would disgrace the disputes of a school boy. They rely on a continual interruption of the course of the reasoning by quoting a multiplicity of cases, few of which have the least resemblance to the points in question. Analogies, on which many of the reasonings of lawyers depend, are thought of but by few, and when neglected justice is not done to the client's cause. The consequence is, that young lawyers of great talent, and some old ones too, who are thus ignorant or forgetful of their clients' interest, are astonished that others, with but half their quickness of conception, should succeed in cases apparently difficult, while they themselves in the most simple ones fail, and are disappointed and disgusted with the profession.

When young men without any guide plunge into the midst of abstruse cases without having a competent knowledge of first principles they must make use of fallacious reasoning and consequently run into error.

A habit of this nature when once gained can scarcely ever be shaken off, it grows upon them, they imagine it the true method of conducting business, and seldom or ever succeed :

"These impediments, (says Mr. Dawes) however, are not insuperable. To defeat them requires an instructor for those Students who want a knowledge of the means to the attainment of ends, and to assist them in the habit of arranging their ideas on points of law, speaking in public, and making them useful. To this end and presuming that such Students are not unacquainted with the four books of Sir W. Blackstone, and giving them credit for a proper share of general reading in history, civil, political, and ecclesiastical, I recommend them to proceed with systematic deliberation on the solution of all questions that may come the nearest to their comprehension. By seeing how these hinge they will be better able to argue them and reach in some degree that portion of legal knowledge they may be so anxious to obtain, while those who study without that previous intelligence necessary for the discussion of points either too abstruse, or for which they are not prepared, will lose their time and find themselves in the end when the hour of trial comes, as unfit for business as if they had never studied at all."

In the Courts at home mediocrity seldom or never succeeds. There are so many whose talents, perseverance, and experience have raised them high in the profession, that there can never be a want of eminent men to undertake any cause, and in consequence the rest must have no practice or retire from the Bar in oblivion. The people there have too much discernment to employ either bad counsel or an indifferent attorney.

Here there is a difference ; no professional man, however mean his abilities may be, meets with disregard altogether ; he will have something to do even though it should be little, and this will continue to be the case as long as there are few of the profession in proportion to the population of the country, and as long as few out of that few are of superior abilities. But the certainty you have of being always able to gain a competence should never allow you to submit to be among the indifferent. You should aim at a higher mark, your determination should be to arrive at nothing short of excellence, and the more perfect you become the more perfect you will wish to be. There are none here but what have talents ; there are none here whose application may not make them sound lawyers, good orators, and raise them to the highest acme of their ambition.

Let me, however, caution all those students who have joined you not to be in too great a hurry to enter into the discussions of the elder students respecting questions which are to them difficult. Let them not regret the time passed without trying their unfledged pinions, it is not lost to them, it is not expected that they should blaze on a sudden, nor is it even supposed they are acquainted with the full extent of their own powers; they will burst out when they least expect it. Let them for a while wait with patience till they acquire a sufficient knowledge of the law and of the practice of the different Courts to enable them to enter into the more simple questions with confidence. Let them in the mean time attend those Courts constantly, and observe the manner practised there of arguing points and other particulars of practice which are all necessary to give them a general idea of the proceedings in a suit, and of points on which many of the questions mooted here turn. By this they will gain experience, which is the soul of all reasoning with regard to facts, and this with a little attention and hard study will enable them in a short time to take their ground here with some hope of success, and without doubt they will be able in due time to take a side in any question here or elsewhere. It may be a difficult matter to say what time of probation would be necessary to the student before he makes his attempt; the confidence inspired by his own acquirements and perhaps a proneness to question the assertions of his brother students would best tell him when to make his debut.

Mr. Dawes says in another place:

"Before the alteration of English Terms, in the early part of the reign of Charles, the writers on Law were of great ability and their books were beneficial to the educated student. Each was his own foundation, and the number was small. They were read with distinction and the sedulous enquirer found little or no embarrassment. Scholastically bred he freely understood the author he studied. But since the general change of the Terms with all their appendages, the consequent disuse of real actions in cases of disputed rights to landed property, and the influx of personal possessions, the fruits of agriculture, manufactures, and commerce, the Law Library hath continually increased until their language hath been reduced to the mother tongue and a door opened for students to pass to the Bar without those solid acquirements found absolutely necessary to our ancestors. This hath occasioned that inundation of books which have poured in upon the profession from the Revolution to the present time. Compilations and breviaries, compendiums and vademecums, abridgments and digests catch the eye of the thirsty student. These he reads until convinced that he hath sought a phantom, and that the substance is only tangible in those writers from whom the principles and spirit of the laws can alone be derived.

Let the well grounded student therefore avoid wandering in such seducing books, and look to the law itself. The law of nature, of revelation, and of nations should be his first professional study. The Municipal or Common Law of England, consisting of general or particular customs, the Canon Law relating to the National Church as a part of the State; the Acts of Parliament and the causes and principles of Equity which are ancillary to the whole for the completion of justice, should be his second study.

Instructed by these he will be prepared for the study of countries subject to the Laws of England, the rights of persons and things public and private wrongs, with all their respective branches of particulars so as to **form one** entire science of jurisprudence, and **apply** it when called for to the **end** of practical and distributive justice.

Without this, eloquence will avail but little. It is not a flowing speed **that** will make him useful at the Bar, when **the** brilliancy of words is **obscured** by the solidity of law, **which with a plain** unvarnished tale will always find a preference.

Tully said that ' True **oratory gained a reputation with** the learned, but with the vulgar for whom it **was used, it was in little** esteem.' And Demosthenes himself says: ' **Words without deeds are empty** and insignificant, and the **more ready we seem to employ them the less credit they will meet with.**'

It is the execution of law business, and not mere talking in the **cause of** it, that will attract employ. The knowledge of the former will facilitate the latter. He who can confirm or defeat a title by his legal discernment, who is acquainted with that heart-string of the law called special pleading, or who by the fire of his conception can shape the case of his client to the spirit and letter of justice so as to affirm or regulate the questions afloat, will draw business toward him like the steel to the magnet, while the ungrounded though pleasing speaker will be lost in his own prattle and do more harm by the freedom of his speech, than good by his judgment."

It would be absurd in me to comment on this, there is so much good sense, so much truth, and so much discernment shewn through the whole, that it is of itself my best excuse for quoting so largely, and should what I have already extracted induce you to look at the original I will deem myself amply **rewarded.**

To benefit by **the instructions to be derived from your books or from those** persons who are **to direct your course in the intricate study of the law, or even to argue here with any hope of** success, requires that **you should have your mind free from all** boisterous passions, nothing should disturb you, **nothing take your attention from** the continued **contemplation of those great principles on which** you are to build your legal structure.

Tranquility is desirable **to aid you in your studies, and to form any decision of importance it requires a calm unbiassed mind ; when your judgment is to bear on any intricate point it must be of** the utmost importance. I do not mean that stupid insensibility which weakens the **judgment,** but a strict attention to your legal affairs and an absence from **foolish pleasures and other unnecessary pursuits which** too frequently **keep the mind in a continual ferment, and are the** destroyers of all **reflection.**

If you have **at heart the respectability of that** Bar to which **you expect** to be called, if you prefer to rise in the world by practising **there, if you wish that** your continued **labours in the** causes committed to your charge may be tempered by the amusement and satisfaction of a cultivated mind arising **from** the sound reasoning and eloquence of your contemporaries, and if **you wish these** contemporaries and their successors to esteem and admire **your** judgment and abilities, now is the time to acquire that eloquence, excellence, and discernment which is to enliven your future prospects ; you may well then be open to every situation in your **country** however high, **and** you may be **one** day its brightest **ornaments.**

On the motion of Mr. Baldwin, the Bencher **was** thanked for this address.

The next entry is **an account of moneys received and disbursed** during Michaelmas Term, amounting to the prodigious sum of twelve shillings, five pence half-penny. One of the disbursements **was :**

Cash paid over **to Messrs. Phelps** and Adams, *Commissioners of the Board of Exchequer*, *to the use of the Treasury.*

Everything seems to have been conducted on the loftiest **principles of** Parliamentary or Inns of Court procedure. **It was** resolved, "That there remains in the Treasury for **last Term the sum of** two shillings and five pence half-penny."

THURSDAY, 20th February, 1823.

The Advocate moves **that the name of George S. Jarvis,** on the black **side of** the roll, be marked called: **also, that the names** John Low, George **Boswell,** James King, Pluto Hawley, **and David L. Fairfield be** engrossed **on the** black side of the roll.

The Prothonotary reports that he did, on the 13th February, 1823, under the direction of the Benchers, file in his office a book, pursuant to an Act entitled, "**An Ordinance to prevent** too hasty a determination **to** admit as members of **this** Society others than students-at-law."

Mr. Smith **gives** notice that he will, on 28th February, instant, **move** to extend **the benefits of this** Society to others as well as students-at-law.

Mr. Baldwin gives notice **that** he will, on some future day, move for **a** Select Committee to take **into** consideration the expediency and **propriety** of admitting others than students-at-law to seats in the Society.

7th March, 1823.

Mr. Baldwin moved his resolution for **extending the benefits of this institution to** others than students-at-law. **The resolution was** then read **pursuant to the** Ordinance.

This question of admitting others than students to the benefits of the Society seems to have agitated the Society to its centre. The cause of the whole matter seems to have been that that clever young man Robert **Baldwin Sullivan,** who afterwards became famous as one of the foremost politicians of the Province, **and** Judge, was knocking at the door of the Society to be enrolled on its books. Here is his petition:

YORK, March 21st, 1823.

TO THE LEARNED THE ADVOCATE SOCIETY:

The Petition of **Robert Baldwin Sullivan**, of the Town of York, Gentleman, respectfully sheweth:

That your Petitioner is a **Clerk** duly articled to William Warren Baldwin, Esquire, one of the Attorneys of His Majesty's Court of King's Bench, in and for this Province: that your Petitioner, from unavoidable circumstances, has been prevented from making application to the Law Society for admission on their books as a Student-at-law; but that your Petitioner, so soon as he can render himself capable of passing the usual examination before the Benchers of that Society, intends to make such application; and that your Petitioner, in the mean time, is desirous of becoming a member of your Society. Your Petitioner therefore prays: that your learned Society will take into consideration the peculiar circumstances in which he is placed, and if consonant to the spirit of your Constitution, and consistent with the independence of your learned Society, that you will take such measures as may be necessary to admit your Petitioner to a seat in your Society. And your Petitioner will ever pray.

Mr. Baldwin and Mr. Robinson were supporters of this petition, while Mr. Richardson, on 29th March, 1823, moved that the Select Committee appointed to take into consideration the expediency of admitting other than Students of this Society be dissolved, and that the Society do now resolve itself into a Committee of the whole for that purpose. Which was lost; and the yeas and nays being called, were as follows:

Yeas.	Nays.
Mr. Richardson.	Messrs. Robinson.
	Baldwin.
	Radenhurst.
	Givins,
	Notman,
	Ridout,
	Henry Baldwin.

From all of which it would appear that Master Sullivan was a very popular young man.

William Warren Baldwin sent in a certificate that Mr. Sullivan was articled to him on 18th March, 1823, and that in due time he intended to apply to the Law Society for admission. The Society required evidence to be given in proof of the facts stated in the petition. There were several motions and counter-motions made, amendments and amendments on amendments, finally the question on Mr. Baldwin's motion, that Mr. Sullivan be admitted to the Society was put, the yeas and nays taken, and Mr. Sullivan admitted by a vote on which he had a majority of one in a full house of nine members. Mr. Sullivan's case caused more commotion, underwent more discussion, and seems to have exercised more voting power than any question that ever came before the Society The question crops up meeting after meeting till finally the petitioner was safely lodged in the Society to stay.

There is a quaint entry in the minutes of the 8th April, 1823. It is this:

> The Bencher informs the Society that Mr. Robert Baldwin has resigned the keys of the Treasury.
> A. CHEWETT, *Bencher.*

Here is another under the same date:

> Mr. Advocate Richardson brought down a message from the Bencher, which having read in his place he delivered at the table, and it was read as follows:
> The Bencher informs the Society that Mr. John Fennings Taylor has resigned the Prothonotaryship.
> A. CHEWETT, *Bencher.*

From the minutes of April 15th, 1823, it appears that this Society was instituted about 1821, and had gradually increased until in 1823, it was composed of students residing in most parts of the Province. That in the infancy of this Institution points of law and such other general questions as were proposed to it by its members were argued or discussed indiscriminately. That in its present state, (1823), it is divided into two branches, one of which under the presidency of the Bencher, argues points of law, costs, demurrer, &c., the other under the Vice-Bencher, discusses nothing but general themes, each of which has its respective laws for the governance thereof.

The Society was a very useful one in its day, **a fit forerunner of the** Osgoode Legal and Literary Society, which **is of so great use in** developing **the** abilities of its members, and improving **their argumentative** and oratorical power. The **Advocates Society has gone to its rest. The** Osgoode Legal **and Literary Society has in full** measure filled its **place.**

Osgoode Hall, **for the education of students, has examinations and examiners. No doubt the students are** well drilled by **these means afforded** them **of getting a sound education in the law. It is to be** regretted that **there is no Law School as there once was, in the time of the Treasurership of the late Treasurer the** Honorable **John Hillyard Cameron, who took great interest in** its formation **and possible continuance. The late Chief Justice Moss was always an advocate of this** School, and the **present Treasurer, the Honorable Edward Blake,** gave it **countenance and support. It, like the Advocates** Society, **has passed away. A writer, a member of the** Bar, in **1880, published in** *The Canadian Monthly,* reasons which **occurred to him as ground for its** re-establishment. **I quote his contribution to the** Magazine, **as it contains many matters worthy of consideration. He says:**

> The enlightened Province of Ontario, in the study of the law is at a standstill. Look at the neighbouring Republic, the decisions of whose Courts are beginning to have weight in our own; whose schools, and none more than those of law, are sending forth men who guide the councils of half a world, who are able to contend in diplomacy with the sages of Europe; whose suggestions are no longer lightly considered in the social and political countries of Christendom. It is a common failing among Englishmen, a failing reproduced in Canadians, to laugh at the American Republic and her institutions—while young—she has now reached her majority, though at an early age her efforts were no doubt feeble and, like those of the school-boy, did not compare favorably with those of the graduate. But we need only turn our attention to the Law School of Columbia College, in New York City, and the departments of Law in the Universities of Harvard, Yale, and Michigan, to find institutions worthy of our consideration, and challenging our imitation, if we are only wise.
>
> In Albany School is such an institution as could be established by the Law Society of Ontario, which should have, to quote from the Curriculum

of that School, "a higher aim than simply teaching young men the law." It should use its best endeavors to teach those who are intending to enter the profession to be lawyers. This is **an arduous** and difficult task. It is training the mind to a right use of its **own faculties.** It is giving it a **power** over its own resources, and enabling **it fully to** avail itself of its own stores of knowledge.

This is to be accomplished in a variety of ways,—principally **by accustoming** the young **man to** do that as a student which will **be required of** him as a lawyer. **We are** fast approaching either the confederation **of the** British Empire, or the independence of the Dominion of **Canada.** We are either to form part of a vast empire, which will **be bound together by** laws as yet unformulated, or **we are to** become a Dominion, and **one of** the powers of the **earth, recognized as** an independent, self-governing body, **and amenable to the laws** between nation and **nation; and yet** notice **the total want of instruction** in international law; **notice the want of instruction in the** science and the art of law in all **our institutions. Our Legislative Halls** resound with the labors of law **makers.**

Ignorantia legis non excusat is echoed by Judge after **Judge, and yet there is** no centre of legal thought.

To quote again from the Albany **Law School circular:**

The student of **medicine and surgery can resort to schools** in which he **can** be thoroughly instructed in **all the principle branches** of his profession; while the student **of law enjoys few opportunities** of acquiring more than he is enabled to **obtain by reading in a lawyer's office.**

Who is to blame for this want, which will soon become an urgent **necessity? Who is to blame for the total want of** any instruction in the **subjects which lead to the degree of Barrister-at-Law?**

By turning to the *Canada Law Journal* of March, 1878, we find as follows:

The consideration of the report of the Committee on the Law School was taken up.

Moved, That the Law School be abolished and cease, from and after the last day of Easter Term next.

Moved, in amendment, That the further consideration of the report of **the Committee on the** Law School be postponed **until the first meeting of** Convocation in Hilary Term next, and that **it be referred to the said** Committee, and the Comnitee on Legal Education, in the meantime, to **confer** with the authorities of the University of Toronto, with a view to **the affiliation** of the Law School with **that** University, **and to** consider such amendments in the system **of legal education** as may appear to be desirable; the said Committee **to report to** Convocation at the same meeting—Lost.

The original motion was then carried.

The writer in *The Canadian Monthly,* to which I have referred, concluding **his** contribution to the magazine said:

Notice the wording of the amendment, "to confer with the authorities of the University of Toronto with a view to affiliation of the Law School with that University." There can be but little doubt that the authorities of Toronto University would have raised no serious objection to affiliation. They might have been so induced as to have **taken** into consideration a partial alteration of their course to the degree of LL.B., so that, on proceeding to the degree of Barrister-at-Law, by a little **extra** exertion, the degree of LL.B. could have been obtained. The committee also were "to consider such **amendments in the** system of legal education as might appear desirable."

The Law Society of Ontario is a wealthy **institution**. At a meeting of the Benchers, in February last, **the** financial report for **the year 1878, as** adopted, shews that the Society had: invested in Dominion **5 per cent.** stock, $50,000 ; in the Government Savings Bank at 4 per cent., **$5.800 ;** besides a large balance, bearing 4 per cent., in the Bank of **Toronto, and** recommends "that the further sum of $10,000 be invested in **Dominion stock, so as to increase the permanent** reserve of the Society to $60,000." The receipts for that year shew the notice **fees as** amounting to $687 ; **students' admission fees, $8,940 ; Attorneys'** examination fees, **$4,350 ; call fees, $6,330—making the handsome total of $20,307,** which together with the other receipts, make up the immense sum of $42,504. The expenditure for that year was $36,233. The surplus on the whole year's operation was $6,361. Thus, at a glance, it may be seen that the students' fees lack only $990 of being the half of the total receipts for the year. Have any of those contributing to that magnificent sum received any return from the Society in the way of instruction?

Each student-at-law pays into the coffers of the Law Society, at the very least, $225 in his course ; and what return does he **receive?** It will be answered, he is to be permitted to practise in the Courts of the Province. Is it forgotten that he will have to pay $17 a year for that privilege? Is it, also, forgotten that he will be taxed for the support of those Courts?

Let the students who are junior members, and who are contributing to the standing of this wealthy Society, demand, in tones not to be misunderstood, a method **of instruction founded on correct principles, and** with the design of instructing them **in the** art as well as the science of the law ; of fitting them **to** enter at once upon the successful practice of the profession ; a course of instruction which will qualify them to take a position in the councils of their country, and enable them to contend not unworthily at the diplomatic board with their **rivals.**

Happily, as I write these **last pages** this reproach is in a fair way of being removed, or **at least** remedied, by the Law Society. An arrangement is being made by the University of Toronto to establish a Law Chair and the Law Society is, none too early, about to admit graduates of the degree to be granted by that University, under suitable regulations, to the degree of Barrister-at-Law.

The Law Society, while it has not founded the Law School, has lent willing aid to the scheme put forward by the University, and we can look forward to greater facilities being given to students, who have been too long deprived of that means of sound education of which they have been so unfortunately deprived in the past.

XXXIV.

Conclusion—Reminiscences

AN actor who has finished his play leaves the stage, but with a lingering look at the footlights. This is my case in arriving at what is intended to be the last chapter in the Lives of the Judges.

I have written of old Judges, old Barristers, old Benchers and Judges of the near and distant past. I have referred to some cases, too, cases in which I was either concerned myself or can tell something about. I have not in the Lives disfigured the narration with any of those little incidents I have known to occur that bear evidence to the wit of the Judges, counsel, or witnesses, which often comes out in Courts of Justice. I did not think it right to disturb the dignity of the Court with these matters, not necessary to the decision of the cause.

In this chapter I am off my dignity, and will recall to mind, and give to the reader something in the nature of dessert at a banquet, or after-piece to a play.

I remember being in a case some years ago at Woodstock, in which I was junior counsel, and the present Chief Justice Hagarty was the counsel on the opposite side. The case was Kerby *vs.* Finkle, and was an action, if I remember right, of slander or libel. The incident I intend to relate, which occurred in this case, will shew that our old Barristers had wit as well as wisdom in their day. My senior counsel, a well known

Barrister of his day and a Queen's Counsel, had very red hair and a partially bald head. In addressing the jury, he took occasion to say that the defendant's case (Mr. Hagarty was counsel for the defendant) was so weak that the defendant had found it necessary for strengthening it to import into the County of Oxford most eminent Counsel—the leader of the Bar; in fact, the *flower of the profession!* I thought this very good; but when Mr. Hagarty stood up to address the jury for the defence, he, in a quiet way, commenced by disavowing all the compliments paid him by the opposing counsel in his address, then, gently placing his hands just on the head of my senior counsel, who was sitting near him and in front of the jury, as if warming his hands, he said: "I protest, gentlemen of the jury: I do not claim to be the 'flower of the profession,' but I do say that beneath my outspread hands there sits the *Sun-flower* of the profession." This was too much. I felt that sally of wit of Mr. Hagarty had hopelessly destroyed our hope of success. And so it did! The jury were carried away by the joke, and speedily returned a verdict for the defendant. It is not too much to say that at the Bar Mr. Hagarty was the wittiest counsel of his day. It is hard for him to restrain it on the Bench: he has many a temptation to give it range, but official dignity forbids.

It is pleasant at times to recall conversations with those of the old Bar; especially those who, in the early history of the Province, had a circuit practice.

The late Henry John Boulton was one of that class. It is he whose name we find as being consulted by the Advocates Society about the propriety of admitting others than students as members. Mr. Boulton was, in his younger days, frequently Crown Officer, and used to go the circuit on horse back, with the regulation saddle bags. This seems to have been the mode in which not only lawyers, but preachers, made their circuits in the early days of the Province.

Mr. Boulton, on one occasion, related to me an incident

which occurred to him which affected me, as it must have affected him at the time, with amusement. Going to London on circuit business duty many years ago, on horse back, he met a man on the roadway three miles from London. The man touched his hat to Mr. Boulton, and said to him: "Be you the King's Attorney?"—"Yes, I am," said Mr. Boulton: "What do you want with me?" "Well!" said the man, "I am in jail for horse stealing, and I want to be tried." How the man came to be *in* jail for horse stealing, and he three miles from the jail, I leave the reader to guess. Mr. Boulton used to tell the story with considerable gusto. It impressed itself on my recollection.

Sir John Robinson, on an occasion when I was travelling with him going from Cobourg to Toronto, related how once when a young man, before the War of 1812, he was sent with despatches from Kingston to Cornwall. When he got to Brockville he was hungry, and in need of refreshment. The mistress of the hotel at Brockville where he stopped stated to her guest that he came to her house unexpectedly; she just then had no fresh meat in the larder. However, an hour after, the table was spread, and fresh lamb set before Sir John. At this he expressed his surprise, and said to her: "I thought you said you had no fresh meat, Mrs. ———." "And so I did," she said; "but since you came to the house I have had a lamb killed, and I am glad to set it before you. I would be sorry if you had to leave my house without fresh meat." It took the good hostess but one hour to receive her guest, have a sheep killed, and give him a good dinner off young lamb. Mr. William Henderson, of the Hartford Insurance Company, who was in the carriage with us travelling from Cobourg to Toronto with the Chief Justice and myself, have often reminded each other of this story of Sir John Robinson's, citing it as an instance of the rough and ready life of the early settlers.

Speaking of Sir John, I remember an incident connected with a case he was trying at Cobourg some years

CONCLUSION. 465

ago, which afforded much amusement to the Bar and to the audience, but sorely tried the patience of the Chief Justice. Upwards of thirty years ago, in a Crown case at the Court held at the Cobourg Court House, then on the hill outside the Town of Cobourg, one Weller had been subpœnaed as a witness for the Crown. The Weller to whom I refer was a fisherman of the Carrying Place, at the head of the Bay of Quinte. It was the custom in those days, when a person trespassed on the supposed rights of the fishermen, to summarily punish the culprit by making him run the gauntlet, as it was called; that is, a double line of fishermen was formed, the offender placed at the head, and given a chance to run between the lines to the opposite extremity, if he could, without receiving a sound bastinadoing from the fishermen, each of whom was armed with his oar or other weapon, with which to belabor the gauntlet runner. The prosecutor in the Crown case had been served in some such way, and the prisoner put on his trial for the offence. It was deemed necessary to make Mr. Weller a Crown witness, though it was strongly suspected that he was himself implicated. Mr. Weller was of the true cut of a Carrying Place fisherman: he was in fisherman's dress, long, black, unkempt hair flowing over his shoulders and parted in the middle. Before the trial came on the prisoner's friends had learned that Mr. Weller was to be a Crown witness, and they deemed it necessary in the interests of the prisoner that he should be treated to something stronger than raspberry vinegar before taking the stand, and treated him accordingly till his brain became so excited that he would interlard everything he had to say with protestations, strange oaths, and modern instances. The case came on, the Court House full, the Chief Justice, Sir John Robinson, presiding. The witness, Weller, came to the stand, which was an elevated one just to the right of the presiding Judge. Then this scene occurred:

CROWN COUNSEL (to witness)—What is your occupation, witness?

59—L. J.

Weller (witness)—Well, when I am **at home** I am a fisherman down at the Carrying Place.

Crown Counsel—Relate what **occurred** there on the day in question between the prisoner and the prosecutor.

Witness—A good deal occurred ; **the** prosecutor was there, I was there and **I guess** a good deal more **was there**.

Crown Counsel—State what happened.

Witness (with an **oath—Can't** you **wait** (hic-cup)? and I'll tell all about it—

Chief Justice—Witness, **remember you are in a Court of justice, and** you are not to swear.

Witness—Well, **go on.**

Crown Counsel—State now what occurred.

Witness—Oh, **what occurred.** Well (a large oath) you know—

Chief Justice—I have told you before **you** were not to swear. I am **afraid you have been drinking, witness. I** advise **you to** be cautious, or **you will get into trouble. I** will commit you **if you swear again.**

Witness—Judge, you can fine, but you can't **commit—**

Chief Justice—Be careful, **witness.** The ends **of justice** require that **what you know of the** matter **should** be given in **evidence, but if** you **swear again the** Court will certainly commit you.

Crown Counsel—Now witness **be calm. I just want you to relate what took place.**

Witness—Well, the Prisoner, that is we, not **the** prisoner, made the **prosecutor run the gauntlet, that we did—yes by**—(a very large oath), **we made him run the gauntlet, we did by**—(another great oath).

At this stage the Chief Justice could not endure it any longer, and so ordered the Sheriff to commit witness Weller to the cells for twenty-four hours for contempt of Court, whereupon Mr. Weller, looking down upon the audience from his elevated position, exclaimed in a loud audible voice to the whole Court. " Well, ha'nt I brought my fish to a pretty market."

The Chief Justice felt that the witness had been tampered with, and for a long time patiently endured his insolence, till at last the propriety of the law absolutely required that he should send Mr. Weller to the cells, and so the witness "stepped down and out." *Sic exit*, Mr. Weller.

It is not often that witnesses have a verdict rendered against them by the jury. It is generally a verdict for plaintiff or defendant, but in a case in which I was counsel on one occasion at Berlin, in the County of Waterloo, tried before Judge Burns, several young men were called who very much defamed the daughter of the plaintiff, who was a witness for her father, stating that they personally knew of conduct of hers, which if true was as disgraceful to the young men, as to the young girl. In my address to the jury in reply, I referred in pointed terms to the disgraceful evidence given by the young men witnesses, and said it ought not to be believed, but if true the young men should be made to pay damages as well as the defendant. I did not of course mean that in that case then being tried damages should be awarded against the witnesses. The jury, however, mostly Dutchmen of the county, retired to the jury room, and in a short time returned and handed up to the Judge a piece of paper on which was entered their verdict, which was, "Verdict for the plaintiff $100 damages against the defendant, and the witnesses to pay $25 apiece." This was truly a Dutch verdict. As, however, the Judge who smiled when he read the paper, could not receive such a verdict, he ordered the jury to withdraw, and I was content to have a verdict for the $100 against the defendant, excusing the witnesses for that occasion.

Another incident occurred during my professional career which struck me as very extraordinary, and to which a parallel is not likely to occur again. It was in the days when John Doe had not yet departed his legal existence. It happened that at the Norfolk Assizes a case came on of Doe Walker *vs.* Walker. I was counsel for one of the parties. The case caused a good deal of interest owing to the fact that it was a contest about property. Judge Draper was the Judge of Assize, and took a great deal of judicial interest in its determination. It happened after a prolonged trial and an admirable charge from the Judge, that the jury was unable to agree, and the time for adjourning the Court arriving, the Judge adjourned the Court to his rooms at the Norfolk House in Simcoe, at nine o'clock in the evening, when he would receive the verdict of the jury, if they had then agreed.

At the appointed time the jury filed into the hotel followed by my client, the plaintiff or defendant in the suit, I don't remember which. Suffice it to say, that my client won his suit. The jury marching to the Judge's room declared their verdict. My client was so much pleased, that forgetting the respect due to the Court, and I believe honestly thinking that the verdict was due to the Judge's charge, the verdict being recorded, thought he would shew his appreciation by an act of Canadian hospitality. So as the jury were retiring after rendering their verdict, he walked forward approaching the Judge and beckoned to him to come forward. The Judge said, "Who are you sir, what do you want?" The suitor meeting the Judge said, "Judge, what will you have to drink?" The Judge was thunderstruck, and said to the suitor, "How dare you, sir, make such a proposition. You had better leave this as quickly as possible." My poor client retreated accordingly, thoroughly convinced that the Canadian law, although inclined to justice, was not yet satisfactorily liberalised. I very much incline to think that if a matter of this kind were to occur at the present day the offender would be committed for contempt.

I have often been upset in my time, but I think never more so than on one occasion travelling on circuit in a sleigh hired by Chief Justice Robinson to take him from Belleville to Cobourg on his circuit. The Chief Justice was always very considerate, and invited me, who had held some briefs at the Belleville Assizes, to share his sleigh. When within about three miles of Cobourg just before daylight, we were suddenly surprised to find ourselves at a standstill. Enquiring the cause we found that our driver had gone to sleep, the horses had in some way got detached from the sleigh, and had left us and the sleigh in a ditch at the side of the road. I never can forget this sight. There was the Chief Justice in a ditch. I at once recognized my unpleasant duty, to walk into Cobourg for assistance. I did walk into Cobourg, but fortunately the Chief Justice was rescued by the driver, who when awake

CONCLUSION.

was equal to the occasion in procuring assistance to carry the Court to the next Assize Town of Cobourg.

I dare say most of the Bar have had the same experience I have had in regard to witnesses. Barristers do not have it all their own way when examining witnesses: they often meet their match, and sometimes more than their match. In a case at the Hamilton Assizes, many years ago I was counsel in a murder trial. A young woman was brought from the cells of the jail, where she had been incarcerated for some minor offence, to give evidence. She testified that she knew a man in some way mixed up with the affair, and as evidence of identity described him as a tall man, and otherwise described his dress and features. I confess to having entered on a severe cross-examination of this witness, thinking to confound her testimony, and at last I said to her, "Now, witness, you say the man was a tall man, now how tall was he?" Looking down from the witness box on myself, who have no claim to be called a tall man, she answered, "Well, sir, to tell you the truth the man was really a tall man, *about your size.*" I thought the repartee so good, that short as I was, I believe I lost something of height, and the Court something of its dignity!

Judicial humour is so common that instances of it are heard every day, but never more frequently than when Judge Sullivan was in the Common Pleas. I was told once of a witticism of his, partially at my own expense. Doctor Connor and I were arguing before the Court. He was prematurely gray, with an abundance of rather long hair, which was rather white than gray, while I at the time had black hair and whiskers, and was rather spare of person. The Judge meditatively contemplated the counsel, and at last asked his brother Judges if they were not strangely reminded of Sir Walter Scott's novels. With surprise the brothers asked which novels,—" Old Mortality " and " The Black Dwarf," said the witty Judge, when his brothers had to admit that the point was well taken.

Robert A. Harrison was not often the cause of merriment in others, but one day the Court got the best of him. He had on a previous day argued in support of a certain point of law, and on this day was dangerously near supporting the other side of the proposition. Chief Justice Richards asked him if he had forgotten his previous contention. Mr. Harrison tried to get away from the question, but the Chief Justice, firmly holding him to the point, said with crushing plainness: " Mr. Harrison—There is a country saying that 'it is hard to chew meal, and whistle at the same time.'"

I think I will not give any more of my personal reminiscences lest the reader may subject me to the criticism of importing into a work of this character something foreign to the principal subject, and relating to myself.

If, during the progress of the work, I have appeared too frequently on the scene, it has only been because my long experience at the Bar has given me so many opportunities of being an actor in the professional proceedings of the past, that I could not bring the suit to a termination without calling up many witnesses, myself among the number.

APPENDIX.

LETTERS OF JOHN O'CONNOR, ESQ., M.P., ON FENIANISM.

ENGLAND'S DUTY.

To His Excellency, the Right Honorable Sir John Young, Bart., P. C., G. C. B., G. C. M. G,, Governor General of Canada, &c., &c., &c.

YOUR EXCELLENCY,—I take the liberty of addressing you through the public press, because although the subject which I desire to bring under your immediate notice is one of vital importance to the public and the Government of this country, and although I am a Member of Parliament, yet I have no constitutional right to tender to Your Excellency privately any advice or suggestion relative to the affairs of this country.

Another attempt, as senseless and futile as it was wicked, has been made to disturb the peace of the country, for the avowed purpose of subverting its Government and establishing in lieu thereof something called an "Irish Republic." This last attempt was again weak as usual, so weak, so evanescent, as to have the appearance of a feint rather than of an intended invasion. But the consequences to this country are, nevertheless, serious. The extreme difficulty, or rather the impossibility of ascertaining in advance the precise magnitude of the threatened invasion, coupled with the rumors invariably set afloat, produces a vague apprehension that the preparations and means of the invaders are commensurate with the end proposed to be effected and the dread of being over-run by marauding bands, who, being subject to no law, no recognized authority, are free from the restraints of all civilized codes, produces panic. I mean not a panic of cowardice, but that which magnifies the danger, and causes greater and more costly preparations than turn out to have been absolutely necessary.

The choicest of the male population are withdrawn from their ordinary avocations; business is neglected, disjointed, and partly paralyzed; and capital which would otherwise naturally flow into, is averted from the country. Great expense is also necessarily incurred; and worse than all else, **unjust suspicion** and consequent distrust of a large and important **class of the people of** Canada—the Irish Catholics—are entertained, and **ill-will** towards them is engendered.

Yet I **verily** believe, indeed I am certain, that, taken as a body, no in this country is more industrious and contented, **nor** is any more loyally attached to the Constitution, the Government, and the Institutions of Canada, than are the Irish **Catholics.**

For the present, however, I **pass this over, and proceed to** the object which I have mainly **in view.** The **results to which I have** referred have recurred frequently **during the six years past.** In fact we have been at **no time** during the period altogether free of the apprehension of danger from the same source.

When is it to end? **Shall we continue to be vexed in** the same way **during an unlimited period?** Surely it is not to be tolerated, if a practical **remedy may be evoked.** I think there must be a remedy for the evil. **I am convinced there is.**

What strikes one as the most extraordinary feature of Fenianism in the United States is, that the Fenians are recognized citizens of that country, with which our relations, both national and social, are friendly. They make no secret of their hostile designs on Canada. They hold public meetings, great and small, and use the public press of that country to advocate their designs and propagate their doctrine in the presence and hearing and within the knowledge of the Government of the United States. They openly avow and boastingly proclaim their purpose to levy unprovoked war against the people of Canada, under colour of the sham pretence of giving liberty to Ireland—a pretence so intensely absurd as to excite no other feeling than one of absolute contempt.

Alas, poor Ireland! Knaves, speculating knaves, are but desecrating thy name to enable them to prey upon the feelings of the warm-hearted, patriotic, and generous sons and daughters, and to filch from them the proceeds **of their hard labour, their honest** earnings. But the real **purpose, the secret** purpose **underlying the** pretences **of** the Fenian ringleaders is not what I **propose to consider.**

Be their real **design what it may, they are permitted in** their course, without any **attempt** at secresy, **to organize bands of** men, to perform military evolutions, to acquire arms, **equipments, military** stores, and to use the public means of conveyance **for transporting them** from place to **place in** the United States.

They adopt and use military **titles** corresponding with those of the **army of the United** States, perform all the functions, and assume the **attributes of** a regular constituted military **power.** In fact, they **have been, and they are** an "imperium in imperio," constituted and organized **ostensibly for** the invasion of Canada.

If all this were **permitted in** relation to Great Britain, and with a view to the overthrow of British power in Ireland, it could be understood, even **though it could not** be justified by the law of nations. But in relation to **Canada the case is** wholly different. It is simply a crime which nothing can excuse or extenuate. History presents no case of like political turpitude. It stands alone—is in the strictest sense "sui generis"—and for obvious reasons.

Canada, or the people of Canada, are in no way responsible for misgovernment, past or present, or for oppression, real or imaginary, in Ireland. On the contrary, Canada is the home—the free and happy home—of many, aye, of thousands, who found it necessary to leave Ireland under circumstances tryingly adverse. Furthermore, the people of Canada, of every national origin, class, creed, and colour, are content with their lot, satisfied with and attached to the constitution, which secures to them the largest measure of rational liberty. They boast with reasonable pride of being blessed with a system of government more truly free than any other under the sun. They desire no change but such as may be effected from time to time, as circumstances require, by constitutional means. They neither desire nor will accept any impertinent interference of people who are not of them, and who are not subject to the same allegiance as they themselves are.

American Fenianism, therefore, in its designs or pretended designs on Canada, stands without that colour of justification which is claimed for, and may in some instances be accorded to those who aid or attempt to aid a people, or a large portion thereof, who complain of being oppressed and are struggling or desirous of struggling for liberty. It lacks immeasurably that justification which is claimed by the savage Indians of the Western prairies when they attack, murder, and rob the white settlers, whom they, not unnaturally, regard as intruders, and even invaders.

The savages can and do urge that they are fighting for their primeval rights. In short, Fenianism in the United States presents an anomaly which is simply hideous.

Attila, self-styled "the scourge of God," with his barbaric hordes devastated Lombardy. But he did it without false pretences, without pretending to advance the cause of political liberty. Barbarous he was, but not a sham. Not so is it with American Fenianism, and yet that is the system which has been nurtured and cherished, until it has grown and become a recognized institution in the United States—recognized apparently by the people as a power in the State, and, if not formally recognized, at least connived at and tolerated by the Government.

If France, great as her empire is, permitted such an abuse towards Great Britain, would the latter brook it? No, not even for an hour. Were Great Britain guilty of such a crime towards France instant war would be the result. When Napoleon the Third found that a few traitors, who had found refuge in England, were secretly plotting there against his life and empire, did he remain passive as if they were beyond his reach? Quite the reverse. He informed the British Government of the conspiracy, and demanded, as he had a right to demand, that immediate and effective preventive action should be taken; and it was done. Thus it should be. So, too, would it be as between any of the powers of Europe, for such is the requirements of international law. The breach of that law would produce war between any of the States of Europe, and in such a war the injured party would have the active sympathy of the other powers of the civilized world. But immeasurably more aggravated has been the illicit conduct of the United States with respect to us in the Fenian matter.

I therefore fully concur in the position assumed in recent leading articles of Toronto papers. I think the time has come when the British Government, in justice to Canada and in vindication of its own honour, should interfere diplomatically, determinedly, and unconditionally.

Canada, the largest, the most loyal, and the most important of Britain's dependencies, has a right to expect such action by the Government of the empire; and should the **worse** come of that action **Canada** will not be **backward, nor will the Irish** Catholics of the Dominion **be the** least forward in maintaining the national honour.

I am, however, strongly impressed with the belief that no **evil will follow from a stand so taken by the British** Government. I have **had, and still have favourable opportunities of** obtaining information on the **subject, and I am convinced that the better, the** more enlightened, **the wealthy and most influential of** the American people have no sympathy **with Fenianism, particularly** in its designs on Canada; on the contrary, **they disapproved of** and disliked it. I am convinced that **to** a large majority of the better class of Americans, **and** even to a large proportion of **the inferior** classes, Fenianism and Fenians are objects of derision and contempt, mingled, nevertheless, with apprehensions for the results of **the system as a political** institution in **the** United States. I have besides an irresistible conviction that if called on in the name of the law of nations, which they themselves invoked not long ago under circumstances infinitely less aggravated, the Government of the United States will enforce the observance of their neutrality laws, and so apply their police regulations as to either extinguish Fenianism, or prevent its being openly offensive and threatening towards Canada. But such a course, **and** by it only, **can** the United States evince magnanimity becoming so great a power. By it alone can they maintain an honorable **position** amongst **nations as a respecter of** the laws of nations.

In the United States, **as well** as in Canada, Vattel **is regarded as authority on** the laws of **nations;** and he states the law **on this subject as** follows:—

"The nation or the Sovereign ought not to suffer the citizens to do an **injury to** the subjects of another State, much less to offend that State **itself.** * * If a Sovereign who might keep his subjects within the rules of justice, suffers them to injure a foreign nation, either in its body or in its members, he does no less injury to that nation than if he did it himself."

And he further says :—"Since the Sovereign ought not to suffer his subjects to molest the subjects of other States, or to do them an injury, much less to give open and audacious offence to foreign powers, he ought to compel the transgressor to make reparation for the damage or injury, if possible, or to inflict on **him an exemplary** punishment; or finally, according to the nature and circumstances of the case, to deliver him up to the offended State, to be there brought to justice.

"This is pretty generally observed with respect to great crimes, which are equally contrary to the laws and safety of each and every nation. Assassins, incendiaries, and robbers are seized everywhere at the desire of the Sovereign in whose territories the crime was committed, and are delivered up to justice. The matter is carried still further in States that are more closely connected by friendship and good neighborhood.

* * * The Sovereign who refuses to cause reparation to be made for the damage done by his subject, or to punish the offender, or finally to deliver him up, renders himself in some measure an accomplice in the injury, and becomes responsible for it." So much for Vattel.

The principles, as enunciated by him, are, I doubt not, a portion of the laws of nations; and founded on the law of nature; and are in accord with the principles of universal justice.

They are necessary to the existence of sovereignties, of nations, of society, to the maintenance and advancement of civilization; of liberty, and to the peace and happiness of mankind.

Great Britain and the United States are friendly; and reasons the most weighty exist for their remaining so. But there are reasons paramount why friendship and friendly relations, not consistent with imperial right, should exist between Canada and the United States. Because, though they are governed by systems different in name, and in some degree in essence, they have nevertheless more in common to be cherished than in Christendom.

To maintain such relations is eminently the interest, and should be the aim of both. I am, therefore, unable to think so meanly of the greatness and civilization of the people of the United States, and the magnanimity of their Government, as to suppose that when properly and formally called upon, the American Government will not, according to the well understood principles by which the conduct of enlightened nations towards each other is regulated. By prohibiting their own citizens and others domiciled in their country, and claiming the protection of their laws, from openly conspiring, plotting, and devising against, and invading the people of Canada, the American Government will do but what is just, and add lustre to their own position among the nations.

I think, therefore, it is the duty of Your Excellency's Government to urge upon the Imperial Government the propriety, the necessity of presenting our case in proper terms to the American Government, and of demanding that they do justice in the premises.

I had intended to offer some remarks on Fenianism and its character, its relation to and effects upon the Irish people in Ireland, in the United States, and in Canada, but I find that this letter is already too long. I will, however, probably take the liberty of addressing to Your Excellency another letter or two on this subject.

I remain,
Your Excellency's humble servant.

Windsor, Ont., May 31, 1870.   JOHN O'CONNOR.

LETTER FROM MR. JOHN O'CONNOR, M.P., ON FENIANISM.

To His Excellency the Right Honorable Sir John **Young, Bart., P.C., G.C.B., G.C.M.G.,** *&c., &c., &c.*

YOUR EXCELLENCY,—In my **letter of the 31st ult.,** I intimated that I would probably take the liberty **of addressing to** your Excellency a letter or two on the subject of **Fenianism.**

I am impelled to **do so by the** belief that it **may be of service, not** only to the particular class to which I belong, but to the **Dominion.**

Since Fenianism in the United States assumed its position of hostility towards Canada, **the Irish** Catholics in every locality have been subjected, more **or** less, **to the suspicion,** vituperation, and contumely of **their neighbors. Of this I have had personal** knowledge in many localities, **and reliable** information **respecting the** country generally. Nor have I **myself** been **permitted wholly to escape the noxious** atmosphere of general **suspicion.**

Hitherto, I **have treated such suspicions, and the** taunts arising from them, with **silent,** but **indignant contempt; because in** the first place, I knew them **to be unfounded; and, secondly,** I considered that a little enquiry **and consideration, guided by a sense of justice,** would shew that those **suspicions were groundless** and ungenerous. Latterly, however, I have arrived **at the conclusion** that a short review of Fenianism, in the relations **mentioned in my** letter already published, **may** be not only not out of place, **but of some service to the country at the** present juncture of affairs; for I **conceive that everything which tends** to dispel **unjust** suspicion, **and to unite all classes in** patriotic sentiment, will add to our country's strength, **and enable her to grapple more** vigorously with adversity.

The existence of the suspicion to which I allude is, I **apprehend, attributable, mainly, if not wholly,** to Orangeism. This I say, **not in a** spirit **of vituperation, but simply** as a matter of observation and of political **philosophy. My object is,** not to rake up the embers of old strifes, but **to trace the wrong of which I** complain to its source, **and** elucidate my **view of it. I will try to explain** my meaning.

Orangeism, **in Canada, is a plant** from Ireland; **and** it possesses and exhibits on **the new** soil **much of, if not all,** the qualities, good and bad, which distinguished it in **the** old. Orangemen in Canada, being mostly from Ireland, possess probably **not** all, **but most of** the prejudices which **they** had in the old country, **relative** to Catholicism and Catholics. As **they** thought and reasoned there, with respect **to** Catholics and Catholicism, so they are prone to think and reason here. This is quite natural; **for a** change from one **place to** another does not, even though mighty waters roll between, change a man's nature, nor does it usually change his principles. And though his opinions and prejudices may be modified **by** the circumstances of his changed position, yet in the main they continue, at least for a long time, unchanged.

The misgovernment in Ireland which oppressed the Catholics, and **caused them to be discontented and** frequently rebellious, made the

Orangemen prosperous, contented and loyal; because the misgovernment consisted of discrimination in their favor. They were, in short, the favored and dominant class. The Government and acts of Government which were most favourable to the Orangemen, were the most oppressive **to the** Catholics. Opposition of interest created opposition of feeling, **from** which arose strife and enmity. The Orangemen being in possession of, and enjoying the favors of Government, supported it, and being **warmly** attached to that which gave them ascendancy, they attributed the opposition and discontent of the Catholics to a perverse and rebellious spirit, engendered in them by their religious principles. Hence **the** Orangemen acquired the mental habit of attributing disloyalty **to the** Catholics, as a normal condition of the Catholic mind. So, by force **of** that habit of mind, the Orangemen of Canada, and others in social **com**munion with them, have suspected the Irish Catholics of **Canada, and** attributed to them sympathy with Fenianism, by reason **of** its professed object being the liberation of Ireland from British rule. But this attribute is an *a priori* deduction from false premises. The fallacy consists of applying a conclusion deducted from premises of a certain character to premises of an entirely different character. This can, I think, be **made clear and** satisfactory.

There are two reasons of omnipotent force, why the Irish Catholics of Canada do not sympathise with Fenianism, and especially with that phase of it in the United States, **which consists of threatening** the peace of **Canada,** and marring its prosperity—two plain reasons why such a feeling should not be attributed to them.

The first is, that Fenianism is not a Catholic **institution; nor has** it the sanction or approval of Catholic authority. On the contrary, it is, in its essential characteristics, simply atheistic; and more inimical to the Catholic Church than it is to the British Government. As such, it has been condemned by the Catholic Church, both generally and specifically. This fact is unquestionable, that it is a branch of, and founded on the same principles as those revolutionary organizations known as Illuminati, Carbonari, &c., which have been so long corrupting the manners and disturbing the peace of nations on the continent of Europe; and that **it** draws its inspirations from the same source. It is part and parcel of **a** general organization formed for the purpose of producing universal revolution, of destroying all legitimate authority, **and of establishing** socialism, with its brutal licentiousness, which is held **up as the** grand ideal of pure liberty.

Therefore, the special organization called Fenianism, as soon as its existence became known and its character understood, was, as its continental parent and prototype had been, condemned by **the** Catholic Church. It was condemned by the Pope at Rome; denounced by Cardinal Cullen, the head of the Catholic hierarchy of Ireland; execrated and consigned to perdition by Doctor Moriarty, the learned, eloquent, and energetic Bishop of Kerry; and discountenanced by other Catholic Bishops and the clergy of Ireland. It received like treatment at the hands of that distinguished Englishman, Doctor Manning, Archbishop of Westminister, who is the head and ornament of the Catholic Church in England. The Catholic Bishops and clergy in England and Scotland generally, and without exception, that I know of, condemned it. In the United States it has been discountenanced by the Catholic Bishops and clergy, and denounced in strong terms by many of them. In Canada it has been universally discountenanced by the Catholic hierarchy and clergy, and denounced in language clear and strong by that eminent Irishman and Catholic prelate, the learned, amiable, and venerable Archbishop of Halifax, distinguished not only by his zeal for the interests of religion, but also for his disinterested and powerful advocacy of Confederation. Nor could anything surpass the uncompromising determination, and the energy of language and action with which the esteemed Bishop Farrel, of Hamilton, sought out, and uprooted, and crushed every germ of Fenianism in his diocese from the outset. The venerable Bishop of Toronto, too, as soon as he became aware of the real character and designs of the infamous brotherhood, placed his foot on the serpent's head. Neither has the learned and pious Bishop Walsh, of London, been backward in exhibiting towards it decided disapproval, disfavor, and dislike; while his senior Vicar-General, the venerable and plucky Father Bruyere, has never flagged in the zeal, vigilance, and determination with which he has labored to expose its character, and prevent its obtaining a foothold in the diocese; and in this his example has been followed successfully by all the clergy.

Strictly in accord with all this has been the practice of the Church; so much so, that no person avowing himself, or known to be a Fenian, has been permitted to partake of her sacraments, or other consolations usually administered to the faithful.

In Buffalo, one of the hot-beds of Fenianism in the United States, the rite of Christian burial has been denied to Fenians after death; and the same has been done elsewhere; and it would be done everywhere if the friends of deceased Fenians presumed to require the rite. Such being the state of the case, it is, I apprehend, too clear to admit of doubt that no Catholic, be he Irish or not, who is attached to his Church, and guided by her teaching, can be a Fenian, or harbor sympathy for Fenianism, after he learns and understands its character. By the mere fact of joining that society, the Catholic incurs the censure of the Church, and ceases to be of her, until he recants.

I desire not, however, to be understood as denying that Catholics have become Fenians. Undoubtedly many Irish Catholics in Ireland and the United States joined the organization, allured thereto by artful appeals to those feelings of dislike for and hatred of British rule in Ireland, which centuries of misrule and oppression had engendered in the minds of most Irish Catholics. But those who were so allured were the unreflecting, many of them generous and patriotic people, who became an easy prey to wiles of initiated knaves and demagogues, most of whom made the whole affair a matter of speculation for profit's sake. Yet these poor dupes, without knowing it, in most instances without even thinking of it, in the excitement and tumult of their roused feelings, forfeited that which, under other circumstances, would be to them of the highest moment, the sanction and favor of their Church—of that Church for adhering to which their forefathers, if not themselves, had endured all the wrongs and sufferings, the memory of which was so adroitly urged to them as an incentive for joining an organization whose principles involve the destruction of that Church as its ultimate and chief object. The Catholics of Ireland, in days gone by, and not long gone, endured the proscriptions of the penal code because they would be Catholics; because they valued the Church and their faith above all earthly treasures; and they adhered to and cherished both when to do so was to incur privation and death. Are they likely now to exchange that Church and its faith for Fenianism—a living branch of the most subtle and deadly enemy with which Christianity has to cope? I think not, except by the ignorant, the unwary, or the malevolent. Thus it has been in Canada. At the outset, when little or nothing was known of the real value of the thing, emissaries from the United States, by representing that the sole end and aim of the order was the liberation of Ireland from British misrule, by reviving the memory of the past wrongs, and by seductive appeals to the feelings thus excited, did succeed, but to a very limited extent, with some of the poorer, but industrious and simple-minded class of Irishmen in Toronto, Montreal, and Quebec city, and duped them for a while. But even this partial success of those imps of Satan was of short duration. The alarm was sounded by poor McGee, who ultimately fell a sacrifice to his zeal. He had had peculiar means of learning the real character of the organization; and his eloquent tongue and powerful pen put the clergy instantly on the alert. The truth became known, and was proclaimed by the sentinels from the watch towers of the Church, and the Irish Catholics who had been allured to partake of the forbidden fruit spewed it out, and cast it from them. A few calling themselves Catholics did otherwise, but they were strayed sheep, foolish ones, who preferred to stray in the wolf's domain.

The second reason, or that, why the Irish Catholics in Canada do not sympathize with Fenianism, in its designs on Canada, is as obvious as the first.

Canada is a free country: there is none more so. Her freedom is real, it is rational, sound, and stable; liberty without licentiousness; restraint without abuse; protection without discriminative favor or its attributes. The constitution is one of wisdom, not empirical, but the product of experience and of practical statesmanship. Its provisions which secure to us the glorious privilege of self-government, are equable and just. Equal rights are secured to all men and classes of men indiscriminately. There is no distinction, no preference. The institutions of the country are in accord with the spirit and character of the constitution, liberal, sound, and healthy. Life, personal liberty, and the rights of property are secured by wholesome laws, impartially administered. Industry and good citizenship are fostered. The country's natural resources are various and immense; fields for the exercise of profitable industry are illimitable. The climate is salubrious, and the soil productive. Particularly, in no other country is the Irish Catholic so free, prosperous, and happy, greatly more so than he is in the United States, notwithstanding the boasted liberty and equality of that country. Why then should it be presumed that Irish Catholics in Canada, merely because they are Irish Catholics, sympathiz with American Fenianism in its mad and diabolical design on Canada The assumption is absurd and unjust. It is unreasonable to presume that the Irish Catholic is less attached and devoted than any other to that which secures to him and his family the enjoyment of life and liberty, and the pursuit of happiness; the enjoyment of civil and religious liberty. Is it reasonable to assume that they would encourage the invasion of their own country, the desecration of their own hearths, the destruction of their own property, by lawless, irresponsible hordes—mere marauders, who are accountable to no nation or recognized authority? Surely it is not reasonable. The Irish Catholics, like all others who have settled in Canada, have made it their home, their country. In it they and their descendants are to blend with the people and descendants of people of the divers other national origins therein, and to form in time, and ere long, a homogeneous, hardy, liberty-loving. law-abiding, and happy people, delighting in, and proud of the title, Canadians.

One more letter, and I shall have done for the present. Meantime,

I remain,

Your Excellency's humble servant,

JOHN O'CONNOR.

Windsor, Ont., June 6th, 1870.

LETTER FROM MR. JOHN O'CONNOR, M.P., ON FENIANISM.

To His Excellency the Right Honorable Sir John Young, Bart., P.C., G.C.B., G.C.M.G., &c., &c., &c.

YOUR EXCELLENCY,—In the letter which I had last the honor of addressing to you, I endeavored to show somewhat of the nature of Fenianism; the position of the Irish Catholics of Canada in relation to it; and the fundamental and principal reasons why they could have no sympathy with or affection for it. And I flatter myself with the hope that I succeeded in doing so to the satisfaction of candid minds.

I now propose to offer for consideration some remarks on the primary end, the main object at which, as it is professed, Fenianism aims; the absence of reasonable ground for expecting that it can attain that end; how and why, as I can conceive, the organization has been so long sustained; what its general conduct has been; and the general results of that conduct in respect to the Irish people, but particularly the Catholic people in Ireland, in Great Britain, and in Canada.

APPENDIX. 481

The professed primary end and object of Fenianism is to ameliorate the condition of the Irish people, by wresting Ireland from the grasp of **British** power, and establishing **there an** independent government, republican in form.

How probable the attainment of this proposed end is, can be judged of, only by looking at facts as they exist, and paying due regard to "the logic of events," rather should I say to the logic of known circumstances.

Ireland is unquestionably, I think, a necessary **part of** the British empire. What I mean is, that without it, the British empire as such, cannot exist. Wrest Ireland from, and make it permanently independent of, Great Britain, and you virtually terminate the British empire. Furthermore, I say, establish a permanent republic in Ireland, acknowledged amongst **the nations as a free, an** independent sovereignty, and **the subjugation of Great Britain by it must speedily follow.** Because, in the circumstances and civilization of modern times, they must **be politically connected, else neither can be an independent sovereignty. This is,** I believe, an inevitable condition of their situation, relative position, and proximity—coupled with **the character and tendency of** governmental ideas in our day. Such, I apprehend, was the opinion of Pitt, when, at **the** beginning of this century, he, by **the use of** means anything but scrupulous, bound Ireland to Great Britain more closely than she had been, by the extinction of her Legislature.

Such, I doubt not, is the belief of the British people and **Government.** Therefore, when Great Britain is compelled to fight for the maintenance **of** her dominion in Ireland, she will fight for her own political existence. Consequently, when Fenianism undertakes to wrest Ireland from the grasp of British power, it undertakes the more **than Herculean task of** overcoming all the resistance which can be made by the **great military** and naval power of Britain, **sustained by her vast resources, her immense** wealth, **her powerful alliances, and above all, by her** millions of loyal people, impressed with the belief and animated by the consciousness that the struggle is not merely for the maintenance of supremacy in Ireland, but for the preservation of her own distinctive nationality—for the existence of British sovereignty. The accomplishment of this by any means within the power of an organization like Fenianism is, I venture to say, not within the range of what the human mind can regard as probable, I may even say, possible.

Empires as great, in their day, as that of Britain—some probably greater more powerful and more magnificent—have existed before, and passed away. The Babylonian, the Assyrian, the Macedonian, and the Roman empires existed in turn, and in turn vanished. The Turkish **empire, once so** powerful as to menace and jeopardise the liberties of all Europe, has dwindled into insignificance. But those mighty changes from magnificent existence and potency **to nonentity or insignificance,** were produced not by the direct agency of human power—not by means devised by human ingenuity for such results, but by a combination or succession of causes—human or providential, or partly both—the effect whereof the human mind could not forsee,—by means, therefore, which the human mind could not devise. The British empire may in like manner decay, and disappear from the list of nations, leaving only her history behind ; and then Ireland may become free, may be a republic or a kingdom, and may even obtain supremacy over England and Scotland.

But that such an event may be looked for as a result of the direct **agency** of Fenianism, or of anything devised or that may **be devised by it,** is, I take the liberty of saying, hardly within the province of possibility, considering the matter as within the cycle of natural causes.

Behold Ireland as she is, every harbor fortified, every city and important town garrisoned ; the navy of Britain, still the most powerful on the ocean, surrounding her, or **ready to** surround her when required ; all being equipped in the highest style, furnished with the latest improvements of steam, **of guns, of** gunnery, and of all the appliances **of war in** abundance. **Last, yet** not least, add to all this, that the people of Ireland are by no means united on the question of independence ; perhaps not even a majority of them consider it desirable, even were it attainable.

It is then probable, nay, **is it possible,** that the notion of wrestling Ireland **from British** power by such means as Fenianism can possibly bring **to bear, should have** entered into any mind possessed of ordinary intelligence ? **I doubt that it ever has ; the** very supposition is preposterous. **Grant that all the men in Ireland** who pant for independence are ready **to fight for it at all** hazards, what could they do, without discipline, without arms, without munitions of **war, as** against trained hosts, supplied with all things needed, seconded by a powerful navy, and sheltered **by** the garrisons of the land. To suppose that arms and munitions of war could be supplied in adequate quantities from America, is frivolous. The mere mention of such a scheme is **'too** wild to be entertained by any mind not controlled by an imagination the most extravagant. **That** such a scheme was ever seriously entertained by men so shrewd as the Fenian leaders in the United States, is too much to be believed ; too much for ordinary credulity. I feel constrained, therefore, to attribute the phenomena exhibited by Fenianism in the United States, in Ireland, in England—everywhere—during the past six years, to **a cause** other than that which appears on the surface, and to the attainment of **an end other than** Ireland's independence.

At the close of the late civil war in the United States, there existed **in the** Northern States a class of politicians who had, during the war **amassed** wealth by ways and practices ill-suited to stand the test of investigation in time of peace. Investigation was, therefore, to be, if possible, averted. The wealth accumulated by those men by their speculations and peculations gave them power and influence, particularly as they had the Government almost wholly in their hands. They adopted a scheme, profoundly laid, of diverting public attention from the consideration of the question of burdensome taxation, from enquiry into the causes thereof, and into abuses generally. Hence was raised the cry for the oppression, for the absolute extirpation of the people of the subdued States, which produced the desired excitement, and the inevitable party warfare in consequence thereof.

But this measure alone was not sufficient. The Democratic party though not in the ascendant, was still powerful, and with the ample materials furnished it, by the past misdeeds of its opponents, it might prevail in the struggle. Safety to the delinquents could be secured only by dividing the Democrats. For that purpose other objects of diversion were required. The times furnished those objects, and they were eagerly seized on and used.

The people of the Northern States had become somewhat exasperated during the war, against England, and partially so against Canada. Hence the mischief-makers resorted to the Alabama claims. So far so good. But the best stroke of all is yet to be told. The Irish of the Northern States were then, and perhaps they are yet, an important constituent element of the Democratic party. They had to be attracted from that party, or, failing that, so agitated within the party as to make the pursuit of a domestic party policy weak, and uncertain, and harmless. For effecting this, a fitting instrument ready made to hand was found in Fenianism.

It was then an insignificant institution, of which Mr. John O'Mahony was the head; and from which he derived an income greater, no doubt than he could have obtained from any honest pursuit, which he was capable of following. But although insignificant then, it contained two elements which, worked and directed by skilful operators, would render it most formidable as an engine of agitation.. It had that mysteriousness which always attaches to secresy, which produce marvellousness, and excites and feeds the imagination; and it had been constituted professedly to procure or effect the independence of Ireland and the humiliation of Great Britain. Than this, no instrument could better suit the purpose of the knaves who had enriched themselves by despoiling their own country, while she was drenched and reeking with the blood of her own people shed in fratricidal strife. It was adapted to answer a two-fold purpose; each useful to the other, and both answering the primary object of the secret operation. Agitation for the payment of the Alabama claims served to embarrass Great Britain, and it stimulated agitation for Ireland's independence, and *vice versa*. Each so materially aided and supported the other that they formed a common cause, having unity of purpose and consistency of end. The proverbial temperament of the Irish race, their keen sense of the wrongs which their country had suffered, and their excitability when the memory of those wrongs is revived, were known to and understood by the shrewd operators; the game was therefore plain and certain.

The wrongs of Ireland were glibly recited, exaggerated, and denounced on the rostrum, on the stump, in saloons, in the Senate, by demagogues who cared as little for Ireland and the Irish, and for their wrongs, past and present, as they did for Arabia and the Arabs. The internal enactments of the penal code were inveighed against, as if they were all still in full force. The atrocities of former days were spoken of, as if they had just happened, and as if they were daily recurring with increased violence. The Irish heart was assailed and agitated, and the imagination tortured by every art and wile which the acuteness of cunning men could devise. Irishmen, many of themselves being themselves dupes, and others doubtless initiated to some extent, if not altogether, were employed **as secret emissaries.** Some of these worked in the United States, others **in Ireland,** and more in England and Scotland, wherever bodies of the Irish people had aggregated. The irreligious character of the institution was so veiled by hypocrisy as to preserve it for a time from detection, and **secure** those who were allured **to it from the salutary and counteracting influence of the Catholic clergy.**

It is, therefore, not astonishing **that** many Irishmen, **Catholic and Protestant,** most **of them** good, kindhearted, patriotic, sympathetic, and **honest,** joined the organization in the United States, and in Ireland and England. Rather is it wonderful that the number of the dupes **has not** been greater.

But the American **politicians—the** wire-pullers in all this puppet show, **have had no desire for a settlement of the** Alabama claims : neither did **they desire** Irish Independence, or intend doing anything to effect it. As reasonably might a merchant be expected to desire the destruction of his stock-in-trade before he **had** effected **an** insurance. Therefore, when **Reverdy Johnson, as United** States Ambassador, agreed with the British **Secretary of** State upon **a fair basis** of settlement for the Alabama claims, **the treaty was** forthwith attacked and repudiated. Johnson, honest, **guileless,** and conscientious man, was not of the initiated ; he belonged **not to the** party, and supposed it was his duty to act honestly for the **settlement of a** dispute which threatened to involve two great countries in war. The foolish old man ; his conscientiousness ruined him.

So in Ireland, the candidates at the late elections who were favorable to the Gladstone Government, which **had been constructed on the basis** of settling the Irish difficulties and removing Irish grievances, were opposed **with the** utmost violence by Fenianism.

Hence also came the ridiculous but painful farce of electing poor O'Donovan (Rossa) for Tipperary, while he was pining in prison, undergoing punishment **as a** treason convict.

Fully in accordance with the purpose which I have intimated, have been the results of Fenianism, and the movements thereof. **It has in no wise improved the condition of Ireland or of the Irish people ; quite the reverse. It increased discontent, interfered with industrial avocations, created heart-burnings and feuds amongst the people, eradicated from the minds of hundreds the principles of Christianity, and imbued them with infidelity instead.**

In America great things were to be done. From America great succor, **overwhelming aid was to go ;** so said the emissaries from America. But **when the day of tribulation** overtook those who had yielded too eagerly **and unwisely to the charms** of the serpent, America, alas, did nothing, **great or small ; nor did succor go.** The duped had to abide the consequences **of their own indiscreetness, and of martial** law brought upon them by **the heralds of** freedom from America. The public mind in England has **been agitated,** panic-stricken at times by the secret plottings and midnight **workings of the** brotherhood, exciting vague fears and terrible

apprehensions; but what benefit has **come to the Irish people from
all this turmoil and** tumult there **or** elsewhere? Some have been
hanged, others imprisoned, and hundreds ruined in their circumstances.
In the United States, the Irish people have been tortured by agitation,
the industrious have been fleeced, plundered **to fill the** coffers of the
institution, and set the principal knaves at fighting **over the division of
the** spoils, resulting in scandalous crimination and **recrimination** amongst
themselves.

In Canada the Irish people have been injured **not only in common** with
the people generally, by the constant alarms **of** threatened raids, but in
especial manner, by the distrust of their **fellow-subjects, from being**
suspected of having sympathy for **Fenianism.**

Such have been the fruits produced. By its fruits the huge swindle
must now be judged. But the secret wire-pullers—the politicians **of**
shoddydom—have gained or nearly gained their end. Time has dried
he festering sores. Mammon may now sit majestically and reign securely
in **the** model Republic; for investigation with a view to retributive
justice, is no longer possible. **Let** us hope, therefore, that we shall hear
no more of Fenian **raids** in Canada. Probably, **too, after** the next presi-
dential election, the Alabama **claims will be settled** or dropped. Then
Fenianism having served the purpose of its **Yankee** keepers, will be
neglected, and numbered with the other ephemerals of the past.

One thing, however, it **has effected, for which it will be** remembered
with shame on the one hand, and with jeers on the other. **It** has attached
the stigma of cowardice to Irish character. **In this way** Pigeon Hill and
Hinchinbrook will long be remembered. **Heretofore** the Irish had credit,
at least, for gallantry, undaunted **valor—heroism** in battle. Without
recurring **to** a period too **remote, mention may be** made of Aughrim,
where Irish valor, **exhibited in fighting for the** cause **of** a renegade
king, **extorted words of** admiration **from** the foreign commander, St.
Ruth. **In the armies of** France, Irishmen sustained their soldierly
character; **and on the field of** Fontenoy, Dillon and his brigade won
fame as imperishable **as that of** Leonidas and his three hundred deathless
Spartans. In **the armies** of Spain and of Austria, Irishmen distinguished
themselves. In **the armies of** England they sustained their **warlike
reputation** on many **a bloody** field; **and** the **"Connaught Rangers,"
dauntless** and defiant **of death, became proverbial for their deeds
of daring.** So in the armies **of the United States, and particularly in**
the recent tremendous struggle **between the North and South, Irish valor
held its own, and** added new military **laurels to Irish fame.**

But Pigeon Hill!! Hinchinbrook!! **Alas! alas! shades of departed
Irish heroes, in justice to** your own **memories, in mercy to** the honest liv-
ing, impart to us the secret of **this inglorious decadence.** I have it.
Thanks, spirits of the brave dead, **for the** inspiration. I will write it.
They were invading an innocent and **peaceable** people who had done no
wrong to them or to Ireland, and incurred no penalty. They were acting
without the sanction of authority. They were violating **the** laws of eternal
justice; committing an outrage on society. The presence of the country's

defenders, ready to do battle in the just cause, forced the truth into the invader's minds, and vivified it. Conscience, aroused by the sense of immediate danger, smote them. The sense of injustice crying to Heaven for vengeance, depressed them. Death stared them in the face; every man shrunk within himself from the hazard of meeting an angry God, outraged by a flagrant breach of his laws. The sword of justice in the hands of the Canadian volunteers, inflamed with vengeance, rushed upon them, and paralyzed with terror, they fled like cowards: like cowards fled men who, before then, had stood with dauntless courage, and acted with heroic bravery on many a gory field where Grant and Lee marshalled the opposing armies. Such, however, was the state of mind and the resulting cowardly conduct which gave opportunity to the plucky little soldier, Chamberlin, to proudly shout, "give the cowards a parting shot." Another effect has, indeed, resulted from Fenianism and its threats towards Canada—an effect more agreeable than any other for Canadians to contemplate—an effect of priceless value. It shews that though sunbeams cannot be extracted from cucumbers, good may ensue to the innocent from the evil machinations and doings of the wicked.

Although Canada has been compelled to incur great expense, and her progress has been seriously interrupted and retarded, yet all is, perhaps, more than compensated by the spirit of patriotism which has been aroused, and of self-reliance which has been implanted, resulting in an army of volunteers, not large, indeed, but well disciplined, and as brave, intelligent, and patriotic, as any age or country has yet been able to boast of. In them Canada has the nucleus of a large and fine army, should her circumstances ever require it, which event, however, may God in His goodness long forefend.

I remain,
Your Excellency's humble servant,
JOHN O'CONNOR.

WINDSOR, Ontario, 10th June, 1870.

THE END.

www.ingramcontent.com/pod-product-compliance
Lightning Source LLC
Chambersburg PA
CBHW021426300426
44114CB00010B/664